The Sett

Ranulph Fiennes was born in 1944 and educated in South Africa and at Eton. He was commissioned into the Royal Scots Greys in 1963 and attached to 22 SAS Regiment in 1966. In 1968–1970 he fought communists in Arabia with the army of the Sultan of Oman. Since then he has led expeditions in remote regions, hot and cold. In 1982 he and a friend became the first men in history to reach both Poles, cross Antarctica and the Arctic Ocean and circumnavigate Earth on its polar axis. In 1992 he uncovered the long lost city of Ubar in the Empty Quarter desert and in 1993 he led the first unsupported crossing of the Antarctic Continent. He has many geographical medals including the Polar Medal with Bar from the Queen. He is the author of twelve books, including the bestselling *The Feather Men* and *Mind Over Matter*.

RANULPH FIENNES

The Sett

Mandarin

A Mandarin Paperback
THE SETT

First published in Great Britain 1996
by William Heinemann
This edition published 1996
by Mandarin Paperbacks
an imprint of Reed International Books Ltd
Michelin House, 81 Fulham Road, London SW3 6RB
and Auckland, Melbourne, Singapore and Toronto

A CIP catalogue record for this title
is available from the British Library
ISBN 0 7493 2161 X

Printed and bound in Great Britain
by Cox & Wyman Ltd, Reading, Berkshire

To Those who Fight Back

Acknowledgements

Dodo Armstrong, Nick Baker, John Bates, Chris Battison, Roger Berrett, Peter Bizzell, Stephen Braden, Roger Bradley, Peter Brant, John Brennan, Dick and Pauline Coombes, Tom C, Joan Davies, B Davis, Richard Dawes, Ken Done, John Donner, JA Dotoli, Nicola Douglas, Clive Driscoll, Mick Eade, James Elkin, Anne Ellis, Rod Ellis, Julian Elston, Stuart and Katrina, Ginnie Fiennes, Bryan Fotheringham, AF, Alex Goodman, Paul Grindley, John de Haan, Rod Hackney, Camilla Hall, Jack Hayward, John Hinchliffe, John Hodges, David and Suzanne Hunter, Grafton Ifill, Clive Jennings, Peter Johnstone, Andrew Jones, John Jones, Peter Jones, Denis Kaye, Mike Lee, Terry Lloyd, Pauline Lock, Lynn Lyddell, Leith Lynch, Tom MacMillan, Charles Mainwaring, Majeed, Raymond Makereth, Roy and Sylvia Maltwood, Glen Marks, Angela Martin, John McCarron, John Meehan, Graham Melvin, Nick Morris, David Murrells, AN, Graham Nielson, Peter O'Donnell, Jerry Ohlson, Louis Ossude, Richard Overall, Frances Pajovic, Owen Pearce, Paul Penrose, Reg Perris, Maggie Phillips, John Porter, John Potter, Power Company of Grand Bahama, Gina Rawle, Derek Reed, Ismond Rosen, John Ross, Paul Russell, TS, Jim Salter, Dick Shepherd, Christopher Sinclair–Stevenson, Raj and Jyoti Soren, Nicky Stafford, Tony and Louise, Telephone Company of Grand Bahama, Hiran Thenabadu, Christopher Thomas-Everard, Victoria Underwood, Hugh Vernon, Ed Victor, Bill Waddell, Tom Weldon, Reinhard Wentz, Charley Wheatley, Ken Whitehouse, Bernard Williams, Cedric Woodall, John Worwood.

'We touched his hand – stone cold –
and he was dead, and they, all dead behind.'
Anthology of War Poetry

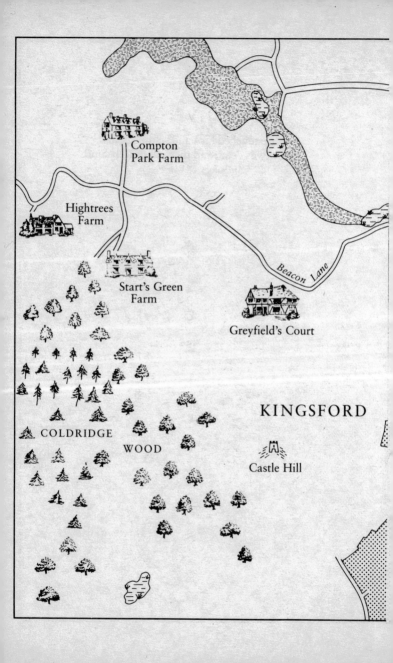

Prologue

I was telephoned at home on 27 March 1994.

'My name is Goodman.' I caught the lightest hint of a Welsh lilt. 'Alexander Goodman. I am so pleased to have found you.'

He sounded apologetic but there was a note of urgency that cut through my irritation at this late Sunday call. He said he had been at Mons Officer Cadet School with me in 1962. That made him about fifty. The previous Christmas, in a London library, he had read *The Feather Men*, a book with SAS connections that I had written two years earlier.

'I am dying,' he said without evident emotion, 'and I want you to write my biography. People must know what has happened to me.'

'Why?' I asked.

'Why?' he repeated.

'Why should people wish to know about you? I do not wish to sound harsh but we are *all* dying and that doesn't usually warrant a book.'

'Your *Feather Men* was about revenge. My last ten years have been the mirror image of your book.'

'I don't understand.'

'Can we meet?' he pressed. 'Do you come up to London? I haven't got a car.'

I tried to put the man off as politely as possible. I had not seen my wife all day. Nor had I any wish to write anyone's biography. People simply do not buy the biographies of nonentities, no matter how thrilling their experiences. They *do* buy the biographies of the

1

famous, however humdrum and tedious their lives may have been. Goodman was irritatingly persistent, refusing to take no for an answer, so I cut him off with an excuse about the toast burning.

The following day he telephoned when I was out and after 10 p.m., which worried my wife. His third call caught me in a more receptive mood and I agreed to meet him in London, if only to convince him that I was a non-starter as his ghost writer or biographer.

I did not recognise the man. Only two of my fellow Mons cadets from 1962 have remained friends over the three ensuing decades. I had telephoned both and neither remembered any Alexander Goodman, so I was suspicious. This may have been unfair, for the Cadet School had closed down twenty years previously. There had been no reunions and I could recall the faces of at best a mere dozen of the other cadets.

I spent three hours at the first meeting with Goodman. We drank black coffee in the lounge of the Rubens Hotel in Buckingham Palace Gate. As the street-lights flickered on, outlining the grimy brick wall of the Palace across the street, I knew that I was hooked. Unless Goodman's story was merely a figment of his imagination, he should be locked up in the nearest 'slammer' for the rest of his days. That was my first impression.

In 1986 I had stupidly become a Lloyd's Name, so I could not consider spending months at work on a book for shared proceeds. I put this to Goodman without preamble.

'If I decide to write your story, any and all revenue must accrue only to me. Would you be happy with that?'

He nodded. Money, surprisingly, was not his rationale. He gave the appearance of a shy, retiring person, not a man crying out for fame and acknowledgement. So what was his motive? Right then this did not matter to me. I could easily check the veracity of any hard facts as soon as he divulged them to me. I would then be able to establish whether the book was fact or fiction and have it marketed accordingly. Reality has since proved me wrong in this assumption. By the winter of 1994, when I began to write his story, I knew at least why Goodman had a nervous tic, why he stared into mirrors and shop windows. Not to return his own haunted gaze but to see who was behind him.

2

July 1984

They had always lived in the gentle land about the Wye and Severn. Welsh border country where the talk was of hops and the weather. Crime, unemployment and the nuclear threat touched only the outer enamel of their awareness, causing little conscious concern.

His birth to Welsh parents in the suburbs of Coventry, a decade before hers in Cardiff, was premature, owing to the Blitz.

Neither arrived to silver-spoon status and both were orphaned in their late teens, though moderate success at their respective grammar schools, Leominster and Worcester, enabled their entry into the safe worlds of rural accountant and shop assistant, where, in 1974, their paths entwined. They married the same year and, nine respectable months later, little Lucy appeared. She remained their only child and the essence of their existence.

I find it difficult to picture the family in any light where niceness and normality do not cling label-like to their upbringing, their thoughts and their day-to-day existence. The sort of people whom God designed in His own image and set down in the epicentre of His most green and pleasant land, a place where nasty things do not occur. Yet, close by in the Cotswolds, as Lucy grew up, a dozen other 'nice and normal' girls were raped, tortured and buried by the respectable West family of Gloucester. Not one neighbour noticed their disappearance, not one relative murmured in concern. How could this happen?

On 22 July 1984 Lucy held her parents' hands as they waved a last goodbye to their cramped but cosy flat in Leominster, the only home she had known. Then they squeezed into the front of their overladen Volkswagen Beetle and headed north, dry-mouthed with apprehension, excitement and hope. That was the day, I think, when God forgot that they were His and the Devil closed in.

On Wednesday, 18 July 1984 an FBI agent, Jed Mason, and two colleagues entered a low, Spanish-style bungalow overlooking the border crossing-point of San Ysidro, in San Diego's southernmost suburb. The house was rented by a Drug Enforcement Administration CENTAC (Central Tactical Unit) team, to which the three men were seconded. Jed, like most middle-aged FBI men throughout the USA, was overworked. Apart from his CENTAC work with the DEA, he was currently handling twenty-eight ongoing cases, the majority California-based, but several stretching across the world of international crime and meshed with allied CIA operations.

He passed the grey Panton R6 binoculars to the taller of his two associates, flipping a centrally mounted lever to the 'smoked' position. 'Try these.' His accent was Boston, his tone tinged with pride. 'Langley's concept but our Bureau wizards handled the design. The first binocs in the world to allow you to see through tinted glass – especially useful since ninety per cent of our top criminals go for black-window limos even before they get their Rolex Presidents.'

'How do they work?' Ridgway asked.

Jed shook his head. 'Ask me another, JR. Something to do with two negatives making a plus to look through a dark glass.' He liked to confuse John 'JR' Ridgway. It went back to the military, where they first met, both rookies from New England but otherwise chalk and cheese. JR had eased into private detection, specialising in arson investigation and insurance fraud, while Jed was head-hunted by the Bureau, at a time when J. Edgar Hoover had lain at rest a mere two years alongside America's other top movers and shakers allotted a Capitol plot close by Abe Lincoln and JFK.

JR and Jed were wont to meet from time to time, as old vet friends do, and, comparing case notes, discovered a mutual interest in Korbi Richter, a suave Los Angeles-based German. Jed had come across the man three years earlier during an international CENTAC narcotics operation, while JR, investigating a disturbing rash of high-tech arson attacks, had traced a call to Richter at an anonymous office suite in a Wilshire Boulevard high-rise.

In 1982 Jed had instigated Operation Caesar, a label for their work on Richter, and in between their many other cases the two men had slowly closed in on the German. There was as yet no actionable evidence and sometimes months would pass with Caesar lying fallow. NCIC, the FBI central computer containing twenty million records, had nothing on Korbi Richter; nor had the criminal files of the DEA and other organisations.

As part of the FBI's declared determination to prevent drug gangs preying on the expected rush of LA-bound 1984 Olympics tourists, Jed had reactivated Operation Caesar by installing basic and illegal snooping gear in Richter's LA office. For weeks Richter failed to show up but, in the last week of June, the name Guzman cropped up in a taped conversation from his office.

'Guzman,' Jed had called to tell JR at once, 'is a top cocaine dealer for Pablo Escobar in Medellín and it seems Korbi Richter's people are expecting him to cross the border out of Baja California on Wednesday. Richter just may have designs on taking over some Escobar business.'

They had agreed to investigate Richter's interest in Guzman.

Jed and his men had followed a black Buick Regal, the car with tinted windows, from Richter's LA office and along the Cabrillo Freeway to downtown San Diego. The largely Hispanic quarter of San Ysidro, named after the patron saint of farmers, is connected to the city only by a narrow corridor down the coastline of San Diego Bay.

The Buick had parked at a Yum Yum doughnut shop on San Ysidro Boulevard. A quick call to Pennsylvania Avenue, FBI HQ, told Jed that Alex Solomon, manager of the Yum Yum, was clean. When the Buick's two occupants, a black and an Anglo type, went inside, a passing Hell's Angel leant across from his Harley-Davidson and snapped a black magnetic strip on to the Buick's roof.

'Easy to spot only if you're looking for it,' Jed muttered to JR. 'Now we can tune into their car talk and find out exactly why Richter's interested in Guzman.'

Pedro, Jed's Mexican FBI aide, snapped photos of their quarry as they emerged from the Yum Yum. They returned to the Buick and parked in a recently vacated space a few hundred yards from the US side of the crossing-point. The Buick watched the border and Jed watched the Buick. JR smoked Camels, Pedro chewed gum and Jed made calls.

James Huberty was only forty-one but his hairline had long since disappeared over the horizon. His features were unrelentingly ugly, and chunky spectacles did little to hide a stare that made people uneasy. Folk from his home town in Ohio called him a man with a chip on his shoulder, an anti-social person who collected guns, kept guard dogs, hoarded food against Armageddon and made his daughters learn karate.

Both daughters and his wife Etna were with him at noon for a short visit to San Diego Zoo following his being fined in traffic court that morning for a double-yellow-line offence. A year earlier the family had tried living in Tijuana but Huberty spoke poor Spanish and found the locals stand-offish, so they had moved to an apartment in San Ysidro. Cassandra was ten and Zelia fourteen. They were uneasy about their father. He had started to hear voices and then began to converse with invisible people. A week before he had lost his job as a security guard.

On reaching their apartment after the zoo visit he told Etna: 'I'm going out to hunt humans.' Then he donned a red T-shirt and combat fatigues.

The previous day Etna had tried to book Huberty an appointment at a mental health clinic. She did not like the sound of his parting remark, but he had never hurt anybody and took no drugs or alcohol.

'Jim is a very sad man,' she told friends. 'He had a broken childhood. His only close friend is his dog.'

Huberty left his home on Averil Avenue soon after 3.30 p.m. and headed for the nearby Yum Yum take-away.

A white Mercedes stretch limo drove from Chapultepec in prime-zone Tijuana, down the main street, Revolución, and, stopping briefly at El Indio, a vehicle body shop adept at cocaine concealment, picked up a creative accountant named Rubi. He was a local, bred in the baked-mud backstreets, desensitised in the stinking brothels and educated in the rules of murder, treachery, smuggling and corruption that pervade most of urban Mexico. With figures he was brilliant. A mixture of well-placed flattery and the right introductions had seen him rise from the service of petty local felons to the senior echelons of the Mexicali cocaine trade. His recent release from the cesspit of Tijuana's La Mesa jail had been engineered by Victor Guzman, a man with an uncanny resemblance to Robert Mitchum; a man friendly with Pablo Escobar, Jorge Ochoa and other Colombian crime kings.

Rubi was shortly due to join his maestro, Victor Guzman, at San Diego Airport and accompany him to Europe. First he had to pay Guzman's corrupt Customs contact, who should be waiting at the first McDonald's on the US side of the border.

The Buick tucked in several vehicles behind Rubi's Mercedes and the Hell's Angel followed them both, calling for Jed as he gunned his Harley-Davidson away from the fumes and bustle of the checkpoint.

Huberty knew that the neighbourhood McDonald's, where he had taken his daughters earlier that day, would be busy and that most of the clients would be Latinos from Tijuana, where he and his family had so recently been given the cold shoulder. He was unemployed, unlike most of the Mexicanos munching at Big Macs.

He carried a twelve-bore pump-action shotgun, a Browning 9mm semi-automatic pistol, an Uzi sub-machine-gun imported from Israel and four hundred rounds of ammunition. True to his word, he was going hunting.

The Mercedes slowed down by the Post Office and turned into 522 West San Ysidro Boulevard, McDonald's parking lot close by the children's Jungle Gym and the Ronald McDonald playslide. Teenagers in blue jeans and beach shirts loafed about as the limo came to a halt. The Buick settled back into its earlier spot in the neighbouring Yum Yum car park and Jed Mason, across the road in the van, tuned into the Buick's occupants while adjusting the Panton's focus. The eavesdropped conversation came across crystal-clear.

The black man in the Buick, a snappy dresser, surprised Jed, for his accent was plainly English; London maybe, though Jed was no expert on Limey patois. 'Hey Pedro,' he shouted over his shoulder. 'Korbi Richter's boys seem to think Guzman's men are about to pay off a Customs contact at an RV in McDonald's . . . The German guy is calling his black pal Tricks. Try that name on the NCIC computer.' Pedro disappeared into the hardware banks in the back of the van. Six minutes later he poked his head through the blackout cloth and shook it. 'Nothing on a black man, six feet-plus and 180lb. Nickname Tricks. English accent. Associate of Korbi Richter . . . No blacks or whites with real or street-name Tricks.'

Jed shrugged. A small man, the ex-con accountant Rubi, climbed out of the Mercedes. JR aimed and focused a directional sound probe, as simple to zero on a moving target as any rifle sight. Rubi waited by the main entrance to the fast-food joint. He looked impatient, furtive or both. JR, his ear pressed to the probe, heard him click his teeth and mouth 'Dios mío' as a fat mamma brushed past him.

A fit-looking sixty-year-old man approached the entrance. Rubi raised his hand. 'Hi,' he said. 'You Mr Blueday?' 'Nope,' the man responded, 'the name's Versluis, Laurence to friends. I come here a lot. This Mr Blueday of yours, he ain't no reg'lar here. I knows all the reg'lars. I never heard of a Latino Blueday and this Micky D's is ninety per cent Latino.'

Rubi waited another five minutes, glancing frequently at his watch. He knew Guzman did not like to be kept waiting at any time and today he had a flight to catch. Rubi seemed to make up his mind. He disappeared into the restaurant but JR could still hear him clearly enough on the probe. The voice was again that of Mr Versluis.

'Hi, pal. Still looking for Blueday? Here, take a seat. Coffee or some other poison?' JR winced as a chair scraped, unseen but sharp to his eardrum. 'Look, Mr Versluis' – Rubi's voice – 'could you do me a favour? I'll pay you . . . Just a matter of handing an envelope to the right guy. He should be here but maybe he's held up in traffic.'

'Sure. I'm in no hurry.' Versluis obviously liked to talk. 'I been in trucks on the highway thirty-nine years and I learnt one thing. Ain't no good to be had by rushing. Do a man a favour one day and someday he'll help you back. That's life, pal, a matter of balance. Balance . . . Say, I may know your Mr Blueday. We get a lot of Sycuan Indians in here with names like that. They run a bingo hall just east of El Cajón. Yeah, might well be a Blueday among 'em.'

'Great.' Rubi forced twenty dollars on the garrulous Versluis. 'If

Blueday shows up real soon and it's likely he will, give him this package. He'll know who it's from. If he's not here when you leave, just mail it next door at the Post Office. He was meant to collect it at 4 p.m. sharp but, too bad, I got a plane to catch.'

'OK, friend. Right happy to help. I'll see he gets it.'

Rubi was a good judge of his fellow-man. Versluis was honesty writ loud and clear. Rubi returned into JR's view and climbed back into the Mercedes, which moved off.

'All you got to do now, JR,' Jed grinned, 'is go have a Big Mac, call yourself Blueday and collect the package. Could help us hang a bribery charge on somebody big.'

'What's with the guys in the Buick?' JR eyed the headphones. 'Tell me, then I'll go make like Blueday.'

Jed nodded. He listened as Pedro twirled knobs on a recorder. In a while he turned to JR. 'Seems like the black Limey Tricks and his German friend are not here to say howdy to Guzman. The little guy Rubi, fresh from a Mexican slammer, is about to join Guzman *en route* to Europe to start major crack rings based from London . . . Richter has his own London thing going under this Tricks and the last thing he wants is Guzman and the Medellín big boys muscling in over there. The idea is for Tricks to get an eyeful of Guzman and his gofer Rubi, so his soldiers can be sure to knock them off as soon as they touch down in dear old London town.'

'So what's in the package in McDonald's?'

'That's what you're about to find out. Probably a fat wad and, with luck, a written note . . . but *wait* . . .' Jed's hands went up and pressed the earphones. He tensed forward, glancing up the boulevard. 'Tricks is shouting something at the German . . . He sounds scared. Says there's a contract killer coming for them . . . Hey, hey. He's right.' Jed's right hand dropped towards his ankle holster. 'You'd better forget Mr Blueday, JR. Take a look at this guy. He's a walking arsenal.'

Huberty opened fire just as Ridgway picked him up with the binoculars. As the blast of the first shot of his 'human hunt' echoed down San Ysidro Boulevard, Jed reached for his phone to call the cops.

Huberty acted with surgical precision. He did not waste bullets on the occupants of the parked Buick because he could not see them

9

through the tinted windows. There was no satisfaction in shooting up inanimate objects. The Uzi jammed, so he discarded it.

As he had expected, McDonald's at 4 p.m. was full of life, mostly Latinos. Three eleven-year-old boys from the nearby elementary school approached, pushing their bicycles. Huberty shot two dead. The third lay doggo with bullets in his back, leg, arm and chest. Earlier that day he and his chums had gone deep-sea fishing. Now they were dead, and as he felt his lifeblood trickle down his crutch he feared that he would soon be joining them.

Huberty was not insane in a medical sense. Or, if he was, he had only been acting that way for three minutes in forty-one years. He was a very standard sort of person with an average marriage and two little daughters that he loved and who were about the same age as the boys on the bikes.

He saw a police car with its roof light flashing and aimed a burst as it blurred by. The police driver later described Huberty. 'No emotion, no expression. Dark sunglasses. A devil walking through his own hell. I'll never forget his face, the look of emptiness and evil.'

An elderly couple had stopped, rabbits mesmerised by the sudden violence. Huberty shot the woman through the head and her husband sank to the ground holding her in disbelief and horror, splashed by her blood. He tried with his trembling fingers to swab the blood from her eyes, to stroke her hair away from her goldfish mouth.

Then Huberty walked into McDonald's. He killed a young married couple close to the front counter. As they died they clutched at each other and fell over the body of their wounded daughter.

Before Huberty's arrival thirty or forty people were in the eatery enjoying their food and each other's company – a scene repeated all over America, all over the world. McDonald's. Civilisation. Huberty was a product of that civilisation. He raised his voice a touch and felt his omnipotence in the terrified cowering of his victims. He told them to lie down flat. They all obeyed. Then he began to kill them, alternating his weapons. He used the pistol for close shooting, held against ears and temples.

He switched on somebody's radio and was impressed that the airwaves were already reporting his first murders on the pavement outside. He looked back out of a front window and saw that the old

10

man was still alive, rocking back and forth and crooning to his dead wife. He put a bullet through his neck.

The three little boys lying slumped about their bicycles looked dead. He saw a policeman and fired a burst, shattering windows and roof lights. Somebody on the floor behind him screamed, so he killed her.

Then he began to walk up the first aisle between tables. Imelda Pérez, sixteen, heard his footsteps and her hand pulled tight over the back of Claudia, her nine-year-old sister. Huberty saw the movement. A single bullet passed through Imelda's hand, killing Claudia. Imelda would have to wait a while.

Huberty murdered Colemanero Silva, a stock clerk from Tijuana, with his pistol, then switched to the twelve-gauge with which he blasted away four-year-old Mirey Rivera's buttocks. Next he killed Señor Rivera, a maintenance man for General Atomic, and sliced shot into a four-month-old girl who was crying – an irritating sound.

At the end of the aisle, those still awaiting death heard him carefully reload his weapons. Maricela Flores, twenty-three, and her family were close to a rear exit. She quietly passed her wounded baby around a door. 'Please take care of her,' she whispered. Huberty finished reloading and killed Maricela. He saw another mother trying to plug her little daughter's wounds with napkins. A single shot put a stop to her ministrations.

A telephone rang with a repetitive jangle. Huberty blasted it from its housing.

By 4.45 p.m. police SWAT (Special Weapons and Tactics) snipers had surrounded the building but could not catch a clear glimpse of Huberty through the cracked windows. They were fearful that a sudden attack would cause more deaths. As they waited, wounded people bled to death.

When Huberty saw an eye blink or a body twitch he pressed his pistol against the head and fired single shots. For long minutes he allowed a hidden baby to cry then he sought it out and the noise ceased.

He moved to the rear lobby at some point where he met John Arnold, sixteen, and aimed his shotgun point-blank. Click . . . a misfire. Arnold was lucky – the second shot merely removed his forearm.

Three girls lay under a booth playing possum. Two were

vegetarians who rarely used hamburger joints. Huberty approached and saw movement. Gloria and Arisdelsi somehow survived but they felt the bullets thud into the body of their friend, Vargas, and her death tremors passed through their bodies as they waited their turn.

Half a dozen young friends worked at the rear of the restaurant. There was always a noisy bustle. A bomb could go off and no one would notice. Huberty was suddenly among them. Elsa Borboa threw a coffee-pot. She missed and he killed her. Seventeen-year-old Wendy Flanagan was enjoying her first job after leaving school. Her friend brought in a tray of iced soda and managed to keep hold of the tray as she died. Four other girls fell among the shiny metal pans but two escaped with a wounded senior manager and hid with him in a closet. The manager stuffed a towel in his mouth to muffle his groans.

In seventy minutes James Huberty killed twenty-one people, mostly youngsters, and seriously wounded fifteen others. It was the worst single-episode slaying in the history of the United States.

SWAT officer Charles Foster, prone on the Post Office roof, sent a .308 bullet through Huberty's chest when he glimpsed him searching around for further prey.

They froze Huberty's brain in the county morgue but found no evidence of tumours, drugs or infirmity. A normal member of the community driven by external pressures to inexcusable action of which neither he nor his family would have previously deemed him capable.

This book is the story of another such man and I have written it because in his case, unlike Huberty's, I can sympathise, indeed identify with, his reactions to the blows that Fate dealt him.

Jed's team watched Guzman and Rubi fly from San Diego bound for London Heathrow and, three days later, the black Englishman Tricks followed suit. Jed applied for FBI authority to wire up Richter's telephones in Wilshire Boulevard back in LA on the grounds of his now proven link with drug dealer Victor Guzman. Within a week the Justice Department granted permission for full covert surveillance of Korbi Richter. JR and Jed felt that, after two years in the doldrums, their Operation Caesar might be showing the first stirrings of success. But they were too street-cynical to count on

12

gaining sufficient evidence for a conspiracy conviction. Richter and his shady colleagues were still beyond their reach.

JR called in a favour from an ATF border police friend in San Diego, who approached an officer working with Captain Ybbandrio in charge of the Huberty crime-scene search. There was no sign of anyone named Blueday. They had traced the body of a truck driver named Laurence Versluis but there was nothing suspicious to be found among his effects, and certainly no cash package. JR naturally avoided any suggestion that such a package might have disappeared during the police search. It was just another false lead. The Richter job, Jed ruminated, seemed to attract more stray bullets than just about any case he could remember. Huberty was not the first foreign body to gatecrash Operation Caesar. Nor, sadly for Jed, would he be the last.

July 1984

Four days after the San Diego massacre, which made headlines all over the world, Lucy moved with her parents to Dudley, a north-western suburb of Birmingham. All her life, school and holidays alike, had been spent in Herefordshire. Her parents were both orphans and only children, possibly one of the reasons they had been attracted to each other, so there were no aunts or grannies to visit. Lucy was a shy little girl, but she had loved her old school in Leominster and dreaded having to be a new girl in Birmingham once her parents found her a school close enough to their new home.

The move had been far too precipitate, as it now turned out. Lucy had made no protest, for she could see her father was excited at the job offer: he had called it 'manna from heaven'. Back home at the hotel and the two shops, he had run everything smoothly and the annual audit was always a success. His employers, the Browns, according to Lucy's mother, should have been named Scrooge, for they never raised Dad's salary and never gave him a bonus. They took his loyalty, honesty and his wonderful way with figures for granted.

One of the brewery companies, with which the Browns' hotel had dealt for years, had come up with the new job and their sales rep had put Dad's name forward. No other credentials were needed. They knew his record and offered a wage far better than he could ever hope to obtain in Leominster. His mistake had been to try for the Army. At grammar school he had shunned the Cadet Corps partly in rebellion against unsubtle pressures from his father. When a car crash killed both his parents while he was at university, he joined up from guilt, to placate his late father's memory. Mons Officer Cadet School had soon confirmed his earlier notions that the Army was for brainless idiots who needed the khaki umbrella to nurse them through life for twenty-two years, then furnish them with a brief resettlement course and an index-linked pension. He knew this was not for him and left Mons before receiving a commission.

He fancied the world of catering administration, for he had often earned pocket money during his school holidays working as a part-time clerk at the Browns' hotel. So, after his hasty retreat from the Army, he went back to Herefordshire and the Browns. Discovering his talents with their confused and often overlapping accounting systems, the Browns realised a considerable saving in professional fees. For his part, he began to study accountancy through the Open University, which led him to tax law and other specialist topics. This became his hobby as well as his living. Somewhat of an introvert and tucked away in the hotel office, he met few girls and bedded only one (owing to a rare state of inebriation one New Year's Eve).

When he met Mary, a recently arrived assistant at one of the Browns' shops, he was thirty-nine. She was nine years younger and socially inhibited to a painful degree. Each knew by the end of their second lunch date that they were helplessly and wonderfully in love. Mary, by then probably the oldest postwar virgin in Herefordshire, discovered a latent sexuality bordering on nymphomania. He responded with fervour and Lucy was conceived in the storeroom of Mary's shop during an audit.

They stayed on with the Browns after their wedding and four-day honeymoon in far-away Clacton-on-Sea. They scrimped and saved over the years but it was a miserable process with a poor outlook for their dotage. This mattered little since they were besotted with each other.

When the offer of the Birmingham brewery job was made, they celebrated with dinner for three at the local Indian restaurant. Life was suddenly and unexpectedly full of limitless potential. The next day the couple finished work early and made love fully clothed on the living-room carpet. They were almost caught by Lucy coming back from school. She held her hand to her lips in delight when she saw the radiant smiles on her parents' faces.

The house in Dudley was semi-detached and in Lucy's eyes 'mega-brill'. This was just as well, since they had sold their Leominster flat with its forty per cent mortgage and taken a seventy per cent loan on their Dudley acquisition. Never mind. There was an oil-fired Aga for Mary, a playroom for Lucy, a separate study for Dad's computer and even a back garden for Lucy's rabbit Munch, whose hutch, back in Leominster, had been squeezed into their cramped kitchen.

The brewery had generously allowed a fortnight on full pay to 'settle in', but in their first week in the new house their dream was shattered by a letter from the company. Owing to unforeseen circumstances, staff cut-backs were to be implemented by order of the Australian-based parent company and, to ensure adequate compensation for the bitter blow that this would undoubtedly be, three months' severance pay would be awarded if the enclosed agreement form was signed by the given date.

Their reaction was to cheer each other up with 'positive thinking'. All was not lost. There must be many other jobs to be found in the country's second city. They would keep their nerve. With the three months' grace he would easily find alternative employment.

They settled down to a new routine: he to the telephone and the newspaper section of Birmingham Central Lending Library, she to home-making and looking after Lucy. On their first weekend in Dudley they had driven out to the nearest countryside. They took Lucy's camera, for Mary had heard there were roe deer which came to Kinver Edge from Arley Forest and little muntjacs if you kept quiet and were lucky.

But luck is a strange potion, concocted, God knows where, to a recipe of devilish complexity. The other ingredients involved in the little family's luck quotient were that very morning coming together many thousands of miles away on the hot river plains of the eastern Punjab.

In 1980 President Jimmy Carter was embarrassed by CIA profiteering, plots to kill foreign leaders and spying on US citizens at home. CIA involvement in Watergate did not help. So he cut down their numbers, their scope and their budget. The KGB were delighted.

A year later Ronald Reagan became President and Carter's various appeasement policies were turned on their head in favour of aggressive action against Brezhnev's 'evil empire' of Soviet-inspired communism. Sadly for Reagan, various Hollywood quick-kill solutions he favoured to crush the Reds were blocked by Congress. Subtlety was required. Annoying but unavoidable.

Most US Presidents have a Secretary of State to control foreign policy and a Director of the CIA to operate covert actions within that policy. Reagan simplified the process by appointing a sixty-seven-year-old businessman (the manager of Reagan's recent presidential campaign) as CIA boss, with an assurance of minimal interference from the government. William Casey took Reagan at his word and then some.

Reagan had no confidence in the body of the CIA but he trusted Casey at their helm. This trust was repaid with unswerving loyalty. Casey, who remained the powerful Director of the CIA from 1981 until his death in 1987, served in two quite separate roles. Openly he was leader of the most powerful secret service in the world. In secret he manoeuvred a group of his trusted chums, many of them millionaires with worldwide connections of their own, in covert operations unknown to the CIA professionals but approved of by Reagan (when Casey saw fit to pass the President details of their activities).

A number of these 'Casey friends' were well known to and frowned upon by the CIA officials at Langley, Virginia. They were called the Hardy Boys and they brazenly used the Director's private office lift at CIA headquarters. They included Swiss tycoon Bruce Rappaport, Brooklyn tough guy Max Hugel (who was briefly elevated to official CIA status) and ex-Eisenhower aide Bob Anderson.

Casey loved all things covert and remembered as the best years of his life his successful World War Two career in the OSS, the precursor of the CIA. Unbeknown to his wife, the CIA, or even his Hardy Boy colleagues, he nursed a secret within a secret – a group of 'patriots', including OSS and Vietnam veterans, business entrepreneurs and top New York lawyers, whose activities were kept a jealously guarded internal secret. They avoided nomenclature, committees and telephone conversations. Their success stood the test of time in that their existence remained unconfirmed despite numerous Congressional and Senate inquiries into potential international crises spawned directly by their machinations.

Only one of Casey's secret group, which, in the absence of an existing title, I will call 'The Friends', was also a member of the

Hardy Boys and visited Casey openly at Langley. John Shaheen, successful ex-OSS banker, as essentially Irish Catholic in his moral ethics as Casey, was chief puppeteer of The Friends. In the early summer of 1984 he and Casey gave themselves elaborate alibis and joined fellow-Friend Albert Redden on board his private Boeing jet to fly to Chaklala Air Base near Islamabad.

Casey had been there two months previously in his official CIA capacity, arriving in a giant black US warplane, to energise his opposite number, General Yousef of Pakistan's ISI. Their joint aim was the defeat of Soviet forces in Afghanistan.

Casey, Shaheen and Redden were flown by military helicopter from Islamabad to a walled mansion on the plain of the river Ravi in the eastern Punjab. This house was owned by the Bank of Credit and Commerce International (BCCI) and run by the Bank's Protocol Department for the specific purpose of impressing foreign dignitaries and prospective BCCI clients.

Casey and his boss, Ronald Reagan, had long appreciated that BCCI was no normal bank. Privately they called it 'the bank of crooks and criminals incorporated'. Seven long years before the Bank of England was to announce BCCI bankrupt and freeze its worldwide assets, the CIA Director knew BCCI as the evil brainchild of a financial magus from Pakistan. BCCI banked for drug barons, terrorists, dictators and spy services. With branches in eighty countries and masterminded from the City of London, the whole crooked edifice was run by Pakistanis under the hypnotic sway of BCCI's founder, Agha Hassan Abedi.

Abedi, a man of impressive charm and the features of a falcon, met Casey, Redden and Shaheen for a late breakfast once they had recovered from their 10,000-mile flight. He introduced a sleekly dressed Pakistani to Redden. 'This is Asaf Ali, a world authority on the sale of arms,' he laughed. 'I should say *the* authority.' Casey and Shaheen shook the man's hand. They had met previously. Casey, well over six feet tall despite his old man's stoop, towered above the others.

'This is Javed Abbas,' Abedi next introduced a small, dark-skinned Punjabi, 'from our Protocol Department. In the absence of Sani Ahmed, Javed from Lahore is arranging a good time for us all once the business is over.' He paused as coffee was poured by

18

uniformed servants. 'The President will arrive shortly,' he continued. 'Quite how shortly I cannot say. He will not want to keep you waiting, Mr Casey, but he too is a very busy man these days.'

President Zia ul-Haq ruled Pakistan with military discipline and Shia Muslim fervour. Hands were cut from robbers, adulterous women were stoned to death. Zia had many enemies and lived in a land of assassins. He controlled the drug trade that produced seventy per cent of the world's heroin yet he spoke fine words to the USA about draconian measures to curtail the output.

Zia's arch-enemy, India, was a nuclear power and Pakistan wished fervently to have its own atomic trigger. Abedi's BCCI was sworn to help the mother country buy nuclear secrets and materials through their contacts around the world. This included a complete uranium conversion plant from West Germany. Officially the USA were against Pakistan or anyone else joining the nukes club and they loudly proclaimed Reagan's war on drugs. But US foreign diplomacy was focused above all else on containing the spread of communism. So long as Zia and BCCI continued to support this aim in Afghanistan, a blind eye would be turned on the lesser evil of the spread of atomic warheads and drugs. This awkward dichotomy was partially behind the visit of Casey and Shaheen to secretly meet the Pakistani President with known crime-banker Abedi as their host.

Casey's travelling companion, Albert Redden, had other reasons for having offered his anonymous jet for the flight. He needed to impress Abedi for his own ends. By arriving in Pakistan with Casey he achieved this. He was as loyal to Casey as was Shaheen and just as patriotic an American citizen as many a vicious Mafioso from Chicago or Miami. But professionally he was an international criminal with irons in many fires and influence in all the right places. Through The Friends he had access to Casey and thence the CIA. Through Abedi's banks he laundered huge amounts of money around the globe and, in the early eighties, invested the filtered results in prime property and real estate.

Redden, a German Jew from Dresden, had fled to the USA in 1945, shortly before the Soviets closed in on his homeland. While all around him people died in the Nazis' extermination camps, Redden, an unemotional realist, blamed them for being caught, not Hitler, whom he admired. Fascism made economic sense to Redden.

Communism was the real menace to his way of life and, from his early days in the wartime Bronx, Redden did all he could to fight the spread of Marxism. The OSS took notice and sent Redden back into the Fatherland during the last two years of the war, when Casey decided to position a generation of sleepers east of the Rhine.

Through the McCarthy 'red-hunting' years and into the early seventies, Redden worked for the FBI as well as the fledgeling CIA, always as a freelance and usually unpaid. One of his tasks was liaison with Mafia families when their support was needed for difficult projects like the Bay of Pigs operation in 1962. He learnt early on never to cross the Mob and never to poach on their territory.

In May 1972, Redden masterminded an ice-cool robbery at 4936 Thirtieth Place, the empty Washington home of the newly dead FBI Director J. Edgar Hoover, one of Redden's few heroes. The stolen documents were gold dust. Those that referred to Redden's own liaison activities with the Mafia in the 1950s and 1960s were destroyed. Others were kept against a rainy day, for their contents were damning to the high and mighty in politics, business and religion in many countries. Their shelf-life was likely to last well into the next century, for the political, financial or religious brethren, and successors of the filed transgressors, would suffer grave embarrassment should the details be released. Hoover was personally far from unscathed, since, for reasons Redden could not even hazard, the old fox had failed to destroy clear evidence that he, the great denouncer of homosexuality, was himself given to dalliance with little boys and had for years kept his FBI agents off the backs of the Mob, who knew about his peccadilloes.

By the late 1970s, based in Los Angeles and his favoured home – the balmy waters of the Bahamas, where he loved to fish and snorkel – Albert Redden had become one of the world's richest criminals.

His watchword was anonymity and he avoided all excesses. Unmarried and bisexual, he used several identities and seldom made love twice to the same person. Boys and girls, usually black or Asian, were brought to him by his staff, who ensured the young prostitutes remained ignorant of his identity and whereabouts.

Redden conducted his business through his long-time companion Korbi Richter. Their relationship stemmed from 1954, when Redden had infiltrated a left-wing student group in Chicago. The students became suspicious and cornered him in a car park. They left him for dead but one of their number, the eighteen-year-old Richter, a fellow German Jew and an activist only because of peer pressure, took Redden to his lodgings and nursed him back to health. For a while they were lovers but Redden soon reverted to younger boys and their relationship became a business partnership with Redden as the undisputed leader.

Richter's émigré father flourished in Peruvian business and had sent his son to the States for a sound education. Richter Senior had been a harsh parent and Redden found young Korbi an unquestioning protégé with a nimble brain. They shared a love of animal games that originated at stevedores' cock-fights in Chicago. Over the years they lost interest in the gambling aspect and gained their kicks through the sheer excitement of watching the naked aggression of the combatants, be they Spanish bulls and matadors or cobras and mongooses.

Javed Abbas excused himself from Abedi's high-powered group in order, he said, to check on the secure arrival of President Zia and to arrange refreshments for the presidential entourage. Like Redden, Javed was not all that he seemed. Abedi had introduced him as a BCCI Protocol Officer. This was not so. Because the meeting was to remain clandestine, Abedi had handed its organisation, including entertainment for the Americans, to a department of BCCI known to the CIA as the 'Black Network' but not acknowledged as such by Abedi. As far as he was concerned, Javed Abbas and his colleagues were a necessary evil who did the dirty work.

The Network – for want of another name – was present wherever BCCI operated and a handful of senior BCCI executives worldwide knew whom to call when they needed pressure to be applied. Gentle persuasion, crude blackmail, disinformation, well-prepared accidents or, in the final analysis, termination. All could be arranged by the well-paid men and women of The Network. Four years previously Javed had worked for The Network in Washington, where Abedi was trying to persuade people of influence to allow BCCI expansion in the USA. Bribery was the main tool. Big sums of cash were involved. This had worked well in the Carter regime but Javed was rebuffed by one of his Reaganite targets, who contacted the FBI.

Soon afterwards an agent visited him, taking care to find him alone. If the Network learnt of this approach, no matter whether or not Javed succumbed to the FBI overtures, his days would be numbered. That, he knew, was the way of his colleagues. Since Jed Mason, the FBI agent involved, made it clear that Javed's refusal to comply would result in compromising photographs of their meeting finding their way back to the Network, he had little choice. He and Jed had since become quite friendly. Javed was well paid whenever he produced worthwhile information.

Javed was no fool: he had watched Abedi tread arrogantly through many minefields and he had heard muted rumours of Washington hounds baying for BCCI blood. Sooner or later the empire would collapse and when that happened he, Javed, saw a rosy future for himself in Asia as an FBI placement.

He did not trust the telephones in the villa but he needed to inform Jed quickly of the unexpected good news. Redden had come with Casey and nobody, but nobody, Javed knew, excited Jed as much as Albert Redden. What should Javed do? Photos? Recordings? Honey trap? He would need to speak direct to Jed, which was fine since at that hour in Washington Jed should be at home in bed with his wife.

Javed's driver dropped him at a village grocery store ten minutes from the villa. He trusted the driver as far as he could throw a rupee. The Network watched one another and Javed trusted nobody. At the rear of the store, for a healthy tip to the grocer, he called Washington.

Jed replied at once and, responding to Javed's report, told him to stick like glue to Redden whenever he and Abedi met.

'After this business,' Javed said, 'they will be entertained locally. I have made the arrangements on Abedi's instructions. A bear fight and the doll-girls.'

'Fine.' Jed's voice was sharp. 'But ensure you record *all* their dialogue, especially at the bear fight. Just the sort of open-air place for talk about laundering Redden's money through BCCI. Miss nothing, my friend.'

Javed thought for a while, then called his apartment in Lahore. Gul Zaman Khan replied. Javed had met Zaman two years before at a meeting between Abedi and President Zia. Zaman was then a member of General Yousef's feared ISI and a personal bodyguard of the President. Javed and Zaman met many times in the course of their work and became friends. They shared the same sense of humour. Zaman, tall and fair-skinned, was no believer in tact. Like all Pathans, he was a fiercely religious Muslim and failed to disguise his frustration at his boss Zia's half-hearted Islamisation of Pakistan.

Zaman's outspoken nature had, some five weeks previously, resulted in his sacking by the ISI and the laying against him of false accusations of corruption. To avoid imprisonment he had gone into hiding and Javed had given him a safe haven in Lahore until the dust settled. Javed had also promised him a well-paid job with 'The Network', a body he painted as being pro-Pakistan and anti-American. He now asked Zaman to help him with a Network task of grave import to the government. 'An influential American businessman,' he told Zaman, 'is to meet my boss, Hassan Abedi, tomorrow at a bear fight. We need to record their conversation and I need a backup. What about it?' Zaman, sensing some test of his abilities by The Network before they offered him a job, agreed without hesitation.

Javed rang off and purchased bags of groceries to cover his sojourn in the store. Back at the villa, gate security confirmed the arrival of Zia's helicopter within the hour.

President Zia sat in an upright teak chair. His mind was razor sharp and given to compartmentalisation, an English word that he used frequently. Fresh from a meeting with his ISI spy chiefs, he relished their reports. Sikh extremists were causing trouble for his arch-foe Indira Gandhi. She had sent tanks to attack the Sikh holy places. They would never forgive her. Her days, he divined, were numbered and his ISI 'stirrers' had assured him they were at work to hasten the process.

Zia's black eyes took in the lack of trappings in the stark, white room – Abedi's way of showing how little he cared for ostentation. Zia disliked Abedi in much the same way that de Gaulle had been irked by Churchill. Proud men hate to be indebted and Zia was as proud as they come despite the Prophet's diktats on humility.

Abedi, he knew, had nurtured his BCCI bank through sound manipulation of worldwide geopolitical trends. The petrodollar boom of the 1970s had helped nourish the bank from its infancy, and, when the oil money showed signs of wilting away, Abedi had

23

switched to arms and drugs. By the time Zia had come to power and found himself economically dependent on Pakistan's drugs income, banker Abedi was on the wave crest. So long as the Afghan war flourished he knew the USA would remain silent about drugs. Drug Enforcement Administration zealots would be kept in check by the CIA.

Zia's ISI and BCCI's own intelligence network were incestuously linked as indeed were the men running the bank and governing Pakistan. They had become interchangeable, each recruiting from the other. The mutual benefit to the two leaders was inestimable. Some months previously Abedi had given Zia a personal cheque for $3 million. Even so, the warmth of their relationship was less than skin-deep.

Zia's vision saw Pakistan under his rule as an Islamic superpower declaring a jihad against the infidel Soviet Communists and for this he needed US aid in huge quantities. But such support must remain *sub rosa*. He had no wish for the Islamic world to brand him as an American puppet. Hence the need for the secrecy of his meetings with CIA Director Casey.

The two men with Casey were, he assumed, mere spooks and gofers. They would not be present unless Casey trusted them. Abedi would mastermind the administration of whatever was agreed between Zia and Casey.

Zia's Presidential Guard surrounded the villa but not with their standard open show of strength. Passers-by on the road leading to the Lahore–Sahiwal highway would note nothing unusual. Javed was responsible inside the villa. He sat outside the only entrance to the meeting room and reflected on his technical arrangements.

Jed had asked for tapes of all Redden's meetings and the identity of anyone involved with him. Javed had found a long-disused larder in the villa's cellar and hidden the recording equipment in two briefcases in cupboards with fronts of perforated zinc. The transmitting microphones had been more difficult to position because of the lack of furnishings in the meeting room. Eventually he had settled on two empty vases, filled them with dirt and taped the transmitters to their inner lips.

Javed's mistake was understandable, for he had no reason to suspect surveillance. After all, Abedi had ordered The Network to supervise the meeting and, within the villa, Javed *was* The Network.

24

But the BCCI Protocol Department, normally in charge of all events at the villa and any meetings involving foreign VIPs, operated their own in-house snooping programmes. Any movement or sound within the meeting room and the bedrooms of the villa was automatically recorded by hidden cameras. At the end of any visit Protocol employees took used tapes back to their headquarters for checking, analysis and filing. So Javed's every move in the meeting room was on record.

William Casey, like Zia, had every reason to keep the meeting a close secret. He was circumventing the CIA, his own agency. In the event of any leakage he could fall back on his ulterior role as Reagan's personal adviser and maintain his actions were undocumented and nothing to do with official CIA business. Where he could minimise risks by having The Friends, such as Shaheen and Redden, represent his interests, so much the better. With the likes of Zia, however, this was unacceptable. The Pakistani President only talked to top men.

Casey was well aware of the fears of Congress, fuelled by advice, in some cases, from his own CIA intelligence analysts. If the USA was seen to arm Zia, the arguments ran, India would be upset and climb even further into Brezhnev's bed. And worse, using American-sponsored weaponry, the Afghan mujahidin were loose cannons. Some had already attacked north into the Soviet Union. This, Congress fretted, could well be considered by the Kremlin as a US-inspired attack on Soviet soil.

Knowing that the Congressional committees would deny him the official go-ahead and budgets to achieve his dearest aims on Reagan's behalf in Afghanistan, Casey had taken his own clandestine path. Distrusting the professionals in his own agency for the work, he used only The Friends. His end goal was the injection of $5 billion worth of clandestine support to the mujahidin, much of it to be sought by Abedi through his Islamic friends in Saudi Arabia and the Gulf states.

The meeting went well. Shaheen and Redden kept their counsel, joining the conversation only when Casey, infamous for his mumbling speech, was unintelligible to both Abedi and Zia.

Much of the weaponry was to come from Third World sources: Asaf Ali gave a detailed rundown on how he would achieve this. His branch of BCCI were past masters at false documentation to simplify the purchase and transport of arms worldwide. Contact with the mujahidin would be through Zia's ISI. Unaccountable monies from within the CIA budget, paid to untraceable BCCI accounts, would oil the machinery inside Pakistan, the launching pad for all operations into the war zone.

'I am assured,' Zia said quietly, 'that the Kremlin is sending forty thousand more soldiers to Kabul next month and intends to start bombing our refugee camps on the border. Their policy is escalation to crush all resistance.'

'We tried that in Vietnam,' Casey rejoined. 'It failed.' They discussed the ongoing work of ISI agents in Kabul to spread heroin addiction within the Soviet forces. Abedi's people were involved in this, mountain men hired by The Network to transport Asaf Ali's weaponry from the Pakistan border, whither the Pakistan Army dumped it, and deep into the mountain strongholds of the mujahidin. Abedi's cut from all this totalled hundreds of millions of dollars annually: Zia and Casey were his golden geese. He was pleased with the results of the meeting.

When the President had departed, Abedi returned to the meeting room. 'I trust,' he smiled, 'you will all join me tomorrow. I promise you the very best in Punjabi traditional entertainment.'

Casey thanked Abedi but declined. He had a hectic schedule and had to depart immediately.

'My Boeing and staff are at your service, Director,' Redden interjected. 'I must stay behind on business. Mr Abedi, I accept with pleasure your invitation for tomorrow.'

Abedi divided his time between a hectic international schedule and a simple domestic existence in Karachi with his second wife, an attractive former airline stewardess. He had a craving for power and any number of visionary Islam-based ambitions for his empire, but he shunned the trappings of wealth. At his London headquarters in Leadenhall Street none of his senior men had private offices. Everything was open-plan. In this American Jew, Albert Redden, Abedi saw a fellow master schemer but one, he suspected, who favoured dictatorship not democracy within his own organisation. This he deduced from a certain hardness of face and manner. He had, as was his wont, sent for the BCCI file on Redden as soon as the man had unexpectedly turned up with Casey. He noted the considerable business Redden's BCCI accounts already generated.

They bore all the hallmarks of criminal sourcing and yet Casey obviously trusted the man: Abedi was curious.

Redden stayed behind when Asaf Ali departed along with Casey and Shaheen. 'Mr Abedi,' he said quietly. 'Might there be a possibility to talk business?'

'Of course, of course,' Abedi was enthusiastic, 'but right now I am late for a conference. When we meet tomorrow at the entertainment, then we will talk.'

Once the meeting room was empty, Javed played back the tapes. Half an hour later, from a public phone booth, he called Jed in Washington and Zaman in Lahore to update them. He gave Zaman the number of Jed's private answerphone in Washington and final briefing details for Redden's attendance at the bear fight.

From his room in the villa Redden called a number in Delhi. 'I need you here at once with cleaning equipment.' He gave concise directions to the villa from Lahore airport. 'Charter a jet. Get here before midnight at the latest. I will be alone in the villa but for the servants. The guards here are all external.'

Nine hours later two Americans in slacks and short-sleeved cotton shirts arrived in a taxi from Lahore. Redden did not enquire about their journey. They followed him to the meeting room. The staff were asleep and Javed was not expected to collect Redden before ten o'clock the next day.

Redden pointed to a ridge of ornamental stucco at standard picture-rail height along a single wall. In two places apertures like mouse-holes peered down at them.

'The owner of this place forbids his architects and designers all frills and excesses. That plaster has been added as camouflage. You are to search this room thoroughly, remove any video and audio recordings you may find, then replace any hardware with care. And, while you are here, check out the other rooms. Wake me when you are finished. You have until dawn, when the staff arrive from their quarters.'

They had finished by 4 a.m. Well-concealed wall panels, allowing access to audiovisual gear installed in wall recesses, were invisible but for the giveaway stucco lining. The technicians replayed a stretch of video to Redden on their portable screen. Only one

27

activity was of interest: the electronic doctoring of the vases by Javed. Redden thanked the men and kept the tape. He had no idea who Javed worked for but he intended to find out.

The technicians soon located Javed's microphones in the vases and his receiving equipment in the cellar but . . . no tapes. Either Javed had failed to record the Zia–Casey meeting or he had sneaked the tapes away afterwards. Redden suspected the latter. When the two Americans were gone, he made a further call before going back to bed.

Javed arrived in a chauffeur-driven BCCI Rolls-Royce. With Casey and Zia gone there was no further need to pussyfoot in public. He treated Redden with the respect shown to all BCCI clients by bank staff. He had planned the day after the fashion of typical Protocol Department hospitality.

Most BCCI customers entertained in Pakistan were Middle Eastern royalty, their princelings and their business functionaries, for whom the fun and games would involve visits to watch and gamble at camel races or to hunt hapless Baluchi houbara buzzards with peregrine falcons, an activity about as skilled as sending leopards after caged mice. When the sport was over, BCCI Protocol laid on sex and drugs in Lahore or, as an expedient, trucked the girls, boys and cocaine, to wherever the clients were ensconced.

Briefed as to Redden's special sporting proclivities, Javed had replaced the camel and buzzard routine with another more suitable Pakistani custom: the bear fight. They sped along poor roads to Gojra, creating mayhem in crowded places. At first Javed tried to converse with his passenger but the latter seemed morose, so he relapsed into the occasional tour guide-type comment on the scenery and, as they approached their destination, a rundown on Pakistani bear fighting.

'Normally there are no fights in summertime. I have arranged today exceptionally for your good self.' He glanced at Redden, who nodded, expressionless. The man was short on the basic graces. Jed would sort the bastard out and hopefully the tapes would help: they were safely locked in the glove compartment. He intended to hand them to the FBI agent in Lahore that night.

'What does your Prophet say about the fights?' Redden asked, glancing coldly at Javed.

'Allah is clear. We must be kind to all animals. The Koran forbids the fights. So does the government, but local officials issue permits in exchange for "*muk-muka*". We stage maybe three thousand fights every year. Everybody involved makes good cash except the organisers, who are local landowners, and they enhance their image by holding the events.' Javed swore as a pi-dog charged across the road and bounced off the side of the speeding Rolls.

'Nobody cares much for animals here. Least of all for bears, who eat sheep and damage crops. Farmers find the dens. Hunters then shoot the mother bears and carry off the cubs in bags by truck to the middlemen, who in turn sell them to Qalander gypsies, the trainers, in Lahore.'

'How do they teach them to fight?'

'Bears have big noses which are super-sensitive. The gypsies burn holes through their palate and their nostrils to take metal rings. For the rest of their lives they will do what they're told to avoid the fearful nose pain. Their teeth and claws are torn out with pliers to keep the fights balanced. The Qalanders control their bears through the medium of constant pain.'

They came to the place of the fight in low scrub country. Javed left the road, following colourful bunting lashed to thorn bushes and leading to a clearing where many cars and oxen, donkeys and vendors of drinks milled about a central area screened off with flags of brilliant hues. Asian music and excited voices jangled from loudspeakers wired to trees. Javed parked to one side and a squad of men in green pyjama suits materialised, bowing their respect as they opened the doors of the Rolls.

Abedi was seated in a place of prominence and Javed led Redden to a leather-backed chair at his side. A group of noisy onlookers squatted in the enclosure right behind Abedi. These were the men who had placed major wagers on the coming contest. Gul Zaman, among them, was shabbily dressed in a khaki *shalwar-kamiz* and a Peshawari cap. He smoked busily, clenching the cigarette between the last two fingers of his right hand with the air of a man just emerged from the wilderness. Even Zia would have had difficulty in recognising his former bodyguard, once a graduate of Kakul, the best military academy east of Sandhurst.

Javed could discern no sign of the directional sound recorder he

29

had sent Zaman the previous day. He hovered close by Abedi, who briefed the American about the entertainment.

Redden relished moments such as this. Power play with one of the world's great manipulators, the opening moves of a new game and, as seasoning, animal sport and sex in the offing. Redden purred within but, outwardly, the thin lips and cold eyes continued to survey the world with disdain.

The loudspeaker hysteria crackled to a sudden halt and the excited crowd of two or three thousand fans abruptly closed about the arena as the first bear was led in by its Baluchi owner. The spectators squatted or stood in a wide circle, blood-lust up and aware that VIPs present for such winter events in summer were as rare as pork-fat sellers in a mosque. Many had recognised Abedi, a local hero, and the gossip buzzed.

'Bad bear.' Abedi leant across to Redden and pointed as the Baluchi yanked viciously at the nose ring of his shaggy Himalayan brown bear, which clearly had no inclination for the fight. The announcer began to sing its merits nevertheless, its track record and its owner's status. Three Qalanders fixed a neck tether, a five-metre rope, to a heavy ground-mounted arena peg and removed their bear's nose lead.

Nobody rated the animal's chances. Its owner trained his bears to dance on red-hot metal trays and this did not help their fighting ability. He sold off some of his best cubs to Chinese restaurants, where the little animals were lowered trussed and alive into boiling water in front of rich Japanese gourmets who ate the paws and meat and then took gall-bladder titbits home as a medicinal remedy. Well-trained bears can fetch £4000 but not the Baluchi's. Some of the crowd jeered his animal as it cowered against the central peg.

The first couple of fighting dogs were announced. Two white Tasi bull terriers owned by a Pathan and specially trained as bear-fighters since puppyhood.

As the dogs were unleashed the crowd went silent. Redden licked his lips and aimed his video at their jaws. They growled in unison, feral hair bristling as they sniffed the fear of the bear. Their lips snickered back across their jaws. Both knew they must go for the nose, avoid the flailing paws.

The bear stood up, brown eyes darting but knowing there was no escape, no alternative but to fight. He was six feet tall and three years old. For two years he'd had a sister but they had taken her away to China to be bled for her gall-bladder fluid. His layer of dense, red-brown underwool should protect most of his body from the Tasis' fangs. His soft black nose was horribly torn from previous fights and from the daily cruelty of his owner. As the dogs began their dance, he whimpered with the sound of a human baby.

Redden's hands clasped the camera. He began to breathe heavily. The dogs rushed at the bear in a well-coordinated pincer attack. One leapt high; the other closed powerful jaws about the bear's tail. The bear swayed like a boxer and slapped at the leaping Tasi, breaking a rib. As the dog fell, the bear dropped down to hold it captive against the dirt floor, leaving both paws free to fend off the other cur.

Two more dogs were brought in as the crowd jeered and whistled. These were of sterner stuff and soon the dust was red with blood from the bear's lips, ears and nose. None the less it crushed more canine ribs and staved off defeat.

A third pair of dogs were released and these were the Pathan's best. They leaped high, crunching sharp incisors into the bloodied nose of the tiring bear. Soon he collapsed and the dogs held him down, their teeth slicing through his face, removing one eye. The fight was over. Redden was content. This was true sport. Abedi watched him and knew that business would be good. They retired to a chocolate-brown Bentley Continental where drinks and canapés were served before the servants withdrew. Only Javed remained in the vicinity of the limousine and neither he nor Gul Zaman was close enough to learn that, for a brief minute, he himself was the subject of the conversation.

Abedi appreciated Redden's breadth of outlook. He felt the presence of a kindred spirit, a man not subject to cramping limitations of vision. Their conversation ranged wide before Redden steered the topic via oil to weapons of war.

The current round of CIA support for Pakistan's Afghan jihad was perfectly timed for Abedi. By May that year the price of oil worldwide had collapsed and Gulf oil revenues had halved within a month. Weapons and drugs filled the resulting vacuum in BCCI's coffers. Two billion dollars of US aid was paid for with Saudi cash and BCCI handled much of the action. Helicopters, mines and howitzers were simple to source but there were other, lesser-known items on the shopping list that were extremely difficult to procure and required great discretion on the part of the handlers. In this BCCI stood head and shoulders above all other agencies.

BCCI was established in countries where the CIA had few assets. BCCI even handled covert transfers of top-secret US technology to Soviet-bloc countries. Irangate was child's play by comparison. The F16a jet fighter – top US sophisticate in the aerial combat field – was included in Abedi's spider's web.

General Zia needed nuclear warhead materials for his atomic dreams and Abedi's men were in the process of obliging him. Pakistan's Special Forces, conducting war games involving raids deep into India, had given Abedi weird and wonderful shopping lists which he in turn had put out to tender. Redden was about to come up with one of Zia's most sought-after goodies.

Early in 1980, with an eye to arson and insurance fraud in big cities, one of the West Coast Mobs had begun paying a retired rocket-fuel expert to develop fire accelerants with the general idea of starting a major conflagration from a suitcase. At first the Mob were happy but rising R&D costs, coupled with a shift of focus away from arson, led them to sell their interests in the scientist and his gadgetry to Redden.

Federal investigators, called in by local fire services worried by Redden's spectacular test fires, had dubbed the unknown arson ingredients High Temperature Accelerant or HTA. By 1984 a 45-gallon drum of HTA could destroy an empty warehouse in minutes.

When the conversation led naturally to the topic of Redden's ongoing research into HTA, the German produced colour video footage of the most recent experimental fire. Abedi was impressed. They talked money. 'There is one small problem,' Redden said, looking at Abedi. 'I need six more months of research to perfect things.'

It was agreed that BCCI would contribute to Redden's further development costs. The cash would come from US and Saudi funds intended for Pakistani arms, so the deal could almost have been described as legitimate.

They moved on to discuss Redden's European plans. He was shortly expecting a heroin shipment in England worth £10 million in cash. Abedi assured him that BCCI London would launder this in minutes.

32

Redden's cocaine empire was based in Miami and supplies came from Medellín, in Colombia, where Abedi had recently purchased the giant Banco Mercantil. Cocaine was now flooding into the USA, where prices had fallen dramatically. So Redden was opening new action in Europe, starting in the UK. Market research revealed that Jamaicans were the undisputed kings of crack in Britain and Redden's Jamaican connection, a corrupt police chief, had introduced him to Tricks. 'If you want a good soldier-boy to handle your business in the UK, you couldn't do no better than Tricksy.'

Based between Tottenham in London and Handsworth in Birmingham, Tricks was mean, arrogant and as streetwise as a tomcat. He and Redden had quickly clicked.

Abedi agreed to open two new special accounts for Redden's burgeoning UK laundering requirements. He also discussed using Redden's hard men in the UK for freelance dirty work on behalf of BCCI where Asians were inappropriate.

They shook hands. Taking Javed with them, they flew to Lahore in the BCCI Bell Ranger helicopter. Javed, during the general bustle after the bear fight, had passed Gul Zaman a package to go at once, with Zaman's own taped gleanings, to Jed in Washington.

On arriving at the Lahore heliport, Abedi's party were met by a businessman in a Western suit whom Abedi introduced as 'Executive Siddiqi'.

'Javed and I will leave you now and meet you for dinner in four hours.' Abedi departed and Siddiqi ushered Redden to yet another BCCI Rolls-Royce. They drove to a low brick house close by the imposing silhouette of the Bad Shai mosque in the Hiramand district. From somewhere within the building issued the haunting sound of a sitar.

Redden passed the next two hours experiencing visual and sensory delights such as few people even dream about. He chose his companions, all trained from the age of nine or ten to give pleasure through titillation and the erotic arts, by watching them play with one another in front of his chair. The cream of the doll-girls and doll-boys of Lahore's Diamond District. None was older than twelve and all were selected for their precocious charms by BCCI Protocol staff.

Siddiqi took Redden away after he was bathed and, somewhere in an adjacent building, he dined alone with Abedi. Business was discussed only after coffee and confined to the distasteful matter of Javed, who had died an hour earlier under interrogation.

'We applied the technique of the hooks,' Abedi's man told Redden, 'and he talked quickly. However, we could not find the tapes where he said they would be, so we gave him a second, more intensive spell, and it seems that his heart was unexpectedly weak. We could not revive him. We cannot be sure who he worked for but we believe it must be an American agency. My people are even now searching the villa, the cars and the place of the bear fight, for we feel sure he did not have the chance to pass on the tapes.'

Redden was annoyed. He suspected that Abedi's men had failed to act quickly enough and he did not share their confidence about the tapes. Javed might have smuggled them out by some prearranged means.

He was not greatly concerned. He would have to warn Casey that his talks with Zia were compromised. He suspected Javed was a CIA or FBI informant but he might even be Abedi's own man. He had no proof after all that an interrogation had even taken place. He had long ago learnt that in the rarefied world of intrigue in which he moved everybody watched everybody else. His own talks with Abedi were anyway not part of the villa tapes. He relaxed.

In Washington Jed took the tapes to the Department of Justice and argued that Redden's very presence at the Casey–Zia meeting made him sufficiently important in terms of national security to warrant a permit for full FBI surveillance of the LA office Redden shared with his criminal colleague Korbi Richter. The permit was granted. The net, it seemed, was falling into place. Now any evidence resulting from the surveillance of either Redden or Richter would be usable against them in court.

When Jed received the tapes from Zaman he found that the recordings were disjointed, but they gave the gist of Redden's HTA proposal and the meat of his UK activities. He called Ridgway from Washington. 'Hi, JR. How are you placed for a week or two in Europe?'

3

July 1984

Lucy was enthralled by the whole thing. And so were her parents. The very newness of the rented colour TV – until then they had made do with black and white – greatly enhanced the dazzling spectacle of the Opening Ceremony of the 1984 Olympics, live from Los Angeles. Hollywood's best ensured that the showmanship and glittering pizzazz, the massed gymnastic displays and giant Disney floats, the incredible laser and pyrotechnic extravaganzas, all served to confirm LA as the showbiz hub of the universe.

They sat side by side on the new sofa, not yet covered, and temporarily forgot their predicament, the alarming mortgage and Dad's continuing unemployment. He looked at his wife and daughter, eyes moistening with a surge of protective affection. He would find work. They deserved the finest of homes and he would find a way of providing everything they wanted. Sunday was about to emerge here in Dudley if not in Los Angeles. They would sleep in, have brunch, then go off for a spin to Kinver Wood, which they had started to explore the previous weekend.

Eight hours later, at Heathrow's International Terminal the Pan Am flight from Los Angeles was overdue. John Potter, top shaker at Pan Am Special Services in Terminal Three, handed over to a pretty blonde supervisor and headed for home. Special Services dealt with the private jets of VIPs and John knew most of them, from George Bush to Joan Collins. He took the frequent tantrums of his customers with a pinch of salt – just as well or he would have been long dead from ulcers. None the less he felt a healthy dislike for the two black gentlemen who had spent the last hour in the cramped Special Services lounge, smoking non-stop and waiting with open impatience for the private 727 from LA. John was no racist but these Jamaicans were arrogant to the point of rudeness.

Tricks turned up the TV as the Pan Am man left. The little blonde was cute but he didn't want her listening. Yet another replay of the LA Opening Ceremony drowned his conversation with Donnie, his chauffeur and general fixer of a dozen years. Tricks appreciated loyalty but seldom rewarded it, for he was above all a selfish man. For the last two years he had run a small army of 'mules' carrying Colombian cocaine from Kingston to Heathrow. Many were caught by Customs but none fingered him, for they feared him more than six years in a British nick where conditions were far better than back home in the ghetto. Most of Tricks's mule-girls were past their prime: their men had left them for younger meat and they depended on the £2000 he paid them for each 10-oz run to Heathrow. When Customs ran a purge at Heathrow, Tricks re-routed to easy-going Stansted.

One practice was to scrape the stuffing from a 10-inch dildo, jam it full of the white powder, seal the open end and insert it in the vagina. Much safer than swallowing even well-lubricated condoms. Two of Tricks's girls had died from burst condoms. Cocaine ingestion caused overstimulation of the nerves, coma and kidney failure. An awful way to go.

Tricks knew the mathematics. His best mules, swallowing 120 condoms, each of several grams, could arrive with a third of a kilo to retrieve from the pan; a messy business but one best closely invigilated to discourage cheating. His Jamaican source, Mascel of Spanish Town, invested £4500 in each 10-oz load. This was split £2000 to the cocaine source, £2000 salary to the mule, £400 air ticket and £100 pocket money. On UK streets and watered down, one load could fetch Tricks £10,800 at £20 per half gram. Good business by anyone's standards but chicken-feed compared with his expectations from his new American bosses; the men he had come to greet.

Tricks used a number of street-names and carefully segmented his associates in different areas of his affairs. His Birmingham reggae partners knew him as Mafia or Spud. To his family he was simply Stafford, and in the States he answered to Tricks or Vix.

For a fortnight his London killer squad had searched for the Colombian Guzman, on Richter's death list. But Guzman had never surfaced. Tricks could only assume the man was avoiding all contact with the Jamaican networks, trying to set things up through South Americans or Turks. If so, he would not get far, for at street level the Jamaican 'Yardies' controlled ninety-nine per cent of the UK crack-cocaine market. Once Guzman faced up to this and made overtures to the Yardies, Tricks would hear and Guzman would die. Tricks used assassins from Jamaica to kill in the UK and vice versa.

A thickset American with a TWA shoulder bag, chrome-edged Raybans and a tennis racket sat opposite Tricks and Donnie. Tricks thought the man was listening to their conversation and gave him the cold eye. This frightened most people but the tennis player continued to stare at the TV monitor. John Ridgway, 'JR', believed in close play when shadowing targets. So long as he avoided eye contact, he found he was seldom compromised by the bold approach and, right now, he needed to learn Tricks's short-term intentions in case he lost him going out of the airport. This was likely, for JR's MI5 contact gave the appearance of being an amateur and he had no other backup in the UK. Jed Mason was in Washington on another case.

The Javed tapes of the Lahore meeting had opened the way for maximum surveillance of the Redden–Richter headquarters on Wilshire Boulevard. The FBI had taken ten years to nail Al Capone and Jed was just as determined to put the two Germans away for life. Whatever tapes, bugs and evidence of money laundering were necessary to blast away the protection these bastards received from on high, he and JR would obtain. What worried them was the inexplicable blocking of previous searches Jed had set in motion at high levels in Washington for existing information on the Germans.

'The CIA are behind it,' Jed was pretty sure. 'They should be called the CYA, "cover your ass",' he snorted. 'They use scum like Redden to help their operations and then they're saddled with protecting this same low life merely to keep their own name clean.'

'Ma Bell' had contacted a dozen firms in other parts of the Redden office block. The whole building was to have new phone systems installed to avoid suspicion. The FBI was footing the bill for all this, proof indeed that Javed's tapes had made the Bureau sit up and take notice. A few years back, in the post-Watergate Carter era, such surveillance would have required a personal OK from the Attorney General. But Reagan, under his wide-ranging Executive Order 12333, had lifted bans on wire-taps and bugging as well as allowing the collection of dossiers on US citizens and the infiltration of suspect organisations.

Following the installation of the new Bell system in the Redden offices, JR had spent three days ensconced in a disused ground-floor office straight across the boulevard. With headphones and two outsize tape recorders, he listened to every call made by Richter and Redden from their executive desks. They would never detect bugs, for there were none. Bell were simply diverting the signals to the FBI as they were legally bound to do.

The previous week, when Richter's secretary had called the captain of Redden's 727 to arrange the flight plan to Heathrow, JR had listened in. He learnt from a subsequent call to London that Tricks was to meet Redden and Richter to discuss the shipment of a £10-million boatload of heroin to London from the Lebanon. With luck and MI5's fraternal cooperation, JR might garner enough evidence in the UK to hook a RICO (Racketeer Influenced Corrupt Organization) conspiracy charge on Redden. The RICO statute, a federal law devised in the early 1980s, was fast becoming the FBI's major weapon against major criminals adept at hiding in the woodwork. By arresting and getting evidence from *any* lowly criminal, some way down a particular crime chain – Tricks, for example – the FBI could, through a RICO charge, prosecute also the main conspirators and bosses at the centre of the web controlling the criminal, even though these bosses were demonstrably not involved at the crime scene itself.

For over forty years J. Edgar Hoover had kept his FBI away from the drugs scene. This was left to local police forces and the Drug Enforcement Administration. When William Webster, the current incumbent, took over the FBI six years earlier, things had changed and the Head of the Los Angeles FBI, Charles J. Parsons, was now as heavily involved in nailing drug crime as was the LAPD.

Two months previously the CENTAC project, set up by the DEA to chase international narco-criminals like Redden, was for political reasons (and because of inter-agency jealousies) handed to the FBI. Jed and JR's ongoing and personal crusade, to hunt Richter and (since the Javed tapes) also his colleague Redden, was beginning to receive the mantle of an official Bureau activity. Their wire-taps and bugs were now legitimate and the ability to call on support from foreign friends, like MI5, was a big bonus.

MI5 had nothing recorded on Tricks but Scotland Yard produced a thin file on the Jamaican as well as general notes on UK-based Yardies of his ilk. So JR knew enough to appreciate the force of the cold stare from the black man in the Pan Am office. He was unfazed by the cold aggression emanating from the drug dealer, for he, JR, held the cards. This guy, possibly the key to convicting Redden and Richter, symbolised to JR the whole evil narcotics trade, currently worth half a trillion dollars annually – more than the total value of all US currency in worldwide circulation. JR's ears strained as Tricks spoke to his minion.

'Call Blackledge,' he instructed Donnie. 'Tell him we'll meet him this afternoon as agreed. He must have enough wagons for all of us, including the Yanks. We don't want our own number-plates associated with this fuckin' animal stuff out in the countryside.' He shook his head. 'Bloody nutters, these Yanks, I tell you. Why can't they stick to business? And hey, Donnie, tell that Blackledge we don't want some place right out nowhere. He should make it close to Brum. OK?'

JR lit up a Camel and mentally reviewed what he had read about his quarry. Born in St Catherine, Jamaica, late in 1949, Tricks had come to England in the early sixties with his parents after basic secondary education at Russell School in Kingston. His parents divorced and his father went to the States. His mother settled in Handsworth, a black ghetto in Birmingham.

At first Tricks had made his money repairing cars, collecting the dole and selling cannabis, but his real talent lay in reggae. He moved between Jamaican communities in the UK, with occasional trips to Jamaica, and acquired contacts among the top reggae groups and DJs. He set up his own sound system, the best around, and his records sold to reggae brothers all over the UK and JA (Jamaica). He

39

called his system Tipper Town, or Mafia Town, or Now Generation. Sometimes he made extra cash from robbing post offices and banks, using 'knife-point pressure', although he carried a big black .38 Smith and Wesson.

The Muhammad Ali Centre in Hackney was his base for a while. In the seventies his wife, Carol, twice instigated hearings against him for actual bodily harm. He had eight children in various cities. In Birmingham little by little he became a big guy, a respected 'don'. In London he was outclassed by nastier colleagues, bigger dons like Rankin' Dred, Tappazuki and Superspade. Dred stole money from him in 1984 and he backed down, knowing Dred had killed seven men in Jamaica and a few more in the UK.

Tricks took his sound system all over, but Birmingham was his chief haunt, dives like the Porsche Club and the Humming Bird at the Leisure Club. He had his records pressed in Shepherd's Bush and bought a shop in Seven Sisters Road which sold Italian clothing.

JR noted that Tricks was a snappy dresser, what West Indians call 'sleek'. Gold Rolex, gold rings and bracelets, crocodile-skin shoes, well-cut two-piece grey suit from Pressburgers in Queensway and a broad-brimmed beaver 'Capone' hat.

In 1983 Tricks lived in Edmonton, north-east London, and stashed his drugs at his mother's house. But Tappazuki double-crossed him and ran off with £15,000 of the takings from a concert. Tricks called a friend in New York, Sal, who flew in at once and stalked Tappazuki for two weeks in Brixton. Bullets flew about until the Met interfered. Tricks had to sell up in London and, back in JA, ran into Mascel, a senior police officer in Spanish Town. He never looked back, for Mascel ran cocaine from Colombia to the UK and USA. Tricks became Mascel's main mover to Heathrow and Gatwick, where the police chief knew bent Customs men.

Early in 1984 Mascel had given Albert Redden a glowing tribute to Tricks and now here he was, the once nobody-man from St Catherine, sitting in Heathrow, with the big boys from LA expected any minute. The immediate business, he knew, involved £10 million in heroin to be brought into the UK by an amateur crew set up by Richter. When the boat arrived Tricks was to seize the heroin, sell it through his urban networks and use the proceeds, banked through BCCI, to commence the expansion of Redden's European crack empire. By 1990, all being well, Tricks would no longer be just another posturing UK Yardie, but Mr Big, controlling the distribution of vast amounts of Colombian coke to swamp the UK and thence Europe.

Linda Forsaithe, the blonde Pan Am Special Services supervisor, approached Tricks. The 727 had arrived. The passengers should be at Arrivals in ten minutes. JR waited until Tricks had disappeared, then took the lift to the first-floor car park, filled with uniformed chauffeurs jockeying to park their limousines as close as possible to the lift about to disgorge their relevant VIPs.

At almost any other airport in the world, including most others in Britain, the rich and the famous can arrive by private jet and, avoiding the official entry and Customs routing, go to a special VIP arrivals lounge or even disembark out on the tarmac to be whisked away by their private transport after an on-board check by Customs. At Heathrow this is impossible. There are no exceptions. JR could be sure that Tricks must meet Redden and Richter at the same Arrivals point as every Tom, Dick and Harry entering Britain at Terminal Three.

The American waited until Donnie had parked close to the first-floor lift in a black stretch Mercedes. Then he moved forward, squeezing between the Merc and a Rolls. He dropped his briefcase, swore for Donnie's benefit and, in stooping to retrieve the case, clipped a magnetic transmitter to the under-lip of the Mercedes' bumper. He did this with care, remembering that Jason from MI5 had stressed such hardware was accountable and he, Jason, did not wish to go through the extensive documentation needed to write off a £3000-plus bleeper-bug.

JR climbed into Jason's blue Ford Escort in Terminal Three's short-term car park. Jason was plagued by dandruff and thick bifocals, but he seemed reasonably adept with the knobs and dials of the bleeper's direction monitor, so JR sat back and relaxed as they followed the Mercedes towards central London.

4

26–29 July 1984

Joe Rowberry from New Cottages worked for the parish council. Despite the loss of an eye in an accident, he loved to walk in the wood with his golden labradors. During the previous summer of 1983 a Manpower Services team had cleared a footpath from Kingsford Lane up to the hilltop which faced towards the sudden escarpment of Kinver Edge. On this wooded pimple they had installed a rough vandal-proof bench. Joe often rested there and watched his labradors sniff the rich leaf-mould for news of other dogs.

Two hundred yards from the bench young bracken shoots and adult fronds carpeted a clearing where badger families had lived for many years. A dozen entry holes led down to their sett. Claw marks on a nearby elder, approach trails and latrine pits indicated recent activity. The Bishop family, who lived in nearby Kingsford Cottage, seldom saw their nocturnal neighbours even though another active sett lay close behind their home. Ken Whitehouse, the National Trust Warden of Kinver Wood, often patrolled the lanes but on 26 July he was clearing brush to the north of the Old Kennels.

A 40lb boar badger slept away the afternoon with his wife and another young sow. His stumpy teeth were set in a hinged jaw of great biting and holding power, but much of his food was easy eating: earthworms by the thousands, beetles, rabbits, voles, birds, apples and berries, supplemented by occasional plunder from some farmyard.

One of the sows was dying from gangrene poisoning due to a wire snare which had tightened around her waist. Before snapping from its pegged anchor the cruel device had cut through and lodged in her stomach wall.

A man who lived to the west of Sheepwash Lane had received a visit earlier that July by two rough-looking men from up Blackburn way. Did he have any vermin he wanted put down? He told them about the brocks he had seen in Kinver Wood. He disliked badgers; they carry bovine tuberculosis, steal lambs and poultry, root out fences and flatten crops. In the past he had pumped slurry down setts to drown the pests.

The two Lancashire men worked at a slaughterhouse in Great Harwood. Both had criminal records for assault and, under the respectable guise of keen terrier men, gained pleasure from digging and killing badgers. Paul Norman Blackledge was ruthless, a hard case even by the standards of the Lancashire region, where he grew up. Badgers were his personal addiction: his trade was drug-dealing for both black and white suppliers in the Midlands, as well as selling guns obtained from an Irishman in Glasgow to West Indians in the cocaine business. Blackledge, well known to the Blackburn police, was to become one of the earliest dealers of crack cocaine in the West Midlands. An evil man best avoided.

Two years earlier Blackledge had been conned by a Wrexham dealer and decided to cut his losses. He invited the Welshman to a badger dig near Pencoed and split his skull open with a pickaxe before burying him. No great sum was involved but Blackledge had to think of his reputation. The police never found the body.

Earlier in the summer a West Indian from North London had paid Blackledge £2000 in cash to arrange 'sport' for two American clients. The Americans were international cocaine barons, or so Blackledge understood from the West Indian, who called himself Tricks.

On this occasion Blackledge was told to find a venue within thirty minutes' drive of central Birmingham, and to be ready by 6 p.m. for the Americans' arrival. As before, they would bring video cameras and wanted to view the action close up. This was a tall order even for Blackledge. Badgers are not available everywhere on call.

That afternoon Blackledge parked his van off Birds Barn Lane. Following the detailed instructions of the smallholder, Blackledge came to the sett and whistled when he saw the prints of the big boar.

'Big fucker, this billy,' he told his colleague. 'We'll need a few good terriers on this one and a couple of vans for the stuff. I'll fix it up tonight. We've only got three days till the Yanks come.' The other man looked up as a car rushed by along Kingsford Lane, a mere two hundred yards away through a thin screen of birches.

'Bit dodgy here, innit?' he said, squinting towards the hilltop bench. 'Plus you got paths all over the fuckin' place.'

'Too bad,' Blackledge replied, and shrugged. 'Lucky to get anywhere active at such short notice. I'll get a couple of extra lads to keep their eyes open for a few quid.'

Driving north up the M6, Blackledge searched the radio bands: he needed a weather report for the weekend. But the air was cluttered with reports about British athletes at the Olympic Games in Los Angeles. He swore. He wanted to know that the good weather would hold: the Americans were more likely to hand out generous tips if not soaked to the skin.

Three days later, at a coffee-shop in Kinver, a couple of walkers with a ten-year-old daughter smiled politely and seated themselves in the curved ladder-back chairs. Joan Davies, the proprietor, clocked them in as 'nice clean people'. They ordered coffee and cakes. Milk for Lucy. She was a pretty girl: high cheekbones, corn-blonde hair and wide blue eyes. 'Will there be deer in the woods today, Daddy?' This was their second visit to Kinver Wood. Lucy's birthday gifts that year had included a little automatic camera and she was keen to photograph wildlife.

It had recently poured with rain but on Saturday, 28 July the weather had been fine as they had driven towards Kinver, working at one another's happiness in the manner of devoted dogs licking one another, for Dad was still unemployed and the mortgage loomed large. Just after a boatyard at Stewponey, beside the Stour, they had turned south and soon reached their destination.

'Let's have tea.' Mary had pointed at the picture-postcard bungalow with the cosy name of The Picnic Basket. 'I like to run my tearooms in a proper, old-fashioned way,' Joan Davies told them. She took meal bookings – but not from 'yobbo' types – and organised charity activities for the church and the scouts.

'She's yearning for the fifties,' Mary whispered to her husband when Mrs Davies disappeared to fetch their order.

Feeling better by the minute, they drank the tea and enjoyed their scones.

'Shouldn't we have walked *before* having tea?' Lucy mused.

'Yes,' Mary said, and they all laughed.

Back in the centre of the village, they asked about a good place for a walk.

'Go up Stone Lane and Compton Road,' the attendant at Lowes Garage had told them. 'Turn left into Kingsford Lane and you'll see a little park place on the right. A couple of fellas recently gassed themselves to death there.' He giggled at this gem of local gossip. 'From the park you can have a lovely walk either side of the lane. The Edge is to the east with caves like Nanny's Rock. Or you can go west up to Lydiates and Vermin Valley.'

Dad wore a Barbour and his old Army boots. He was proud that they were all wearing sensible colours that would blend in the woods. They might spot a deer and he knew how happy Lucy would be to take a picture of one. Mary held Lucy's hand as they walked into the brush ahead of him. He realised that, whatever might happen with the job and the house, he was blessed a thousand times over. These two people were his whole world. So long as they were together and happy, how could he possibly be downhearted? He began to whistle. Then he stopped himself as Lucy turned with a grin and a finger to her lips.

The full heat of midsummer had begun to ease with the slow passage of the afternoon. Blackbirds chackered in the undergrowth but there were no other walkers about as they came to the outskirts of Valehead Farm.

Most weekend visitors to the woods, whether tourists or locals, preferred the more interesting paths beneath the cliffs of Kinver Edge on the other side of the lane. Moving quietly by gorse clumps, through sunny glades and up to a little hilltop, the family came to a lonely wooden bench and sat there for a while, squeezed together and whispering, for it seemed the right sort of place for sylvan animals. It was then that they heard the distant yapping of dogs. If only the breeze had been blowing in the other direction, the sound might never have reached them.

5

29 July 1984

At 4 a.m. on Sunday, 29 July the police officers left their Metro car in an invalid bay by the Holly Lane ambulance entrance to the Midland Centre for Neurosurgery, known locally as the Neuro Centre, in the Birmingham suburb of Smethwick. Ben, the fatter of the two constables, had never seen the place so quiet, but then he normally found himself here on Friday or Saturday nights, prime time for alcohol-inspired injuries. He breathed heavily, trying to keep up with his junior colleague. 'Hold it mate. What's the rush? It's a mugging, not a murder, you know.' Both men were from Wombourne village police station, the quietest place on God's earth. Because Kinver was in their parish and that was where the bloke had been found, here they were at the hospital.

The Neuro Centre delighted Ben. Pretty, uniformed women flitted by as he wiped beads of sweat from his eyebrows. They found Ward Ten and the nursing sister, Anne Ellis, who had phoned the station. She was in her early thirties and Ben found her attractive. She noticed his admiration and became less twitchy. Four a.m. was her least favourite hour. Patients were at their lowest ebb at this time and so was she. 'Come to my office,' she growled. 'There may be chairs if they've not been borrowed again.'

She even organised tea. But no biscuits. The patient she wanted them to see had arrived an hour earlier with suspected brain damage from a head injury. Cause unknown but probably a blow from a heavy blunt object. He was nauseous, dizzy, sick and drowsy.

The policemen followed Sister Ellis and the Duty Night Sister down shiny linoleum corridors to the Intensive Care Unit. There was no evidence of third-party involvement. The patient might have simply fallen over and hit his head. There were no identifying papers on him, no cash – nothing.

'Any indication of his being mugged and his belongings stolen, Sister?' Ben had his notepad and pen at the ready.

She shrugged. 'Possibly. Whatever happened to him, there are no witnesses that we know of. He was found three hours ago by a motorist passing through the village of Kinver. He was conscious and his wounds had stopped bleeding. His Good Samaritan dropped him at the nearest hospital, then disappeared leaving no name. The Corbett in Stourbridge, the hospital in question, closed down their casualty department eight weeks ago, so he was shuttled on to Russells Hall Hospital in Dudley.'

'Are *they* clued up on brain injuries?' Ben flashed his brightest smile. 'Like you are?'

Sister Ellis experimented in looking demure; difficult at 4 a.m. 'They did some initial testing in their general ward but decided to pass the buck on to us. They usually do if there's any chance of severe neurological trauma.'

'Have you spoken to him?'

'No.' She shook her head, one hand touching at her neatly tucked bun. 'He rambles, mostly incoherently. Keeps asking who he is and where. He may have been unconscious for hours.'

'What about an X-ray?' Ben asked.

'Of course,' the sister was curt. 'As soon as the ambulance brought us the patient from Russells Hall our registrar, Graham Flint, assessed him and sent him to Radiology. But the scan found nothing untoward. No blood clots nor evident brain damage.'

They followed her to a curtained-off bed. The patient's name card, hooked to the bedstead, was blank.

'He will get a registration number shortly in place of a name,' she announced.

The man's eyes were bloodshot and barely visible beneath puffed-up and discoloured eyelids. Bandages covered his face apart from his nose, which was that of a rugby player who had walked into a door. His right arm lay on top of the bedclothes, revealing a splint attached to one of his fingers.

'The finger is lacerated,' the sister commented. 'The Dudley report indicated that a sharp blade had been used to cut across it.'

'Torture, you mean?' Ben's colleague brightened up.

She shrugged. A young nurse entered with a thermometer and dish.

Sister Ellis spotted the instant directional change of Ben's antennae, blatant to the point of rudeness. She dismissed this inwardly, being much used to the fickleness of men.

'This is Doreen, our auxiliary nurse and very efficient.'

Doreen dimpled. Sister Ellis smiled, 'Show the constables anything they want to see, providing they behave themselves.'

Sister Ellis departed and Doreen showed Ben the patient's clothes. The officers examined each item with care but found nothing which might help identify the man in the bed. A tattered Barbour jacket, corduroy trousers with a couple of well-repaired tears and well-worn Army boots. Jockey underpants, a vest and carefully darned black socks completed the ensemble. The boots were well dubbined. A keen walker, Ben thought. No mud packed the treads but then the ground had been dry the last day or two in most parts of the country. They found grains of red sand in the pockets of the Barbour and inside the boots. Ben looked at the man's fingernails for traces of this sand. There was none, but someone at the hospital might have scrubbed his hands before sewing up his damaged finger.

When they had finished, Sister Ellis was nowhere to be found but Doreen promised that Ben would be notified once the patient was in a fit state to be interviewed.

Three days later Ben returned by himself and was taken to see Professor Hitchcock, the neurosurgeon who was handling the case, an impressive professorial type.

'You can see the chap right away,' he told Ben. 'He's been moved to the Bury General Ward as there's no apparent need for surgery. His scan and X-rays are all clear so his current memory loss is likely to recover slowly but surely. We will keep him for a while for neurological observation. My juniors put in fourteen stitches to the head and finger wounds and, all being well, he should be as right as rain in a few days. He is probably a bit of a loner. Otherwise somebody would surely have enquired after him by now. Or else he's on holiday and is yet to be missed by his nearest and dearest. A simple case of mugging whilst walking in the woods, don't you think?'

'Quite likely,' Ben agreed 'but we must remain open-minded until we can speak to the man.'

Professor Hitchcock's secretary found a porter to take Ben to the patient's new home, a noisy mixed ward with many visitors. The man was propped up with pillows and Ben nearly failed to recognise Doreen in a pretty, flowered shirt and short skirt, sitting beside his bed.

'Can't keep away from him?' he joked.

'He's got no one else but me.' Doreen's smile was infectious. 'Meet Sandy Goodman,' she announced with a flourish.

'Hello there,' Ben addressed the patient's intelligent blue eyes. 'So your memory has come back. Well done. That's good.'

Goodman proffered his left hand and spoke slowly. 'I wish it had. I only know my name because Doreen has given it to me.'

Ben's eyebrows rose.

'Well,' said Doreen 'he was all sandy when they undressed him at Russells Hall and still a bit sandy when I first washed him. I know he's nice, so I chose Goodman. There you go! Until he can come up with the original, he's Sandy Goodman. It's more friendly than a hospital registration number.' They laughed.

The noise made Goodman wince. Doreen was instantly solicitous, her hands to his shoulders. She looked back at Ben. 'He has giddy spells and a headache that he calls a burning pain.' She laid her hand on Goodman's forehead. 'Ben is from the local police,' she said gently. 'He is trying to help find out what happened to you.'

Goodman opened his eyes a little. He seemed to dislike direct light.

'What can you tell me?' he asked Ben. 'What have you found out? Who am I?' He put his good hand to his forehead. 'I get these vicious headaches, like somebody is pressing rocks into my skull. When I wake up I can sometimes remember things. My mother's face. Whole chunks of life back at home when I was little. Vanna the grocer and Dad doing carpentry. But not our name. Each time I try to remember my name, it seems to be Goodman. But, of course, it isn't. That's just Doreen's invention.'

'Can you remember anything about how you received your injuries?'

49

Goodman shook his head. 'Sometimes I feel a dreadful thing happened. With other people. But it's useless to try. It just brings my headaches back. A picture begins to form but then jumbles up and fades into the pain.'

'Did someone hit you? Were you on foot? Do you drive?' Ben was desperate to write something down.

Goodman shook his head. 'I had hoped you would be able to tell me. Has nobody asked for me? No abandoned car? Something from my life out there?'

Ben assured Goodman that the police would let him know just as soon as anything turned up. He went back, as agreed, to Professor Hitchcock. The Professor was looking more relaxed, and invited Ben to join him for a coffee. He began by distinguishing amnesia with an organic cause from psychogenic amnesia. In Goodman's case, X-rays and a brain scan had revealed no damage. Moreover, when there is an organic cause, social awareness is likely to be impaired, yet Goodman had shown no signs of this, remaining well-mannered to the medical staff at all times.

However, when Ben asked him about the psychogenic angle, Professor Hitchcock admitted he was on unfamiliar ground. 'Less simple, and not my field,' he said, with a tone of mild disdain that Ben could not fail to notice. 'I am a neurologist, not a psychologist. I like to think my science is a lot more precise; less awash in theories.

'As with the so-called Rape Trauma Syndrome, psychogenic amnesia can appear without a blow, without concussion. The brain simply decides to blot out an awful memory. Perhaps of an acute financial loss which might, but for the intervention of such amnesia, lead to suicide by the devastated businessman. Soldiers haunted by hideous scenes of military butchery are prone, of course, but each of us is involved in the process every day of our lives in a minor way.'

Ben looked lost.

'Listen,' the Professor explained. 'When you drive on a fast motorway in foul weather or walk through town in the dark, you wilfully suppress the natural fears of what you know could happen, given a touch of bad luck. Instead you try to think positive. You selectively focus your thoughts and suppress the fears simply to get on with your life. This natural mental mechanism to obliterate unwelcome fears is not so far removed from full-blown psychogenic amnesia.'

'Are you talking about a conscious act of forgetfulness?'

'Sometimes, yes. Forty per cent of all homicides and violent criminals practise psychogenic amnesia when interviewed about their crime. This chap we call Goodman is unlikely to be a criminal. His memory loss, if it is sustained, could be caused by brain damage undetected by our machines or a protective mental function to fend off the memory of something fearful to him.'

For the moment, there was nothing more to add. Ben thanked the Professor and took his leave.

Back in the ward, Doreen had gone and Goodman lay awake. He wanted desperately to touch and to talk to somebody who loved him, to reassure them that he was alive. But he did not know where they were or indeed if they existed. Nobody had come forward to claim him. Perhaps he was alone in the world, a man without friends or family. This dread possibility increasingly haunted those periods when the burning in his skull allowed him to think.

6

August 1984

The skipper, Keith Jones, did not like the feel of things. He was an Essex man from Southend, born to the smell of the marshes, and he respected the sea. For thirty years he had handled boats in tricky situations but this was different. He feared the people behind this voyage; he suspected they were out to cut him from his rightful share or even get rid of him. Perhaps tonight. He opened the flares cupboard on the bridge of the *Robert Gordon* and loaded the Colt and the Smith & Wesson pistols, the only weapons on board.

The last day of August 1984; some forty sea miles north of stricken Beirut. Terry Waite, he thought, is out there somewhere. Rimming the dusk-dashed seascape, a twinkling line of lights from the coastal villages disappeared to the north-east towards Al Kabir at the Syrian coastal border with the Lebanon. In other circumstances Jones, part-time seadog and pipe-puffer, would have been happy enough. As it was, he just wanted the whole job done with – get paid and get out. He swore to himself he would never again mess with the likes of Baker and his fellow-bastards.

It began back in 1983, when Bryan Baker, an Essex car dealer and golf-course owner, agreed on a deal with his long-time buddy Frank Simway. For some time Simway had happily run a neat little business importing cannabis from Amsterdam to Sheerness in a fruit and veg truck. Bryan Baker, 'respectable' Bentley dealer, was his partner and, early in 1984, they agreed to blow out the Dutch, who were getting greedy, and run with some powerful new Middle East contacts Baker had made in Cyprus.

Jones cursed the day he became involved with Baker. While in Brixton jail for petty fraud he had met up with some of Baker's cronies who had later remembered his tales of sea dramas, and when Baker wanted a skipper for his newly conceived Middle East run, he made Jones an offer. Jones accepted out of fear. He knew Baker's reputation.

Simway was to be responsible for pick-up and distribution within the UK. Baker would mastermind the foreign connection from the Cyprus villa where he and his girlfriend, Gina Great, enjoyed the sun and dreamed of Essex pubs.

Jones found the *Sallykins* dry-docked in Majorca in June 1984 and Baker sent out John Nicholls from Burnham-on-Crouch, a skilled carpenter and no criminal, to build a secret compartment into the hold. The boat was bought with £35,000 cash from Baker's Bentley business account.

Back in London, Simway continued the last of his Dutch runs but ran foul of the Customs, who caught him, in his BMW, and his greengrocer lorry-driver from Hayes, unloading marijuana bales in the lorry park at Scratchwood Services on the M1. Simway and Co. were put away, which removed Baker's distribution network overnight.

Jones meanwhile tried to sail the *Sallykins* to the Lebanon to collect Baker's first load of cannabis. But major engine defects soon surfaced and he retreated to Majorca. Baker was furious. With Simway in prison, he decided to handle all distribution himself and approached three Harlow friends, two of whom, John Bridger and Geoff King, were heavily into the North London drugs scene.

That June one of Bridger's dealer friends had talked to the wrong man, a friend of Tricks. Tricks had called Richter in Los Angeles.

With his new London network in place, Baker switched his attention to skipper Jones. He appeared unheralded on board the *Sallykins* and made Jones quickly aware of what further delay and failure would mean. Jones remembers the experience. He is himself a stocky man but Baker, a vicious six-foot-five bodybuilder, lifted him up one-handed by a hank of T-shirt and crashed him against the cabin wall. 'You muck up one more time, Jonesy, and I'll fucking tear you apart.'

Jones was told to search for a suitable successor to the *Sallykins*. 'Spend up to £75,000, including what you get for this tub. Then get

53

over to the Lebanon fast. Any expenses, I want to see the receipts. Even your phone calls . . . OK? Screw up again and you're fish food.'

Scared witless, Jones agreed to find a better boat. His girlfriend drove out to Gallow's Corner on the A12 to meet Baker's henchman, Terry Guy, a well-known face at Baker's golf club. He gave her bags of cash for Jones and later called on her by night at the mud mooring under Malden bridge where she lived in a houseboat. 'Nice place this,' was all he said. The threat was unmistakable: if Jones stepped out of line, Guy knew where his girl could be found. That June, Jones had purchased the *Robert Gordon* in Majorca from a pretty Scottish girl. Just in time to keep Baker off his back.

At midnight on the bridge of the *Robert Gordon* Jones ran a hand through his curly, grey-flecked hair. He had spent his time in various nicks over the years, mostly for cheque fraud and petty theft but this was for real. Big-time stuff with all the risks. He was forty-one and felt every bit of it.

'Red light at eleven o'clock,' the Greek deck-hand, Nikos Kefarakis, shouted from the bridge wing. Jones focused his binoculars. In a while the light, on a level with the horizon and just south of the glow of Al Mina, began to pulse a repeated signal, the Morse code for 'K' – dah-di-dah – and Jones recorded its bearing. He nosed forward until, well within the Bay of Tripoli and bobbing among hundreds of moored boats, he told the other deck-hand, Hill, to return the signal with the spotlight. Crude but effective. He smelled rather than heard Sally Erthaimon arrive at his shoulder. He had signed her on at Rhodes as their chef. The deckies' morale had soon perked up with her arrival. Good to ogle and no mean cook. He hoped she would keep her sense of humour when she found out the nature of the cargo they had come for.

They had kept the radio tuned on the agreed frequency but no message had come from Baker in Cyprus. Just a burble and clatter of conflicting conversations pierced by Morse. Greek, French and Arabic predominated.

Tibi Somogyi was a Hungarian war orphan and a rare child survivor of Auschwitz. He did not hate Arabs, because his quotient of loathing was focused solely on Nazism. A deep-seated fear simmered beside the hatred, kept at bay so long as Tibi never left the borders of Israel. Only within the protective portals of the promised land did he feel safe from the dread possibility of a sudden pogrom, another Holocaust. Perhaps an intelligent shrink with great patience could have rid Tibi of his terrible insecurity and the black, haunting shadows of his dreams. He had, at a tender age, witnessed what no human being should ever suffer at the hands of another.

He and his twin sister had been selected by Dr Josef Mengele, Auschwitz's 'Angel of Death', as ideal for genetic research. They had been forced, aged twelve, to couple in incest many times over a six-month period. They had watched the daily trains of death arrive, from Hungary and elsewhere, to disgorge hundreds of thousands of men, women and children to feed the gas ovens and the roaring flames of the crematoria. Tibi still remembered the death screams where others conjure childhood memories of bird calls and schooltime laughter. For him, the smell of burnt flesh instead of baked cookies.

So long as Mengele needed Tibi to copulate with his little sister, neither child would join those other twins, their usefulness over, for phenol injections to the heart and the short wheelbarrow ride to Mengele's pathology slab. So they had begun to actually look forward to each summons to his laboratory. The guilt feelings would never leave Tibi. His answer was to give his life to his new country. He could never enjoy a woman but he could live every day to help protect Israel, his only love and his sanctuary.

Tibi worked for Military Intelligence, that much John Ridgway knew, but for which department and in what capacity he did not ask. JR liked Tibi at once when the gaunt Israeli came to meet him at the airport. Jed, who had worked with Tibi before, had his own Mossad (secret service) and Shin Bet (intelligence) contacts well isolated from normal CIA–Mossad channels. The FBI was slowly expanding direct liaison with certain secret services as a result of repeated bitter experiences where the CIA had failed to respond, often with vitally needed information, because of inter-departmental jealousies.

Bureau Director William Webster had led the way to the establishment of direct contact with foreign agencies and many agents, like Jed, soon developed useful connections with the agents of Israel, France, Germany and a growing number of other nations where, in J. Edgar Hoover's day, they could only have made contact through laborious State Department channels.

Tibi took JR by car from Tel Aviv Airport to the city's Kaplan district and a top-security area inside the Ministry of Defence. 'These' – he showed JR a sheath of pink transcripts – 'cannot leave this room. Indeed you have never seen them.' JR nodded his agreement and spent the next thirty minutes memorising the contents of the edited and translated eavesdroppings of the Israeli electronic ears on the Golan Heights. For immediately after the 1967 capture of the Heights, the Israelis had established, at 8000 feet above sea level, sophisticated listening devices to cover every inch of Lebanese soil and far beyond into northern Syria.

'Amazing.' JR's admiration was genuine.

'Yes.' Tibi was pleased. 'Every conversation between Syrian command in Damascus and all outlying units in the Lebanon, no matter how small, is covered every minute of the day. Each scrap of radio traffic between the PLO, the Lebanese Army and the terrorist groups is sifted by Golan and an army of translators in Qiryat Shemona. The best computer technology available in the world makes it possible for our small land, surrounded by those that hate us, to survive by knowing in advance when the least enemy mice begin to squeak.'

Tibi was fond of Americans. After the Death March from Auschwitz in early 1945 he would have starved but for the kindness of passing GIs.

'So what can we do for you?' he asked as JR replaced the last file.

'Is there a chance I could observe the pick-up? The men I am after, German Americans, will supervise the operation. If I can record the hand-over, that could help us to indict them and many of their colleagues.'

Tibi did not need to check with his bosses. Israelis at his level are trusted with far more latitude of action than in any other developed country. This absence of stultifying controls has saved Israel money, time and lives.

'No problem.' Tibi smiled at JR. Twenty-four hours later, on the last day of the month, the two men, accompanied by a Ministry of Defence surveillance agent, flew by helicopter to the coastal town of Nahariya, a favourite target of Hizbollah raids from Tyre and Sidon. After dusk an inflatable, manned by Israeli sailors, delivered them to a low-silhouette patrol boat bristling with weaponry and surprisingly quiet considering its forty-knot cruising speed. In three hours they reached a point ten nautical miles north of El Batrun and a thousand metres west of the intercepted grid reference of the PLO rendezvous.

Tibi's cameraman set up shop on a patch of steel decking unencumbered by rope coils or ammunition bins.

'Rome's paparazzi would give their front teeth for that gear,' Tibi told JR. 'You could identify the sex of a flea in a film star's crotch from a distance of two miles and through a sea mist. We will photograph your targets for you – providing they make an appearance.'

The Israeli patrol boat skipper, whom JR judged to be not yet twenty-five, joined them on deck and handed his binoculars to Tibi. 'We have them on radar now,' he said. 'The bigger boat is directly under the loom of that high promontory.' Tibi focused on the *Robert Gordon*. He could see no lights and no life aboard her.

'Now go right two fingers,' the navy man instructed, 'and you will see the PLO boat, a local fishing smack.'

Tibi whistled. 'I would not like to be aboard the *Robert Gordon*. There must be twenty or more heavily armed men on the PLO boat.' He passed the binoculars to JR. 'Do you see your American gentlemen?'

JR was disappointed. Neither Redden nor Richter was yet in evidence. He settled back to wait. Maybe his quarry would emerge on deck only when the two boats came together.

Tibi never liked inactivity. With the waiting came the uninvited memories. The twins, Mengele's Children they were called, had privileges. One was the facility to wash. The Doctor liked them clean for the ongoing experiments. Too late Tibi had learnt where the camp soap came from. He still awoke sweating from dreams in which his mother's face smiled at him from the waxy surface of a square yellow soap block.

Tibi had never learnt how to squash out such images, yet he remained sane. He dreaded retirement and had applied to continue work as an unpaid clerk for Mossad (the Hebrew word means 'Institute'), specialising in the correlation of data on all East European *sayanim* – Jewish sleepers who may never be asked to perform any service for Mossad but who remain always ready for the call from Israel. None is ever paid and all remain citizens of the land of their birth. In Hungary in 1984 there were 200 *sayanim*.

With the *sayanim* job, Tibi hoped that he would keep his mind active and, one never knew, he might come across some long-lost member of his family to have escaped the Holocaust.

The lights of Al Mina and Tripoli glimmered along the north-eastern horizon, once the site of three great Phoenician cities; hence the Greek name Tripolis. Tibi reminded himself, as he stared at the countless stars above this Arab 'capital of the north', that everything was constantly changing emphasis, that futility lay in dwelling upon a single evil, no matter how appalling, for nothing remains but shrinking memories. For how long, for instance, would he and JR remember this evening's events?

Tibi looked at JR, whose world was wrapped up in his hunt for two men. He envied this quiet American who, he knew, had passed two 'exciting' years in Vietnam. If only he could magically exchange his own war memories for JR's he would be the happiest man alive. He raised the binoculars and watched the PLO boat become one with the bulk of the black schooner.

As quietly as a ghost vessel, the Arab fishing ketch arrived from the south, her bulk hidden by the backcloth of the Al Qalamun coastline. Unseen hands flung lines and, as the two vessels nudged, men sprang aboard the *Robert Gordon* and made fast.

Whoever they were they had done this before. Jones was impressed by their seamanship.

A scrawny Arab in dark fatigues and *shemagh* head-cloth appeared on the bridge. '*Alaikum salaam. Kayf al haal.*' The voice was high and nasal, the features sharp, birdlike.

'Hallo. Good to see you.' Jones felt inadequate. He had assumed they would speak English.

'*Wayn nahut a gooneeyaat?*' Where should they put the cargo?

The little fellow must be the boss, for nobody else came on to the bridge, though Jones could now hear the babble of a dozen or more Arabs on board the schooner.

He shrugged his shoulders. '*Parlez-vous français?*' he tried. He thought people spoke French in the Lebanon. No response. Perhaps these guys were PLO or Syrians. At least he had not been shot on sight.

'We are here at your service,' he said, attempting to look obsequious, a dog on his back pawing the air. 'Please treat the boat as yours. *Le bateau est pour vous, monsieur.* Welcome. Please.' Acting on inspiration, he grabbed at the chart drawer. Instantly the Arab thrust the hard nose of a sub-machine-gun against his ribs. He straightened, hands high. 'Whisky,' he whined. 'I was only getting you whisky.'

The gun remained in his side as the man checked the drawer.

'*Whisky zift*,' he spat. Then, pointing at himself, he said: '*Shia*.'

Jones counted eighteen Arabs, all heavily armed with a miscellany of weapons, including the ubiquitous Soviet AK47 rifle. Most were clad in army-style camouflage and *shemaghs*. None greeted Jones but all leered openly at the blonde cook. They formed chain gangs and soon the sickly-sweet smell of cannabis resin mingled with the odour of PLO sweat and Jones's pipe tobacco.

Hempen gunny sacks and polythene-wrapped half-kilo slabs were flung into the hold, the cabins, the bridge and all over the deck. When they had finished four and a half tonnes of top-quality Lebanese Gold cannabis resin lay higgledy-piggledy aboard the 70-ton black schooner.

The head Arab again appeared. This time he thrust a clipboard under Jones's nose. Jones could not read Arabic but he signed at once. He knew the PLO grew cannabis in the Bekaa Valley, to the east of the Lebanon mountains. The PLO love European hostages. Jones wanted only to go. He would have signed over his own mother to get rid of these unwashed brigands.

The fishing boat disappeared into the night. Jones glimpsed the deck-hand Hill groping the cook on the forecastle. He found himself shaking hands with the Greek deckie. In high spirits they moved the *Robert Gordon* through 180 degrees and set full speed towards the south coast of Rhodes.

The PLO leader left the fishing boat at nearby Al Qalamun and commandeered a café owner to drive him to the Tripoli villa of Zaheer Gillani, a wealthy Asian from BCCI's Beirut headquarters.

Gillani came to the door and, after effuse greetings, gave the PLO man a fat envelope. 'The balance as agreed,' he grunted. 'Such is my trust in you that it is yours before even we hear your news. God is generous.'

Seated on floor cushions and after further greetings, the two men and Korbi Richter discussed the *Robert Gordon*. The English of the

PLO thug, who had spoken only Arabic in front of his men, was now perfectly adequate.

'The captain,' he told Richter and Gillani, 'is strong enough but that is all. The rest are rubbish. Two servants and a woman cook. No sign of weapons and no security but for standard door locks. How they will hide the bags, I cannot say but I doubt they can conceal much of so large a load.' He paused and stared hard-eyed at Richter. 'I guarantee the load at four and a half tonnes as agreed. My work is done and none of my people knows of my contact with you.'

Richter looked at Gillani, who nodded. The three men shook hands and Gillani summoned his servant for refreshments. The air-conditioning was affected by yet another power cut and the room felt hot and sticky. Richter would be back in Los Angeles in thirty-six hours; he was pleased with himself. There had been setbacks over the past two months but now everything was in place. The PLO were paid off and cannabis worth £10 million was *en route* to Tricks, who would make short work of the carriers.

Tricks had lately gained himself high marks in Richter's eyes. He had picked up the original cannabis rumour on the North London dealers' sensitive grapevine. Two Harlow dealers, John Bridger and Geoff King, had talked to one too many people in a Walthamstow pub. Tricks had put a man into Harlow, promising payment on results and, when the source was revealed as the Lebanon, had called Richter, who, in turn, phoned Gillani. The PLO in Lebanon banked with BCCI, like terrorists the world over.

Sailing homeward with his sweet-smelling cargo, Jones decided to spend three days in Gibraltar. It was not a wise move since all private vessels passing through the Straits between Gib and Algeciras are closely monitored. Algeciras is known as 'the mari-juana gateway to Europe', being the unloading point from Tangier and the Ceuta enclave for most 'camels': the jeep and truck drivers of hash loads from the Rif.

Police and Customs of all West European countries cooperate in an efficient and closely guarded series of operations against runners emanating from both sides of the Straits. Jones was lucky. If he had been caught and the cannabis confiscated, his life, in jail or out, would be filled with fear of Baker's revenge.

Twenty-five days after the *Robert Gordon* left Tripoli Bay, Inspector Nick Baker in his ground-floor office at Customs House in

London's Lower Thames Street, lowered his phone and looked at one of several wall charts. He placed a single red magnetic pin beside Cape Trafalgar on the Atlantic side of the Straits of Gibraltar. You could almost hear him purr.

7

August–September 1984

Sometimes, during the first two weeks, he would wake screaming and the nurses would wipe the sweat from his forehead and around the stitches where his hair was growing back. He was always apologetic. 'Whatever he's forgot,' he heard one say, 'it's not his manners. Right charmer is our Sandy.'

He disliked Sandy and hoped it was not his real name. When Doreen next came to see him he asked her several times. Had she really christened him Sandy Goodman or had the ambulance men told her that was his name when they first brought him to the Midland Neuro?

Doreen, wanting to make him happy perhaps and sensing his growing frustration over his memory, began to procrastinate. It had been a busy time. Perhaps someone *had* told her the name. She really couldn't be sure. Maybe she'd invented it, maybe not. Goodman nodded to himself. 'Either way,' he told her with his quiet Welsh lilt, 'I can't have been Sandy . . . Alex, yes, or Alexander, but not Sandy.'

She laughed and held his good hand. 'How's things?' She meant his memory.

He shook his head slowly, frowning. 'You know how it is when you waken suddenly from a morning dream? You can often recall the flavour but not the content of the fading images? Well, I think once or twice I have caught glimpses from my past. From long ago when I was little. But they vanished as soon as I tried to pin them down.'

He smiled weakly and Doreen thought how nice he must look

62

without the pallor and the semi-shaven skull. 'I should be thankful that at least the headaches have eased,' he said, 'They come back with sudden noises or movement but they're mild now compared with a few days back.'

They had moved him back to Russells Hall Hospital from the Neuro Centre after four days of observation. Bed space was always in demand at the Centre and he seemed to be in fine shape apart from his amnesia. Professor Hitchcock had passed his file to an Asian doctor at Russells Hall, Ram Mohan, who assured him he could stay until they discovered his identity.

After a fortnight and thanks to excellent nursing, Goodman found he could walk about without suffering sharp head pains and dizzy spells. He could leave his ward and wander the linoleum corridors to the only recreation area, a narrow, grassy bank outside the surgical ward, where he sat in the sun and gazed across to Bough Hill, with its high religious monument and fields of grazing cattle.

Sometimes in the pre-dawn hours he heard a rush and roar as the British Steel Corporation furnaces at Round Oak opened up and turned the night sky red for miles around. He wondered whether his was a town or country background. He certainly felt more at home with the browsing cows than the industrial clatter.

A doctor called every morning to question him and monitor his progress. By the third week he began to taste his food. There was no bleeding or regression. The recurring headaches, dizzy bouts and sudden panics subsided. But his past remained a book which somebody was reading to him by night, starting at Chapter One and snapping shut the moment he awoke. This left him increasingly frustrated.

B24 was a mixed ward ruled with a rod of iron by Sister Cox, a jovial forty-year-old, with a navy-blue uniform and well-permed auburn hair. Every morning one of the staff would sit by him for a while and ask him questions about his early life. Was he married? Children? Pets? Anything to prompt a reaction, stimulate a response.

Most of the time, like everyone else, he watched television, trying to ignore the rasping shouts of elderly ward neighbours, distressed or partially deaf. Endless TV hours were devoted to the emotive topic of the five-month-old national coal strike, with miners' leader 'King' Arthur Scargill ranting and Coal Board boss Ian McGregor denouncing. Bitter fighting between strikers and 'scabs' cornered the headlines, along with running battles between police and miners, the latter hurling stones and bags filled with urine.

Asked whether he remembered Scargill and Maggie Thatcher, Goodman replied that he thought he did. They were both generally familiar yet he could not isolate any specific memory of either person.

The police visited him once at Russells Hall – an officer named Ben who said they had talked before at the Midland Centre. Goodman said he did not recollect the man or the meeting but he found himself attacking the poor constable as though it was his personal fault that no trace of Goodman's identity had as yet been unearthed.

Ben was indignant. 'Look, sir, we are undermanned to a ridiculous extent due to the miners' strike and we have to treat enquiries on a strict priority basis. With all due respect, your case can only be considered as of lesser urgency to the dozen or so burglaries and car thefts we get daily.' He paused, keen to phrase his words to avoid causing offence. 'You have not pressed charges against anybody or complained of any offence. No third party is necessarily involved. You may have been mugged or struck by a hit-and-run merchant, but we have no proof. As far as the law is concerned, we just don't know where to start. If you could give us just one lead or clue as to your identity, we could maybe do something. Of course we hope that somebody will come forward to "claim" you but, if they don't, I'm afraid there's nowt we can do but live in hope. If . . .'

'What about my belongings? Did you not inspect them for clues?' Goodman interrupted.

'Your clothes' – Ben gestured to a neatly folded pile on the locker beside the bed – 'were thoroughly searched. Some string, sweet papers and a biro. No car keys. No old bills. No identity. We could tell from your hands that you were not a manual worker and from your accent that you are Welsh. Your Barbour jacket, corduroy trousers and boots suggest you had been walking through the woods for pleasure. The red sand clinging to you was from the Kinver locality. The expert darning of your socks might suggest that you are not wealthy but have a loving relative, mother, sister or wife. Unless of course, sir, you are a bachelor and a dab hand with a needle.'

Goodman nodded. He apologised for being abrasive. 'You will let me know if anything does come up?'

Ben promised he would, then left.

Doreen visited Goodman again during his third weekend at Russells Hall. She was attracted to his gentle eyes and shy ways. She thought him tragic and could imagine mothering him back to happiness.

'When you doodle,' she told him, 'it's nearly always figures. You know, mathematical stuff. I reckon you must be an engineer. Maybe a top professor at the university.'

He smiled at her and patted her hand. 'Think, Doreen. Try to put yourself in my place. What if I've got a loving family out there? They may be crying their poor eyes out for worry about me. Or maybe I'm a bachelor boy up from Wales on a day's visit to a secret lover in the village of Kinver. Perhaps I had sand in my clothing because I was digging her vegetable garden for her and then I had a fainting spell and fell on my shovel. How about that?'

She thought there was a twinkle in his eyes. She loved the Welsh way he said 've-ge-ta-ble', lingering on each syllable as with four separate piano notes.

'If I am a bachelor,' he added, 'I could be a highly mobile yuppie with a Porsche and a penthouse flat. Just think of that. Even now the place may be full of burglars stealing my hi-fi or squatters making love in my jacuzzi.'

She laughed. 'No, Sandy . . . I mean Alex. I think you are a lovely single man with more sense than money. I hope you are single! Think about it now. If I was your wife or your mum and you had disappeared, I would be screaming at the police, calling up the news reporters, visiting hospitals and putting adverts all over. This is the 1980s, remember, with high-tech communications. It's easy to let people know things. If you do have a family, it must be an auntie or an old mum that you go to visit once every few months and they've not missed you yet. But you can't have a live-in lover or they'd be shouting to the rooftops for you and we'd know about it.'

He nodded slowly. She could be right. He put out his hand and she held it with both of hers. She felt her eyes prickle. His loneliness and confusion were worn on his sleeve. She kissed his forehead. Briefly, for nothing was private in B24. She promised to return, but they were not to meet again.

The ward was full and his original doctor, the protective Ram Mohan, had left the hospital. The authorities 'want your bed', Lisa, a plump Australian nurse, warned him unofficially. He had not relapsed, his physical health was fine and his wounds, the stitches long removed, were healing well, so there was no reason for him to remain hospitalised. Only the fact of his continuing amnesia and the lack of any friend or relative to care for him prevented the authorities from discharging him at once.

Lisa did some reading on amnesia for him. His memory, she told him, should have returned within a week or two of his accident. But in some cases partial amnesia could remain for up to eighteen months.

'It seems us medicos know very little about the mind,' she said. 'In fact doctors aren't even sure where it is. They can't actually point at an X-ray of the brain and say, "That bit's the mind." All they know is that the memory is a function of the mind and the mind is part of the brain. But their knowledge is constantly increasing and I'm not at all up with the latest know-how.'

Sometimes Goodman found himself close to panic at the thought that his memory would never come back, that a loving family were somewhere longing for his return but he would never know where to find them. Every day that passed was taking him further away from his elusive 'nearest and dearest', for whom he yearned. There must be something he could do, some tiny clue he could follow up. He would finger through every fold of his clothing, stare for long minutes at the soles of his walking boots, avidly search the Personal Columns of newspapers. He grew increasingly despondent. If he died tomorrow, nobody would know or care. It was as though he had arrived from another planet, dumped like some unwanted child in Kinver Wood with no certainties beyond his little cubicle in Ward B24 and a forlorn pile of worn clothes. Even his name might merely be the joke of a hospital nurse.

Then, idly watching ITN evening news on Wednesday, 29 August, almost a month after his accident, Goodman experienced a miracle. He recognised a man shown on television. Since his memory was in tatters, this was surely impossible. The man's face was as familiar to him as oft-recurring television images like Reagan and Gorbachev, but this fellow was a nonentity unlikely ever to have featured on TV before. Goodman jumped to the inescapable conclusion that, if he knew this man, the man must know him. He leaped from his bed and moved closer to the screen, desperate to pick up every word of commentary.

Junior Social Security Minister Tony Newton and others were being interviewed about the Benefits system. Pickets were shown parading outside a DHSS office in the Erdington district of Birmingham. The problem under discussion was an increasing flood of demands for benefits which, the angry DHSS workers claimed, would soon bring the Social Security Services to a grinding halt. Not exactly compulsive viewing, but that applied to ninety-nine per cent of Goodman's TV menu for the past month.

Now, however, he was ecstatic, for a tall man wearing a light-brown coat and with an Afro hairstyle appeared fleetingly, but clearly, four or five times over a period of some sixty seconds. His colouring and features, in silhouette and full frontal, were those of a half-caste. He stood in the Department of Health and Social Security waiting room with the listless expression of a Muscovite in a bread queue. Goodman clenched his fists to his temples. There was no doubt. He knew this man.

Back in bed he collected his thoughts. One or two neighbours stared at him in concern. He grinned back at them. Suddenly he felt on a par with all the other B24 inmates. Soon he too would have an identity. Lisa had mentioned a 'discharge letter' the other day. This would involve his GP and, since he had none, he decided to ignore such bureaucratic banalities. He would not talk to anybody. They would only make a fuss, involving social workers and documentation. They might even send him to some hostel for the unidentified, if such a classification existed. No, he would go at once to the Erdington DHSS office and find Miracle Man. He decided to wait until the ward's quiet time, around 9 p.m., when he might best slip away unobserved.

He left a note under his pillow thanking those staff that he knew by name, especially Lisa, for their kindness. Another note, which he left to be given to Doreen, explained that his memory had suddenly returned and, knowing the authorities needed his bed, he'd thought it best to get out of their hair with minimal ado.

His clothes fitted him but only just in the case of his trousers for he had put on weight at the hospital. He left intending to walk to Erdington, using a map he had torn from a reference book in the library. Only a mile from the hospital, he felt faint and rested on a bench on Castle Hill which runs beside the grounds of Dudley Zoo.

When Goodman failed to reappear in the ward two hours after his exit, a nurse told the duty sister, who checked with Reception. 'He often wanders about in his dressing gown,' the sister said, 'but not after hours. And his clothes have all gone.'

'Well, we've seen no sign of him.'

Then the nurse found Goodman's notes and the sister called the police. They, of course, could find no criminal file on him.

'Did he say where he intended going now his memory's come back?' asked the police duty officer.

'No,' the sister replied. 'Unfortunately not.'

'Do you think he'll be able to cope?'

The sister thought for a while. 'Well, we've been worrying about his being here for quite a while. We wanted to discharge him. He should be fine if he's got somewhere to go and he doesn't have a sudden relapse.'

The policeman promised the sister to inform beat officers of the situation and that was that.

Goodman was out and on his own. Given his unprepossessing appearance and lack of funds, he did well. Taking a bus from Dudley to the centre of Birmingham, he fetched up in Queensway, having successfully appealed to the good nature of the ticket collector with a story, rehearsed in the ward that afternoon, that he had been mugged at the zoo. This was possibly the first time in his life that Goodman had knowingly broken the law, the first step on a long downward path.

He carried his Barbour over his arm, for even at that hour the city was humid. He followed the ticket collector's directions to St Paul's Square, in the vicinity of which he found four churches. All were closed and a policeman directed him instead to a Salvation Army hostel by Snow Hill.

The William Booth hostel looked bleak, seven storeys high and built on the bank of a gloomy canal. The main entrance door was locked but a night receptionist soon appeared and introduced Goodman to a Major Moffat, the duty officer, who took his personal details.

Aware that the police might be on the lookout for him, Goodman gave a false name and explained that his papers had been stolen.

Again his recent head scar and his easy, open manner helped ease his way through the red tape.

Major Moffat agreed to a free bed for one night plus breakfast but after that: 'You must pay £4.50 per day or £54 full board per week. Tomorrow morning you must go straight to Social Security to claim. We close the building to everyone from 8.30 a.m. after breakfast, until lunchtime.'

Goodman agreed and was shown up to a five-bedded room with two snoring inmates. The place could hold 240 men and women and forbade alcohol, drugs and smoking in the bedrooms.

In the morning Goodman woke early, washed, shaved with an abandoned razor and engaged his room-mates in conversation. One was a morose traveller whose wandering life consisted of seeking jobs from town to town, but the other, a gambler, was affable and interested in the story Goodman had concocted and already tested on Major Moffat.

'I got mugged,' Goodman said, brushing his head wound with his hand. 'All my papers, money, everything, whipped and my memory box smashed. They threw me out of hospital yesterday after only a month. No money, nowhere to go. They said they needed the bed.'

'Dreadful,' the gambler tutted. 'Thatcher's causing dreadful grief. Dreadful.'

'Is there any chance of borrowing cash until I get a job?' Goodman looked the man straight in the face, knowing that his eyes were his best guarantee of honesty. 'I will pay back twenty-five per cent interest on a small loan and give my only possession, my Barbour, as collateral. Two weeks is all I need. A hundred pounds would be ideal.'

'Sounds good to me,' the gambler laughed. 'But I'll have to set you up with Alfie upstairs. He's flush at present and anyway I'm off to other pastures after breakfast.'

In the rambling dining room, already full of mostly males in their fifties and sixties eating breakfast, the gambler introduced Goodman to Alfie, whose keen Irish eyes checked him out in seconds as he listened to his story. He agreed to the loan, provided the interest was forty per cent and he paid Goodman £10 daily, not a lump sum. He took possession of the Barbour then and there.

Goodman was happy to leave immediately after breakfast. He decided to spend minimal time in the hostel. The residents, some of whom looked decidedly shifty, included alkies, druggies, mental cases, ex-offenders, folk on the run, wife-beaters and those who simply couldn't cope with job and family.

He walked to the DHSS office and trotted out his cover story with an added twist. His amnesia prevented him remembering which hospital had discharged him, although a dated rail ticket he said he'd found indicated that he had arrived the previous day from London. The DHSS took down his false details with care and issued him with a temporary voucher for his bed and food at the hostel.

At 10.30 a.m. he caught the 102 bus from St Chad's Circus up the Lichfield Road, beneath the concrete horror of Spaghetti Junction at Gravelly Hill, and into the centre of Erdington. He found the DHSS office that he had seen on television, at the junction of the Kingsbury and Wood End roads. He settled himself against a wall fronting the local secondary school and began to browse through a copy of the *Sun* purloined on his bus journey. By noon he grew impatient and joined a small queue inside the office. He asked the official behind the window if he could register as unemployed. 'Not here.' The man sounded bored. 'That's at Washwood Heath, two miles away. Separate office. When you get set up, then you come here weekly for Supplementary, Sickness and Unemployment – if you've no fixed address.'

Goodman, unaware of the status of the Miracle Man whom he sought, returned to his observation post until 3.30 p.m., when the DHSS office closed. He had no option but to continue this daily schedule and be thankful for the ongoing fine weather. He did not consider failure for a moment. As soon as the staff locked their doors, he moved quickly to the nearby Job Centre and checked the work cards. After jotting down any job available in the Erdington district, he walked to the relevant recruiting offices, where he soon grew accustomed to negative responses. On the fourth evening he thought he had landed a job as a fork-lift driver at the AMAC fettling shop, moving vehicle pistons from stack to stack, but when he checked back the following afternoon the job had gone, with no explanation offered. So he wandered along Wood Lane, trying SU Carburettors and Valor Gas. No luck there.

At his next port of call, Dunlop Tyres, he struck lucky. Dunlop's Base Stores was an imposing, though somewhat dilapidated, brick building amid a sprawl of subsidiary office structures, serried lines of factory blocks with high metal chimneys and dozens if not hundreds of smaller, often abandoned outhouses. The whole Fort Dunlop site, covering 360 acres, had once been a self-contained community of 10,000 Dunlop workers with its own fire brigade, laundry service, plumbers, gardeners, two dozen carpenters, in-house security and even a typewriter repair department.

By 1984 all this had changed. No more than 2000 people were now employed and most non-core business services were contracted out. Goodman was offered casual labour on the understanding that the work might change from day to day. Anything from mowing large areas of grass to cleaning up in the rubber-mixing shop and moving scrap tyres and rubber, empty chemical bags and used pallets to the scrap yard. He agreed without hesitation and was told to turn up the following Monday.

At 11 a.m. on Wednesday, 12 September, at his observation post outside the DHSS office, Goodman dropped his newspaper as though stunned, for the Miracle Man slouched past, mere yards away and crossed the road to disappear into the office. He was in every way familiar to Goodman, in fact more so in the flesh than on television. His Afro was now dyed a faded orange whereas on the TV it had been dark brown. His general appearance was stooped and emaciated, not, as seen on ITN, upright and fit. Goodman knew he had met the orange-tinted, etiolated version and the memory 'scent' felt recent. He was beside himself with excitement. All he needed was the man's address. Then he could confront him and call the police. In no time he would learn his own identity.

The man stuffed his unemployment cheque into his trouser pocket as he left the DHSS. Goodman followed him at a discreet distance to a post office in Erdington High Street, where he cashed the cheque, and thence to The Roebuck pub, some fifty yards away. Goodman entered after a short pause and, noticing his quarry deep in conversation with two men at one end of the bar, he ordered a Watney's Red Barrel at the other.

Moving to a table close to the bar but facing the street, he strained to listen to the conversation immediately behind him. He heard his man being called Trevor but the accents were Irish and piped music added to the general din. He edged sideways and watched the group as he sipped his beer. Trevor paid money to a skinny youth whose accent was impenetrable to Goodman. In return Trevor was given a wad of what looked like red capsules stashed in cling film. He unwrapped them roughly and counted them out. Satisfied, he pocketed the package. 'Cheers, mate,' he grunted and left the pub cursing a young Alsatian that he tripped over.

'I don't like that bastard,' said a 15-stone bouncer as he appeared from behind the bar. 'If he touches Ludo again I'll string him from the ceiling.'

'Shouldn't be bothering yourself with the loikes of Trevor, Soapy,' one of the Irish bar-proppers advised. 'He's stoned out of his toiny moind most of the toime.'

Goodman left without finishing his beer and followed Trevor down the High Street to the Six Ways roundabout. The half-caste crossed Wood End Lane without appearing to heed the traffic. Brakes squealed and drivers cursed. Trevor lifted two fingers high above his head and shortly turned left into Cecil Road. Halfway up this street he let himself into a rundown basement flat. Goodman noted the number and withdrew. He felt elated but determined to take one move at a time. He deserved a self-congratulatory coffee and cakes but, with just enough cash for the bus back to the hostel, instead he cruised the High Street coffee-shops to find lodgings. An Italian waiter directed him to a bed and breakfast, only £5 per night, above a sandwich bar run by his relatives. Goodman saw the room and told the landlord he would take it next week.

The following Monday at 7 a.m., with a generous four days' loan cash from Alfie, he moved into his new digs in the High Street and reported to Dunlop at 8 a.m. His work consisted initially of ferrying by dumper truck waste materials from a number of dispersed collection points to a central incinerator. He quickly learnt the basic layout of the whole complex.

Goodman's supervisor was easy-going, as was the entire set-up. Having lost their way over the previous decade, the company's survivors were scared stiff of joining the majority on the dole and, like stunned rabbits, they awaited take-over by the Japanese. Security was all but non-existent. So many tyres had been stolen over the past four years that watch-towers had been erected. These were no longer manned and whole areas behind the main work-shops lay derelict, a post-apocalyptic scenario symbolic of Britain's industrial decline.

Away from his work, Goodman spent every available minute

watching Trevor's movements. Not a demanding task, for the man was about as observant as any other drug addict busily doping himself to death. In The Acorn, another of his favourite haunts, Trevor smashed a beer bottle against his chair and lunged at one of his drinking companions without apparent provocation. A doorman appeared and evicted him. Outside he swallowed one of his red pills and headed home. Goodman once saw him selling blue pills in a nearby Ladbroke's betting shop but suspected most of his business was with the itinerant hippie crowd he observed flowing in and out of Trevor's squat, one of many in Cecil Road. The local police appeared to ignore the flagrant trading activities of Trevor and his fellow-dealers and Goodman decided to confront the man in the hope of catching him unawares. That way he would be sure that they had met before.

The next evening, a few minutes after Trevor returned to the squat with a pint of milk, Goodman knocked at the basement door. A young child of indeterminate sex with a snotty nose let him in as though he was expected. The smell was overpowering, a weird blend of joss-stick and sewage. At least two radios blared pop on different channels.

'Trevor?' Goodman asked the child, which took its thumb out of its mouth long enough to point at a figure in the dingy hallway. Hearing his name, Trevor turned and, for an instant, Goodman saw his mouth form a dark circle of surprise. Then a darting glance at Goodman's hands.

'What you want, man?' Aggressive.

'Hi. Good to see you again, Trevor.'

But the moment was gone. The man, if indeed he had briefly recognised Goodman in the gloom, was determined not to acknowledge the fact.

'What you mean? I never seen you before. Who are you?'

'Alex Goodman.' He could think of nothing else to say. He realised with a sinking feeling that his opening move had failed. He stared at Trevor. There could be no doubt. He *had* seen him before.

'Fuck off, man. If you're from the pigs, you got fuck all on me. I'm clean. Go on. Beat it.' He shouted towards the back bedroom. 'Terry, come here.'

But Goodman did not wait for the reinforcements. He let himself

73

out into the fresh air and returned, via the shops, to his own cramped garret.

Sitting on the floor, he used his bed as a table, for the room was short on furniture. His purchases were simple. Black coffee in a Styrofoam cup, a cheap writing pad and a soft pencil. He wrote 'PLAN' at the top of the first sheet then waited as a wave of shooting head pains surged and eddied. They came less frequently, thank God, as the days went by. He was somehow more confident armed with the paper and pencil. It felt right.

If he went to the police now and pressed charges against Trevor – for he was instinctively convinced the man must have been involved in his head injury – he feared they would do nothing but ask what evidence he had. Recognition alone would not be enough. He must force a confession from Trevor, but how?

The man's weakness was his addiction: his life centred on the buying, selling and consumption of little red and sometimes blue pills, supplemented by a weekly visit to the dole office.

Goodman dismissed the thought of interrogating Trevor at the squat or in his own room. He further accepted that he must use guile, not force, since he was neither fit nor capable of striking a mouse, never mind another human being. Two hours later he reviewed the detailed steps of his neatly prepared action plan. He would start work without delay.

On Wednesday, 26 September, as soon as Trevor returned to his squat, Goodman appeared at his door, giving him no time to object.

'Listen, Trevor, I was just checking on you last week. I've been watching you at The Roebuck and The Acorn. I'm nothing to do with the coppers. I just want to do us both a favour. Look, I know you're on barbs and so am I. I'll give it you straight. I can undercut the Irish by thirty per cent and I can deal any time, twenty-four hours, from my place in the High Street. No more hassle for you when you run short in the night or whenever. What do you say?'

Trevor's addictive greed quickly suppressed his natural suspicion of strangers.

'How do I know your stuff's gen . . . hundred per cent?' But his face betrayed him. Goodman was offering him a dream.

'Want to see my stash? I can offer you a dozen free up front if you agree to deal long term.'

Trevor nodded. 'Sure. Sounds good, man. Let's go. How far?'

'Maybe ten minutes.' Goodman did not wish to put the man off. He was nearly there.

'I thought you said the High Street.'

'I did. That's my flat. But I keep the stash hidden on the industrial estate.'

'OK,' Trevor approved of this set-up. 'We'll go in my machine.' Goodman was surprised Trevor owned a car. He'd assumed the druggie would have long since sold any possessions of value to support his habit. Perhaps he stole cars as a sideline. He followed Trevor to a battered yellow van parked up Wood End Lane. For an instant he thought he recognised the van.

They drove through the main gate at Dunlop because, although Goodman was headed for the west end of the site, he knew the east and west gates would be locked.

A stream of contractors' vans and cars passed through the main gate and Goodman waved at the security man, who recognised him. They drove past successive blocks of workshops, skirted round Tyre 7 and headed northwards up West Road to turn left into the more derelict zone north-west of the Machine Tool block, Steel Shop and Carbon Black Store. Over to their left a flat waste area gave on to the test track and tyre-proving ground.

Now they entered Goodman's work zone, passing by the incinerator block to the Salvage Area between the West Car Park and the Crude Materials Store, an area of many abandoned buildings, piles of scrap for reuse and sub-standard products for sale to employees.

Goodman told Trevor to drive straight into his chosen shed. He had rehearsed every detail with care. Trevor helped him close the doors behind them. A small cardboard box sat by itself on a heavy workbench surrounded by a thick carpet of metal lathe filings. Trevor crowded him as he made to open the box.

'Here,' Goodman said. 'Tell me what you think of this.' He handed Trevor the box. Reaching to one side, he felt for the plastic handcuffs, clicked one deftly on to the addict's wrist, then stepped back out of reach.

'You can scream the place down if you wish. Nobody ever comes here. No one will hear you. But if you do make a nuisance of yourself in any way, you get no barbs.'

Trevor scrabbled at the box lid and the scrunched-up polythene

75

inside. Nothing. No candy. No red pills. He made to rush at Goodman and swore as a chain brought him to a sudden halt. The dog chain, padlocked to the cuffs, was also bolted to the workbench. Goodman busied himself with the two sheets of black cloth, a hammer and roofing nails. In minutes both the room's grimy windows were blacked out. The radius of Trevor's available movement allowed him to sit or lie on the workbench or the floor. Goodman reversed the van away from his reach and took a coil of silver foil from his trouser pocket.

'I got these nasty little Seconal 100mg capsules from Danny at The Acorn, same as you do. But I didn't attack him with a broken bottle. You get very nasty sometimes, don't you, Trevor? I'm not taking any chances. I will bring you food, drink and change the bag in your bucket daily, providing you behave.' He indicated a fire bucket beside the workbench. 'All mod cons, you see. Nothing but the best. But these' – he withdrew six red pills marked 'LILLY' from the foil and placed them one by one on the floor, just out of Trevor's reach – 'these will be yours only when you tell me all about me.'

'What do you mean? Man, are you crazy? You're the biggest fuckin' freak. What do you want from me? I never seen you. Never. Never. Never. Listen, you made a mistake. Maybe somebody who looks like me done you in.'

Goodman's blue eyes surveyed the lanky, agitated figure. For an instant he felt a mix of doubt and sympathy, but he fought this down.

'When you first saw me you looked at my hands, Trevor. You know about the cuts on my fingers. But, even without that, I have no doubt in my mind and you will stay here until you tell me everything you know about me. What happened to me? Do I have friends? A family? You see, I have no key to my identity but you, and you're staying right here, without your precious pills, until you help me find out who I am.'

He ignored the rush of foul invective, the threats and the renewed protestations of innocence and drove Trevor's van back to its usual spot in Wood End Lane, pocketed the key and walked home. Twenty-two hours later he took bread, fruit and Coca-Cola to Trevor, whose demeanour was considerably changed from the previous day. A stench of diarrhoea filled the room. Goodman changed the bucket's liner bag. Trevor was sweating and paced back and forth, dog-like, on his chain.

'You fuckin' bastard, give us the fuckin' downers.'

'How many?' Goodman asked, needing to know.

'I need six Seccies a day, every day.' His eyes were alight with hope now.

'OK,' said Goodman. 'They're yours, right now. Just give me the information I need.'

At this Trevor buckled and fell to the floor, his back and head striking the bench. He sobbed, cursing and promising Goodman, alternately, death, shattered kneecaps and forgiveness if he instantly freed him. Cramps then attacked his stomach and he rolled about the oily floor groaning in pain. When the bout subsided, he sat back shivering and sweating at the same time. He told Goodman nothing and was given no pills.

The following evening Goodman dumped six more red barbiturate capsules on the floor just beyond the point which Trevor might reach with an outstretched foot. He had visited the Erdington Library and studied barbiturates. He reckoned Trevor could not have been addicted for long, since, despite his emaciated appearance, he did not answer medical descriptions of the worst cases. 'The barbiturate addict presents a shocking spectacle,' he read. 'He cannot co-ordinate, he staggers, falls off bar stools, goes to sleep in mid-sentence and drops food out of his mouth.'

As with opiates, barbiturates relax the addict, remove stress and quickly make the body chemically dependent. Cocaine and cigarettes are merely mentally addictive. You only think you need more.

Of the various available barbiturates Seconal, containing quinalbarbitone sodium, is a short-acting toxic depressant whose withdrawal symptoms are even more horrific than those of opium. They include terrifying hallucinations and convulsions that can cause permanent brain damage. Goodman was keen, of course, to avoid any damage to Trevor's brain, his only possible source of the information for which he was so desperate.

On the third evening Trevor cracked. 'Blackledge,' he screamed as soon as Goodman arrived with his daily bread ration. 'He's the bastard you want. And the big black fucker Tricks with them Americans. He took your wallet. Thought you were a pig or RSPCA. All I did was drive the diggin' boys. You got to believe me.'

Goodman was elated. It was working. He had known he was right but all the same there had been creeping doubts. Now his actions were justified. He was about to discover for himself what the police would never have learnt.

'Give us the Seccies,' Trevor groaned. 'Come on, man, I'm fuckin' dyin'.'

But Goodman was firm. He held all the cards. 'You get your pills just as soon as you finish your story.' He placed a can of Coca-Cola within Trevor's reach. The man's stomach was in a bad way. Goodman changed the bucket bag, then took out a small notebook and pencil. 'Go on.'

Trevor's tale was straightforward but no bells began to clang for Goodman, no sudden flood of memories was triggered. Trevor had earned drug money from time to time by running errands for Blackburn hard man Paul Blackledge when the latter had cause to operate in the Birmingham area. This work had sometimes involved using his van to transport labour, local Erdington lads prepared to earn a bit on the side and keep their mouths shut.

Trevor was from Leyland, Lancashire, where he had known Blackledge since their schooldays. Blackledge had his own badger-baiting mates but occasionally, as with the black guy Tricks and his American bosses, he kept them well out of it, preferring to use local Brum lads through Trevor. He would use his own dogs and meet Trevor and the labour force at a pub, or some other easy-to-find rendezvous, from where they would convoy to the day's site. The Kinver dig at the end of July had worked that way, Trevor told Goodman.

'Blackledge calls me, I don't know where he is these days. An' I don't want to know. That's one mad, bad bastard. Look, give us just one red devil.'

Goodman shook his head impatiently.

The Kinver site, Trevor continued, was vulnerable, what with a minor road through the wood a couple of hundred yards away and weekend dog walkers liable to stumble on the sett any time. So Blackledge had divided his labour force between watching out for snoopers – who might, if they saw what was going on, call the police – and wielding spades at the sett.

Trevor himself had stayed by the action, attentive to any new order from Blackledge. They had located the badgers and the

78

Americans were having a great time when he, Goodman, had suddenly appeared at the scene from nowhere shouting at them to stop what they were doing.

'You got fuckin' balls, man. I'll say that.' Trevor put one finger to his temple. 'But you're nuts. You try that stuff on the likes of Blackledge, you're lucky you're still around.'

Blackledge had apparently thrust the barrel of a twelve-gauge shotgun under Goodman's chin, had him frisked and given Tricks everything they found, from his wallet to a Kodak film spool. Trevor heard them argue that the intruder was unlikely to be an official since he had wilfully broken his cover and seemed to be alone. After a while Tricks, keen to keep his Americans happy, had ordered Trevor to truss Goodman's hands, gag him and dump him in the bracken beside the sett. They then carried on as before.

Goodman could not decide how much of Trevor's ramblings, if any, he should believe. Would he, Goodman, have behaved in such a way? He had no way of knowing.

A few minutes later, Trevor continued, Blackledge had suddenly fired the gun into the dense, man-high bracken above the sett. He, Goodman, had started thrashing about at this, so someone had bashed his head with a spade.

Cursing Blackledge, Tricks had apologised to the Americans and suggested it would be prudent to end the day's sport, and the action had been wrapped up. 'But' – Trevor's voice indicated he was coming to the point – 'as Blackledge and my boys packed up, I heard the fuckin' Yankees talk real serious with the black boy, Tricks. I can't tell you every word but what I do recall clear as I can see you was the date. Fourth of October. Fourth of October at The Anchor on the Crouch. Yank said, "nine to midnight". They was on about how many men to take and what fire-power. A boat. Four tons of weed. Sounds like a heist to me . . . That's all. That is it. I done like you said. Told you all I know. Now give us the candy and let me get out of this fuckin' hole.'

'Hey, hey. Hold on.' Goodman waved his hands as though bidding an orchestra to play softer. 'You've not told me anything that will help me.'

'What you mean, you bastard?' Trevor snarled and advanced to the end of his chain, stirring the air with his stench. 'I've told you every fuckin' thing I fuckin' know. The Yanks and Tricks went off,

79

and as soon as Blackledge had the lads tidy up he told me to take them back home. He paid us and we fucked off. I didn't want you dyin' 'cos of your head bein' bashed, so I came back and dropped you off in the village. End of story. So now you give me the Seccies and let me piss off.'

Goodman ignored the outburst. 'Where's my wallet?' he pressed Trevor. 'Did they throw it away once they'd looked at it?'

'Nah.' Trevor was emphatic. 'Black boy took it. The Tricks guy, he had it in his pocket.'

'How do I find him – or Blackledge?'

'Blackledge moves round a lot but his dad's from Blackburn way. That's as much as I know. Ask the Blackburn pigs, they'll tell you all you want to know about that bastard. Give us the reddies, you fucker.'

'And Tricks?'

'I told you. You don't fuckin' listen, do you? Fourth of October. Nine o'clock. Anchor pub on the Crouch.'

'The Crouch?'

'The river, man. The fuckin' river.'

'What river?'

'The Crouch.'

'Yes, but where?'

'How do I know where? But it's got to be a river, ain't it? Ain't no sea called Crouch, and Anchor pubs are beside water. So it's got to be a river.'

Goodman was nodding. This looked good. Too involved for the man to be lying to him. Maybe a lot of his story was rubbish, but the Anchor bit and the whole cannabis boat thing could hardly have been invented by Trevor. His brain could scarcely have produced such a scenario, Goodman guessed, even before he started pickling it with barbiturates. The fourth of October was six days away. He would find the River Crouch at the library. Use Trevor's van and keep its owner safely locked up here until he got back. If the foray led him to Tricks, his wallet and, pray to God, his identity, he would happily return Trevor to his Cecil Road squalor. Meanwhile he would continue to feed and water the man and give him a single capsule daily since he was beginning to look seriously ill.

Trevor swallowed the 100mg Lilly and instantly begged for more, sobbing and screaming, then when Goodman turned to leave, switching to violent threats. 'The black bastard will kill you. You know nothin' about these mean cunts. You're way out of your depth, man.'

Goodman closed the double doors and went home feeling better than he could remember.

8

4 October 1984

In September and October 1984 the Investigation Division of HM Customs and a number of police units cooperated in a complex operation, code-named Bischop, to net Bryan Baker and his cannabis gang. At the time no love was lost between police and Customs officers, who competed with one another for financing and power. Memories rankled of operations rumbled through interference or overlapping by the other service. But for eight weeks, as tension mounted and the *Robert Gordon* crept to and from the Lebanon, liaison and cooperation between the Bischop operators continued to go miraculously well.

Before September the Crime Squad and the Central Office organisations at New Scotland Yard were huffily upset when they first learnt that Chief Nick Baker and his Customs men were targeting various Essex and North London criminals, suspected of a major importation, without telling local or central police agencies. Lack of firearms facilities forced HM Customs to come clean and bring in the police. At that point all the Bischop information gleaned by HM was fed from the Customs computer CEDRIC into the central NDIU (National Drug Intelligence Unit) police computer at New Scotland Yard and the two forces began to work as one.

On the morning of Thursday, 4 October, a dull, grey day in coastal Essex, John 'The Fish' Nicholls, a lobster man from South Fambridge on the River Crouch, found an A4 envelope on a pavement in the village. It contained a set of colour photographs of the *Robert Gordon*, dropped in error, a few days earlier, by a plainclothes police officer snooping in the village. Nicholls mentioned the photos in the village pub and the story, corrupted, passed quickly to other drinking places along the Crouch. Somehow the wrong ears failed to connect with the gossip. Otherwise thousands of man-hours of police and Customs time might have been wasted.

Later that morning two local bobbies, knowing nothing of Bischop, parked their panda car beside the Ferry Road slipway at North Fambridge on the Crouch. As they unwrapped their sandwiches a sharp call sounded from their speaker: 'Move at once. You are compromising ongoing activities.'

At Harlow, well north of the Crouch, the central police station received a call from a resident. 'Last night I saw a van being moved in our street here, Red Willows Road.'

'How do you mean, moved, ma'am?' the duty officer enquired.

'Well, not exactly stolen. If it had been, I'd have called you at the time. No, these geezers pushed the van – it was a Luton Transit – some fifty yards down the street from outside number one: that's the house of the man what's rented the van.'

'Couldn't you have called us then?'

'Not really. We don't have a phone, see. The call-box is down the road and I'm alone with baby.'

'I see. So what happened to the van?'

'Well, two blokes in dark overalls fiddled with the motor for half an hour, then pushed it back up to outside number one. Real weird, don't you think? Anyway, I thought I'd call you in case it's a bomb or something.'

'Thank you, ma'am. Where's the van now?'

'Oh, it's right there still.'

The police operator took the caller's details in case she was needed later. Then he made a call. Five minutes later a very senior officer telephoned back with a raised voice. 'Do nothing! Leave it. If the caller persists, just say the matter is being looked into.'

Three tiny blips in the normal course of local events. Small oversights or just bad luck. Any one of them could inadvertently have warned off the Essex-based members of the drugs ring. Bischop's fortune held however and the *Robert Gordon* continued her voyage towards the Crouch.

Keith Jones set course from Dungeness and Ramsgate on 3 October but failed to appreciate the dangerously shifting nature of

Foulness Sands off the mouth of the Crouch. At the Black Deep No. 9 buoy, some ten miles east of Foulness Point, Jones rammed the schooner fast on to a sandbank. He had no option but to radio for help. His distress call was answered by Coastguard Kibbles at Walton-on-the-Naze, who launched his lifeboat.

Fortunately for Jones, a rising tide floated the vessel free of the sandbank before the lifeboat arrived and, with only a slight leak in the stern, he steered under cover of darkness for Holliwell Point at the mouth of the Crouch. After mooring briefly to use a phone box in Burnham-on-Crouch, Jones goose-winged at ten knots upstream and reached Fambridge at 7.30 a.m. He anchored in mid-river.

After a catnap he went ashore by dinghy and met up with one of the land-based team, Terry Guy. They agreed to unload the cannabis after dark. Eight of the gang would be present. They did not anticipate trouble.

Guy's henchman, Bridger, had rented two vans from Hoddesdon Motors and delivered one to his driver, Geoff King, in Harlow. This was the vehicle which undercover police technicians had doctored the previous night, wiring an electronic bug to the van's electrics. A police radar van, a mile from Red Willows Road, picked up a signal as soon as King drove off to rendezvous with Bridger, in the second Luton van, and Guy in a Ford Fiesta containing £25,000 in cash to pay off the gang. After dark on 4 October the three vehicles, using only side-lights, drew up on the North Fambridge slipway to await Jones's dinghy with its £10 million cargo.

Static Customs observation points at key road junctions and on an undercover vessel anchored in the Crouch reported the progress of the van convoy and at 8 p.m. over a hundred officers of No. 5 Regional Crime Squad and armed members of the Essex Tactical Firearms Unit closed in around Fambridge. The trap was set. People could still enter, but not exit from, Fambridge.

Tricks and six heavies armed with two Uzi sub-machine-guns and a mixed array of small arms had arrived at dusk. Their two car drivers had sensibly retired to a pub in South Woodham Ferrers, four miles away, ready to respond to any walkie-talkie call from Tricks. The Jamaican wore a navy-blue track suit and black trainers. He carried light-intensifying binoculars, his Motorola and a Beretta pistol. The low-lying farmland on either side of the Crouch is liable to flooding, so earthen floodbanks had been raised on both sides of the river. Tricks had met up with his hired guns in The Anchor and chosen the north bank for the heist, since a quick glance told him that all the boat-landing facilities were there. Two of his men took a drink in the nearby pub, the rest lay low in the scant undergrowth set back a few yards from the floodbank. Tricks expected the drugs would be landed at the jetty at 10 p.m.

Inside the North Fambridge pub, The Ferryboat Inn, the landlord, Bill Noyce, dealt with a dozen or so customers. Regulars Phil Slade, a metal broker, and Aubrey Stockford, a designer of braking systems for Ford, stood at the bar, while Dave 'Woody' Woodford was installed in Woody's Corner celebrating his wedding anniversary. He would not say which one.

Noyce had been Mayor of Dagenham before Ind Coope leased him The Ferryboat. He loved the place. Not just the position beside the river but the general feel of the low floodlands, the call of curlews and plovers, the family atmosphere in the village. His missus had transformed the pub with warm lighting from old ships' lanterns, open coal fires in Parker back-boilers, red velour with Regency stripes on all upholstery and the dark shine of their solid-oak bar.

Two strangers had entered the pub towards 8 p.m., polite enough but somehow tense. Noyce had a bad feeling about them and noted the unmarked white van in the car park outside. The publican's motto, developed while he was still Mayor of Dagenham, was: 'You spot trouble before you know it's trouble, and there'll be no trouble.'

Goodman had excused himself from work at Dunlop an hour early with 'a blinding headache' and driven via the M1 and M25 to Brentwood and Wickford. He had discovered from Directory Enquiries that there was indeed an Anchor pub on the River Crouch, in the village of Hullbridge. He arrived at 7.30 p.m. and, after a thirty-minute vigil, began chatting to the publican, a Mr Green. There was, he soon discovered, another Anchor in the smaller village of Fambridge a few miles along the river. A more likely place, according to Mr Green, to meet friends arriving upstream by boat.

Goodman took his leave and drove on to the Fambridge Anchor. Here he ordered another pint and dallied for a further half hour. Nobody remotely resembling Trevor's description of Tricks entered the pub. Again Goodman approached the landlord, one Steve Clift, and this time learnt to his dismay that although this was indeed The Anchor in Fambridge, if he was wanting to meet friends off a river boat, he would do better off in North Fambridge.

'Only two hundred yards away on the other bank,' Steve Clift smiled, pointing out of the window. 'Just a stone's throw but a good thirty minutes by car.'

Goodman moved on again. At 9.25 he finally coaxed Trevor's sluggish van into North Fambridge and left it in the middle of the village in a private driveway. On foot he followed the road south and soon came to The Ferryboat Inn beside a wooden house on stilts, a relic of pre-floodbank days.

Nervous, he found himself glancing into the undergrowth and down into the dank mere bordering the boat-yard beside the pub grounds. He walked towards the jetty with tidal mud-flats to the west and the flapping of burgees on the yachts in the boat-yard to his east. He was pleased to have his Barbour back, for the night was clear with a sharp autumnal breeze.

Over to his right the outline of five quaint fishermen's cottages, built as two units, bothies really, established the river boundary of North Fambridge. He moved as quietly as possible along the sea wall above the slipway approach lane and stopped when the river appeared in the moonlight. Any closer, he feared, might expose him to Tricks and his ambush party. This would hardly help his aim, which was to identify Tricks while remaining unseen; then to follow him and establish his address. If Trevor was right, it would be somewhere in North London.

He stopped and listened. As his eyes grew accustomed to the semi-gloom, he made out the silhouette of a little boathouse, the North Fambridge Yacht Club, set on piles driven into the river mud. Beside it a long ramp led down to a T-shaped pontoon jetty over tidal mud-flats. Sudden swirling eddies and the shifting breeze played on the surface of the river. Strange sounds to Goodman, but he neither heard nor saw any signs of human activity. Perhaps the gang had yet to meet up in the pub. He walked back briskly, for he was getting cold.

He scrutinised the other patrons in the bar, a friendly place but, despite the glowing fires at either end, a touch draughty. Bill Noyce, hand-pulling a pint of Ind Coope, asked in a friendly tone, 'What's yours, sir?'

'I'll have an IPA, if I may.' Goodman had spotted the trade name on a hand-pump. 'Have one yourself.'

'Don't mind if I do. Thank you, sir.' Noyce extended a hand. 'From Wales, are you?'

Goodman smiled and they raised their glasses. The publican began to tell him about Fambridge, glancing every now and again at the two men drinking at the far corner table. They looked shifty, Goodman mused, but surely not the type to engage in armed robbery and internecine drug warfare. Noyce saw the direction of Goodman's stare and lowered his voice.

'We get all types round here you know,' he confided. 'Mostly respectable middle-class professional folk – on the face of it, that is.'

At that moment the two men from the corner table came to the bar for their bill. One stared at Goodman, a cold professional once-over. Noyce shook his head once they had gone. 'Up to no good, I'd not be surprised. You get so you can always tell, doing this job.' He glanced up at two wall-mounted pairs of boxing gloves. 'They're the sort of blokes I keep the gloves ready for.' He grinned, then added 'Very proud of them I am. Bought them at a sports auction. Muhammad Ali and Joe Frazier wore them at their historic fight in Manila. Piece of history, that was.'

Shortly before 10 p.m. Goodman, who had explained his presence in Fambridge to Noyce by saying he was a bird-watcher, took his leave and again walked down to the jetty. This time he kept to low ground and stopped every few minutes to listen. Things had changed. Racing nimbus clouds set moon shadows chasing over the grassy silhouette of the floodbank and Goodman clearly saw the outline of men, crouched along its rim, either side of the ramp leading down to the jetty. He climbed through a fence into the boat-yard and crept into low brush beside a trickle of a stream. Between his hide and the ambush group only some fifty yards and a line of up-ended dinghies obstructed his forward view. Once the action commenced, he decided, he would close in and use the inevitable commotion to locate the man Tricks.

But events did not go as planned for either Goodman or Tricks. A camouflaged policewoman, dug into a mudbank and observing the jetty, whispered her report into a throat microphone. 'Two vans and car, parked on slipway, with three males. Inflatable dinghy from schooner with two crew now returned to mother craft. Cargo of sacks loaded into one van.'

Minutes later, around 10 p.m., she continued. 'A man, probably local boat owner, arrived and spoke to van drivers. Probably checking they weren't thieves or vandals. He's now gone but the van men are spooked. They are leaving now. Not waiting for more cargo.'

Over a hundred police and customs officers within a radius of two miles listened in silence to her message. Twelve hundred yards away to the north the jetty road crossed a railway line at Fambridge station. As the drug collection vans arrived there, a police car slammed across the road and a dozen blinding Dragon Lights flashed on. Tough man Bridger soiled his trousers, vans collided and heavily armed police closed in wearing Balaclavas and flak-jackets under navy jumpers. Three weeks earlier one of their number, Billy Bischop, had been killed in a post office raid, so they were not gentle.

Goodman had heard the vans depart from the slipway but Tricks's men had made no move. He crouched low and felt cold; then stiffened as he recognised the outline of a body not four yards away and partly hidden by the leaves of a hide. The owner of the body must have watched Goodman arrive and, sensing that he himself had now been seen, turned and the two men's eyes met. Neither was armed and both, aware of the need for silence, remained warily motionless.

'Who are you?' Goodman read the man's mouthed query.

'Police,' he whispered.

'Me too.' This rejoinder coincided with the sudden clatter of a helicopter that appeared overhead as though by magic and began to hover a hundred feet above the river. A searchlight mounted in the belly of the aircraft lit up the river and blinded Goodman. Minutes later a member of the helicopter's police crew began to address the *Robert Gordon* by megaphone. If anybody in Fambridge was still asleep, they would need to be clinically deaf.

Goodman felt his shoulder clasped. His companion in hiding had squirmed up beside him.

'Howdy.' The accent was unmistakably American. 'Which force are you from?'

Goodman's vision was returning to normal. The stranger had a round, friendly face. Definitely not one of the Tricks group. He was much relieved. 'I'm with the River Crouch Regional Force.' He immediately wished he had chosen something that sounded better but the American seemed unfazed and rolled sideways in order to proffer his right hand. They shook and said hello.

'We'd better keep quiet,' the American whispered. 'Talk later.'

Illuminating flares fizzed high into the sky, unnecessarily since the helicopter's searchlight lit up every detail on board the schooner as well as on both banks of the Crouch.

Skipper Jones and his crew were arrested and driven away. Before the searchlight was switched off Goodman saw that Tricks and his men had vanished – assuming it was indeed them and not part of the police ambush that he had seen.

Three hours later, stiff and very cold but fairly certain all police elements had withdrawn, Goodman and his American companion retired to the village and Trevor's van.

'I'm John Ridgway. My friends call me JR.'

'Alex,' Goodman murmured. 'Pleased to meet you.'

For a while they fenced about at random while JR lit up a Camel and breathed in with relish after his long enforced abstinence in the no-smoking zone by the floodbank.

Goodman instinctively liked the American and found himself enjoying the experience of simply talking to an intelligent human being – a rare commodity in his life since he had left hospital five weeks before.

JR, with MI5 support limited to minimal appearances by the myopic Jason, had traced Tricks to The Ferryboat Inn earlier in the evening and watched as his gang set up their riverside ambush. He had been tipped off by MI5 that the village was targeted for a police operation and had assured them he would not end up embarrassingly netted. His original hope had been the arrival of Richter, or even Redden, at some stage following the river heist and their proven involvement in what was to prove Europe's largest-ever seizure of smuggled cannabis. That was still his intention but the British Customs involvement and their successful seizure of the drugs had cut down any chances of Redden's arrival to near ground zero. Maybe, he thought, this stranger in the bushes would prove to be a fresh facet, a new angle from which to ensnare Tricks and Richter. After all, although Goodman was quite clearly not a policeman, he seemed an intelligent and straightforward enough sort who was involved in observing Tricks for reasons of his own.

JR made up his mind to find out Goodman's real status. He started by showing sympathy, for the Brit was obviously in need of a shoulder to lean on. JR was no shrink but he was a good listener and the man was keen to talk. His story was simple. He had woken in hospital with amnesia after an accident. By chance he had come across evidence implicating a drug dealer. He had somehow incarcerated the man, who had led him to Tricks. The sole aim in life of the lonely 'Alex' was now to trace his own identity. JR decided to accept this story, for the moment at least, and tag along with Alex in order to meet up with Tricks's minion, the dealer Trevor. There was no telling what information he might be able to extricate from a malleable drug addict which could prove usable RICO material against Redden and Richter.

The two men drove north to Birmingham and Fort Dunlop. Goodman appeared to accept without question Ridgway's cover story that he was a Drug Enforcement Administration liaison officer with British Customs investigating the *Robert Gordon* and believed Trevor might be involved with the smugglers far more than he had admitted to Goodman. As a DEA officer of many years standing he was an experienced interrogator and, he assured Goodman, he would soon find out anything that Trevor was holding back.

Goodman was as usual waved through the Dunlop main gate. They arrived soon after 9 a.m., the DEA having subsidised a major breakfast meal at a Little Chef restaurant on the way.

'What happens if you can't find Tricks and never learn your identity?' JR asked.

Goodman looked up sharply from his cooked breakfast. 'I will find him. I will get my wallet back from him and with it my personal details. I *must*. I think there is someone, somewhere, who loves me and is desperately searching for me.'

JR nodded, his mouth full. Goodman was clearly a shy, intelligent man, good-looking enough in a simple, unexciting way. Warm, friendly voice. Probably about forty and almost certainly married with children. He felt sympathy for him.

When they arrived at the derelict shed and Goodman jumped out to open the double doors, JR marvelled that this mouse of a man could have plucked up the courage to apprehend a drug dealer. He climbed from the van and retched at the smell of faeces and vomit. When his eyes grew accustomed to the gloom he saw the dealer asleep on his back on a workbench.

Goodman finished blocking the doors from inside and joined JR.

'That's odd,' he said, 'he's normally all over me for pills as soon as I arrive.'

Trevor lay motionless, staring at the ceiling, his mouth agape. JR, suddenly suspicious, felt the man's pulse. Then he touched one eyeball.

'He's dead,' he said. 'Your addict's not going to tell me much, I'm afraid. He's gone to that great addict emporium in the sky and he sure ain't comin' back to answer any questions from me nor any folk else.'

Goodman stared down at Trevor's body, ignoring the powerful stench and unwilling to accept that the one possible key to the secret of his life had been stolen from him.

'He can't be dead,' he whispered. 'I left him food and water. He was fine yesterday morning.'

'He's dead,' JR repeated, 'and at an educated guess I would say he's had a mighty big overdose. Where did you keep the capsules you said you were weaning him with?'

'There.' Goodman pointed at the floor in the middle of the room. 'About a dozen were left and they were definitely out of his reach. I measured the chain and estimated his reach. He could not possibly have got to the pills.'

But there were no pills in sight.

JR turned the body sideways. The odour worsened if that was possible.

'Look at this.' He lifted the stiff right arm.

Trevor must have forced his hand out of the single cuff with which Goodman had secured him to the bench. JR could not imagine anyone being able to inflict such damage and pain upon themselves: the dead addict's hand appeared to have been brutally flayed with a surgeon's knife. Great hanks of skin and flesh hung away from its back and sides.

'There are trickles of dried black blood from his nose and mouth as well as vomit . . . Poor fella.' JR replaced the lacerated hand. 'I've seen many cases just like this in LA. Less now than five years ago, but still a major cause of death with the addicts. All it needs is a few too many tablets. A guy slowly takes more and more, builds up his body's tolerance so he can take what would kill you and me. But if he goes turkey for a bit – like our Trevor here – then he'll lose that tolerance pretty quick, you bet. I guess Trevor stuffed the whole damn shoot, all the bombs that you left on the floor, right down his throat. That's a massive dose of barbiturates. Could have killed him in minutes, a few hours at most. All his body functions would slow. Maybe he suffocated on his vomit or maybe his heart just gave out . . . Whatever, he's dead and it could be said you killed him.'

'What will I do?' Goodman was stunned, unable to think clearly.

'Who knows you came in here? Into this place?'

'I think nobody does. But I couldn't swear to it. Sometimes other workers did come round this part of the site. I saw them and they just may have seen the van. The gate security people know I use a yellow van but nobody knows where I live and I've given false names; said my documents were stolen, I was mugged, showed them the scar on my head.'

JR's brow furrowed. 'If I was you, pal, I wouldn't leave bozo here. Sounds like nobody from that squat of his will miss him. Get rid of him – at least from here – as soon as you can. Look, I'll help you put him in your machine. Then I'm going to have to get my ass back to town.'

They left no traces of occupation in the shack except for a lingering smell.

From Fort Dunlop they drove, with the windows fully open, to a car park in Erdington. JR gave Goodman a telephone number in Los Angeles.

'If ever you need help with these guys you're chasing and you find yourself Stateside, you call this number. Right?'

Goodman nodded. He could think of nothing to say. He felt drained, helpless.

'Do you have an address? Any means I can contact you?' JR pressed him.

'Nowhere,' Goodman said.

'Look, friend, here's some cash to tide you over a week or so. When we meet again you can pay me back. If you get some address where I can find you next time I'm over here, you send it to this postbox in LA. OK?'

They parted in the car park. Then Goodman drove aimlessly

north into Derbyshire. That night he used one of Trevor's two trenching spades, relics probably from his past involvement with the badger men, and disposed of the sad and soiled remains in a shallow forest grave. In another place he threw away the spades and the sacking he had used, which smelled of the body. Then, slowly and lost in a trance of dejection, he returned to Erdington and, the following day, to work. The thought of ending it all crossed his mind more than once but one thing kept alive the smallest spark of hope. Somewhere, he thought, there is somebody who loves me.

He would stay in Erdington only long enough to stock up some cash. Then, in North London, he would find a tall black dealer in drugs, a Jamaican called Tricks.

He had come a long way, without help, since leaving hospital. He was not going to stop now. He had worked his will on Trevor. Tricks was next.

9

Autumn 1984

Barry Smart adored Amy. Making love with her was jungle, acid rave and rose petals all on the same magic carpet. The *Kama Sutra* and then some. Yet, with her clothes on, she could act the most innocent, wide-eyed and pony-tailed of eternal schoolgirls.

When he first met her at university two short years before, he told her he would do anything for her. And he had meant it. This was just as well, for now he was in the shit, right up to his neck, on her account, and he was very frightened.

Raddle had cost nothing, being from the Battersea Dogs' Home, and was affectionate despite his loveless background. His credentials, on which they were relying, were the multiple scars about his eyes, mouth and jowls and the obvious signs of battle damage to his front legs. They had paraded Raddle at game shows, dog shows and terrier meets through the summer and autumn and had reached the stage where they recognised many of the terrier and lurcher men.

Amy had spent her first year at Durham University with a group of Animal Libbers, two of whom were very active. One of these, Animal Liberation Front code-name Francis, had discovered by chance that the demure and divine Amy was a nympho in heavy disguise. He could teach her nothing in bed but he did imbue her with his genuine hatred of cruelty and a powerful disdain for 'the talkers'. 'Never forget,' he would lecture her, 'as far as the tabloids are concerned, if it bleeds it leads, and for us a single line in the media is worth a thousand committee debates.' Amy learnt a great deal from Francis but only in theory because he forbade her presence on his 'missions of mercy', his animal liberation outings.

When Francis left Durham, Amy fell for a number of virile young men but none found even her undoubted attractions worth the effort and embarrassment of involvement in ALF activities. So she moved on until she met Barry Smart. Wild female-student gossip related that the dapper young Smart, doing social sciences and philosophy, was able to maintain an erection for twenty minutes of ferocious activity, so Amy had bedded him in a high state of anticipation.

Needless to say Barry's staying powers, only marginally less unimpressive than the average British male student's, proved a bitter disappointment, but he compensated with oral virtuosity copied from the Danish 16mm movies he had watched at a cousin's 'working-men's club'. Barry fell for Amy at first sight and learned from one of her previous lovers that 'The only way to Amy's *heart* is not through her muff. If you want her undying devotion, then join the ALF, become a furry anarchist and burn every leather handbag shop in sight.' Barry had taken this advice to heart, and in the summer of 1984 he and Amy had become a noted menace in Durham and surrounding districts with a number of fur-shop fires to their credit.

Amy's ownership of a venerable Morris Minor was invaluable to their activities, as was her continued membership of the university ALF group. Although weak on the action front, their group intelligence was good and included a senior RSPCA insider. Early that summer the nine-person ALF group, including Amy, had watched an RSPCA undercover film on badger-baiting in Cumbria. Copies of RSPCA files on some of the badger-baiters, including their addresses, were also supplied, but, despite horror and indignation by all present, it was agreed by an 8–1 vote that no personal action could be taken against the 'bestial thugs identified but not arrested by our RSPCA friends'. Amy was disgusted and, after a spectacular half-hour sex session to release her pent-up emotions, she told Barry that they must do something to have Blackledge and his evil digger gang put away. Nobody else seemed able or prepared to try, so it was up to them. Barry saw the hard glint in her eyes as she looked down at him while still straddling his fading manhood. He could see she meant business.

They had searched for a war-scarred lurcher and found Raddle, swotted up on David Harcombe's *The World of the Working Terrier* in order to 'know the enemy', purchased used Barbour jackets and tweed caps in charity shops and exchanged Amy's beloved Morris Minor for a black Renault van. At first they simply walked about at the shows and listened to the dog men, soaking up the terminology and the badinage.

'Get yourself a Northern terrier or a lurcher,' the RSPCA contact had advised Amy. 'Two would be better, but one will do. That'll get you on the same wavelength as these people. Don't open your mouth, lass. Let your bloke do the talking if he has to. Best of all is to break the ice by complimenting them on their dogs. Things to say? OK . . . "He's nice, in't he! Real good-looker. Deep chest, thick neck, good legs." Remember a lurcher's in his prime at two or three and the pundits like to say he should have "a neck like a drake, tail like a rat and feet like a cat".'

Amy's accent was poorly disguised upper-class, but Barry was ethnic Wirral, a version of Liverpudlian which would not raise antennae among the earthy terrier fraternity. Amy simply kept quiet and wore a tight T-shirt under her unzipped Barbour. That way, dumb but sexy, she was an asset, like Raddle.

'Ask them about their dogs,' the RSPCA man had suggested. 'That's the best way to get them talking because they always love to brag. How good their dog is, what it can do and take? They may not immediately specify badgers or foxes. They'll probably say, "it's steady on all quarry". They'll maybe go on to say, "thirty rabbits in a night, a dog fox single-handed without a problem" and "straight down the beam to the quarry", meaning with a searchlight and, usually, a fallow deer.'

'So how do we bring the talk round to badgers without raising their suspicions?' Amy asked.

'Don't you worry. They're often not the brightest of people, these bastards. They'll spill the beans about everything their dogs can do and more because they're so keen to impress. I mean, within an hour or two, especially if you buy the rounds in the drinks tent, these geezers will tell you how many deer they've poached even though they've never met you before. And badgers . . . they'll tell you how they find the best setts, and once they start on their "stripey" stories there's no stopping them. Most of Britain's fox hunters and their terrier men frown on cruelty to badgers. But the sort you are after are the vicious minority who give the hunt a bad name by mistaken association.'

At first it had seemed surprisingly easy, especially when they discovered that Blackledge was well known about the circuits, indeed almost revered by some. He was an active member of the Fell and Moorland Terrier Club and a fanatic about his own brand of Patterdale terrier, black dogs mainly, sired originally by a prime badger killer called McCoy. Blackledge named his strain the Real McCoy and took his best dogs to many of the shows in the north when not engaged in his professional capacity as slaughterer at Slinger's Butchers or gun and drug running with various northern nasties. Blackledge was high on the list of criminals wanted by his local Great Harwood police. He knew this and enjoyed the consequent enhancement of his tough-man image.

Barry and Amy met up with a Lancashire dog man named Terry at one of the shows and struck up a canine conversation based on Raddle's fine collection of battle scars. Terry openly admitted to knowledge of badger diggers and, in the beer tent, he went so far as to say he had himself been on a great many digs all over Britain.

Attempting to sound casual, Barry introduced the names of some notorious badger men, past and present, and included Paul Blackledge as an afterthought.

Terry warmed to the badger talk and they left on good terms. A month later they met him again and Barry, a touch too blatantly perhaps, steered the talk straight to Blackledge.

'I've heard say he's the king,' said Barry, looking suitably adulatory, while Amy let her fulsome lips fall apart slightly. 'Any chance of meeting him?'

Terry stared at his feet for a second or two as though deep in thought. Then he looked up with a fine smile. 'Of course, mate. I'll fix it . . . You going to the Barrowford meet next Wednesday?'

They nodded as one, though neither had ever heard of the place.

'Right, then. See you there. Paul will tell you things you won't believe. His dogs have done it all.'

And now here they were in an obscure Barrowford pub, not far from Burnley, at the bimonthly meeting of the Fell and Moorland Terrier Club. They kept a low profile all morning. Terry had stopped by and, rather curtly Barry thought, told them that

Blackledge would meet them 'later on'. Amy spent an uncomfortable morning trying to ignore the lewd comments and coarse jokes. She felt a dozen pairs of eyes undressing her and more. Barry knew they were both out of place. He felt sorry for her, but then she had only herself to blame.

Barry's reservations were increased ten-fold when, soon after lunch, Blackledge appeared, all groin-bulge in tight jeans and great biceps bursting out of his T-shirt. He stared at Amy as he shook Barry's hand, a calculated taunt which seemed to say, 'I like your bird, mate, and if you want to make an issue, be my guest.'

Besides Terry, there were three other men. Amy soaked up every detail, as Francis had taught her back in Durham, for regurgitation to the police. There was a Tony something, a Roy and a big Irishman called Patrick.

Blackledge looked at the others, who left, except for Terry, and took a seat, switching from menace to charm in one easy movement.

'Like the slides, did you, lass?' he asked, referring to the morning's collection of members' photos showing their dogs at shows and at digs.

She nodded. 'Very nice,' said Barry.

'Like some weed?' They declined and he rolled himself a marijuana joint while stroking and inspecting Raddle.

'How does he perform?' he asked.

'Aah . . . Excellent. Excellent.' Barry gave a frozen grin.

'Really?' Blackledge's lip curled a touch. 'He looks a bit flat-footed.'

For twenty minutes Blackledge chatted about his terriers, firing the occasional question at Barry. Then, without preamble he looked up, all black hair, beaked nose and jutting beard on the solid bull body. Amy remembered that Terry had said Blackledge was a bare-knuckle fighter back home and at events like the annual gypsy horse fair in Appleby. She could picture his hammer fists and cruel pig eyes as the blood and spittle sprayed and the crowd roared him on.

'Ever done any gardenin'?' he asked.

Barry, remembering his RSPCA training on diggers' slang, replied: 'Yes. Once or twice. Had a bit of fun.'

Blackledge then looked up. 'How'd you like to come on our next trip, then?'

'Very much,' Barry tripped over his tongue. 'Be great, wouldn't it, Aim?'

Amy nodded, baring her teeth to stress her delight.

'Good.' Blackledge smacked his knee. 'Give us your phone details then.'

This seemed like a bad idea but, with little choice, Barry obliged on the back of a beer-mat.

'In a week or two, then,' Blackledge said. 'On a Saturday. Probably down south and startin' very early. Oh . . . and don't bring your dog this time, OK? Maybe another time, when you get the way of things.'

And that was it. They shook hands and left. The royal audience was over and they were greatly relieved.

'Phew!' Barry said, stopping their van at a teashop in Hexham. 'I don't like that guy one bit and I certainly didn't fancy the way he kept looking at you.'

'He's not the first,' Amy protested, but she was pleased. She liked Barry to be protective.

'I think the man is evil and I seriously believe we ought to drop him like a hot brick. I don't wonder the RSPCA have found it difficult to convict him. They're probably scared stiff . . . I certainly am.'

'That's not fair,' Amy's voice began to rise to her combat octave. 'The RSPCA did not drop the case. They would love to get Blackledge but, as yet, they don't have enough hard evidence. That video alone would not even allow a court to confiscate his dogs, never mind imprison him. Don't you see, that's what *we're* doing. Compiling evidence. We need to pinpoint in advance exactly when and where Blackledge will dig badgers so we can get the RSPCA and police to set up witnesses and pre-position cameras. It's not enough to film haphazardly and record his dog's backside disappearing down a sett. He could say they were after foxes and that's legal.'

Situated opposite an ugly multistorey car park and beside a busy shopping complex, the Swan Hotel netted a mixed clientele, but the publican, Walter Buck, kept his nose clean and to the casual visitor the place was warm and friendly.

Blackledge and Terry met at a fish 'n' chip shop in Corporation

Street then moved to their usual spot at The Swan. Blackledge was troubled.

'I've called that bastard Trevor on four separate nights this last week. I got his girl this evening. She's worried about him. Hasn't seen him for weeks. Says she thinks someone was after him.'

'So what?' Terry commented. 'Always thought the lad was a right bummer. Don't see why you did business with him in the first place. Askin' for trouble, I'd say.'

'He's useful. He lives in a part of Brum which I can work in. One of the few places not sewn up tight by local lads. And he's got a quick line into the NHS for cheap barbs. There's not many folks has that.'

'Not many nowadays as wants barbs neither,' Terry commented sourly.

Blackledge ignored him. 'Well, he's been useful to me when I got work down that way and he keeps his mouth shut. I don't want him doin' a disappearin' act on me, so I'm goin' down there at the weekend. Can you see to the dig?'

'Sure,' Terry nodded. 'What you doin' about them toffs with the lurcher?'

'Nowt,' Blackledge said, looking down as he often did when he was lying. 'I think you're too uptight, Terry. If they're snitches, then I'm a bleedin' Dutchy. Mind you, I'd shag that bird, no problem.'

Terry left and Blackledge called a friend in Hampshire who specialised in violence against his fellow-humans, not badgers. Then, taking a torn piece of beer-mat from his bomber-jacket pocket, he dialled the Durham flat of the toffs with the lurcher. Their interest in his digging activities was too pointed, too personal.

The day before they drove to Southampton, Barry purchased a knife in a Durham camping store, among a display of lethal hardware ranging from throwing knives to CS-gas guns, all apparently legal. He decided on a three-inch knuckleduster knife, the Urban Skinner, with a clip-on belt sheath. This helped his morale, but not much. He had tried hard to dissuade Amy right up to the moment that they packed their sandwich packs and gumboots in the Renault. But she was adamant. When Blackledge had phoned, with instructions to 'meet his man' outside Yorkies Fish 'n' Chips in Cowes at 7 a.m. the following Saturday, she had been thrilled. She called her RSPCA contact then and there, at 11 p.m. on a Sunday, with a briefing as to 'her intentions'.

The ferries were running every two hours, with heavy Friday evening traffic returning from the mainland. Barry had reserved breakfast at Yorkies under an assumed name. He thought this ridiculous but Amy had insisted, her ALF indoctrination to the fore. They had discussed taking the video camera but she had eventually agreed this would be too dangerous on their first outing with Blackledge.

There were two of Blackledge's men, Len and John, waiting under the archway outside Yorkies. Neither looked welcoming. Barry, as instructed, followed their Bedford van to Apse Heath via Newport, a journey of thirty minutes with two short stops which, Barry assumed, were to spot would-be tails. Close to the junction between the A3056 to Sandown and the B3327 to Ventnor, both vans left the road and joined a third already parked in a lay-by.

Blackledge and a friend they had not seen before were waiting, each with a trenching spade. Blackledge gave Amy his charming but wolf-like smile and bade them follow him via hedgerows and a nursery garden to a wood with thick undergrowth that ran south of and parallel to the Newport road. His companion moved behind them while Len and John disappeared, presumably to keep watch.

'Private land, this.' Blackledge kept his voice low. 'Called America Wood.' He walked easily despite his bulk. Barry and Amy felt clumsy behind him as they moved in single file through tangled brush. Amy estimated that the setts, when they reached them, were half a mile from the road junction. Blackledge concentrated on a large and obviously active sett with at least five visible entrances.

Barry flinched as an aircraft passed low overhead without warning.

'Sandown,' Blackledge said. 'Just north of here and we're right under the flight path. Light aircraft only.' He took them through thick gorse to the rear of the sett, where they found four dogs tethered. One began to growl but quietened instantly at a sign from Blackledge. A man in a woollen hat glanced up from the five-foot-deep hole he was digging. 'Hi,' he said. Barry thought he looked quite amiable, different from the others.

'This is Paul,' Blackledge nodded. 'Good fox man.' Barry had the impression this was said with a sneer. 'Builds boats for a living. Takes all types, don't it?' He stood over the hole, his great forearms crossed and his beard thrust forward. The autumn morning was fine but cool. Blackledge, in faded blue T-shirt, jeans and black boots, appeared impervious to the chill.

'Your first time down south, then?' He looked at Barry.

'Yes. We're real grateful to you. There's nothing like learning from the maestro himself.' A touch of flattery will get you everywhere he thought to himself. Looking at Blackledge above the pit, he found himself thinking of Dante and the Devil incarnate.

Earlier that morning Blackledge had loosed his best dog into the big sett and almost at once had heard the frenzied yap of contact. They had not brought electronic collar bleepers to simplify the job of locating the underground dogs, so the only way to extricate them, along with any badgers or foxes located in the sett, was to dig down until they reached them. Barry and Amy were told to park themselves above and beside the work pit, from where they might best view the action.

'Give over,' Blackledge said to the boat builder.

'That's OK. I can stick at it some more.'

'Did you hear, lad?' Suddenly Blackledge's tone was icy. 'I said give over.'

This time Paul Martin levered himself up from the pit and handed the spade to Blackledge. 'Sure, Paul, sure.' All honey and flowers. Another frightened man, Amy thought.

The boat builder crouched beside them as they watched Blackledge attack the pit. The big man was entirely absorbed in the act of digging. For two hours with scarcely a pause and without a word, he sank the shaft at first deeper and then laterally towards the tunnel where his dogs could occasionally be heard to yap. His eyes were out, his face working.

Paul Martin discussed the waiting dogs with them. 'They all belong to Blackledge. Digger, the rough-haired black there, is one of his specials. This is my first dig with Blackledge, but I know all about him. His fame precedes him in the terrier world.'

Amy noted the dogs' scars and remembered what Francis had once told her. 'Badgers hide their heads under their front legs when attacked, then bite from underneath so badger dogs end up with wounds to their lower head and mandibles, whereas injuries from foxes or other dogs are mostly to the upper head and muzzle.'

Martin indicated Blackledge's other colleague, who had accompanied them from the van. 'That's Jamie. He's digging down to a stop-end to make sure the stripies don't retreat into other parts of the sett as we get close. He's a mean lad.' He lowered his voice. 'Don't cross him.'

Amy had always known she would sooner or later have to confront cruelty face on and witness horrible things short term in order to achieve long-term justice. At noon that day the moment of truth arrived when Blackledge, seemingly tireless, broke through to his dogs and Amy imagined the helpless terror of the badgers at bay a short distance under her feet. Her nightmare thoughts were interrupted by the strong animal odour of Blackledge, who levered himself up from the pit and squatted in front of her.

'Like it, girl?' he leered into her face. 'Great, eh? Nothing beats the dig . . . almost.' He switched suddenly from crude to menacing. 'Did you come all this way to join the dig, did yer? Really? Well, I'll not disappoint. Fun's about to start. You'd like my home, lass. I've got forty brocks stuffed. Reds, albinos, great boars, a little sow what killed two of my best dogs, only the best, I tell you. Jamie, come on up here now – we're all ready.'

Jamie looked no more than nineteen. He stood immediately behind them holding his spade. Amy was glad they had not tried to bring the video. The next hour was full of pain for her. She clenched her fists and averted her eyes, but the noise of the killings would stay with her for ever, as would the image of the corkscrew device.

There were three badgers in all. When the dogs dragged the first sow clear by her head, Jamie forced her from them and held her aloft, laughing with pleasure as her legs paddled the air and blood poured from her mouth wounds. With his free hand the man stabbed a scout knife into her buttocks, then flung her to the two untethered dogs. Ten minutes later the sow finally died and the two fresh dogs were set on a second sow. This, Blackledge said, after a short while, was a poor fighter. He killed the animal in the pit with his spade.

The third badger was a fine red boar and Blackledge was delighted. 'I'll get eight or nine hundred smackers for him from the

Chelsea pit-bull lads.' He dropped his spade and shouted up, 'Pass us the screw will you, Jamie.'

Amy had heard of these instruments of torture but this was the first she had seen in use.

Blackledge deftly caught hold of the big boar's tail and, shouting at his dogs, wrestled the struggling badger from their jaws. Quickly he skewered the animal's neck with a long-handled 'corkscrew', a dog-tether ground spike, and began to twist. The corkscrew tip slowly dug deeper, entrapping fur and flesh in its tightening grip. The badger began to throttle.

'Here, darlin',' Blackledge shouted to Amy. 'You should be looking happy, shouldn't you? Here's your chance to show what you're made of.' He thrust the long handle towards her and she found herself holding the heavy boar badger as it slowly strangled. Jamie held out a gunny sack. 'C'mon, girl. Put the cuntin' critter in here.'

She hesitated. Above all she wanted to drop the horrid tether and set the poor animal free. Her emotions were clear to all. Barry sat there, frozen in indecision, used to Amy making all the moves but seeing her dilemma.

Jamie, disgusted, took the decision for her. Cursing, he swooped the sack up and under the hanging boar then tore the tether from Amy's grasp.

'You're all tit and no spine, bitch. Give it here.'

Blackledge's eyes had gone hard. The elation of minutes before was gone.

'Terry was right,' he said quietly. 'Jamie, when you've secured the stripey, go get the others. We got us a problem here.' He strode over to Amy. 'You're a libber, ain't you? One of their clever little snitches, infiltrators, whatever.'

From the corner of his eye he saw Barry move. 'Paul, keep tabs on Lord Fauntleroy there, will you. Smack him if he does owt.'

The boat builder, spade to hand, closed behind Barry, who found his legs painfully stiff from five hours of sitting and squatting on damp soil.

'Who are you with, girl?' Blackledge snarled. 'What've you told them so far, eh? Terry says you been traipsing around for weeks at the shows droppin' my name. Who did you get my name from, then? Somebody up Durham way?'

104

Amy's fear had been swamped by her horror at the death of the sows and the boar's suffering. Her eyes sparked. 'I'll tell you bugger all, you bastard, and I'll set the police on you for what you've done to these dumb animals. I know where you live,' she spat. 'And I'll see you suffer as they did and all the other helpless creatures you've killed. You're a bloody monster. Prison will be too good for you.'

Blackledge shot out an arm. A ham-like hand caught her under the chin and squeezed till her eyes stood proud and her tongue appeared.

Barry lunged clumsily at Blackledge's rock-like paunch but Amy's body partially blocked his move and the Urban Skinner fell to the ground as Blackledge's free fist caught Barry's mouth. Blood and tooth fragments choked him as he tripped over backwards into the pit.

'Get the tether,' Blackledge told Martin. 'I need to make her talk, but she's a stiff little vixen and we don't have all day. She's got hot pants for the lad and she'll talk fast enough if you fix him with the tether in front of her.'

Martin slipped off into the undergrowth to where Jamie had disappeared with the bagged boar and the corkscrew. As he left he saw Blackledge's bruised hand begin to fondle the half-throttled girl's crutch.

The men would be back from the road junction within ten minutes, Martin estimated. He had to make his decision quickly. This was not his first badger dig but he was above all a lover of terriers, all dogs come to that, who fancied the occasional fox dig at a farmer's invitation. He had been fooled by bad elements within the island's hunt fraternity and ended up acting as guide to the notorious Blackledge. He had met the man socially at shows but this was his first dig with the bastard. Paul had seen the man's propensity for violence and he feared the worst for the two students or whoever they were. A minute after leaving the sett, he made up his mind.

Amy was paralysed by Blackledge's neck-hold. She felt him unzip her jeans, force them down and explore her with his horny fingers. He was rough and, as he became aroused, she heard rather than saw him wrestling with his own trousers. Her head began to sing as, unthinkingly, his thumb and index finger tightened about her windpipe.

Then she heard shouting and saw a blur of movement. Spitting profanities, Blackledge released her neck and she collapsed gasping.

'Police.' Martin was back, breathing hard. 'I got to the stash where Jamie left the kit when I heard their voices. I looked through the brush by the road and saw them. They're coming straight at us, sweeping the wood from the runway side of Cheverton Farm. It must be these two here that rumbled us.'

Blackledge nodded. 'We'll have to leave the stash and hope they miss it. You head back to your car in Wroxhall. I'll go to the vans and warn the others. We'll go back up to Cowes by the Newport Road. It's unlikely they'll have roadblocks up just for diggers. Cheers, Paul. See you.'

Blackledge fetched his dogs together and left the sett. Amy croaked Barry's name, relieved when he replied from beside her, having crawled winded from the pit, blood dribbling from his chin.

Martin reappeared. 'Can you walk?' They followed him along game trails. These were his woods. He explained what he had done: the false alarm. When they arrived back at their van, the badger men's Bedford was gone. Barry did not speak because cold air on the nerve ends of his broken teeth was painful.

'They'll kill you, won't they, Paul?' said Amy. 'Come back to the mainland with us.'

'I think I'm OK. They'll not know there were no police. But you take it carefully. If I were you I'd lie low till Monday. Blackledge is likely to head back on the ferry before Sunday midnight. And please don't muck around with his sort ever again. You will always be the losers.'

Amy kissed the boat builder, aware of the evil consequences he had risked on her behalf. She told Barry she had better drive. She wondered, as they headed north for Cowes, how his smashed mouth would affect him in bed.

Blackledge stopped off in Erdington, a stone's throw from Junction 6 on his M6 route north from Southampton. He felt like batting somebody and that bastard Trevor had failed to respond to his instructions for over a month. Getting sloppy! He parked by the Cecil Road squat and was pleased when Carol came to the door. He was always amazed how such a bird could fall for, let alone stay around with, a divvit like Trevor. Perhaps it was out of deference to

Trevor's only evident asset, his quick line to a reliable source of barbiturates.

For old times' sake Blackledge gave Trevor work of a not too demanding nature when it suited him and he needed to keep his dealings clear of the Blackburn mob. But he must keep a tight line on the donkey.

Carol kissed Blackledge and brushed her knee about.

'Hi, champ,' she cooed. 'After Trevor, are you?'

'Course not,' he laughed. 'Not while you're available. But, yeah, where is he? Been ill, has he, or off to Benidorm with his auntie?'

'I thought *you* might know, love,' she said, turning serious. 'He's been AWOL since weeks back. Not a word.'

Blackledge's libido was still smarting from the Apse Heath trouble. He could picture the sexy blonde libber even now. Given another five minutes he'd have given her something hard to forget. Very hard.

'Carol,' he said. 'Place full, is it?'

'No,' she purred. 'They're all out at The Acorn. Why?'

'I need to talk.'

'Talk?' She moved against him.

'Yeah, well.' Blackledge knew he was home and dry.

They had been giving each other the eye on and off ever since he first saw her with Trevor two years back. Now, it happened as easy as stabbing a brock. Once, quick and rough. Then two relaxing spliffs – Blackledge never touched anything stronger than hash – then he lay back and let her play about for an hour, confirming that she was definitely wasted on Trevor. After the second main event, he turned businesslike. She didn't mind.

'So how am I goin' to find your lover boy?' he asked her.

'I've told you. He just went. Never said nowt before and he's not called since.'

'He owes me.' Blackledge gave her his hard look.

She shrugged, breasts jiggling, and sucked at her spliff. 'There was a bloke, come to think of it. Could have had summat to do with it.'

Blackledge said nothing.

'Well, this fella, looked like a town clerk on the dole, called here way back. I'm no good with dates. My kid told me about it. This bloke comes to the door, says he knows about Trev, but Trev fucks him off sharpish. Afterwards Trev farts around like he's seen a ghost. That night he wakes up, clutches me and grunts, "They were dead. I know they were dead." "Who?" I ask him. "Them at Kinver," he says. Then he clams up tight as a tick.'

Blackledge looked up sharply, scratching his chest and fiddling with his heavy gold medallions on their neck chains.

'I thought the geezer must be some undercover drugs pig,' she went on. 'Saw him hang around watching Trev for days. Real weird. He went off with Trev in the van the day Trev disappeared.'

'What was his name?' Blackledge asked.

'I didn't hear and Trev never said.'

Blackledge asked her a great many questions but he could see she knew no more. Trevor had simply vanished and there was no proof the scruffy little clerk was involved. But Blackledge disliked the reference to Kinver. He called Tricks and repeated what Carol had told him.

Tricks asked the same questions. If this 'clerk' had seen Blackledge's driver Trevor at Kinver, had he followed him back to Erdington? What was he after? If he didn't look like a pig or a nark, what the hell was he? Could he have seen the Americans?

Blackledge had answers to none of these questions.

'Well, keep your eye out, man,' Tricks told him. 'Any sign of this clerk, you hold him and you call me. Right?'

10

February 1985

Goodman lost his job with the ever-shrinking Dunlop workforce in February 1985. He took his savings and his Barbour jacket and moved to London, although his plan had been to stay in Erdington until April and warmer weather before making his break. He had done what little research he could at Erdington Library on the geography of West Indian drug dealing in British cities. Tricks operated in North London and that meant, if police regional drug statistics were to be believed, that he should initially focus on the contiguous districts of Tottenham, Stoke Newington and Hackney.

People in London struck Goodman as less friendly than Brummies. The uncaring face of Mrs Thatcher's capitalism was blamed for this by most folk with whom Goodman shared a table in coffeeshops. His driving aim was to find a job and a roof, but after three bitingly cold days walking the streets of Finsbury Park he was not hopeful. Unemployment across the land had reached three million, an all-time record not helped, so those affected snarled, by Norman Tebbit's comments on bicycles. Laws designed to protect tenants had scared off a great many landlords, so that affordable rented accommodation was in short supply.

With his meagre savings in a cloth wallet on a money-belt next to his skin and a natural inclination to frugality, Goodman set himself a tight budget and no rental offer he had yet found came within its limit.

Erdington, he decided, was a quiet suburban paradise compared with his new London pastures. Every form of vice and fraud was rampant, drugs were everywhere and the police presence hopelessly inadequate.

Café gossip indicated well-priced rentals in Haringey. Goodman began his search there early on his second day in London and by nightfall was following up leads in the Green Lanes district. One recommendation led to another. In a so-called 'Greek area' he called at a Turkish kebab house, an Armenian fruit shop, a Cypriot car-hire firm, a number of Middle Eastern greengrocers and a Lebanese charcoal grill.

At midnight the streets were still alive and full of bustle, but Goodman was exhausted. A deaf Cockney octogenarian directed him to the 'Passage', famous since Dickens' day for its twenty-four-hour mugging service. A hundred years ago the Passage was an open sewer running between Green Lanes and Wightman Road. Nineteen parallel streets link these two roads to form the 'Green Lanes Ladder' and the Passage bisects them all – a narrow, dingy place at noon and a fearful haunt after dark.

Eventually, having failed to find the flat he sought, Goodman gave up looking, and at the southern end of the Ladder he emerged at the entrance to Finsbury Park. Dog-tired, he spent the rest of the night there, shivering in a cricket hut with a snoring alcoholic. In the morning he was woken by the man, who appeared friendly, erudite and at least temporarily *compos mentis*. Would Goodman treat him to a dram?

They ended up in a scruffy sandwich bar near the Manor House Hotel, Finsbury Park's nerve-centre. Henry, the alcoholic, had no advice on specific bedsits but plenty to say about the area. He had lived there for some twenty years, surviving by a mix of *savoir faire* and state hand-outs.

'I'm an alcoholic gent,' he informed Goodman, 'not a wino. They're horrible. Vermin of both sexes. The dregs of humanity, stinksome and diseased. In the Park they kill, rape and bugger one another.'

Otherwise, Henry assured Goodman, it was a 'perfect spot' in summer. He was an ex-army man and a good judge of bivouac sites. There were, he said, plenty of comfy hidey-holes in the bushes where local police never checked. 'Mind you, one needs to know who to placate round here. Do the wrong thing to the wrong face even through ignorance and you could wind up dog meat in the West

Reservoir. I used to make sure, for instance, to pay my dues weekly to the Afghan kings.'

Goodman's eyebrows rose.

'These brothers, their dad was an Afghan and their mum a redhead Scot. Each twin was six foot four, rough, lean and fiery. The younger was a psychopath, and an armed robber by trade. One August noon I was surveying a pretty woman lying in the grass in her swimsuit and perusing a magazine. Afghan Two was out jogging through his territory when he spied her and decided on rape. She screamed, so he nutted her – that is the term we use for a headbutting – and carried on . . . Do you have a fag?' Goodman shook his head.

'Leastways a good friend of mine, Paddy the Wino, was dossing beside my bush and saw Afghan, who he hated for his Park tax extortion, and he upped and hit him right then and there as Afghan tupped the lady in his track suit. Paddy hit him hard as he could with his VP sherry bottle. I cheered, I tell you, from my bush. But Afghan simply withdrew from the tourist lady and set about Paddy. They fell into the pond, we call it our lake, and struggled among the lilies until the police came. The law gifted Paddy £25 and Afghan got eight years. His brother soon disappeared and the Park's been a tax-free residence ever since.'

On Henry's advice Goodman walked a few hundred yards down Seven Sisters Road to locate the GLC temporary works office, which, according to Henry, was good for casual labouring jobs on the nearby giant Woodberry Down Estate, with its ten thousand inhabitants.

At the works office a notice instructed work seekers to try further up the road at the site, so Goodman made his way to a deserted place of scaffolding, skips and heaped building materials. At length, behind a concrete mixer, he found a security guard, who told him that the works office was closed until 4 p.m.

'Meanwhile,' warned the man, looking furtive despite his impressive American-style black uniform, 'don't hang around here. The gangs will get you and there's nothing I can do unless I see them at it. I have to stay right here by this phone point.'

Goodman had nowhere else to go. He'd decided not to suffer another night out but to delve into his precious cash for a bedsit. He would concentrate on finding work first. 'I'll wait if I may,' he told the security man, who seemed glad of the company.

*

111

Sara was a Gujarati Hindu from Surat. She had few memories of India, or of Kenya, where her family had lived from when she was four months until her *karnavedha*, when, aged three, her nose was pierced by a goldsmith. All her memories were of London and most, despite her good nature and resilience, were unhappy. If she now owned a tiny flat and ruled her own life, free from black pimps, it was thanks entirely to Sailor, Columbo and the rest of The Family.

She smiled warmly at Columbo. At eighteen and three years her senior, he was streetwise and sleek. He had pretty girls at his beck and call, she knew, but she did not mind for he was like an elder brother, not a lover. They had been at a North London comprehensive school together where Columbo had shielded her from the taunts of both white and Jamaican bullies. He was a karate fighter with respect from his peers despite being from Trinidad. Trinidadians are 'Smallies' or Small Islanders in Jamaican eyes and in North London the pedigree hard men among blacks, at least in their own eyes, are all from Jamaica.

Sara had fled school despite Columbo's protection, for he could not be everywhere. She became a hostess in a West End topless disco soon after her only surviving relative, an old aunt, died, leaving her homeless and destitute, a casualty of the flaws in the welfare system. The same year she aborted her first pregnancy but lost her job. To obtain lodgings she fell prey to a Jamaican pimp whose girls worked Wilberforce Road in Finsbury Park at £5 a turn, which translated into £1 a minute to kerb-crawling punters.

In the summer of 1984 Sara's pimp dropped her off at a house in Green Lanes to service an Asian drug dealer named Sonny Guha. He introduced her to heroin and paid her pimp a lump sum to take her on full time. For two months Guha's clients at Green Lanes treated Sara as their plaything. She got on fine with Guha, who was kind enough, but his bosses were brutal and she soon fled. With neither money nor a source of heroin, she tried to kill herself with a razor-blade. She was then only fourteen.

A Jamaican trainee nurse at the Whittington Hospital recognised Sara as an old school mate and remembered Columbo's attachment to her. Columbo took her to his penthouse flat in Haringey as soon as her wrists were sewn up and nursed her day and night through the dreadful weeks of withdrawal. He was at the time a cat burglar and when he had to 'work', other members of The Family stood in to watch over Sara, who was incarcerated, for her own good, in a windowless bedroom.

She had pulled through and Sailor, head of The Family, had given her 'life lease' on her little flat. She went back on the game, her alternative to the dole, but on her own terms and able to veto clients as she felt inclined. Life had very definitely improved over the past year.

'See you next week, love,' Columbo said, pressing her hand. 'Do nothing I wouldn't.' He winked at her and jogged away up Towncourt Path in his £90 Nikes. Her flat was in the Keynsham block, deeper into the Woodberry Down Estate. She was passing the building repair works area when rough hands closed about her waist. She tried to scream and to struggle but a dirty cloth was wedged between her teeth. There were two of them carrying her and another two waiting behind the blocks of concrete.

They took her handbag and ripped off her silver wrist-clasp, a present from Sailor. For an instant her hopes soared that she would merely be robbed: she never carried much cash with her.

Three of the assailants were white skinheads, the fourth a burly teenage black. One ripped her shirt off and held her fast from behind. Another pulled up her miniskirt and grabbed at the tights. They were brutal and when, dog-like, they decided to turn her about, the gag fell free and she screamed her lungs out. A shout of 'Police! Stop!' resounded, followed by raucous shouting. Her attackers dropped her to the ground, where she lay sobbing, curled up in a foetal ball. In a while she heard a gentle voice and looked up into the concerned blue eyes of a uniformed policeman.

'You OK?'

'Thank you. Thank you,' she whispered.

'Here, put this on. You'll get cold.' Her rescuer took off his uniform jacket and she saw that apart from it and his peaked cap, he was scruffily dressed. A second man then appeared, who took and donned the peaked cap.

'Well done, good on you,' he said to Sara's rescuer. 'I'd have done the same myself but for my eyesight. Blind as a mole, I am. I rung the police – they'll be here shortly if they're not too busy.'

Goodman lent the Asian girl his Barbour jacket as her shirt was in tatters. He offered to take her to a café for hot soup but she shook her head.

'I'll be all right,' she smiled her thanks. 'Would you like to come back to my place for a coffee? It's not far. Then you can have this jacket back.'

She limped at first and noticed how gently he supported her elbow. She was not accustomed to deference. Back at her flat the answering-machine regurgitated two messages, both from regulars, but thankfully there would be no visitors for an hour or two. She felt both drained and shocked.

'Shouldn't you see a doctor?' Goodman fussed. She could see he felt awkward.

'No,' she said. 'I'm OK. My name's Sara. What's yours?'

'Alex. Alex Goodman.' He offered it quickly as though keen to confirm that he had a name.

'Stay for the coffee?'

He nodded eagerly and she noticed he was unshaven, a touch rumpled, almost like a tramp.

'Are you hungry? I can easily do us a fry-up.'

Her accent was North London, not Asian nor Cockney, and, he guessed, she was seventeen despite her little-girl looks and shape. He could see why the gang had singled her out. She was stunning. He wondered who she lived with in this tiny flat. There was no sign of male occupancy.

'Well, I wouldn't say no, since you ask,' he said with a grin.

'You local?' she asked as she busied herself at the cooker.

'No. I've only been in the district a few days. Looking for work. That's why I'm on the estate. Thought maybe I could do casual labour for the council. I've tried for three days to find digs around here but there's nothing reasonable at all.'

She switched on a battered Roberts radio; the automatic gesture of people who live alone and need voices. Bob Geldof's 'Do They Know It's Christmas?' competed with the spitting bacon fat.

'Tell me about yourself,' she said. 'How did you scare off those bastards?'

He was happy to talk. The room was delightfully warm, a real haven after the past week. He tried to be modest but secretly he was quite pleased with himself. He'd been sitting with the security guard, sharing his Thermos, when they saw Sara attacked. The guard had grasped Goodman's arm. 'We'll call the cops. Keep down or they might see us. They'll have knives.' Goodman, seeing the need

114

for quick action, begged the guard to lend him his uniform and identity disc. Holding the disc like a police badge, he had rushed up, making as much noise as possible and dreadfully frightened that the yobs would turn on him.

'I was amazed when it worked. I'm only sorry I didn't get to you sooner.'

'Listen, Alex. You look like a nice bloke. You must be or you'd recognise me for what I am – a hooker. I make my brass on the job so rape don't mean as much as it might. As for my things, they only took my bag, a tenner and a bangle. Don't you worry, I'll be fine – thanks to you.'

She thought for a while, prodding the pan. Goodman's hunger stirred at the smell of bacon and eggs.

'Go on then,' she prompted 'tell us all about Alex Goodman.'

At first he was hesitant. Since leaving hospital he had told nobody but the American John Ridgway, 'JR', about his identity problem. Back in Erdington none of his Dunlop workmates nor his Italian landlady possessed a shoulder he wished to cry on and, in any case, he was wary lest the police enquired into Trevor's disappearance. Sara was different. He felt somehow that she would sympathise. Although she was young, her great brown eyes were full of understanding. So the words came out and she listened, so fascinated the toast burnt.

'And now?' she asked when they had eaten and he had finished his story, omitting only the fact that Trevor had died.

'It depends on my memory, I suppose.' He felt that he had known her for months, not a mere two hours. 'Over the past few weeks my headaches have stopped altogether, my ability to taste things is fully recovered and I rarely feel dizzy. More important, I wake some mornings with knowledge of my childhood which I am sure was not there the previous day! I know now that I lived in a vicarage beside a red-brick church and my father was the rector. My mother took Sunday school and I always won prizes at primary school for mathematics. I had a beagle dog called Fez which wore a red collar and was run over.'

'That's great,' Sara's laughter tinkled like crystals. 'Soon everythin' will come back.'

Alex looked doubtful. 'Somehow I don't think so. In hospital they said full recovery normally takes days, rarely weeks and only

115

occasionally months, unless there is a self-inflicted subconscious desire to forget, in which case I may never recall the event that caused the amnesia or any associated memories. Childhood memories are an encouraging sign but I can't bank on the full works.'

'Poor Alex. You could be heir to the throne and you wouldn't know it. If you've got a family, it's surprisin' they've not made a fuss, innit?'

'That's right,' he agreed. 'But there again, maybe they *have* tried to find me, desperately, and somehow we've just not connected. You read of mothers and children, brothers and sisters who, despite searching, lose each other for decades. There's no Missing Persons Bureau, you know, no central computer. The police told me they hear of sixteen thousand individual cases yearly and they reckon that's just the tip of the iceberg.'

'That don't help you though, does it?' She tapped the table with a finger. 'What are you goin to do to find this bloke Tricks? You tried a private dick?'

'How do you mean?'

'You know, an agency. They chase hubbies on the loose and catch them on the job so's their women can get anemone.'

'Alimony.'

'Yeah.'

'You mean pay an investigator to locate Tricks?'

'Why not?'

Goodman considered the idea. 'Where are these investigators?'

'You could try Yellow Pages for a start.' She stretched for a tattered phone book. Everything was in reach in her kitchen. She yawned, remembering with displeasure that a client was due in just under an hour. She wondered if she could fob him off without full sex as she was still sore from the attack.

Alex sensed her change of mood and reached for his jacket.

'I must go. I've spent enough of your time. The meal was wonderful. I hope you're really OK, Sara.' He said her name for the first time; it felt good on his tongue.

'Listen,' she said. 'This place is lousy when you want to be private and for the next couple of hours it'd be best if you're not here.' She looked rueful. 'Can you take me out tonight? I really want to talk with you, Alex.'

116

He felt warm and happy in her company and agreed with immediate enthusiasm to return at dusk.

That evening, after they had eaten in a Chinese restaurant, she refused to let him pay. 'Listen. It's the least I can do after this mornin'.'

He wanted her to talk about herself but she switched deftly to other topics as though her own life was unsavoury. He did learn that she lived by herself but often stayed with a group of valued friends she called The Family. Her hobbies included the nursing of two outsized window-boxes and reading whatever she could find about the Hindu faith, into which she had been born but from which, following her parents' early deaths, she had lapsed.

She asked him back for coffee, and they returned to the flat, avoiding the building site.

'What'll you do tonight?' she asked.

'I booked into a hotel,' he said. 'Just down Stroud Green.' Sara said nothing. She lifted the sash window to check her flowers. 'Buggers,' she swore and squinted upwards into the dark. 'They do it every night like clockwork. About one in four land in my boxes.' She held up a used condom with her fingertips, then let it drop into the dark. Her flat was on the second floor. She turned and faced Goodman, catching him ogling her legs.

'You don't want to waste your precious brass on no hotel, Alex. Listen, I'll make you a business proposition. You pay me a fiver a week and share the doin's and you can have the spare room.'

'But . . .'

'Wait,' she said, holding her finger out to hush him. 'Look, this place ain't no great shakes but it's a roof and I can see that's what you need.' She opened the two sliding doors that led from the sitting room-cum-kitchen. Her 'big room' was actually a medium-sized bedroom in which she conducted her business when not 'visiting' in response to a call.

'And this one's yours,' she said, indicating a tiny room with a folding bed but no space even for a bedside chair unless the bed was folded up.

A pair of Doc Martens and a black bomber jacket, XL size, lay on the bed. She saw him wondering. 'That's Columbo's,' she explained. 'He's like my brother. You'll like him.'

Goodman wondered if this Columbo would like him.

'Really, he won't mind you bein' here.' She read his mind. 'He's got his own place. Just uses my pad when it suits. So do the rest of The Family. Sailor's the chief. He owns this place.'

Goodman let this go. Doubtless everything would make sense later. Right now he was over the moon. Cheap lodgings with the loveliest girl in London. He held his hand out to shake on their agreement. She laughed and kissed it.

'You're a right caution, you are,' she said. 'It's a deal then, starting tonight. House rules . . .' She ticked off her fingers. 'You keep in your place when there's a client in the big room. You use the shower and toilet in the back of the big room when I'm out or in the kitchen. Likewise the TV, opposite my bed; I have to keep it there 'cos the clients like the videos. You keep quiet when I pray to Krishna. . . . And watch it with matches. Too many flats round here go up in smoke. Some of them for no known cause at all. Whoompf! They call it immaculate combustion but I think it's folk playin' with matches.'

'Spontaneous,' Goodman murmured.

'What?' she said, turning abruptly.

'Spontaneous,' he repeated. 'Not immaculate.'

She ignored him and pulled aside a curtain in the sitting room, revealing a tiny shrine with a sandalwood image to a Hindu god, half human, half elephant. 'That's Ganesha,' she said. Further images of clay, brass dishes, bowls, a bell and an incense lamp shared her little shelf with the elephant god and Goodman smelled a blend of turmeric and other spices as she closed the curtain. He felt like shaking his head to clear it but feared to do so in case it was all a perfumed dream of heaven and he woke to find himself back out on the street.

Over the next few days Goodman did his utmost to find a job, but although he was ready and willing to turn his hand to any unskilled manual labour, there was nothing available. Sara sympathised when he returned after dusk. They remained on friendly, easy terms. Columbo called; a powerful young man, as Goodman appreciated when they first shook hands. For his part, Columbo saw a wimpish but honest-looking white guy, who, judging by the way he had helped Sara, must in fact be pretty gutsy. Sailor and he had already been to the building site to sort out the yobs who had attacked her, but there was no trace of them. For a while Columbo felt ill at ease with Goodman in the flat, accustomed as he was to receiving Sara's full attention. But he slowly recovered his natural bounce, and when he heard from her the details of Goodman's own problem, he even offered to help search for a 'good private dick'.

Giving up his futile job-hunting, Goodman went with Columbo to a phone box from which, using ten-pence pieces covered with heavy silver foil, Columbo could make free any calls he liked, including long-distance gossip with his folks back home.

'On you go,' he said, flashing his gleaming white teeth at Goodman, then, seeing his hesitation, added: 'Go on, mate, it's a public box, innit?'

With this logic ringing in his ears, Goodman called a number of detective agencies listed in Yellow Pages. They promised expertise in divorce and matrimonial matters, debugging, surveillance gear for hire, fingerprint analysis, process serving, credit reports, bodyguard provision, missing person location (including debtors and witnesses), photo and video evidence collection and covert surveillance.

'Don't go for the two-pint, one-horse, shitty set-ups,' Columbo warned. 'They'll rip you off and do sweet Fanny Adams for yer.'

Goodman made nine calls, which reached answering-machines or otherwise failed to connect, before catching a warm-sounding, middle-aged female who called him darling. She belonged to Associated Detectives at 85 Tollington Way, Holloway, and she re-routed him to her 'Head Office in the City'. He made an appointment, and the next morning stood outside a smart building in Queen Victoria Street, opposite The Sea Horse pub and the rear end of the *Financial Times* building. If they could afford City rates, Columbo had advised him, they must have plenty of work and that meant a good reputation.

He ascended four floors and an efficient receptionist admitted him to an inner sanctum where three 'detectives' handled active phones and full ashtrays. A wall notice in capital letters announced: 'The Seventh Commandment is Thou Shalt Not Admit Adultery.' Two empty desks testified to absent agents doubtless out on the trail of adulterous spouses. Goodman was impressed. Sadly, however, the detective he spoke to was transparently unimpressed by Goodman. For a start he wanted to see proof of identity, which, of

119

course, was not available. Furthermore, when it became clear that Goodman's 'quarry' was a dangerous West Indian drug dealer with no known clues as to his location, other than the street-name Tricks and the likely general stomping ground of North London, the detective shook his head in disbelief.

'That, sir, will take a great many man-hours. That is needle-and-haystack stuff in a very – I repeat, very – unhealthy area. You are going to be presented – make no mistake, sir – with a monster bill. I tell you this now because we believe in total honesty upfront. We take no customers – unlike the competition I have to say – without telling it to them straight.'

'Monster?' Goodman had no idea what sums were involved.

'If I say a minimum of £5000 plus expenses, plus VAT, I would not be exaggerating. Could be a great deal more. A great deal and, of course, we shall need that proof of identity and the £500 standard upfront payment against cancellation or non-payment. Fees thereafter, needless to say, depending on how things progress, paid in instalments to be agreed. Drug dealing . . . North London . . . West Indians. Maybe a great deal more.'

Noting Goodman's despondent manner that evening, Columbo said he thought that the detective's adverse reaction was quite fair and his estimate reasonable.

'You'll get the same sort of reaction with all the dicks,' he advised. 'They're shit-scared of Jamaican dealers. Who isn't?'

'What else can I do?' Alex asked.

Columbo and Sara looked at each other.

'I'll ask Sailor,' Sara said at length. 'He may think of somethin'.'

'Alex here's goin to need ident and cash,' Columbo told Sara. 'Even if he finds a right cheapo dick. They'll do nothing without readies and ID upfront.'

'I'll see what Sexton can fix, startin' with National Insurance.'

Alex looked mystified.

'Sexton,' Columbo explained, 'reckons our Sara's the ultimate – which, of course, she is – and he busts a gut to keep her happy so she'll always be around when he calls. He's from Lagos. Them boys use their brains. In Lagos there are schools where they teach one subject only: how to suck the UK social services dry. Boy, they are classy. You want anythin', they'll get it. Not cheap but good-quality

120

stuff that'll fool ninety-nine per cent of the fuzz ninety-nine per cent of the time.'

'And if,' Sara added 'they hit the one per cent, they don't care too much. A British nick has a lot better livin' standard than what they get back home.'

'How much will all this cost,' Alex asked, 'to fix my identity?'

'Forget it,' Sara said. 'This one's on the house but it may take a couple of weeks dependin' on how busy Sexton is.'

'How does he get official documents?' Goodman was sceptical.

'I'm no expert,' Sara said, 'but I know the basics. You go to St Catherine's House in the Aldwych and ask for Births, Deaths and Marriages. Tell the official you want to look at your family tree. You take a seat at one of their computers and if you like the sound of the name Smith, tap "SMITH" into the machine and see what you get. Maybe a few hundred Smiths. Choose one that suits you who's died and would be about your age if he'd lived.'

Sara warmed to the subject. 'If you're usin' the old Somerset House ledger books rather than the computers, never choose a name that has a pencil mark against it in the index. That will mean somebody's been there before you, a Nigerian probably, and already used *that* Smith's identity. OK, now you got your chosen name and birth date, nip across to the Birth Certificate Applications Department, a different part of St Catherine's House, and tell them you've lost your birth certificate, along with all your other papers, and you need a new one. This will cost you £4.50 but you'll come away with a birth certificate in your new name of Smith. Now you go to the nearest DHSS office and tell the officer you've been abroad fifteen years and all your papers have been pinched. You produce your new birth certificate and any service bill with your new name and the address of your squat upon it.'

'How do I get that?'

'Off the Nigerians. They'll forge you any bill you like; for instance, an invoice on official North Thames Gas or British Telecom paper. They'll print in your new name, Smith, and if you like, this address of mine as your current residence. The DHSS will then send you your official UB40 benefit book and a National Insurance Number in your new name. You can use this to get credit cards, provisional driving licence, whatever. Also, of course, to claim the dole – £72 a fortnight.'

121

'And that's it?'

'Yep. Sexton charges a West African illegal, just smuggled into the UK, about £300 for that and another £200 for a British passport because, for that, he needs an "official" referee to sign the photos and to say he "knows" the bearer. This service he'll get from a West African London solicitor using a false address. If you then want free health care and full housin' benefits, Sexton will provide the relevant advice at a small extra cost. He knows every welfare scam in the book and he's nothin' special. There are thousands of other Sextons in the UK and hundreds of thousands of freeloaders bloodsuckin' the taxpayers.'

'You must be joking,' Goodman said.

Columbo grinned. 'Listen, these boys are proud to fleece Britain. They say that the English stole the wealth of *their* countries for centuries. Now it's their turn to get it back.'

'I don't like it.' Goodman was shaking his head. 'It's not right.'

'Why not?' Sara prompted.

'It's criminal.'

'When you pretended to be an official security guard to help me,' Sara said, 'you were breakin' the law.'

'That was for a good cause,' Goodman protested.

''Course it was. And so's this. You need the money in order to catch this bloke Tricks, who is, by the sound of it, a criminal right down to his boots.'

Goodman yielded, for, when all was said and done, he could see no alternative. He must have an identity and some seed money in order to raise the very considerable funds he would need to undertake the search for Tricks.

Eventually, true to Sara's word, Sexton produced a birth certificate and UB40 for Goodman, which pleased him mightily since, even though they were false, they were a great deal better than nothing. Even so, he could not see how he could amass the '£10,000 clear' that Columbo told him he would need once he started messing around with detective agencies.

Columbo casually suggested the answer.

'I do blags, armed robberies, as well as the "cat" work, and I'm good. I don't mess about, man. Folk fool with me and they're down, down for good.'

122

'You've killed people?' Goodman looked at Columbo anew. He had previously seemed a rough but gentle giant.

'Well, man,' Columbo confided. 'I tell you true. I done bad things in my time and I'm no saint. But since The Family took me in, I don't like to kill unless there's no easier way. Sailor and James have made me see the light. Life is precious in the eyes of our Lord, so I don't take it away from folks any more so long as they do nothin' stupid when I go across the pavement, like.'

'The pavement?'

'Yeah, man. Blaggin'. Robbin' at gunpoint . . .' He paused then eyeballed Goodman. 'Hey, man, you drive? Drive good?'

Goodman nodded without hesitation. Since his accident, he'd driven fork-lifts, dumpers and Trevor's van. He had no reason to think he would fare less well with fast cars, which was doubtless what Columbo had in mind.

'How you fancy a quick fifty thousand greeners for one night's work, Alexo? With that sort of cash, friend, you could hire a bleedin' fleet of dicks right away and find your Yardie man, Mr Tricks, no problem. Sounds good, eh?'

'Why do you need me?'

'OK. All my normal jobs have been shoework. But this one's big and needs wheels. The machine's got to sit in the right spot, at the right time, or I'm in deep shit. But if a black brother's sittin' there smilin' at passin' pigs and bananas, they will blink twice and say, "Uh-huh, we have here a black geezer about to do a blag." But you, Alex, with a newspaper and a sandwich, they goin' to ignore you all right, for sure.'

'Bananas?'

'Yeah, CID. They're bent, yellow and hang around in bunches.'

'What is the target of your blag?'

'Emby.'

'Emby?'

'Emby is a loan shark. Big and black like me, but twice as sharp. He operates from the Finsbury Park Tavern, and that's one mean place. No-go area for the fuzz. Full of Yard-men from Jamaica. Only a few knows about Emby. He's rich on account of bein' a ghost. He's there but nobody knows it. He calls in his tickets once a month and never the same place twice. Ten days from now he'll be at the Tavern and I ain't tellin' you how I got to know.'

123

'Tickets?'

Columbo smiled. 'I'm beginnin' to know, Alexo, when you ain't comprehendin'. Tickets is what Emby's callin' back. Always cash and always in tens. Tens of thousands, that is. Loans.'

'Doesn't he have guards?'

'Sure he does, but less than you'd think. A ghost don't need too many soldiers. His crew's real tight. Maybe two good boys close by, but he's relyin' on nobody knowin' he's there. Usually he's right. At the Tavern he'll be wrong 'cos we'll be there and we're goin' to lighten his load just before he quits the place.'

'Fifty thousand pounds?'

'That's minimum and all yours. All you got to do is be there. I jump in and you drive off. You got it?'

'Drive where?'

'You and me will sweep the plot in a few days till you know the route blind.'

Goodman slept on it but the decision was not hard to make. This was a chance to gain the necessary funds in one fell swoop without involvement in anything more violent than a quick unarmed car ride from Finsbury Park to places as yet unknown.

Columbo met Goodman one evening when Sara was at bingo with a girlfriend.

'What do you think about Sara?'

'I like her,' Goodman replied.

'You sleep with her?'

'Of course not. I'm her lodger.' Goodman was shocked.

Columbo looked at him, uncertain whether or not he was being sent up. Then, seeing Goodman was genuine, he burst into deafening hoots of mirth. This was partly through relief since he was jealous of Sara, as any man would be, despite his platonic, big-brother relationship with her.

Columbo had brought Cokes and crisps. He intended to show Goodman the area of their intended crime. They sat and talked as they waited for dusk and Columbo's life story spilled out in short bursts of bitter-sweet humour. His parents had arrived in Stoke Newington in 1967, when he was two years old. His father disappeared when he was eight. No explanation: 'he just blew', and his mother never really recovered her spirits.

124

Columbo had three elder brothers and two little sisters. Rudderless, they learnt self-sufficiency in an uncaring world. At twelve, Columbo was sucked into the sad and dangerous world of London rent boys to help supplement the family income out of school hours. He would catch the 253 bus along Seven Sisters Road and cruise known homosexual pick-up points such as the public toilets at Manor House and Clapton Ponds. For £15 he would accompany one, sometimes two, elderly men down backstreets to dark doorways.

Since most of the rent boys were white, Columbo did good business on the rarity ticket. However, he kept well clear of West Indian men, whose traditional reaction to 'battyboys', their name for gays, is violent assault.

At weekends Columbo and a group of younger school friends from Stoke Newington, all white and mostly abused at home, would explore the gay Meccas of Piccadilly, Victoria and West End bars such as Richard Branson's Heaven, with its 16,000 gay members.

Some of the boys were natural homosexuals and some were merely effeminate. The majority, like Columbo, found gay fondling distasteful, certainly not arousing, but an easy way – their only quick means – of earning money. Back at school they tended to stick together and jealously guarded their secret for fear of bullying and 'queer' taunts.

Columbo had taken to amphetamines at the tender age of twelve and, maturing more quickly than his white friends, found he was no longer so attractive to pederasts favouring younger boys. To pay for his drugs he started to procure for closet homosexuals, mostly married businessmen commuting from the stockbroker belt. His headquarters was a restaurant close to Parliament Square and his clientele expanded by 'word of mouth', for he was easy to locate. A black boy holding a rolled *Financial Times* in a place where blacks were a rarity was unlikely to be a police plant. He was paid £15 for a teenager and more for younger boys.

Columbo found many of his boys at railway stations, fresh from areas of high unemployment.

'Glue sniffers were my main source,' he told Goodman. 'Here on the Woodberry Down there are plenty of sniffin' dens with boys as young as seven and they do anythin' for cash. I'd been at school with quite a few or with their big brothers, so they knew me, they trusted me.'

Columbo stuck to his amphetamines and Ecstasy and thought the solvent-sniffers were crazy. He saw the nightmares they went through when fully conscious. One girl of eight, whose favourite 'sniff' was to kneel with her head under a refuse bag positioned over the petrol tank of a parked car, used to scream and scratch walls until her fingers were bloody. 'Keep them away . . . the snakes,' she would cry.

'Another kid used to steal fire extinguishers from the landings and inhale the bromine fumes as he triggered them. He said his mother made his baby sister sniff felt pens when she cried too much.'

'Felt pens?'

'Yeah,' Columbo nodded. 'Anything with fumes . . . Tippex and Evo-Stik are easy. Hair sprays, fly sprays, nail varnish, paint stripper, shoe polish – you name it, they sniff it.'

He had seen a young friend, Jason Swift, at a sniffing den on one of the Woodberry Down landings, light a cigarette while another girl, not yet pubescent, was sniffing from a butane gas cylinder under a bin-liner.

'She was lucky,' Columbo explained. 'There was a bang and the bag burnt up in a flare. But only a bit of the gas had released, so her hair and eyebrows were singed but her skin was OK. Others get their faces and hands burnt bad.'

He had witnessed a young Scots lad, frightened by the screams of a fellow-sniffer, die from a sudden massive heart attack – the result of months of abuse.

'And he was only twelve,' Columbo added. 'He used to spray aerosols straight into his mouth, which, Sailor says, clogs up your lungs and freezes your throat so's it swells and you throttle.'

Columbo sighed. 'It got so I could spot a sniffer even if they was in Sunday school. Mostly young Jason, who didn't sniff himself, would tell me where the dens were and I got to recruit the bumboys that way but other times I could tell a sniffer from his red eyes, the smell on his breath and the spots round his mouth. "Ever go with a punter?" I'd ask them. "Make lotsa ackers in five minutes, no problem." Sooner or later they'd say yes, OK, and I'd take them to the punter. I'd get cash on delivery or no deal.'

'When did you stop it?' Goodman asked.

'When I heard about the paedo mob, Interchain, and what they did to the kids. After that I didn't want nothin' to do with it.'

'Interchain?'

'They're from Zurich, New York, Hamburg – all over the bloody world. They pay subscriptions for videos, magazines and addresses. They're into dirt and the younger the better. Real sado-bastards. RFI with ten-year-olds. That's "rectal fist insertion" like you saw in Al Pacino's *Cruising*. There's a couple of hundred UK Interchain pervs and the fuzz know all about the bastards. They done several murders of young bumboys as well as clean lads they kidnapped. Last year they got my mucker little Jason. I know who done it but the fuzz won't ever catch the sods.'

'Why don't you shop them anonymously?' Goodman was shocked at Columbo's apparent indifference.

'Look, mate. If I open my mouth to the law, I'd be up in open court and these buzzards would nail me sooner or later. They don't muck around. Six of them took an hour to kill Jason. Buggered him every which way, stuck knives up him, then suffocated the poor little kid with a pillow. I've left the rent-boy scene, Alexo, and I ain't goin' back. Me and two others switched to blags about a year ago. Chemist – he's got Aids – will be with us next week.'

'Next week?' Goodman's voice raised.

'Yeah, it's on for Friday. Didn't I tell you?'

'Emby, you mean?'

'Yep. You, me and Chemist. Me and him used to do tube-muggin' folks on Fridays – pay-day. Piccadilly was favourite on account of Chemist livin' Hammersmith way and knowin' the line. We carried big lock-knives and a squirter full of bleach.'

'What about the Transport Police?'

'Nah, mate. We didn't do nothin' on the trains. We'd picket the target durin' the trip then follow her – women is always best – outside and grab her in a side-street or car park. No hanky-panky, just a straight bag and sparklers snatch and off you go while she's still gaspin' like a goldfish and wonderin' why she's not dead meat.'

Columbo looked at his watch. 'We'd better get our act together,' he said. 'Wait while I call Chemist.'

Goodman sat in silence contemplating the past achievements of his new partner in crime. At least, it seemed, he was not teaming up with a novice. Any Columbo-inspired raid should stand a reasonable chance of success.

'The fucker's got a relapse.' Columbo slammed down the phone furiously. 'He can't make it tomorrow for the sweep, the practice, and he thinks he'll be in St Anne's for two weeks' treatment. Says he's sorry. Sorry! The cunt's done us proper this time.'

Columbo immediately made another call and conducted a lively conversation in West Indian patois, only partially comprehensible to Goodman.

'You sure? . . . Midnight dead for the pigs?' He nodded to himself and stared at his gold Rolex as though it was a stopwatch. 'OK, man. See you Friday at Walker's. No more talk.'

He turned to Goodman, white teeth flashing in a wide grin. 'That's my friend, Art. Chemist can go fuck himself at St Anne's 'cos we, Alexo, are goin' to make ourselves a fortune from ol' Emby.' He extended his long arm and slapped Goodman's fist in an Afro handclasp, a sure sign of his improved mood.

'What was all that about?' Goodman asked.

'The Tavern has been Jamaica territory maybe five years but a few months back the owners put in a new guy. Irishman, with an army of heavies, Paddy hard men, behind him. These boys didn't scream for the fuzz when they got threatened, they just threatened back. Errol Braithwaite, a big local black boy, kept at the Paddies but a fuzz undercover job got him. Emby was warned off last week. He ain't goin' to The Tavern no more but my friend says he'll be at Walker's same time, same date. As for our practice run, we'll carry on like planned.'

The rehearsal that night went well. Goodman listened to Columbo's every instruction and memorised the route, double-checking it later in an A–Z. He felt nothing could go wrong. Soon he would be able to pay an agency to find Tricks and this uncertain existence would end.

Columbo wore an all-black outfit, Nehru jacket, leather trousers and rubber-soled, calf-leather sneakers. Visor-shaped Polaroid glasses, heavy silver at neck and wrists and a white Homburg completed his 'top-sleek' ensemble. He had considered borrowing Tosh from Sailor for the evening to enhance his overall look since white baby-mothers were in fashion. With her slim, six-foot frame, legs up to her armpits and flaming-red dreadlocks, she would give him definite brownie points with the brothers at Walker's. Tosh would love the excitement, he knew, but Sailor would never forgive him if she was hurt, and in the mayhem he anticipated, that could not be ruled out. So he was alone. And apprehensive.

Walker lived in Crowland Road, an offshoot of Tottenham High Road, where, at number 157, he owned the best place in London. If you were black and a high-ranker, Walker's was the place to go. Sexy white girls could be seen and maybe even heard but white men stayed clear. Fridays and Saturdays were favourite and top dealers vied with each other for that key commodity, 'respect'. BMWs, Mercedes, Alphas, lined both sides of Tottenham High Road, as far as the eye could see from Walker's.

This was no 'front line' or flashpoint – just a party place. By 11 p.m. the club was bulging at the seams with hardly room to move and blacks parading the streets all around in their finery. Eighty per cent of the new cars, gold chains, Gucci, Hermes, Armani and other high-fashion accessories were funded from drugs, but Taff Jones and the rest of the Tottenham Crime Squad were generally pleased with Walker's. What trouble occurred, stabbings and the occasional shooting, were kept low-key within the black community. Only forty per cent of black killings were actually reported, and since most of the dead were illegals, few ripples were caused.

Taff, only two months out of the uniformed boredom of the local Beat Crimes Desk, was happy as a sandboy in the Crime Squad and intended to stay out of uniform for a good many years. He was Welsh, canny and proud of it. An ex-bricklayer and landlord of The Beehive pub in Tottenham, he had joined the police later than most and was thus rich in the life experience lacked by most of his straight-from-school colleagues.

Taff stretched across for the binoculars. With an hour to go till midnight, it was his job to ensure that the Governors were informed of any unexpected happenings at the target site. He reported all quiet on his hand-held radio and lay back against the sloping tiles. The daffodils were out in nearby Finsbury Park but he wore a heavy donkey jacket, for roof duty at night was never exactly warm. He noted idly the stumpy white man in the Barbour jacket still waiting in the badly parked Escort. He had a jumpy, unsettled look about him. Taff decided this was understandable. The fellow was obviously from out of town and, waiting for some woman, felt intimidated by the all-black ebb and flow in the street about him. Taff sympathised, his eyes continuing to rove the streetlamp-lit areas below.

There would be over 200 constables involved in the coming raid, possibly more, so Taff did not anticipate trouble. Things would be different if this was a front-line dealer's shebeen or one of the local white discos, The Royal or The Eagle. Blood spilled in such places every Friday, raid or no raid. No, Taff decided, there was no colour bar to violence and crime in Tottenham.

Walker's rumbled to the steel clatter of a passing train. South Tottenham BR station overlooked the shebeen, but none of the gathered black assembly noticed the vibrations, for Walker's emanated its own sound: wild reggae too loud for its denizens to hear each other speak. Nor could they see a great deal in the dimly lit blue swirl of smoke from joints and Havana cigars. Only in a tiny room upstairs where Emby took scheduled visitors could a cat's yowl be heard above the patois hubbub, the smash of dominoes on tables and the all-pervading beat.

Emby's two bouncers, Doug and Latto, were built like teak wardrobes and mathematics was not their greatest talent. So Emby did his own counting and always had since the sixties, when the Arabs had murdered his family and hunted him from Zanzibar. He had fled to London, abandoning his first amassed fortune as a loan shark but saving his life.

'You are short by a quarter,' he told his client. 'Twenty-five thousand is a lot of money, my friend. Don't you agree?'

The tall Afro-haired Jamaican spread his hands. 'I done my best, Emby. You got to believe me. I need maybe two more weeks and I'll clear with you.'

Latto's arm swung across and the supplicant found himself airborne. His navy-blue Hardy Amies blazer creased as he swung in the gorilla's grip. Doug reached over, grabbed the man's scrotum and squeezed. The resulting scream made no impact beyond the room. Only Columbo, on the other side of the closed door, picked up the sound. He was crushed against the wall in the crowded room and feeling tense. There were only minutes to go.

Emby nodded and Latto let the man drop, moaning and winded, to curl up on the floor.

'You got two weeks, man. Fourteen days. We'll let you know the place. Stay around.'

The man struggled to rise. He managed to nod his compliance.

'And listen,' Emby purred. 'Next time, Latto here will cut them off.' Latto fingered a four-inch serrated blade on cue and the debtor left the room. Doug shouted 'OK' and another man pushed past Columbo to keep his appointment with Emby.

Then a piercing whistle sounded and the reggae ceased. Everywhere the guests began to secrete capsules, foil-wrapped sensimilla and resin blocks. Mouth, vulva or anus. Take your choice and take your time. The fuzz would be slow and ponderous at Walker's. They seldom raided but when they did the sheer numbers of patrons frustrated any attempt at efficiency.

A hundred officers closed in from the rear and a similar number from the High Road side. The reggae was on full volume again, making police orders from the loud-hailer difficult to hear.

'The fuzz are all over,' Columbo screamed at Doug and Latto. As the two bouncers stared down at Emby for instructions, Columbo sprayed CS gas at short range into their faces, switching immediately to Emby. He snapped shut Emby's case and slung it through the window into the darkness. Within seconds he had closed Emby's door behind him and was firmly pushing his way around the perimeter of the crowd towards the stairway. He knew the accepted reaction by Walker's habitués to a raid was to stay put until forced outside, thus making things as difficult as possible for the police. But he needed to exit at once. Goodman and Art would keep to the agreed timings. Even as he made the stairhead he heard the siren and grinned.

Taff laid down the binoculars. Everything was off to a fine start. No unforeseen embuggerance factors this time. He knew there would be only limited success because the law forbade body searches, so only the drugs of a few addicts, too spaced out to hide their goodies, would be netted. But the Squad would be seen by law-abiding citizens, criminals and the local media to be flexing its muscles and doing so in sufficient force to discourage trouble.

Taff heard the siren and then saw the approaching blue lights. Hopefully nobody had been stabbed. That was Taff's first thought, for only three months earlier he would have been one of the uniformed lads down there and he knew what it felt like to move through the menace of a crowded room. Your serge uniform felt as thin as cotton and the hair down your neck bristled at the thought of a blade thrust from behind. Too many freaked-out addicts had stabbed too many of his unarmed beat friends for Taff ever to relax in such conditions. But the ambulance, which he could see now was a standard white Peugeot estate, flashed up the High Road, kept clear as part of the operation. The blue Escort, from immediately below Taff's vantage-point, nosed out in front of the ambulance and the two vehicles screeched off past the shebeen and the milling crowds outside, to halt by the railway station. Taff picked up his radio but the airway was busy.

As the ambulance passed the shebeen, the dark figure of Columbo slipped outside and, taking advantage of the momentary diversion, evaded the police ring about the house. Easing himself thirty yards down the street to a nearby shop, he took a back alley to 157's rear garden, where he picked up Emby's case and, unobserved by police back-stops, he returned to the High Road. A second, shadowy figure followed Columbo and stabbed him in the back and neck as he opened the door of Goodman's Escort in front of the railway station.

Columbo, collapsing, screamed to Goodman and dropped the briefcase on to the passenger seat. Too late he recognised Emby's loan client. He should have gassed him too.

'Get out of it! Now!' he shouted. 'Go!' He slammed the door and stumbled away.

Goodman surprised himself by the speed of his reaction. The engine was ticking over. He reversed into Columbo's assailant and leapt out to pull Columbo back into the Escort.

Two police officers were investigating the ambulance from which Art had fled into the station, leaving siren and blue rotating lights in full swing. Both men now ran back to the Escort but Goodman reversed again, swung into a side road and followed the route he had rehearsed over the previous week. For a while he thought he could hear following sirens but soon he knew he was clear and stopped in a

Stoke Newington backstreet. Columbo was bleeding freely. Goodman had never seen so much blood. 'Take me to Sailor's,' Columbo whispered.

As he drove to the new address with Emby's briefcase beside him, Goodman reminded himself that he was not a criminal. He was doing this to catch criminals.

11

Early summer 1985

Taff Jones and his colleagues wore bomber jackets and carried binoculars. For days they had watched 7 Alfoxton Avenue from an upstairs room in The Green Gate pub and plotted the movements of residents and visitors alike. They categorised most of the inmates as white New Age Travellers mixed with anarchists and general layabouts.

Most of the cocaine and heroin was delivered by a smart young man in a souped-up Cortina responding to specific orders by phone. He sourced his supplies from a local Turkish gang and the proceeds went to fund the Animal Liberation Front, two of whose members lived, on and off, at number 7.

'This lot's new,' Barry Walker, Taff's team mate, said, indicating the arrival of a grey mini-van. They watched a tall woman in a black beret, dark glasses and white mackintosh stride to the door. She carried an attaché case. A black man waited in the van.

Taff nodded and reached for the Nikon's telephoto lens. The police photographer was downstairs chatting to the landlord.

'I've seen the driver before somewhere,' Taff muttered, taking a few shots as the black beret lady reappeared. 'Good-looker this, even with the shades. Take a squint while she's in the light.'

Barry looked and whistled. Through the binoculars he saw the bountiful auburn hair spilling from under the beret, the freckled ivory skin, the model's legs and the full breasts. Under the unfastened mackintosh, she wore a blue denim miniskirt and a white tank top in keeping with the flaming July day. Taff noted the time and the registration number of the departing mini-van in his surveillance log.

'Shit,' Barry said, his ear to a transistor radio. 'Boris Becker's won Wimbledon and he's only seventeen.'

Chemist drove the mini-van with a deft hand. If anybody was following they would have a devil of a job keeping up as he wove his way south to Peckham. Tosh noticed that he was not his normal talkative self. She knew many Aids sufferers and sympathised with Chemist. Columbo had rescued him from the rent-boy circuit and introduced him into The Family. He had been with them for three years now and was indispensable at the lab. They had all been as shocked as he when, four months ago, the HIV-positive diagnosis had confirmed his growing health worries. Most days Chemist managed to push aside all morbid thoughts and think positively. Some doctors were saying a high percentage of HIV carriers would never develop full-blown Aids. Others said ninety per cent would die within ten years of contracting the illness.

Chemist parked along Commercial Way and entered the Dickensian maze of the North Peckham Estate by an entirely different route to Tosh. Like other members of The Family, they kept the location of 'the Home', a set of three interconnecting flats, a well-guarded secret. All the addicts Tosh was 'cooling' were taken in and out by night along the labyrinthine walkways. Sailor tongue-lashed anyone whose vigilance lapsed. A cautious approach was especially valid when returning from a cannabis or amphetamine run, as they were now. They met again on Hordle Promenade, both sure they had no unwelcome tail. Minutes later they reached the concrete rise overlooking the flats and, as usual, stopped to check things out.

Tosh grasped Chemist's wrist and pointed at the side door. A body lay in the walkway. They split up and approached in the deeper shadows. Tosh reached and saw the intruder first, peering through the letter-box. She stunned the man with the heel of her hand and immobilised him by reversing his jacket, an old UVF trick from her Belfast days. Then she ran back to find Chemist cradling Columbo's head. The big man lay inert, seemingly lifeless. She felt underneath his chin.

'Weak but OK,' she whispered. 'But we'll need the doc, so we will.'

Chemist let himself into the interlocked flats of the Home and dialled the Pakistani doctor who attended The Family both legitimately and when circumstances inflicted injuries that would arouse police interest if they were to use regular NHS facilities.

'Who is the bastard you smacked?' Chemist asked Tosh as they dragged Columbo into the building. Somebody had tied a makeshift handkerchief dressing over his neck wound but his blood-soaked trousers smeared the lino in the hallway. Tosh left Chemist in order to follow the blood trail back some two hundred yards, along passages and down stairways, to the nearest car park space. She found the briefcase in the Escort and removed it, along with the car keys, after driving the car well away from the start of the tell-tale smear.

She dispatched Chemist to swab down as much as possible of the staining and dragged the inert Goodman down to the nearest of her coolers, already occupied by a young heroin patient. The cubicle was soundproof and secure.

Chemist removed most of the bloodstains and went to wake James, the only Family member in residence. He was not in the best of moods as he had slept little all day and had tended to the coolers the previous night. But once Tosh told him about Columbo he was immediately solicitous. Sailor, he said, had been away two days and was expected back during the night.

They assumed Columbo had been attacked by a rival amphetamine gang, an ever-present hazard and realised Art might also be in danger. They tried his mobile but received no reply. 'They may have attacked him at the lab,' James thought aloud. 'You'd better check it out.' Tosh and Chemist took handguns from the nursery and departed, leaving James to await the doctor's arrival.

'If Art is dead or Columbo dies,' Tosh said as she left, 'I will surely to God skin and boil that fecker.' She nodded towards the cooler where she had dumped Goodman.

James did not respond. His was a gentle nature by comparison with the rest of them. They should wait for Sailor's return, he thought, before deciding what to do with the white man in the cooler. They had no proof as yet that he was responsible for Columbo's knife wounds. The latter had said not a word and appeared to be breathing ever more faintly as time passed by with no Dr Khimji.

James was not Columbo's greatest fan within The Family since he disapproved of the young tearaway's lifestyle. He had lectured him a hundred times on following the Rastafarian way and Columbo had always grinned at him and said he intended to improve. But the robberies had continued. Since Columbo was always generous to The Family with large portions of his ill-gotten gains, it was not easy to berate him. Some sage had once uttered an inanity that Columbo kept regurgitating at James: 'It is easier, brother, to fight for your principles than to live up to them.'

James considered himself as guru and, at forty, patriarch of The Family. He had studied the Rastafarian faith in depth and held steady in the paths of righteousness inasmuch as the Lord permitted, given the wicked world in which The Family was forced to move and make its living.

Sailor, his younger brother by two years, was an ox of a man, fierce and fearless. With a razor-sharp brain, his ways were as devious as the Scriptures but to James he was always Little Brother. If business parallels were sought, Sailor would serve as executive director to The Family, James Rasta as moralising chairman and the others as workers with full rights to be heard in council – and ignored. Measured tolerance was stressed a good deal by James. Turn the other cheek, unless to do so means death, in which case an eye should be taken for an eye with the speed of light.

He looked down at Columbo, with whom he had, these last few years, been extremely tolerant, and he realised how fond he was of him. Everything, James knew, was for the best or the Rastafari Jah would not have ordained it so. Perhaps the Columbo who survived these wounds would be a less impetuous lad.

There was a gentle rapping at the side door. Dr Khimji had arrived, a busy little man who had tended the brothers since they had first come to the Peckham 'Home' in the mid-seventies. James rolled a joint and sat back, ready to fetch whatever the doctor might need. The room filled with the sweet aroma of sensimilla. He ran his fingers through his long, greying dreadlocks and sighed. He and Sailor had come a long way since leaving JA but he could never be sure they had done the right thing. True, they had escaped the hell-hole of West Kingston, but, as he looked down at Columbo, he reflected that South London was no longer a haven of peace for a brother. Killings and torture, rape and theft were on the increase, and all, in James's opinion, due to the advent of the accursed cocaine.

'Man,' he sighed, 'I love the weed. It's so sweet. Nobody never got dead of the herb. But crack belongs to Satan. Only a crack user will spend her last dime on her cravin' instead of food for her little pic'ny.'

Ganja was non-addictive, as harmless as Players No. 6 or Tennant's bitter. In fact, as a medium to help relaxation and contemplation of the Scriptures, James recommended it. Without cannabis, he admitted, Sailor and he would still be in the JA poverty trap. Thousands of Yard-men – to a Jamaican 'Yard' means home or hearth – have become rich beyond their dreams over the past twenty years thanks entirely to drugs and, initially at least, that meant cannabis grown Yard-side and exported worldwide.

The newly emerging 'Yardies' soon became the terror of expanding crack ghettos throughout the big cities of the English-speaking world but chiefly in the USA, Canada and the UK. Single-minded, ruthless violence carved a rich field of operations for Yardies in North America at the expense of the Mafia and Cuban and Colombian gangsters. This held true from Miami to Seattle and from London to Toronto.

Local black American drug dealers were picked off by Yardie gangs or posses, who quickly established their own ghetto bases in every major city.

Unlike Chinese, Italian or even Colombian crime groups, Jamaican posses are divided and unstable, doubly dangerous through their spontaneous, almost natural violence towards one another as much as to outsiders. They control street dealing in cocaine and crack by exercising extreme brutality and cruelty even when they could get their way by mere threats. With no code of ethics and virtually no ties of internal allegiance, the posses fight within themselves and then split to form further factions which quickly turn on the original organisation. All this makes them specialists in disorganised crime and creates a nightmare for pursuing lawmen.

The West Indian centres of Britain's inner cities were hit hard from the early eighties and onwards by successive waves of violent Yardie illegals, and those most affected were the previous wave of emigrants. Among these were people like James and Sailor, who had earlier survived by practising the only skill they had brought with them from their native land: the cultivation and sale of marijuana. Now their trade included amphetamines. There were fewer inter-gang killings in Britain than in North America because of the stricter firearms laws and the tighter grip of the immigration authorities, but many of the brothers' friends died. They themselves survived by tight adherence to security and anonymity.

In a world where enormous importance is placed on respect, the brothers' mania for low-key 'minimal silhouette' operations was unique. Every 'trader' in the ghettos of Brixton, Stoke Newington, Peckham, Tottenham, Clapton, as well as the corresponding black districts of Bristol, Birmingham, Nottingham and Manchester, knew all their rivals and what they were up to. This helped the police, since Jamaican informers with grudges were two a penny. It also facilitated the work of Jamaican enforcers when searching for contract targets in UK cities.

The brothers' methods of conducting business incognito included use of several 'street-names', Yardie terminology for nicknames, and the dispatch of junior Family members to carry out street business. They lived in Peckham, South London – Sailor had been loaned one flat and would later enjoy the use of the two adjoining ones as well – but operated their amphetamine laboratory in North London, moving its location every year or so, sometimes just ahead of raids by police or local drug gangs.

The Family lived dangerously, the more so thanks to their cooler activities, cherished by James and Tosh, tolerated by Sailor and the rest. Sailor, more than the others, hated the violence of the Yardies. He steered clear when he could but fought fire with fire when he had to or when folk he considered weak and innocent were being victimised. He was not fussy as to his methods and would cooperate with the law, on a favour-for-favour basis, through two Peckham 'plods' who had risen to positions of some influence since their first street-level meetings with Sailor.

The Family had made many friends who knew of their where-abouts and many enemies who did not. One secret of their survival untouched by the Yardie wars, James reflected, was their business flexibility in dealing with West Africans, white Brits or Turks while maintaining a rigid line against dealing in heroin, cocaine or crack, despite the resulting loss of potential income. To James, and to all true Rastafarians, cocaine was an evil concoction from the cauldron of the Devil and one that eventually destroyed all who dealt in it.

'He will live,' Dr Khimji announced as he emerged from Columbo's bedroom. 'He has lost a lot of blood and should have a cross-match blood transfusion in sterile conditions immediately. But I recognise the circumstances so I've fixed up a saline drip and given him a big shot of penicillin to prevent infection. His wounds are all stitched up and dressed. I can do no more right now. I will be back in two days to check on him unless he regresses, in which case, call me.'

James nodded.

'Give him these penicillin tablets four times a day,' Khimji continued. 'Keep an eye on the drip and allow him as much food and drink as he can take. Check that he urinates correctly. This is vital. The blood-loss shock may have shut off his kidneys. As his blood pressure climbs he will regain consciousness; any time now. Keep him in bed, James. This is not the first serious wound I have treated for that young man and I know he hates to be inactive.'

James thanked the Pakistani and paid him cash, as was their custom. He took the proffered prescription and promised stern supervision of Columbo. It was as well for the white man in the cooler that the stab wounds had not proved lethal. Sailor should return soon and retribution, James knew, would be in kind. He had twice witnessed his brother's wrathful reaction to killings of Family members.

Goodman sat upright in one corner of the tiny padded cell. The girl's naked legs lay across his, her Marks & Spencer panties were printed with smiling images of Mickey Mouse, around the edges of which curled her black pubic hairs. This fascinated Goodman, since the girl was a peroxide blonde. Thank God she had fallen asleep. He hardly dared move for fear of waking her and prompting renewed amorous advances or, worse, one of her screaming, frothing fits. Once upon a time, he mused, she must have been strikingly attractive in an emaciated way.

They had thrown him in with her and locked the only door. But he was not tied up, and seeing a paper file in a wall slot, he stretched out for it without moving his legs. The file was a copy of an original and labelled simply 'CAROLE'. Her age was not given in the appropriate slot. Whoever was supervising her treatment appeared to know nothing of her background and the sheets dealt only with the likely explanations of her physical state.

Her left hand and the upper half of her left leg were both bloated and pitted with poisoned ulcers, deep, suppurating abscesses. Old, inactive needle ulcers pocked the lines of her main veins, especially on her forearms and thighs. Even her jugular showed evidence of needle pitting. Many of the sores were 'barb burns' from injected barbiturate powder which had missed the veins. Other ulcers, according to the report, were from injected Diconal tablets, which should never have been ground up and diluted.

An HIV test had been taken the previous day and the results were awaited. Carole's teeth were in a state of advanced decay, a fact which Goodman had already noted during her earlier attempt to rape him. This decay, he read, was caused by Carole's inability to absorb calcium due to her artificially stimulated metabolic rate. The file went on to chronicle a variety of suspected sexual ailments, malnutrition, bronchitis, urinary problems and rectal boils.

Goodman felt sorry for the girl although still recoiling with repugnance from her earlier behaviour. If I had a daughter, he decided, I would want her to see the miserable state of this young addict. She had, at first, stayed curled up in her corner, twitching as though in pain and staring at him from under half-closed lids. Soon she had started to moan and to itch as though ants were crawling all over her. She had then begun to tear off her clothes, along with plasters and bandages smeared with blood, pus and yellow ointment. Bouts of screaming followed and then, as though in a trance, she had begun to finger herself. Goodman had averted his eyes but she had settled herself in his lap, fastened her lips to his and attempted to undress him. A terrible screaming session had followed his rejection of her before she had finally dozed off.

For long hours Goodman lay there unable to sleep and plagued by half-recognised vignettes from his youth. He had remembered, a month or so previously, that he was once an officer, or at least a cadet at some barracks in Aldershot. A flood of detail followed but, for him, Memory Lane ended in a cul-de-sac. He knew nothing of military matters generally, yet he could clearly recall the finer points of infantry drill movements and the stripping down of a rifle. He must have been in his late teens at Aldershot. Why, he asked himself again and again, should he recover so much of his early memories yet experience a black void thereafter? He had studied medical books at libraries and knew that his amnesia symptoms were rare and almost certainly self-imposed through a dread of recalling some past shock.

His father had developed epilepsy after receiving shrapnel wounds in the Second World War. Although there was no proof, it was probable that the car crash which had killed both his parents was caused by a sudden fit when his father was driving. He now remembered the familiar stab of guilt he had often experienced after the crash. Yet, at the same time as he wondered how he knew about this, he realised he was still unaware why he should feel guilty. He was sure, again without knowing why, that he had been nowhere near the crash and certainly not in the car. Maybe he should have been driving at the time but had let his parents down.

His thoughts were interrupted by a click from the door of the cell. Two large black men stared down at him. One he recognised as Art, Columbo's friend, who had driven the Peugeot ambulance. His hopes surged. Art beckoned and Goodman rose cautiously. Carole's legs slumped outwards but her bronchial snoring continued uninterrupted.

Goodman followed the men past three other soundproof doors and along a dark, twisting corridor to a high-ceilinged room which smelled of stale ganja. Art gestured Goodman to a ragged armchair. The five others sat themselves around him as though in readiness for some kangaroo court to commence.

'Tosh!' said the heavy-set Jamaican who had arrived with Art. He addressed the white woman who sat on a window-sill away from the rest.

She nodded. 'This fella was up to no good, Sailor, that's for sure. I caught him snoopin' through the letter-box.'

Northern Irish, Goodman thought. Her voice was attractive; a touch on the husky side. 'Chemist and I were just back from the Alfoxton drop and found him pokin' his nose about,' she said. 'Col was bleedin' at his feet like a stuck pig and I wouldn't be surprised but that he did it.' She waved briefly at Goodman.

'Art!' Sailor, chairing the gathering, eyed the youngest Family member. Tosh and Chemist had found him over at the lab, whither he had returned after the Peugeot ambulance run, for it was his lab duty night. They had caught him on the bed in the lab with a fourteen-year-old Jamaican schoolgirl, despite the firm Family rule of no outsiders knowing the lab's whereabouts. As yet Tosh had not told Sailor of this indiscretion.

'That's me, guv.' Art threw a wide, guilty smirk at Sailor.

'Don't clown, boy. Say what you know.' Sailor's mood was dark. He had returned from two days in Nottingham, setting up a business for a Korean friend from Los Angeles, and disliked leaving London. Now he had returned to big problems, or so it seemed, from an unidentifiable enemy, since the white man Tosh had caught was clearly neither police nor standard gang material. Unless proof was quickly forthcoming of the man's innocence, he would have to dump him with Troon's Korean boys. Troon disposed of people with finality as though they had never existed. Enemies of The Family who threatened their existence were usually sent to Troon's.

Art had been horrified to hear about Columbo and overjoyed to learn he would recover. Seeing the look in Sailor's eyes, he became serious. All Art knew was that Columbo, needing two drivers for his latest job, had given him the ambulance detail and made a deal with some white guy to act as his own wheels.

'Did he tell you who this man is?' Sailor asked.

'Yeah. He lodges with Sara. Pays her room rent.'

'But who is he? What's his work?'

'Search me,' Art said with a shrug. 'Never spoke to him.'

'Can you think of any reason he might want to put Col away?'

'Nah. Unless he's workin' for an oppo crowd and Col didn't know it. But, that bein' so, why would he bring Col back here bleedin' and half croaked?'

Sailor nodded. 'Usin' your brains now, Art. However, if the guy's workin' for the competition but Col thought he was a friend, when he got stabbed he would have told the guy to bring him back here despite our security rules.'

'Troons, then,' Tosh said, 'before he can tell his bosses about this place.'

'Ain't you rushin' things?' James suggested. 'You don't know this fella's guilty. Justice and truth. That's the Lord's way.'

Sailor looked at his brother. 'We're all down 'cos of Col. Maybe we should watch we don't act rash. But Tosh is surely right. We got to keep this man locked up real tight and send him to the Troons if he is a competition spy.'

'What if he's the law?' Chemist asked. He was feeling sick and low. He wanted the meeting to end so he could just get to sleep and forget the whole lousy world.

'He, the law!' James snorted, 'and I'm a white man.'

'Be safer to top the bastard, whatever,' Art suggested.

'Art, you bloody eejit,' Tosh growled. 'Oscar said that God, in creatin' man, greatly overestimated his ability. I look and I listen to you and I know Oscar was right.' She had read all Wilde's works and quoted them at the least excuse. She removed her beret, letting her shoulder-length red dreadlocks fall free. 'I'm goin' to check on brother Columbo,' she announced.

She was back in a minute. 'He's awake an' talkin'. He wants to see everyone right away. I'll stay with this fella. We don't want him doin a runner while we're all cuddlin' Col.'

The four men disappeared and Tosh, back on her window-sill, said nothing. She watched Goodman with cold eyes. He decided not to appeal to the colour of her skin since, if it was possible, she seemed even more hostile than the others.

In a while Sailor called them to Columbo's room. Tosh prodded Goodman close up to the bed. Columbo lifted his right arm and clenched his fist. Goodman, greatly relieved, responded with the black handshake. He knew he would be cleared as soon as Columbo could make himself understood. That did not take long. Sailor knelt beside the bed and Columbo whispered in his ear.

Later, back in the main room, the atmosphere was palpably more relaxed.

Sailor spoke. 'Mr Goodman? Alex Goodman?'

'Yes. Alex . . . call me Alex.'

'OK, Alex. We owe you an apology. But I hope you understand we got to be careful – all the time and with everybody.'

Goodman nodded violently. He understood.

'Columbo,' Sailor continued, 'tells me he would be dead or in the lock-up but for you. He says you done real good and he wants you to keep his share as well as yours. Tosh, would you count the money and give Art what he needs for the pay-offs, the cars from the Troons, the Babylon contact and Col's grass at The Tavern. What's left over all belongs to Mr Goodman here.'

Goodman was astounded. One minute he feared for his life. The next he was rich. He thanked them profusely and said he ought to be getting back to Sara's flat. He refused to accept Columbo's share.

Sailor raised his hand. 'Alex, boy, we love Columbo here, and when you risk your freedom to save him, you become like a brother, like one of us. But when we do a bust that gets police attention, we has a Family rule. Anyone involved chills out for a week, stays home, watches TV, whatever, but no partyin'. A week is maximum attention span for Emby's soldiers and even less for the Babylon, but until then, you and Art got to stay low. OK?'

Goodman guessed that this was an order more than a question. He nodded smiling.

'I understand, but can I call Sara?'

'Sure you can,' James laughed. 'Sara's part of The Family. She is like Col's little sister.' He was effusive, obviously a keen Sara supporter.

Goodman was given a room or rather a bunk the size of Carole's cooler. He left a message for Sara, who never answered her phone after midnight. He slept well and woke late in the morning as they all did.

Art left early to dispense the pay-off cash and Chemist, whom he dropped at St Thomas's special Aids clinic, would be away for a fortnight. After pay-off deductions, the haul came to £226,000 and a gold Rolex, which Emby had presumably accepted as a loan repayment. Columbo decided to gift the Rolex to James, who was forever glancing enviously at Columbo's own mega-gadget Seiko.

'Bruncho is up,' James announced to Goodman. The Rasta wore three clothes-pegs hanging from the dreadlocks, close to his right ear. At first Goodman desisted from querying the religious significance of the pegs but, since the atmosphere at 'bruncho' was considerably more relaxed than the previous night, he eventually popped the question.

'Ah,' said James, obviously pleased to be asked. 'I never have colds due to my moderate ganja intake, so I never carry a handkerchief.'

Goodman digested this and, when no more was forthcoming, asked if the pegs were part of the Rasta's ganja-smoking process.

'Gracious, no,' James chuckled. 'I have memory problems, maybe senile dementia, so I need to be remindin' myself of many things,

145

especially when I'm on cooler duty. I cannot tie big knots in my handkerchief so I have a peg hittin' my ear for every item to remember. On a bad day there may be eight or nine. This can be very confusin'.'

'Brother James,' Tosh, holding a plate of baked beans and spiced Trinidadian sausage, muttered to anybody listening, 'is usually confused. If he stopped tryin' to convert the rest of us he could spend time de-decodin' his own contrary impulses.'

'It is my duty to improve us all,' said the Rasta, wiping a Heinz bean from his goatee and looking happy.

'Oscar said' – Tosh liked to have the last word – 'that women who moralise are invariably plain. That's why I don't. Also that men who moralise are usually hypocrites.'

Before James could retaliate, Sailor, who had finished a heaped plate of curried goat, opened the briefcase and placed the thick wads of notes on the table.

'These,' he said to Goodman, 'are yours and they are well deserved. Columbo, our beloved brother, has told me all. I shake your hand.'

He did so. James stood and did likewise, most effusively. Tosh took off her dark glasses, raised one hand and wriggled her fingers at Goodman. She almost smiled. He saw that her eyes were as green as Ireland and her freckled skin wonderfully white except where a thin scar marred one cheek. She was, apart from Sophia Loren, the most beautiful woman he had ever seen. Her cleavage, magnificently visible between the lapels of her woollen dressing gown and, from Goodman's viewpoint, swaying gently just beyond the spiced sausages, was hypnotic.

'What will you do with the money, Mr Goodman?' Sailor asked.

'Please call me Alex.'

'Alex.'

'How should I address you?'

'Sailor.'

'James.'

Tosh said nothing.

'Call her Tosh,' James said. 'And ignore her moods.'

'Sara banks for me,' Goodman said simply. 'This money is the answer to all my problems.'

'You have problems?' Sailor prompted.

146

Goodman nodded but did not elaborate. Nobody pursued the topic.

'Would you like to work with us? While you keep your head down, maybe you can help us some? With Chemist away, Col knackered and Tosh about to bring us two more wrecks for coolin', we could do with manpower.'

'Person power,' said Tosh.

'Yeah,' said Sailor. 'We need persons.'

'I'd be happy.' Goodman meant it. These people were warm and genuine, like Sara. He needed to belong. 'And now I've the means to pay for my lodgings.'

Sailor shook his head. 'That's on the house, in return for your joinin' our work roster here and in the lab. You and I can have a talk later so you know the house rules. OK, man?'

Goodman spent the day with James caring for Columbo and with Tosh, who was preparing a cooler for another addict due in shortly for detoxification, a service for which addicts' parents paid The Family big sums in cash, but based on results as well as the assurance of total confidentiality.

'Och, you'd be surprised,' Tosh told Goodman, 'where they come from, the parents or guardians. Some are politicos and big business. Others are real nasties, Kray types. Sometimes you can see they are desperate 'cos they adore their junkie kid, but mostly they are terrified of exposure, like embarrassed to hell the press will tell the world and they'll be treated like lepers 'cos their kids are crack-heads.'

'Is there not a dichotomy?' Goodman ventured.

'You mean are The Family not a bunch of hypocrites makin' their money from dealin' with the one hand and nursin' turkeys with the other?'

'Well, if you put it that way . . .' Goodman found Tosh's flame-coloured hair and her directness rather intimidating.

She laughed but did not smile. 'There is a lot you may learn about us if you stay around and' – she paused – 'maybe we will learn about Mr Alex Goodman too?'

That evening Sailor drove Goodman to Woodberry Down. Car parking and approach techniques were discussed on the way.

'Security is the thing,' Sailor repeated. 'Art needs a heavy refresher course on the subject.'

'I understand,' Goodman said. 'I will not let you down but, as a white, won't I stick out like a sore thumb?'

'No way, boy. Woodberry is a mixed salad. You get them all here. Every country from the old Commonwealth spat out their dregs to the estate. Then you got to add every refugee from every revolution anywhere in the world. Afghanis, Viets and Kurds are big this year. Plus plenty of Paddies and Scots. So long as you don't raise no eyebrows by bein' different in a different sort of way, nobody's gonna look at you twice.'

Sailor pointed out the relevant estate block, Peak House, and the walkway approach. 'I'll leave you here. Knock the Morse letters for Art on the door. Like this.' He demonstrated. 'See you later.'

Art started by explaining to Goodman the workings of the laboratory and what could go wrong. From the flat's tape-darkened windows, through eye-slits, he ran through a list of various signs to note in order to detect unwelcome observers, whether police or other drug dealers. In case of a raid, he produced a sheet of paper with The Family's emergency phone numbers, that of their Korean tough-boy friends, the Troons, and the carefully planned escape route.

'Remember, the apparatus is very basic and should run itself, but watch the ventilation, the water system and the top-ups. The containers are all clearly marked. These are for Ecstasy. The proper name, in patois' – Art favoured Goodman with a flash of his perfect dentures – 'is methylenedioxymethylamphetamine, which must be a Welsh word. We call it MDMA. People will tell you it's harmless, OK? Don't you believe it. You can get kidney failure, heart failure and brain damage from MDMA tablets.'

They moved along a shelf of marked but empty plastic tubs and metal cans. 'These here are for amphetamine sulphates, our biggest line. Overdose and you die. Like all our competition, we add a few cheap flavours. In fact our finished product averages about eight per cent pure. The rest is made up of bulk-outs: caffeine, lactose, glucose, mannitol and paracetamol. Good for the client's health and our margins. Each gram of our finished powder retails on the street between £8 and £15. That'll last most punters about two weeks but your heavy user'll need maybe eight grams a day. So he'll have to bust a lot of banks to keep himself in dope.'

'Where did you become a scientist?' Goodman asked.

'Me a boffin! Take a jump, mate. I skipped school long before O-levels. To me "O" means opium, not physics. You don't need no knowledge for this lark. Chemist is The Family expert. I learnt a bit in Brixton – I was "on ice" there for two years. Most folk get moved on to other nicks but I stayed and I listened. I tell you, a lot of heavy-duty bad boys passed through while I was there. The boxes of cornflakes and thickos would sit around in one corner, but for any upwardly mobile lad, like me, Brixton is your Harvard and Yale. You can meet all the big names who you'd never get the time of day from outside, get their advice and their phone numbers. In fact, more business goes on inside than out and you get what you want through tippin' the screws. Drugs in, letters in and out.'

Goodman learnt that Art was always on the prowl for new lab premises. If, at any time, signs of a bust were suspected, The Family were instantly able to move lock, stock and barrel to another site because Art always maintained one ready for use. He simply broke into rundown squats, rarely checked by the council, especially amid the chaos resulting from the abolition of the Greater London Council, changed the locks and kept the keys.

Goodman liked Art. They spent quite some time together in the lab over the next few days. Art trained him in streetwise vocabulary and ended with an oral test. Goodman had learnt the alternative names of amphetamines. These included: A1, beans, bombido, bumblebees, cartwheels, chicken powder, co-pilots, crank, cross-roads, diet pills, eye-openers, footballs, French blues, greenies, hearts, lightning, line, macka, miniberries, roses, speed, splash, sulph, thrusters, toffee whizz, truck drivers, turnabouts, wake-amine and zoom.

'What's yellow submarines or bennies?' Art asked.

'Benzedrine.'

'When do the fuzz turn your drum over?'

'When they raid.'

'A stuffer wired to the moon with sputnik, temple balls and wacky baccy?'

'A vagina or anus drug smuggler high on opium mixed with Pakistani cannabis, street cannabis and cannabis resin.'

'Big John necked the embalming fluid and connected Cecil with pasta from the travel agent?'

149

'The undercover police swallowed the PCP and bought cocaine with coca paste from the street dealer.'

Art clapped his hands. 'Not bad, boy, for a novice. Even Tosh would give you the thumbs up.'

'She doesn't seem to like me,' Goodman said.

'Da, you want to pay no notice. Ol' Tosh has had a life that would have turned most folk crazy, but she don't mean no harm. Did Sailor tell you about her?'

Goodman shook his head.

'Well, seein' as how Sailor and Brother James have taken you in, there's no harm in my tellin' you. We love her and, make no mistake, she's mean as a bitch with puppies if somebody threatens The Family.'

Goodman then listened, incredulous, to Art's pocket history of The Family's only white member. Tosh was born in Belfast in 1953, to Protestant parents of Scottish stock. An only child, she grew up adoring her father and fearful of her iron-willed mother: he a powerful Freemason and Loyalist organiser, she a narrow-minded society climber and strict puritan. Until the age of sixteen Tosh was sexually checked after each and every date with a boyfriend. She longed to help her father with the cause, to gain his admiration through some heroic act for the Orange Order. But, as he gently but constantly reminded her, she was his only and much beloved daughter. She need only behave like her mother to be an asset to the cause. He would pat her hand and hurry off to another covert meeting which would doubtless set back the wicked Republicans in their latest evil plotting.

When Tosh was sixteen, Harold Wilson sent the British Army to take over security after the Royal Ulster Constabulary lost control of nationalist rioting and the loyalist backlash. She saw the British soldiers as hugely romantic and, not long afterwards, began a liaison with an infantry officer she met at a Protestant ball. Pregnant and unable to face the wrath of her mother or the shame of her father, she sought succour from the UVF.

The Ulster Volunteer Force, started in 1912 by Sir Edward Carson, her father's hero, had 1500 members and a number of closed activist cells that raised cash through racketeering and kudos through beating up Catholic civil rights people. Following her abortion, paid for by her UVF cell leader, she became an active

150

'soldier' collecting second-hand intelligence about the IRA by seducing both Army and Special Branch officers.

In 1972, in the aftermath of internment and Bloody Sunday, she was promoted to an armed UVF unit in the South Armagh IRA heartland, where she met and fell for an English corporal attached to 14 Intelligence Company. They helped one another's intelligence units a great deal until the corporal was killed by the Irish National Liberation Army and Tosh, beside herself with grief and hatred, began what she nowadays called her 'black time'. For four years she assassinated people at the behest of the bosses of the Ulster Freedom Fighters killer squads, to whom she had switched her allegiance. In 1976 she was moved, by way of recognition of her undoubted skills, to 'foreign' targets. These included enemies in the Republic, mainland Britain and the United States.

By the summer of 1978 Tosh was based in Dublin and living with two English contract killers, Rod Jenkinson and Dinko Maynard, who sometimes disappeared to fight communists in Angola as a change from the standard contract 'quick chop'. They taught her a few new ways of disposing of folk and, when relaxing, how best to 'improve sex and be happy'. This turned out to be a euphemism for smoking heroin – 'chasing the dragon' – and Tosh took to the practice with abandon.

Dublin in 1978 was fast becoming a favourite European drug-dealing centre among erstwhile bank robbers and jewel thieves who liked the idea of less risk and bigger profits. Two things happened to Tosh that summer. She learnt that her father had died, and an INLA killer arrived in Dublin with her name on his list. Dinko Maynard happened to be dozing in their flat when the assassin arrived. Maynard died and the INLA man was fatally wounded.

Jenkinson moved to London at once and took Tosh with him. A month later he disappeared to Africa and never came back. By then Tosh was a junk-head and, with nobody to keep her in dope, she began to sell her still-ravishing body on Finsbury Park's Wilberforce Road, the nearest hot spot to Jenkinson's pad.

Sailor, out searching the area for his very first lab site, spotted Tosh's red beacon hair and explosive silhouette and for the first time in his life he crawled the kerb. They had never looked back.

By the time Art joined The Family, early in 1984, Tosh was 'washed up' – she would never touch another drug, not even a cigarette, and the greatest kick she now gained in life, apart from Sailor, was the 'folding up' of wasted junkies. This required infinite skill, patience and psychology and Tosh, Art assured Goodman, was the best.

But Art's potted biography of Tosh was, as Goodman would later learn, a highly sanitised version. His first work beside her, with Carole and two other sad specimens in the coolers of the Peckham Home, revealed a sensitive and gentle woman. Tosh had spent years as Dr Jekyll. Goodman was seeing only her better side.

She told Goodman of past visitors to her coolers dying of poisoning after eating Phalloides and Virosa fungi, raw and immature, mistaking them for the hallucinogenic Liberty Cap or Semilanceata variety. She had dealt with the victims of virtually every drug on the market and sometimes with mothers wondering if they should have young babies 'put away' because they'd been born 'all wrong'.

'This,' Tosh explained, 'usually means the mum took massive doses of phenobarbitone in pregnancy and the poor wee nipper has a horribly cleft palate and weird distortions of the face and hands. Even alcohol, if taken heavily when pregnant, can cause hideous damage in the baby, giving it a flat Eskimo face, no lips, nostrils with no nose, hearing-holes with no ears and for good measure, generous splatters of purple birthmarks.'

'Why do you take them on, Tosh?' At first Goodman had felt like calling her 'ma'am', for she overawed him and mere 'Tosh' seemed wrong.

'It's just so great when you finally drive the divils out and you get to see the real person that's left. Also there are, for sure, some laughs from time to time. Last month there was a lass who'd heard I could cure anythin'. She was afeared of doctors thinkin' she was crazy and so she came to me. Or rather I went to her for she was clearly no druggie. I read up my medical books after I'd seen her and cured her in ten minutes! She had a pica!'

'Pica?' Goodman was lost.

'Tá. Yes,' said Tosh. She had retained the incongruous habit of lapsing into the odd word of Irish ever since, as a teenager, she had noticed how much it annoyed her parents and Protestant peers. Tosh had always loved to buck the system and the habit had stuck. She pointed at the fridge. 'That's pagophagia – addiction to ice, or sometimes soil, and sufferers keep eatin' great quantities. Pregnant women can be susceptible. They crave for ice. My patient was losin' money havin' to buy successive sets of new dentures as she cracked them up chewin' ice cubes.'

'How did you cure her?'

'No problem. The medical dictionary always gives the answer once you have diagnosed the illness and there was nothin' ambiguous about an ice-eatin' addict. I prescribed pills for iron deficiency and the ice cravin' disappeared within four days . . . If only the Good Lord made them all that easy.'

Sailor received reports that Alexo, as they had all begun to call Goodman, was good news. Ten days after Columbo was stabbed, the tough young Trinidadian was sitting up in his bed and Dr Khimji had pronounced him clear of any ongoing problems. Chemist was back in business and Sailor's Finsbury Park spies reported that the Emby furore had died down. The loan shark was back to his routine regime and his soldiers were no longer on the prowl for anyone resembling Columbo, Goodman, or Art. Sailor told Goodman he should feel free to return to Sara and get on with his life.

'Art will drive you back with the money. Give Sara love from The Family. Tell her not to be a stranger. Long time no see. And, listen Alexo, we like you, boy. You're welcome here at the Home. Any time.'

Goodman felt great. He had been happier than at any time he could remember. For days he had been turning over a possibility. Now the time seemed right. Sailor could always say no.

'Sailor. Two days ago you said The Family would always help me if I met trouble . . .'

Sailor nodded. 'What I say, I mean.'

'Well, I am in trouble. I asked Sara to tell nobody and I would ask you the same.'

'My ears await. My lips are sealed with superglue.'

Goodman told Sailor everything. Even those things from his youth and childhood which had returned to his memory. When he was done, Sailor took his hand.

'Man, you have had a raw, raw deal. I have heard some stories but yours breaks the cane . . . This Tricks guy, he seems like the only answer. You got to find him.'

153

'That's it,' Goodman said, 'and I feel inside me that I must hurry. What if I have a wife or fiancée somewhere. She may give up and marry someone else. Maybe I own a house and land which lawyers might pass to some relative – if I have any. I had intended to raise enough cash and get an agency to search North London for Tricks. But then, when I met you and got to know The Family, it struck me, that, maybe . . .'

Sailor stood up, his left hand in the air.

'Alexo, I am pleased, very pleased, that you honour us with this. You should have no worry now. I will tell nobody more than they need know to find your man. But it will be difficult. Very, very difficult. North London is a big place and there are many, many big black men dealing drugs.' His laughter rumbled. 'Of course not many will be called Tricks but all of them will have a street-name, some of them four or five street-names.'

'This one,' Goodman reminded Sailor, 'associates with Americans and with badger diggers in the Midlands.'

'Yeah, yeah. That could help . . . Listen, I will take this on. You saved our brother Columbo. This is the least we can do. There will be costs, of course. The Family has better contacts for this search than any detective agency in London but for such information we will need to pay a good many ears in many areas.'

'Do I have enough?'

Sailor laughed again. 'I reckon you do if you have no other commitments.'

'Only Sara's rent.'

'OK. I will start enquiries right away. Don't expect no miracles but rest certain I will leave no stone unturned.' Sailor thrust his fist at Goodman, who returned the black handshake and no longer felt alone in the search for his past.

At St Anne's Police Station, off Seven Sisters Road, DC Taff Jones collected his mail and studied two photographs received from Scotland Yard's photographic branch. He called Clive and Barry Walker, the other members of his Crime Squad, and they discussed the photos. Two days later, using the vehicle's registration number and by searching through the local Collator's Indexes, they came up with the goods.

The driver of the mini-van at 7 Alfoxton Avenue, the suspected

ALF drugs base, proved by comparison of photographs to be a Jamaican, street-name Chemist, who had been charged following a lab raid by the Holloway CID in November 1983.

Taff looked happy. 'So, our lad Chemist is into labs. Hence his name. Looks like the white woman with the black beret may be dealing direct from a lab. Next time we get a sighting of either of them, or the mini, we get a surveillance team a.s.a.p. OK?'

Taff returned to his Wood Green home. His wife, Maria, was worried they were at risk there. Too many nasties, arrested by Taff and then released, lived in the district. And the atmosphere on some of the nearby estates was reaching boiling point. Beat police were being kicked and stabbed.

Taff shrugged off the bad thoughts. At least he had a good new lead.

12

August 1985

Los Angeles, only a few decades ago a paradise of verdant park and sandy beach, is now a concrete hell locked into a spiral of crime and armed response. Media accounts of killer youth gangs maddened by crack, and senseless car-borne shootings, have led to a fortress mentality.

The authorities try to contain the lawless to certain zones like Skid Row, east of Broadway. The weak and the helpless poor are forced jowl to jowl with the evil in such places. Skid Row now contains arguably the most lethal ten square blocks on earth, ruled by gang warlords, slashers and night stalkers.

Beyond this heart of darkness, whole suburbs are cordoned off, with thoroughfare forbidden to all but residents and their invited visitors. Private lawns show signs announcing 'Armed Response', the rich hide behind electronic surveillance and armed guards. Shopping malls bristle with cameras and razor wire.

John Ridgway and his family lived in one such fortress city, the 'gated community' of the Bradbury district. JR's wife argued that he had made many enemies through his job and the children might be at risk from 'God knows who'. Whenever he read about dreadful attacks on simple citizens in lawless LA, JR was glad of the security. Forty minutes' drive from home, he parked in a reserved underground space and, without leaving the building, walked up to the Operation Caesar room, where Jed Mason was already at work amid tapes and video gear. JR lit up his first Camel of the day, ignoring Jed's habitual grimace.

Jed switched on the projector and both men sat back to watch his surveillance material from Washington.

'Our target, this guy' – Jed pointed at the screen – 'has just been drinking with a Secret Service contact in the Fraternal Order of Police private club. The FOP includes individuals from all branches of Washington law enforcement. They get cheap booze and nobody minds them socialising fully armed like so many cowpokes in a saloon bar.'

The smartly dressed man of about forty who had issued from the club now hailed a yellow cab. His hair was close cut and his bearing resolute.

'Military?' JR asked.

'Yep. A US Marines officer and he's *en route* to see CIA Director William Casey at the Washington residence of our pal Redden. A meeting intended to be as private as was Casey's Pakistan visit last year when poor Javed disappeared.'

The undetected surveillance of a single taxi in heavy Washington traffic, JR knew, could easily involve four, even five, coordinated shadow units using cars, vans, motorcycles, and numerous pedestrians in various guises. Jed's film was ample proof that the FBI was still right behind Operation Caesar despite their continuing failure, after three years, to indict Albert Redden and Korbi Richter.

JR was well aware of their increased clout with both the FBI and the DEA once Javed had provided evidence that Redden was involved with the CIA's Director. The Bureau hounds were keen to catch any sniff of wrongdoing in high quarters and Jed had been quick to take budgetary advantage while the Casey connection continued.

Jed had attached Pen Registers to various Redden telephones. Although these could not eavesdrop – and therefore did not require a court order for installation permission – they did reveal which phone numbers were contacted by the user. Jed was then able to check out these third-party identities and in turn put Pen Registers on their lines.

'Title III' wire-taps, which do require constantly updated Justice Department permits, were in place on those of Redden's lines which were not already being recorded by the line owners, Bell Telephones.

The DEA central NADDIS computer, incorporating the old

CENTAC Pathfinder data bank, was able to match many of the numbers revealed by the Pen Registers (and checked against the DEA's EPIC computers), with subscribers' names and addresses. In consequence, Caesar's store of information on Redden's contacts, including a number of known criminals, was now impressive. But to obtain an indictment against a man with such high-flying connections, they still had a long way to go.

'OK,' Jed explained as the video switched from the US Marines officer in his taxi to a well-furnished drawing room. 'This is Redden's Washington city pad. I only had the place wired six months back but it's paid off, as . . .'

'How come,' JR interrupted, 'nobody's used our information to attack Casey? The Javed tapes were dynamite about him and the BCCI bank. Casey's got plenty of enemies. But none of our stuff seems to have caused any stir even though you passed it to the Justice Department, the DEA and the Bureau.'

Jed grunted. 'Passing our info upwards is all we're expected to do. What goes with Casey is not meant to concern us. The trouble is that Redden seems to enjoy protection based on his very closeness to Casey and that we have got to break through.'

'He looks ill.' JR meant Casey.

'What do you expect? The guy's in his seventies and his job's not the easiest. He has high blood pressure, lives on bottles of pills and rarely sleeps.'

Thick spectacles clouded the CIA man's grey eyes. Stooping and all but bald, he resembled a wizened and ancient chimp well past his prime but still capable of creating mayhem. He sat, as though hard of hearing, with one ear poked sideways at his long-time friend and OSS comrade John Shaheen, a small, sallow man with the appearance of a shady Arab merchant.

Redden, at sixty-two looking no older than a fit, tanned fifty-five, sat relaxed with a long drink, listening carefully to Casey and Shaheen. Since Casey's enunciation was poor at the best of times, close concentration on his lips was imperative. Casey's boss Ronald Reagan, according to Shaheen, was too polite to constantly ask Casey to repeat himself. He would simply nod in agreement. This made it easy for Casey to say: 'I have the President's agreement.'

Two other men, both in their sixties, were in attendance. Jed had not been able to identify either but thought they were, like Redden and Shaheen, members of Casey's Friends.

Jed Mason froze the video. 'What do you know of Casey?'

'Not much. Just the standard stuff in the press. I reckon he's done a good job after Carter cut the CIA down to a group of spastics. He's restored their morale and their capability.'

Jed nodded. 'Fair enough, but you need to look back a bit to understand his principles – or lack of them, some would say. He was brought up with the moral prejudices of an Irish Catholic with a strict Jesuit education. The priests made him logical, concise, a hater of dithering.'

'Sounds like you,' JR said.

'Thanks! Well, when Casey joined the fledgling OSS, or "Oh So Secret", as the Washington wits joked, the organisation was full of ex-polo players, high-society wasters and White Russians; well-heeled romantics wanting to play at spies. Casey was very different. He became one of their ablest wartime planners and leaders, able to inspire and mobilise even the weakest material. His watchword was efficiency and he brooked no bureaucratic delay, no red tape. In the 1950s he supported Senator Joe McCarthy's witch-hunts for communists, explaining: "Don't you understand. The Nazis are finished but the communists are still unbeaten." To him anti-communism was almost a second religion.'

'Did he stick at intelligence work after the war?'

'No way. He reached the top of half a dozen other professions. Law, business, book writing. Amazing guy. One of his books was on how to avoid tax: he originated the idea of the tax shelter. He only re-entered the world of spooks in 1976 after a thirty-one-year absence and took over the CIA four years ago in '81.'

'Surely these covert meetings don't say much for his judgement. He's got the whole of the official CIA at his command and yet he fools with sons of bitches like Redden.'

'To him these fellas are the salt of the earth. He's known and trusted them since the best days of his life, the OSS war in Europe, and he knows they'll keep a secret. When he wants something done that Congress won't approve, he keeps clear of his official CIA staff at Langley because he knows they can't keep their mouths shut. State secrets nowadays have to be revealed to the members of half a dozen committees and their staffs. What Casey has to include in his briefings to Congress is often leaked to the press in a corrupted fashion, so as to damage Reagan, Casey's hero. Casey, therefore, when he wants to forge ahead with a plan that must be kept close to his chest, naturally gets his private army to fix it – people like Redden.'

The video moved on. The US Marines officer arrived at the Casey meeting.

'Listen.' Jed struck the table between them. 'Casey has two pet loves and he can give neither the support he thinks they need because of Congress interference. Number one, the Contras. Number two, the Afghan mujahidin. If Congress was to lay its hands on this video, Casey would be in trouble, and so would Reagan, who does what Casey suggests. There is now an office *in the White House* from where this US Marines officer handles crooked arms dealers, the likes of Adnan Khashoggi, in order to follow up Casey's foreign policy, already banned by Congress.'

'Should we not disapprove?' JR looked across at Jed in the dark.

'You can do! I'm a Casey supporter except when he smiles at Redden.'

'Do you think he knows the half of what Redden's up to? The drugs, the cruelty . . . ?'

'Possibly. But why should he worry himself? He believes Redden to be an important weapon against this country's enemy, communism. If Redden's got a few warts, so what? That's his business. Take the HTA experiments on other people's property. The FBI would put Redden away for years for involvement in arson and the death of fire-fighters. But from Casey's point of view Redden is merely underwriting research into a weapon which is wanted by an important ally, Zia of Pakistan, and part subsidised by the BCCI bank, itself an institution uniquely able to help the CIA worldwide. Understandable double standards, you could call it.'

Jed restarted the video and increased the volume. Redden could be seen handing Casey a thin file and, at the nod of the CIA Director, he passed copies of the contents to the others. For twenty minutes the conversation could only be described as obtuse, if not unintelligible, to anyone not in possession of the subject material. 'Managua' and 'Moynihan' were mentioned. 'Olin', the name of a chemical corporation, the 'Seattle Fire Department' and two chemicals, both thermite compositions, 'Cadweld' and 'Thermoweld', were all discussed. Jed and JR played back parts of the conversation several times but reached no conclusion except that the matter under discussion was probably the use of HTA arson materials against the Soviets in Afghanistan.

'So what's new?' JR asked, looking disappointed.

Jed played the video to the point where everybody rose and Redden saw them out of the room. Shaheen, the last to leave, asked Redden: 'With these continued delays, how much longer can you keep Abedi underwriting the R & D costs?'

'No problem, John. In a month or two we will be ready to test a new mini-pack version. BCCI will be impressed by the results and Abedi will continue to pay until we have a monopoly on the deadliest saboteur's tool in existence.'

The video screen went blank and numbers flickered across it. Redden's face then reappeared.

'Same room but several days later,' Jed advised.

This time Redden's lone visitor was his partner Richter and the conversation covered a number of topics. Richter reported that drug baron Pablo Escobar's envoy, Victor Guzman, had decided to set up shop in Paris, not London.

Richter's information came from a contact within the Service de Documentation Extérieur et du Contre-Espionage (SDECE), the French CIA, whom he trusted. Guzman had met, in Tijuana, an influential heroin dealer named René Santamaria, born in Marseilles and a member of the infamous Ricord group, which had offered to help Escobar's ambitions to expand into Europe. Guzman had heard of the Ricord mob and had shown cautious interest.

During the Second World War the Gestapo used Corsican criminals to murder communists in Marseilles and Gaullists later hunted these 'collaborators', who fled to South America. Auguste Ricord was one of them. Based in Buenos Aires, he had founded a Corsican crime syndicate with an international network which, in 1965, organised an attempt to kill President de Gaulle in liaison with elements of SDECE. Over the next twenty years an unholy alliance in the drugs trade was cemented between these same intelligence officers and the Ricord group. It was a mutually beneficial arrangement which, Guzman could see, would give Escobar a far better launching pad into Europe than via Yardies in

London or via Madrid, the European city most favoured by Escobar's partners, the Ochoa family.

Guzman and his maestro accountant, Rubi, Richter told Redden, were currently setting up meetings between Escobar and Ricord representatives, with Rubi as the key mediator moving nimbly through a minefield of suspicious, volatile gangsters.

Redden and Richter discussed a number of courses of action which might set back this Colombian–French cocaine alliance and, at length, agreed to concentrate on the major meeting, engineered by Rubi, to be held between the two groups in Miami that autumn.

'Get Tricks over for your October visit to Mexico,' Redden told Richter. 'I want him to meet all our key players and I have a feeling Mexico is developing well as our main alternate to Miami.'

The meeting broke up and the video ended.

'Do you intend getting in on this Miami meet between the guy Rubi and the French mob?' JR asked.

'Maybe. I am taking the risk of not passing this tape to CENTAC HQ or DEA. Too great a chance of leakage. Miami may be our best chance yet to nail Redden doing evil things to Rubi's mob.'

'What exactly?'

'I don't think he's decided yet. When he does, we will hopefully get to hear about it in time for us to "be there" if only in the electronic mode.'

'What about Tricks when he comes to Mexico?'

'Sure. That's a must. I can see what Redden's up to long-term. With one hand he hopes to delay the big Colombians, Escobar and his pals the Ochoas, from expanding into Europe via England or France. With the other, he prepares a belt-and-suspenders set-up in case Colombian vengeance disrupts his existing and known cocaine route to all his US retailers from Florida. He'll be setting up some system of routing his Colombian powder over the Mexican border as a separate entity to his Miami distribution network. By following Tricks we may learn exactly what Redden has in mind.'

'With all this evidence, when do we pounce?'

'You getting impatient, JR?'

'Of course.'

'Well, my advice is: don't. This thing has got to be tight as a colt's ass. Redden has more influence in Washington than we can bust with a few tapes, videos and Pen Register-traced calls to mobsters. We have got to get his laundered accounts.'

'How's your guy in BCCI doing on that?'

'We spoke last month,' Jed grimaced. 'He's found nothing on Redden at BCCI Luxemburg, where he's been able to check the system thoroughly.'

'And the Caymans?'

'His BCCI Caymans friends are not in key positions, so they have had to take things slowly to avoid raising suspicion. Redden's secret accounts are obviously known only to a handful of BCCI staff. They are almost certainly not run from the Caymans but from the Leadenhall Street BCCI headquarters in London. This being so, we will need to place our own long-term mole *in situ* there as the place is a labyrinthine maze of cross-accounting and strict secrecy, riven by sectarian jealousies. The ideal man to insert, my guy suggests, would be a Caucasian accountant, since they have recently been recruiting non-Asian, preferably ex-Price Waterhouse accountants, who are willing not to be too fussy or alert. The bank uses these guys, who they entertain lavishly in all sorts of ways, to interface between their internal auditors and the official mob, who are, of course, Price Waterhouse. Know anybody suitable, JR?'

'Is that an order, boss?' JR smiled. Jed rarely gave instructions except as gentle suggestions. So gentle they were sometimes missed altogether.

'Can you think of someone? To be honest I am up to my neck at present. Never mind the mob and Redden, we've got ongoing investigations with the Yakuza, the Shower Posse Yardies, the Chechen and Armenian gangs, Hell's Angel Chapters, the Sicilian Mafia, black, Korean and Puerto Rican turf warfare, plus Triad and Tong killers all hard at it. So, yeah, it would be great if you could spend time thinking of a nice white accountant to plant among the London Pakis.'

Back home in 'Fortress Bradbury', JR unlaced his deck shoes and settled his Cuba Libre and his Camels beside his rocking chair. His wife and daughters were playing tennis with a neighbour, the mimosa smelled good around the porch, and he cast his mind about for a BCCI mole. A Brit, he decided, would be the least conspicuous choice, although his roll-call from the old country was minimal. He could check the Bureau's London files, but so much better to deal with a known quantity.

He had worked in the UK twice, and once, investigating a suspicious oil-tanker explosion in 1977, in Ireland. Most of his British contacts were professional insurance assessors and security officers, none of whom would be in a position to take a sabbatical working at BCCI. His last visit, concerned with Redden's intended heist of the cargo of the *Robert Gordon*, had been brief, involving few contacts other than Jason and a couple of other MI5 agents. Then he remembered the owl-eyed Goodman he had met in the bushes of North Fambridge. A well-educated man with a sense of humour and somehow – JR rarely made snap character assessments – a thoroughly honest sort of fella.

A great believer in happenstance, JR tried to list the qualifications of the quiet Welshman for the BCCI role. Goodman had seemed to him to be a genuine case of an innocent 'good citizen' being in the wrong place at the wrong time and running into trouble. He had inadvertently fallen foul of Redden's mob, who had, in passing as it were, stolen his identity in the form of his memory and, more practically, his wallet. He was now a lost soul searching endlessly, to mix metaphors, for a needle in the woodpile of North London.

He, JR, could have helped Goodman on his way by telling him Redden's LA address. But to have done so would have signed Goodman's death warrant. He was glad he had kept quiet.

Goodman had been in poor financial shape then and perhaps he still was. He might respond to an offer if the pay was tempting. I could even suggest helping him search for Redden, for his identity, JR mused. If he agrees, it should not take too long to train him in the basics of accountancy: maybe two or three months. Better to find the right man and teach him the skills rather than try to insert the wrong character, however clever a mathematician.

The more he thought about it, the more he liked the idea. He telephoned Jason at MI5, gave him the best description he could of Goodman and, when the response was less than hopeful, he said, 'Come on, Jason, my friend, you wouldn't want to let down the great sleuthing reputation of the British bloodhound. Of course you can trace the guy. There's only sixty million folk in your little ol' island. We've got four times that over here. C'mon, you can do it. Put your deerstalker on, pal.'

Jason promised he would try. JR relaxed and poured himself another drink. What the hell, he thought, the whole effort's only pissing in the wind. Only the previous day he had heard Reagan announce: 'We are winning the war on drugs.' A fine example of PPB – prime presidential bullshit.

Lying back, he began to think of all the golf courses he had ever walked. He wondered if Goodman played the game.

13

September 1985

Sara made the tea stronger than usual. Her friend Basu from Tottenham had cried her eyes out for half an hour and now she was quiet. She looked pallid, like a sheep awaiting death; quite a different person from the jolly, slightly podgy schoolgirl Sara remembered from six years back, when Basu's family had first moved to Tottenham from Handsworth in Birmingham.

Two days earlier, on Monday, 9 September, Basu's cousins, two brothers who ran the post office in Handsworth's Lozells Road, had been burnt to death in violent riots following the local festival. The brothers had long protested to the local police about the activities of West Indian drug dealers at the nearby Villa Cross pub, and during the riot the dealers had paid them back. The police, heavily outnumbered by rioters, were unable to rescue the brothers despite telephone calls begging for help as they were 'about to be killed'. Property worth £42 million was destroyed in Handsworth, most of it owned by small Asian family businesses.

For Basu the murder of her cousins was no isolated trouble. Since moving to the Broadwater Farm Estate, her parents had suffered constant threats from bad elements, black and white, who hated the Asians.

'It's hell on our estate,' Basu told Sara. 'The black drug dealers rule us and the police daren't touch them. Most of the time there are only four police on the entire estate and they're as frightened as us.'

'You're unlucky,' Sara said, choosing to forget her own recent rape attack. 'We've got plenty of black neighbours here too, but the crime's not all that bad and the police stamp on any gangs that get too big.'

Basu sighed and wiped her eyes. 'Your tea is good, Sara. I feel much better because you listen with sympathy in your heart. I am alone now with my mother and her mind is not as it was. I keep her in the flat all the time, like a dog who might otherwise be run over. It's no life for her and there are so many other terrified old people waiting hour on hour for the next hammering on their door . . . dog mess or flaming newspapers through their letter-box . . . hate messages. And now the murder of my cousins. I have not told my mother as the shock might kill her.'

The Broadwater Farm Estate had witnessed see-saw troubles for five years between blacks and police. This was partly due to a small knot of criminals whose activities led to firm reactions from the police which were labelled as racist aggression. The police then increased their patrols and arrests of any young blacks, which in turn irritated many innocent members of the black community. Individual beat bobbies in Tottenham were over the years attacked and stabbed and the whole estate achieved a notoriety which tended to make police response to cries for help from estate inmates like Basu both slow and inadequate.

A black social worker, Dolly Kiffin, had gradually built up a social centre and Youth Association in the estate block called Tangmere – the drab, concrete warren where Basu lived. This, by 1985, boasted a number of facilities, shops, cooperative businesses and a central venue for Tangmere's youth to come together. Throughout a damp and dismal summer tensions had run high in the block, but Dolly Kiffin's influence was such that the worst elements were kept in check. Unfortunately, that July she and other youth leaders had gone on an official visit to Jamaica and drug dealers from surrounding areas had moved into the estate, which, in Basu's words, quickly became an open-air drugs market. Roving gangs terrorised the estate throughout the summer attacking postmen, firemen and even refuse collectors. Life for the old, the weak and the infirm was especially hellish.

Basu looked increasingly disturbed, as the afternoon wore on, at the thought of returning to Tangmere. The previous evening she and her mother, hands to their mouths, had watched television coverage of the Home Secretary, Douglas Hurd, being showered with bottles and bricks by angry blacks in Handsworth. But for the quick action of a police van driver, the minister might well have been killed, such was the fury of the mob. As they watched the anarchy played out on the screen, Basu had heard the baying of a crowd in the concrete walkways outside the flat. Gingerly she had slipped the chains and watched from the balcony as two policemen were cornered by a mob on the deck below. She heard a raucous shout: 'Touch your radio, pig, and you're bacon!' Terrified, she watched as the police broke free and a hunt began along the corridors and down the maze of walkways. Both officers were seriously injured.

'I must go now,' said Basu, picking up her black scarf. 'I wear this to look as unattractive as possible. Gang rape is common on the estate. I carry no handbag and only minimal cash in my shoe to cover the shopping. I sometimes wonder if honest folk in the assassin districts of Bangladesh live in such a state of fear as we do in London.'

The two friends hugged each other and Sara sent a silent prayer to the goddess Laxmi, with thanks for directing her to settle on Woodberry Down and not Tangmere. As she prepared the bedroom for the busy evening period – Essex regulars on their 'way home' from the City – she found herself worrying about her lodger. While she was delighted that The Family had opened their arms to him, she sometimes feared for his well-being at the lab, where he now spent most of his time. Columbo, Art and the others could well look after themselves when things went wrong but Goodman – she liked to call him that – was such a gentle soul she wished he could find some solid, risk-free job. She had grown accustomed to his presence in the flat, the cups of tea he often brought her and above all the respect with which he treated her, despite her profession. When he had given her the cash proceeds of the Emby job to bank for him, she had flushed with pleasure at the confidence he was placing in her. She decided to wean him away from the lab.

Taff Jones and Barry Walker sat in the Seven Sisters Café, legs splayed and mugs of tea steaming. Both appeared to be engrossed in their tabloids but their lips were moving in what they called dumb-speak. They had become adept at conversing in a way unintelligible even to their closest neighbour. In the street they watched black dealers mouth-kiss white prostitute punters, passing over foil-wrapped 'rocks' of crack. The man they were hoping to tail was Chemist, last seen at the Alfoxton Avenue address and hopefully a likely lead to his lab. He had twice been spotted dealing at the local William Hill betting shop, easily visible from the café.

The street was strangely deserted by many of the local Yardie 'faces' who, Taff knew, frequented the locale. A police van cruised by, virtually ignored by the dealers. Eight frustrated Special Patrol Group officers stared out of the wire-reinforced windows. They were on a 'high-profile' patrol but they were well aware, as were the local cocaine dealers, that current police policy and prevailing inner-city tensions made it highly unlikely that they would leave the van for anything short of a murder perpetrated right under their noses.

For Taff and the seven other plain-clothes constables in his group, from the St Anne's station, life was especially hazardous at such volatile times. Many local criminals knew them by sight. They could easily be cornered by a ruse, by a false phone call. One of their covert surveillance points was an empty flat on the fifth deck of Tangmere. Barry had been there three weeks earlier, observing a suspected amphetamine laboratory, when two uniformed bobbies had been brutally stabbed and beaten senseless following a bogus rape call from the fourth deck. He had been powerless to intervene. He still boiled internally at the memory.

The previous day an armed officer had shot a black Brixton resident, Cherry Groce, in bed while searching the house for her son, thought to be armed and likely to shoot the police on sight. This tragic error sparked off a full-scale riot in Brixton, featuring cutlasses, sledgehammers and petrol bombs.

'They smashed a local photographer's skull open last night,' Taff murmured.

'Yeah,' Barry replied, 'and gang-banged the daughter of an MP after beating up her boyfriend. Reduced her to a mental cabbage by all accounts; near enough split her open, according to Capital Radio.'

'The latest strategy from the Yard,' Taff said, 'and I got this hot from Clive, is to seal off the big estates and keep out till they cool off.'

'So what happens if some poor bugger inside a sealed-off estate calls up to say they're being burgled or worse? Do our boys ignore them?'

'Seems like it, yeah. Tough titty.'

'Does the seal-up rule apply on our ground?' Barry asked.

'Mostly.'

'Woodberry Down?'

'Nope.'

'Tangmere?'

Taff shook his head.

Barry's eyebrows shot up. 'But that's one big death-trap. Everybody knows it. If anywhere needs a no-go seal-off response, that's it.'

Taff nodded. 'I agree but who are we to question Newman and his think-tanks? Most of their strategy boyos have never been at the sharp end. They tell us to appease when we need to show a firm hand and they advise "aggressive response" when we should be displaying tact.'

'Do you think all the riots are linked? Planned?'

Taff shrugged. 'Could be, but I doubt it. Some of your basic cause is general frustration. Standard have-nots keen to knock the system 'cos others are better off than them. What's called inequality-driven frustrations back on the Hendon psychology course. But mostly it's the big drug dealers orchestrating the troubles on their patches. The best way to keep us off their territory is to make the top brass scared of provoking riots. So, yeah, I'd say a good deal is organised by the dealers and, round here, their prime new patch is Tangmere.'

'You think that's due for big troubles?'

'I'm sure of it. Tinder-dry. Just waiting for a trigger event. '

Dave 'Ears' Norton specialised in fading into the furniture. On Thursday, 3 October he was alerted by pager to call at the Yard. He was delighted at any excuse to escape the boredom of his current job, watching the Ministry of Defence main building in Whitehall or, to be more precise, observing the habits of certain car and van drivers outside that great concrete monolith. This was not as difficult as it seemed since all parking around MoD property was rigorously controlled and unusual visitors who parked and 'sat' in their vehicles could be spotted with ease. Norton had an excellent standing arrangement with the headquarters of the traffic wardens responsible for Horseguards Avenue and Whitehall Place. A dedicated mobile channel allowed wardens to alert him of suspects and he could warn them to stay clear of certain vehicles.

An IRA grass, Norton's sergeant informed him when he got back to the office, had warned the department of an imminent attempt in Sloane Square 'on a senior Army personality'. Computer checks on likely targets spewed out 'NIL' but a telephone call to Chelsea Barracks put Norton on to the Duke of York's Barracks next to Sloane Square, which, at that time, housed the headquarters of Britain's Special Forces. He was informed, in the strictest confidence, that the Director of the Special Air Service Regiments was wont to walk between the barracks and Sloane Square tube station twice daily, usually wearing a scruffy white mac.

Norton assured his informant that he would tell nobody but that the IRA already appeared aware of the SAS brigadier's Sloane Square movements and he would be pleased if such perambulations ceased forthwith for the VIP's own safety. Norton's department had arranged for a look-alike in a dirty Gannex mac to keep to the brigadier's usual schedule so that Norton and his colleagues could locate any Irish gentleman who showed untoward interest in the Gannex as it traversed the busy square.

Norton had been assured that the SAS man (and therefore the look-alike) should normally be expected to remain inside the barracks through standard working hours. He therefore took the opportunity of turning a quick buck while loitering away the day in King's Road close to the barracks. He used his mobile to call Sailor and they arranged a midday meeting in the window seat of a cheap restaurant opposite the gates of the barracks.

Norton's path to Sailor and the excellent two-way relationship they had enjoyed over the past year, was long and devious. Orphaned early in Glasgow and shipped in the early 1960s to foster parents in Sydney, Norton developed an early entrepreneurial flare which had brought him brief fame on the circuit of Australia's roughest nightspots, as the seventeen-year-old promoter of a novel gambler's sport which he called dwarf-throwing. But already, at that tender age, he had begun to specialise in falling foul of the law and/or vested interests; nor did he restrict himself to one continent. After a series of mishaps in Cairo, he escaped with his life to England.

Norton's luck held out, for in Cairo he had supported an Oxfam worker helping the homeless. The lady in question gave him free lodgings in Oxford and a bed, her bed, while he sought employment and British citizenship, a long drawn-out process because he had long since lost touch with his foster home and his birth certificate. Love and passion bloomed with the Oxfam lady throughout the late seventies, during which period Norton cleaned Oxford streets, rented out bicycles and river punts and then did well as a security guard. In 1981 Oxfam posted his loving landlady to India and Norton joined the Metropolitan Police Force at the advanced age of twenty-two.

His promotion from a local Beat Crimes Desk was rapid and in early 1984 the CID posted him to the Metropolitan Police's Diplomatic Protection Squad, on special liaison duties with MI5. A previous job with the Flying Squad, under an officer named Griffiths, had involved undercover work with a Turkish Cypriot, police code-name Keith. A long-time information gatherer for Sailor, Keith had earlier that year helped identify the head of a protection racket trying to pressurise The Family's Seven Sisters network. Sailor, without giving too much away, had put Keith on to Goodman's search for Tricks. In turn, Keith had subcontracted the task to various friends, including Norton, who had access to police computers. When the latter claimed he had struck gold, Keith collected a modest payment from Sailor and introduced the two men to each other.

Sailor arrived by taxi at the Peter Jones department store in Sloane Square and, punctual to the minute, sat down beside Norton, who was studying the shiny plastic menu. They shook hands.

'I understand from Keith that maybe you have found the fella,' said Sailor.

'That's right. He fits your description to the inch. Keith tells me your offer is £30,000 if I've hit the jackpot and £10,000 for a likely cert.'

Sailor nodded. 'And you have reason to believe this guy's a dead ringer?'

'Hundred per cent. Listen. I've had all the Regional Squads' West Indian files checked, not just the northern sectors. About five big reputed Jamaican dealers called "Sticks" showed up. There are none called Tricks and there never have been. Three of the "Sticks" are too old and one was on ice at the time of "the incident in Birmingham". But the fifth fits your description perfectly, is known to be into reggae gigs, visits Birmingham fairly frequently, and dresses in snappy designer clothes. Like I say, a dead ringer.'

'But,' Sailor complained, 'your guy is called Sticks not Tricks. Just about every tall fella from JA is called Sticks. If I was hunting a John and you came up with a Don, what good is that?'

'Who's your client?' Norton asked.

'Who's sayin' I have a client?' Sailor countered.

'Let's say that you do, for the sake of argument.' Norton had an infectious smile. 'Would he or she, your client, recognise this Tricks they're trying to locate?'

'Why?'

'Because I can produce my Sticks any time for identification once you agree to my introduction fee, which is your upfront ten grand.'

'My upfront offer, which Keith should've passed to you, was for a "dead cert" Tricks. You've come up with a dead cert Sticks. That ain't good enough.'

Norton wasted no time. He could see the point. 'Five grand and you get your info.'

'OK. Keith says you're good on your word. Five tonners down for my guy sees your Sticks.'

Norton and the head of The Family shook hands in the restaurant opposite the headquarters of the SAS Regiment and moved on to discuss quite how Norton would 'introduce' Sticks to Goodman. Norton's definition of an 'introduction' fell a long way short of the Oxford Dictionary version but Sailor decided not to withdraw. It was not as if any of his other scouts had offered leads on a likely Tricks.

'So where exactly is this grocery shop where you say I can have my client view your Sticks?'

Norton had the decency to sound a touch embarrassed. 'Tangmere,' he said. 'Sticks is thought to deal narcotics from a grocery store in which he's a partner on Tangmere deck, part of the Broadwater . . .'

'Yeah, yeah.' Sailor's voice had risen from its normal growl. 'You don't have to lecture me on Tangmere's geography. If you'd said where this Sticks was before we shook on the deal . . .' He shook his head negatively. 'Broadwater. The Farm. Tangmere. You got to be jokin'. My boy's a nice, clean English boy and you want him messin' on Tangmere.'

'White, is he?' Norton fished.

'I didn't say that.' Sailor gave Norton a hard eye. 'You're a lucky man that I'm feelin' generous but, OK, you produce a Sticks answerin' the exact description I put out through Keith and you get your five tonners.'

They talked over the details and discussed how to communicate. Then both men went their separate ways.

The laboratory was adequately ventilated but, waiting in the walkway, Sailor detected the unmistakable whiff of amphetamine. Goodman heard the first three letters of Alexo in Morse sounded on the buzzer, checked the spyhole in the door of the flat and unfastened the heavy bolts to let Sailor in.

'Tea?' he asked.

'Why not. Listen, man, I may have the news you been waitin' for. But don't get excited. If Tricks is who my scout thinks, then we have one big problem on our hands to get you anywhere near him – never mind askin' him for your lost wallet!'

Goodman poured two mugs of tea. Sailor rolled himself a joint. He saw that Goodman was perched on his chair edge and spilling his tea on the concrete floor.

'Hey man. Stop pissin' yourself. We got a long, long way to go and there ain't no guarantee this guy's the right man. He surely sounds exactly like your Tricks, that's true. But for one thing his name is Sticks, not Tricks. How's that grab you?'

Goodman looked at his shoes, brown brogues from Church's, which Sara had made him buy along with other good-quality gear from the West End. They had gone there together not long after she had announced him 'a rich man' with over £130,000 in his 'bank' under her floorboards, where she kept much of her own earnings.

Sailor said nothing. He liked Alexo a lot. Tosh, whom he loved with his life, was still gruff towards the timid Welshman but she had decided he was 'OK' and that was a big vote of confidence coming from her.

Goodman thought back carefully to his interrogation of the drug-crazed Trevor. Had he definitely said 'Tricks' or could it have been

'Sticks'? On reflection he could not be sure. Trevor's Lancashire accent had been as thick as a triple club sandwich.

'It's possible, yes,' he told Sailor. 'He could well have said "Tricks", or "Dicks", or "Ticks", or "Sticks". I thought it was "Tricks" but, yes, it could equally have been "Sticks".'

Sailor sat up and looked hard at Goodman.

'Listen then, Alexo. This is the situation and it ain't exactly plain sailin'. Unofficially my information comes from the police and is, in this case, liable to be accurate. Assumin' this guy Sticks is one and the same as your Tricks – and it does look that way – what do you want from him?'

'The wallet that he took from me a year ago.'

'Will you recognise him?'

'Difficult to say. I recognised Trevor, so maybe I'll recognise Tricks.'

'But you don't know what he looks like.'

'True. But nor did I have a visual image of Trevor. I still recognised him though when I saw him, even fleetingly, on TV.'

'Well, we're goin' to have to get you to speak to the guy if you recognise him because the only other way won't work.'

'The other way?'

'Honey talk. Pillow talk. I pay one of our good-time ladies to give Tricks a good time and, when he's all fired up, steer the conversation softly round to Birmingham and badgers. That way we can be pretty sure he is, or isn't, the right guy without a fuss and even if your money fails to click with him.'

'That's a good point, Sailor. What if he is Tricks but I don't recognise him?'

'Exactly my meanin'. But in his case I can't see a honey trap workin' 'cos he's got himself a steady girl, a beautiful lady that works in the City and by all accounts he don't mess around on the side. So, my friend, I'll tell you how I see the best plan. OK?'

Goodman nodded. Sailor could see he would agree to anything but inaction.

'There's only two places we can be sure to get you in position to see this guy. One is Tottenham Police Station, where he has to sign bail every day. He's known as the big guy, the king of Broadwater Farm. People live in fear of him. The black brothers hold him in great respect. He was in Borstal for robbery, involved in many fights, acquitted of a stabbing murder in '79 and of knifing the Ol' Bill in '83. In 1980 he was best man at a weddin' attended by Roy Jenkins and Shirley Williams, and a few months back, when Princess Di visited Broadwater, he told her she wasn't welcome since her visit didn't help the Tottenham unemployed.'

'Is that why he's on bail at the moment?'

'No way,' Sailor chuckled. 'You don't get done for bein' rude to royalty. And don't forget, she's only a princess. Sticks is king of Broadwater. No, he's on bail for another murder accusation. Last Christmas a boxer called Smith was stabbed at a dance in Hackney. He died with his heart and stomach cut open, his lungs punctured and his face slashed. He'd been fightin' Sticks.'

'So, even if he's the man I'm after, he's not likely to come clean about my wallet?'

'I doubt it. You may even get a knife in your ribs if you try pressin' the point. What we got to do is set up the right situation. That's what I do best, boy: set up situations. What exactly do we want? Number one, for you to recognise him. Second, for him to listen to you without pigstickin' you out of hand. And, three, for him to give you back your wallet, OK?'

'Right. But how?'

'It'll cost money.'

'Of course.'

'Like I was sayin', there are two places we can be sure to locate Sticks. One is Tottenham nick and that don't fit with my plan. The other place is at his grocery store on Tangmere. The word is he deals from there. The police have been watchin' him closely. They are expectin' big trouble on the estate any time now and Sticks, they are sure, will be the ringleader. I know two battyboys on Tangmere who, for a price, will let us use their place close to the grocery store. We'll need six of our boys but I'm usin' nobody from The Family 'cos it's risky. So that's another cost. When Sticks calls at the bail station, my guy there will call us at the battyboys' flat. When Sticks reaches the grocery store, three of my boys, all black, will attack him. He will think they are from the Yankee Posse out to kill him for the murder of their fellow Yankee, Smith. You with me so far?'

Goodman was.

'Then you arrive on the scene lookin' like a typical Broadwater Farm poor white with three black pals. The four of you scare off his

176

"attackers" and Sticks sees that you have a gun, which gives you respect in his eyes. He thanks you. He can see that, but for you, he'd be raw meat. You say you're lookin' for him because you are bein' paid a big sum of cash to locate some Brum guy's wallet. You tell him you know that he took this wallet and that you will pay him £10,000 for its return with all its contents.'

'Why £10,000?'

'Because he's goin' to realise somebody has a very good reason for thinkin' the wallet is important if they've spent over a year lookin' for it. He will not part with it for small beans. He will ask you who wants it and why. You, of course, can't tell him the real answers, so your only lever is money. And Sticks by all accounts loves money. He will ask for more.'

'How high do I bid?'

'He'll test you. Don't go no higher than £20,000. Then let him think about it. If he still possesses the wallet, he'd be a fool not to take twenty grand.'

'When can we do it?'

'Right away. There's big trouble comin' any day now on Broadwater and he'll be in the thick of it. He'll have to be, to keep his reputation as the big boy of the estate. That means the law will probably nick him and put him away – maybe for a long, long time. We either do it now or you risk a big delay.'

14

October 1985

Sunday, 6 October was hot and humid. After a damp summer, the autumn had blazed away, with early October temperatures higher than recorded for half a century. Life within the concrete estates was even more miserable than usual.

Before Goodman left the previous evening, Sara had warned him about estates in general and especially Broadwater Farm. Basu had told her of white, mixed and Asian families who had lived there for fifteen years but were now moving out. Old folk had their invalid cars smashed. The Tenants' Association was controlled by a few West Indians who ignored the Asian and white minority. Fifty-five per cent of the 3000 tenants were Jamaican. Gangs ruled by day and by night, their hate-filled graffiti daubed all over the estate. To attempt to wash the messages from a flat's outer wall was to invite retribution. And since only 10 per cent of tenants paid their full rent, the council could ill afford to remove graffiti or in any other way improve the look of the estate.

The construction of Broadwater Farm started in 1967 and ended in 1973, a twenty-one-acre estate of ten four, five or six-storey blocks and two eighteen-storey monsters. Most of the units were built on stilts because the River Moselle, which flowed across the site, was prone to flooding. The Department of the Environment gave the estate an award for 'good housing' and the Planning Committee's Chairman, Roy Limb, told the press: 'Broadwater Farm will be an everlasting memorial to my committee.' For a short while the first tenants were content but the arrogance of the money-not-tenant-orientated planners and architects was soon shown up. Rain and wind battered their monstrous blocks, roaring with katabatic violence through concrete tunnels and passageways.

No thought had been given to the weak and elderly, nor to police access to catch rapists, muggers and thieves preying on the tenants. Cars were vandalised and stolen, their drivers beaten up in the dark car ports of the basements. Flat roofs and burst pipes in upper storeys flooded flats. Lifts and heating systems broke down and were not repaired, window frames rotted and doors hung off their hinges. Ventilation systems gave easy access to flats for germs, cockroaches, rats and exotic varieties of flea. Lighting was poor and broken bulbs were seldom if ever replaced. Condensation and fungal slime skeined concrete walls that never dried out. Privacy was non-existent and the corridors amplified noise so that the sounds of footfalls on the walkways, neighbours snoring, screaming and playing radios were magnified and transmitted day and night into the flats.

Refuse chutes were too small to take full rubbish bags, so they jammed and the stench filled the passageways. Fearful of entering the lifts and corridors below, tenants threw bulging bags off balconies to the rats at ground level or left them in the walkways to rot.

Urine covered the ground, and excrement and used needles lay about like autumn leaves. Old folk had been killed by young motorcyclists playing chicken along a tenth-storey walkway. Waste areas between blocks were heaped with litter, glass and the faeces of dogs kept by tenants for company and protection.

The safest place for the lonely and the ill was to stay double locked in their prison-like flats but this was impossible, for planners had allowed for minimal community services. Vandals terrorised postmen and milkmen. Nothing was delivered and nobody would come to do repairs, thanks to Broadwater's fearful reputation and its air of alien menace. Nothing could be left outside a door, otherwise it would soon be smashed or stolen. To buy milk or bread, to collect a newspaper or post a letter meant a long journey through the corridors of fear.

No minicab driver would risk a visit, nor, after a bad experience, would friends or relations. Shopkeepers in neighbouring suburbs gave no credit to 'Broadwater people', such was the stigma of the place as a 'sink' estate. Nobody wanted to live there, so the council increasingly used it as a dumping ground for drug addicts, the mentally and physically ill, alcoholics and 'ethnics'. The bullies reigned supreme. Neighbourliness, once a strong point among Farm people, fell away as individuals grew wary of one another. Feelings of hostility were so pronounced in some quarters that new residents preferred to remain anonymous to avoid the possibility of confrontation.

At any one time eight unarmed policemen, in four pairs, were meant to patrol the nightmare acres of the Farm. During the fortnight before Goodman's arrival in Tangmere, four of these constables had been assaulted and three were badly injured. They could not protect themselves, let alone the tenants. The law of the Farm was truly the law of the jungle.

Sailor's friends, Jack and Tender, were both Jamaicans and their flat on Tangmere was two decks above the grocery store belonging to Sticks. Goodman and the half-dozen Peckham Jamaicans with whom he had arrived the previous evening were made very welcome in the surprisingly spacious flat. Sailor had briefed his paid hands with care but they were initially dependent on Jack and Tender for local know-how.

Goodman was left alone but for one or other of these two, while Sailor's men roamed the block, chatting and gaining information about Sticks. A growing number of unsavoury characters from outside Tottenham, including 'heroes' fresh from riots in Birmingham, Liverpool, Brixton and Peckham, were inflaming the locals to defiance. The house of an ex-Broadwater family had been searched by police the previous day and the housewife, Cynthia Jarrett, had died of a heart attack during the search. The cry was out: 'An eye for an eye.' Feelings were, according to Sailor's men, running high but there was as yet no trace of Sticks himself.

Jack and Tender were a happy couple in their late twenties and both struck Goodman as a touch androgynous. They knew The Family well, following some trouble Sailor had once helped them with. They chatted freely with Goodman in the kitchen, tucked away from the noise, ganja fumes and Red Stripe beer cans of the living room.

By the Sunday afternoon, with still no sight of Sticks but all the signs of an impending riot, Goodman had established excellent relations with Jack and Tender but was taken aback when they began a frank and explicit description of their love life. They asked him, under no circumstances, to mention anything to their fellow-Jamaicans next door to whom, they said, any form of sexual deviation was abhorrent.

'Should I not even talk to Sailor about it?' Goodman asked.

'Oh,' Tender smiled. 'Don't mind what you say to The Family. They know all about us. They're as liberated as you.'

Jack explained that he and Tender had met and fallen in love at Newcastle University nine years before. At that time Jack was an attractive young girl named Jackie and Tender a shy lad called Tom. Both came from hardworking, middle-class Jamaican immigrant families who knew nothing of their children's latent gender unease.

A happy fate had brought the two together and, soon after they left university, they decided to save all their earnings in order to *both* obtain sex-change surgery.

Goodman's lower jaw dropped as Jack launched into a surgical dissertation by way of explanation.

'Would you like to look?' Jack said.

Goodman hastily declined. 'Do you know Sticks well?' he asked, changing the subject.

'Of course,' Jack said. 'His shop downstairs is very handy when he or his partner are there.'

'What is his real name? Or is he like lots of people I've met of late, with only a street-name?'

'Silcott,' Tender said. 'Winston Silcott.' She switched up the volume of her radio and raised her hand. 'Quiet a bit. It's Bishop Tutu. He's just been seeing Mrs Thatcher and the Archbishop of Canterbury. They . . .'

The door slammed next door and Leon, one of Sailor's men, burst into the kitchen. 'Sticks has left Tottenham Police Station,' said the pocky, rat-like lad. 'He signed bail there at 6.30 and they say he'll be here in twenty minutes. It's real bad down there.' He gestured outside. 'A crowd of boys from off the estate, some of them white skinheads, caught one of the local beat coppers on patrol and smashed him with a concrete block. There's cars on fire all over, Ol' Bill vans bein' smashed and a council of war is just endin' in the Youth Club down by Sticks's shop. Alexo, you'd better get ready, man. There's a war startin' out there.'

Leon paused for breath. 'I've been in the meeting. It's just broken up and they are angry, man. I mean they are goin' out to kill Ol' Bill.'

'Sticks?' Goodman asked.

'He's still not been seen.'

'So he wasn't at the meeting?'

'Well, if he was, I wouldn't have recognised him. But there's lots of different big dons cryin' for pig blood. I think a lot of them come from other parts but the local brothers on the estate feel their time has come. You see, all the other brothers have done their thing, riots and that. Brixton, Bristol, Toxteth. Now the Farm lads want to show some spunk. The lid's off the bin and they won't cool it till they've cut the fuzz up. If we're goin' to catch Sticks, tonight's our best chance. In the dark while all his friends is beatin' up the cops.'

'Do you want to go now?' Goodman asked.

'Nope. All the boys is out scoutin' for Sticks and cuttin' up shirts for masks like the rest of them. Some of the locals have promised to tell us when Sticks arrives. Then we'll come and get you.'

'What's that smell?' Jack asked.

'Burnin' rice,' Leon said. 'They've set fire to the Paki supermarket. It's a trap. Once the fuzz come up, they'll close in with knives and petrol from behind.'

'Hadn't we better clear off before the police come up here?' Goodman had visions of ending up in prison for being in the vicinity of police murders. 'Otherwise we'll never get near to Sticks when he does come.'

'You leave this to us, man.' Leon was firm. 'We never let Sailor down yet. Just you come when we call.'

The three men sat at a small table in the canteen of Wood Green Police Station. Keith Blakelock, a home-beat officer from the middle-class suburb of Muswell Hill, was ten years older than Dick Coombes but had experience outside the Force, unlike many of their fresh-faced teenage colleagues raw from Training College. The third man, Alan Tappy, was a couple of years younger than Dick but both men had been firm friends since Alan had joined up and was introduced to the beat by Dick.

Five years earlier Blakelock had tried to join his local Northumbrian Police, keen to do a meaningful job to help the community. Northumbria would not take him because of his age. So he'd moved with his family to North London and was soon a popular character with colleagues and public alike. His wife Elizabeth and their three sons were, he suspected, sitting at home anxiously watching television news reports on the escalation of violence in Tottenham.

'If we get a riot tonight,' Coombes said, 'I hope the powers that be act firm and don't pussyfoot about.'

'Depends who we get, doesn't it? As always, it's a question of the boss on the ground, no matter what the Commissioners pass down as policy.'

'You'd have thought Maggie Thatcher would've straightened things out by now but she hasn't. Once we'd stood by her over the miners and she by us, things began to slip back to wishy-washy "community policing" – another way of saying, "Don't confront. Don't upset the whingeing liberals. Protect the criminal." '

Blakelock shook his head. 'I don't think you can blame Thatcher. She's not a dictator even if she'd like to be. This country, right or wrong, is ruled by the civil servants and, never mind Tories or Labour, they steer the ship. There's no way they're going to upset all their legal friends by sensible rules such as removing the right to silence. If they do that, half the work of defence lawyers is removed and therefore half their fat fees. The solicitors, the barristers, the beaks. No way will they allow such a sensible change to the law.'

'One of the problems,' Coombes added, 'is a number of Chief Constables with virtually no operational experience. They have a social-welfare outlook to policing. Nice enough blokes, many of them, but out of touch with the sharp end. Want to run the police as a corporate function and it won't work.'

As dusk closed in, outside the canteen, young policemen in uniform moved about with cups of tea and buns. There was an air of tension and uncertainty, people talking in quiet knots with one ear on their radios and one eye out for the arrival of their officers with news or orders. A hundred or more blacks had thrown stones at Tottenham Police Station that afternoon, after Cynthia Jarrett's death from a heart attack. The crowd had screamed abuse, including threats to kill police officers and their families. They had dispersed but promised further trouble.

Later in the afternoon three officers had been injured, one all but blinded, on the edge of Broadwater Farm. The radios in the canteen crackled. The occupants of District Support Unit (DSU) van number Y32 had been attacked with petrol bombs and machetes. Wood Green Control was mobilising further units to go to the estate. As these arrived they found all four road entrances blocked by blazing barricades and hundreds of rioters, including a vociferous minority of white youths, hurling missiles from the concrete balconies above the barricades.

Tappy, Blakelock and Coombes were summoned by their commander, Sergeant David Pengelly. Their group, Unit 502, consisted of ten men, only half of whom were trained in riot control. All were from the Wood Green and Hornsey stations. Pengelly told them to draw riot gear from a mobile van, truncheons, fire-retardant overalls, helmets and shields. They then squeezed into a Sherpa DSU van which Coombes volunteered to drive. No time for last calls home.

Wood Green Control sent them to Seven Sisters tube station, where there was trouble. On arrival they found those responsible had vanished and another call rushed them to assist officers being stoned on the edge of Broadwater Farm. Then pell-mell off to the south-west entrance to the Farm, where the Avenue meets Glouces-ter Road. By now blazing vehicles blocked every entrance to the estate. From the concrete balconies immediately overhead, a lethal shower of petrol bombs, rocks and bricks rained down. Isolated squads of police rattled their shields as if to ward off the threatening din of yelling youths, exploding vehicle tanks, tyres and petrol bombs.

Pengelly dismounted his little group as fire engines arrived and extinguished the nearest blaze. Reports followed of a fire raging in an Asian supermarket on the second floor of Tangmere which threatened the occupants, including many old people, on the floors above. The local police chief, Colin Couch, decided to risk sending in firemen protected by Pengelly and his men.

The night was dark, with a gentle drizzle. Most of the Farm's public lighting had been vandalised in the car ports under Tang-mere. From his position on the road Pengelly could see a grass bank, sloping away down into the gloom of the car port area, where a forest of concrete stilts supported the Tangmere block. Enemy territory but, so it seemed, presently free of rioters. Couch, in Chief Superintendent's uniform, walked down the slope and into the car port close to where concrete steps led up to the first-floor walkway of Tangmere. Nothing happened. He returned, and despite the complete lack of back-up units, decided to send the firemen in with their hoses, escorted by Pengelly's men.

At about 9.30 p.m. the unit moved forward from the road, through the mist of black smoke from burning tyres. They soon vanished single file into the darkness of Tangmere. Coombes was entering what for him and his family would prove to be a lifelong nightmare.

As Unit 502 left the road and filed down the damp grass, Coombes noticed a council sign which read 'WELCOME TO BROAD-WATER FARM'. As quietly as possible the little group of five firemen dragged their hoses over the grass and on up the concrete stairways towards the blazing shop on the second storey. Pengelly's men escorted them, eyes peeled for sudden attacks in the darkness. Constable Tappy, thirty-one, kept close to his old friend Coombes. Five of the men had long, heavy riot shields and five carried short, round, lighter models.

As they reached the first floor, mocking laughter came to them from five white skinheads on the fifth-storey balcony above. Ricky Pandya waited at the rear of the column as Keith Blakelock conversed in a low voice with Pengelly. The sergeant detailed Blakelock, Howells and Pandya to stay down on the first floor to tell residents to keep inside their flats. Pengelly and the others disappeared up to the second storey.

Pandya heard the sudden smashing of glass from the balconies above and, down in the darkness of the car port, Coombes glimpsed the movement of many silent, running figures. He felt the hair on the back of his neck rise for the first time in sixteen years with the Force. He could see they were caught in a death-trap.

Pengelly, reaching the second-floor walkway about the blazing shops, saw graffiti on one wall of the Asian supermarket: 'TAN-DOORI SHIT GET OUT. NIGGERS RULE.' On his squad radio he learnt that, four hundred yards away to the far side of Tangmere, four hundred police had been shot and more than two hundred injured at the Griffin Road entrance. He wondered how long before he and his men were noticed *inside* the lions' den. From a distant part of Tangmere he thought he heard the clang of a handbell.

The firemen had not long begun to set up their equipment when thirty or forty men in track suits, combat fatigues, black jackets and makeshift masks ran up a second set of steps and advanced along two separate corridors towards the firemen. They carried machetes, stabbing knives, long, sharpened steel rods and boxes filled with petrol bombs. They halted a few yards from the five long shields of Pengelly's detachment.

'We're only protecting the firemen,' Pengelly shouted. 'Let us do our job. Then we'll go.'

For a moment there was hesitation. Then a brick was thrown and the pack's adrenalin surged. With shrieks of fury and hatred a hundred and fifty rioters, most but not all black, closed in for the kill. Coombes heard yells of 'Fuck off, pigs', 'This is the Farm', 'No pigs here' and 'You'll never get out alive.' The individual taunts soon merged into a steady chant: 'Kill, kill, kill the pigs.' Coombes realised the only way to escape certain death was to work as a group and, above all, stay calm. Easier said than done. Petrol bombs exploded, chunks of torn paving smashed against helmets, sharpened machete blades sliced into the shields and Pengelly shouted for an orderly retreat behind to ensure the protection of the firemen.

By the time Coombes and two others reached the stairs, their long shields locked as they retreated, a hundred armed youths screaming 'Kill the filth!' and 'Burn the bacon!' were bearing down on them. Coombes froze as he saw, through the scarred plastic of his visor, an attacker trying to light a flame-thrower. The police were all soaked in petrol from petrol bombs which had been thrown unlit. Now he knew why. Luckily the apparatus would not ignite.

Somehow 502 and the firemen, some wounded but all still mobile, survived the terrifying descent of the stairs, stumbling on fire hoses, until they reached the last step and ground level. There they were met, under the faint light of a single security lamp, by an ever-growing crowd of rioters intent on cutting off their retreat.

Once the last man was down from the block, the unit split up, every man for himself, for the roadway was a hundred long yards away over the killing ground. By now the drizzle had turned to heavy rain and Keith Blakelock lost his footing. As he stumbled thirty rioters closed in on him with a variety of weapons. 'Kill, kill, kill,' they screamed. His truncheon, his shield and his helmet were torn from him, so he raised his hands to protect his face. They slashed at his arms, chopping off fingers and exposing his head.

Stakes and knives were plunged into his chest and his neck but he did not die.

Coombes saw the crowd 'like a flock of murderous birds in a feeding frenzy, hacking and jabbing' at his colleague Blakelock. Fire Officer Trevor Stratford from Romford and nineteen-year-old Constable Maxwell Roberts grabbed at the wounded Blakelock, but both were themselves attacked. Stratford's back was struck by a brick and Roberts was knifed. At this point Coombes, running back to help Blakelock, was blocked by a number of rioters brandishing various weapons. A vicious blow knocked him down. He was then set upon by the pack, his visor torn off and his neck slit open with knives. His jawbone was shattered by a machete blade and he lost consciousness. Masked rioters set about his inert body with knives and clubs.

Pengelly was being hunted by a separate group, and as he turned to face them, not far from the safety of the road, he glimpsed a mass of rioters, their arms rising and falling, about Blakelock's body. With great bravery Pengelly charged back through his own attackers, truncheon flaying and short shield swinging, to single-handedly attack Blakelock's assailants. His truncheon work was effective and three other constables fought their way back to help out. Stratford, Maxwell and Alan Tappy dragged Blakelock to his feet and Stratford screamed at him: 'Run, man. Bloody run!'

Pengelly recognised Blakelock only by his moustache, for his face was a bloody mess. The handle of a knife, driven four inches into the back of his neck, stuck out from under his ear and a gaping wound ran from his mouth to the back of his shoulder, almost severing his head. Somehow he was still alive and managed to take four or five paces before finally collapsing. A youth tore away Pengelly's truncheon and, by the time they had dragged the dying Blakelock back to an ambulance on the road, the sergeant had stab wounds in his neck and shoulder.

Other constables, Ken Milne and Mike Shepherd, had managed under attack to pull Coombes, blood pumping from his face and neck, to the roadway. Coombes would suffer from crippling epileptic fits for the rest of his life.

If the Welshmen of Rorke's Drift once showed valour in the face of overwhelming odds, Pengelly's Unit 502, though unsung owing to political correctness, should have their place in history, even though Broadwater Farm is a less romantic setting than the bushveld. The Farm's marauders, both black and white, had now scented blood and began to prowl in chanting mobs about the estate's perimeters in a state of heady, if rain-sodden, euphoria and keen for 'more of the same'. About half an hour after the battered occupants of Pengelly's Sherpa van returned to Wood Green Station, the word reached Leon that Sticks was holding court in the Tangmere car port.

'If we don't go down now,' Leon insisted, 'we'll never get him.' Five of Sailor's men, soaking wet and wearing muddy trainers, were not looking happy. They had witnessed the horrors of the night and now they feared an imminent and massive police backlash. They wanted to leave the estate at once. Leon was of sterner stuff. Goodman could see why Sailor had hired him. Small and weasel-like, he was possessed of a strong will and a sharp tongue.

'I say we get down there now. Find a good spot, away from the crowds, and get Sticksy to come to us.'

'Oh yeah?' queried one of the doubters. 'If he's the big badman round here, he ain't gonna come to nobody.'

'Tell him that I'm Willy Haggard, Rankin' Dred, or some other big don and I'm real proud of Sticks and the Farm brothers for their work tonight. That will make him feel big. And curious as to what a number-one don is doin' on his patch. Once he's away from the crowds we do what we come to do. Then we go.'

This carried the others and they left. Goodman held his hand out to Jack and Tender, thanking them. They embraced him and wished him well.

Sailor had lent him a small revolver, but he left it behind in the kitchen, fearful of the police catching him with it.

Goodman found the gloom of the car port disorientating. At first he followed the whispers of Sailor's men towards the laughter of some hidden group but he soon lost them. As his eyes grew accustomed to the darkness he began to pick out the concrete foundation pillars and the occasional car. The whole area stank of excrement and urine. Old beer cans, wheels and refuse bags littered the ground as he made his way towards the sound of voices.

A torch flashed at him as he trod on a broken bottle, and shouts of 'Pig!' and 'Spy!' rang out. He felt panic, and turned and ran, but he was not fit. He slipped in the mud and heard the cries of his pursuers closing about him. A steel-capped boot thudded into his back, another smashed against his skull. The darkness seemed to blaze and flash in his brain as he lost consciousness.

15

October 1985

His hands were gently parting the high fronds of bracken. His breathing quickened. There were at least eight men in and around the clearing and half a dozen dogs, terriers of different sorts.

Mary and Lucy were safe. Back on the bench where he'd left them. God, this was loathsome. A summer's afternoon in a lovely English wood, a public place for walkers and nature-lovers. He had heard of badger diggers, and not that long ago he'd seen an RSPCA film describing the cruel tradition and advising viewers, should they ever see diggers at work, always to call the police but never interfere, for they were often dangerous men.

He heard the sound of steel crunching into soil and the muffled snarls of dogs underground. He froze as bracken crackled beneath his boots but the diggers and the two smartly dressed men with shooting sticks and video cameras were mesmerised by the action.

He wondered if the badgers felt fear and decided that everything living had the fear instinct in order to survive. The poor animals must smell the dogs and men and cringe at each approaching blow of picks and shovels as their home was cruelly invaded and their approach tunnels caved in. He watched as the man they were calling Paul laid down on the earth with his ear to the ground. 'Dig further towards the left,' he grunted.

Goodman's fist clenched tight around the bracken stalks. The faces of the black man and the two voyeurs with American accents were clear. Goodman stared at them, and then at the others, determined never to forget their features until he could help the police select them from a line-up and put them away for as long as possible. Such people were vermin. The law should allow their extermination. Goodman's skin crawled as he watched and listened.

A cry went up as a further tunnel section collapsed and 'Paul' thrust his arm downwards, grabbing a sow with his long-handled badger tongs. He clamped the metal jaws about the neck of the terrified creature and triumphantly pulled her clear of the sett. The sprung jaws bit into her hide and punctured her muscle layer. With squirming, cat-like contortions she managed to bite at the instrument, but now, held high by the clamp, all struggle was useless. Below, the three dogs still above ground yelped and strained at their leashes.

'Bastard!' The tongs man swore. 'She's got a snare around her guts. She'll be weak. No good for a fight.' He turned to the black man. 'Shall I chuck her?' he asked. 'Makes sense, 'cos there's others down there bound to put up a better fight.'

The black man looked at the Americans, who nodded.

The clamp was released and the snared sow dropped to the ground to be pinned by a shovel while two of the dogs were released. Ten long minutes later her grunting died away. Goodman had watched the dogs tear her limb from limb. Down in the remnants of the sett, the other members of her family had listened to her die. Now it was their turn. The digging and the barking began afresh and Goodman's impotent anger mounted.

They found two more badgers in the sett and dispatched the first, another sow, using all five dogs and, at the Americans' behest, some well-aimed shovel blows to enhance the video.

Some twenty minutes after Goodman's arrival, the big boar was held aloft in the tongs and his size was proudly promoted by three of the cognoscenti present. An argument ensued as to whether, owing to the Americans' busy schedule, they should crush the boar's paws or snap his jawbone to 'even things out' before the fight commenced.

At this point Goodman found himself beyond the restraints of logic and common sense. His voice screamed, 'Stop! Stop! Police' and he forced his way through the bracken. The Americans seemed more likely than the brutish-looking locals to respond to his appeal and he had taken a single step towards them from the edge of the clearing when the bull-like tongs man caught hold of his jacket.

'Here, cunt. Who the fuck do you think you are?'

Three of the others closed in and seized Goodman.

'Trevor, Jake,' someone shouted. 'Check the bushes.'

The black man sauntered over to the captive Goodman.

'Who are you, then?' he asked. 'And who are your friends?'

'I'm just a lone walker and I don't have anyone with me. I simply came to ask you, beg you, to stop hurting these badgers. They've done you no harm.'

The black man gestured to the tongs man. 'Blackledge. Search the geezer, will you. He seems like Joe Public, but you never know. He may be RSPCA or CID.'

In the pockets of his Barbour they found a used Kodak film from Lucy's camera, the house and car keys on a ring and his wallet with cash and cards.

'There's nowt here,' Blackledge said, handing keys, film and wallet to the black man, who pocketed them. Everybody seemed to relax. 'Sorry about the delay, Mr Redden.'

'Time's getting short, Tricks,' said the American.

The black man nodded and turned to Blackledge.

'How long for the boar?'

'Well, he's a fine, strong brock. I reckon, with all five dogs on him, it could take twenty minutes, maybe more, unless we even the odds a touch.'

They decided to video the handicap ceremony and aim for a ten-minute fight. With the cameras in place and the big boar firmly clamped, they smashed his front paws between two spades, rendering useless his great digging claws.

Goodman watched speechless. By now his main emotion was of regret that he had come forward and fear lest the searchers, one of whom had a shotgun, should come across Mary and Lucy. He cursed himself for not having taken his wife and daughter quietly down the road, stopped a car and called the police. But now it was too late. He had blundered into a hopeless situation and done nothing to help the badgers. He prayed silently that Mary would hide Lucy away from the badger men and that, realising he was no threat, they would simply leave him behind when they packed up.

With the tongs preventing movement, Blackledge further crippled the badger's defensive ability with a heavy hammer blow to its lower jaw. Once all five terriers were ready, their quivering *muzzles bloody from the sow, Blackledge released the tongs and the boar dropped down to the waiting pack. Despite his injuries he managed to sever one terrier's jugular, crunch through the front leg of another and remove most of the muzzle of a third. But within Blackledge's predicted ten minutes the boar was blinded, disembowelled and torn to pieces.*

'What to do with Noddy here?' Blackledge asked Tricks as he tossed the three mauled badgers into sacks.

'Tie him up and leave him in the hole.'

The searchers returned. The one named Trevor lashed Goodman's hands painfully behind his back and, leering at him, placed a foul-smelling sack over his head.

A piercing scream sounded from close by and Goodman ducked, trying to shrug off the sack. Then the world exploded.

Slowly, through the mists of his dream, Goodman returned to the reality of Monday, 7 October. Sara, kneeling beside his bed, was watching him. Her wonderful saucer eyes creased with pleasure as she realised that he had woken and was conscious of her presence.

Goodman's brain tried to distil the messages emanating from two separate levels of memory, those of his beloved Mary and others, more recent, of Sara. He felt a sense of unease, the same disinclination which, for the past fifteen months, had forbidden his brain to delve into that memory compartment which held knowledge of the Kinver Wood happenings. Why should he not? Because such knowledge would be too painful to bear. Far better to shut the memory off than to live with the thought that, through a moment's blind stupidity, he had endangered them. The only people he had ever loved and would willingly die for might never return because of him. How could he live with such a memory?

So, like a scab congealing over some ghastly wound, the automatic mental function known to psychologists as functional retrograde amnesia had clamped down like a smog, leaving Goodman unaware that he had ever taken his loved ones into the wood or indeed that they had ever existed.

Since his emotions were still every bit as tender fifteen months after the Kinver event, why should the memory block have now suddenly withdrawn? His mental state as he was kicked unconscious beneath Tangmere may or may not have approximated to his

Kinver experience. Whatever the reason, Goodman had fully recovered his lost identity by the time he awoke in Sara's flat. A blank still remained, but it covered merely the period between his hearing a scream, shortly after his head had been hooded, and his revival at the Midland Centre for Neurosurgery. This memory lapse was of a duration to be expected after any concussion.

He could likewise remember nothing from the moment the previous night when he had been mistaken for a police spy and kicked senseless, until the time of his first conscious stirrings in Sara's flat eight hours later. Even as he looked at Sara and felt her squeeze his hand, as she leant forward, kissed his forehead and whispered, 'Welcome back, Alex', he thought only of Mary.

Why, in my dream, did Mary and Lucy not come back? Why are they not here with me now? Why am I in bed? I was searching for Tricks to learn my identity but now I know my identity and I am not Alex Goodman. I will tell nobody that, but I'm not. My head aches abominably. I left them on the bench, my darlings. Surely they hid. Oh God! Save them from the badger men. Trevor and another man called Jake were sent to search the brush but they came back with nobody . . . So my loves *are* all right. But then why have they never come back to me? Why, over all the months, have they stayed away, never advertised nor searched for me? But then perhaps they have and by bad luck we've just missed one another.

This last thought made him illogically hopeful. 'Sara,' he said aloud. 'I'm OK but I must tell them at once. Will you have them brought here?'

'Who, love?' She was confused.

'Mary, my wife, and Lucy, my daughter.'

For an instant Sara felt shock and a heavy sinking of some unacknowledged hope. But she smiled brightly and clapped her hands as with delight.

'Alex! Your memory's back. Great. Great. I'll call Columbo and the others. Fantastic.'

She rushed out, made her call, and came back with herbal tea. 'Are you hungry?'

He smiled weakly. 'Only for news.'

She grimaced. 'Well, you were at Tangmere lookin' for Sticks when some baskets attacked you and were busy puttin' the boot in when Leon and the others pulled you clear and brought you back here.'

'Did they get to Tricks?'

'Nah. Not a sign. Leon says if he was there, he was all geared up with a mask on and keepin' out of sight of police cameras since he knows the Ol' Bill always picks on him.'

'So it was a waste of time?'

'And lolly,' Sara added. 'But look on the bright side, Alex. You got your memory back, ain't you? And that's what it was all about.' Then she fell silent, before adding: 'How can I get your wife and kid for you? Do you even remember your home number?'

'They can't be there still. It was heavily mortgaged. Unless I found a job we'd never have paid our instalments. But the estate agents may have something on her. I must go up to Dudley at once.'

'Dr Khimji said you should stay here till he says you can move.' Sara tried to look fierce. 'I'm to put you under again if you don't behave. He says it shouldn't take long for you to recover. Mostly you're just badly bruised, includin' the biggest wallop on your thigh not an inch from your dick.'

Goodman's eyebrows rose.

'Yeah,' Sara said. 'I had to help Doc Khimji bath you and check you all over. You needn't worry. I see quite a lot of blokes in the raw.'

They laughed.

'You rich, were you?' she asked.

'How do you mean?'

'Before it all happened. Did you come from a big upper-class family, like? Lots of dosh?'

'Lord, no.' Goodman luxuriated in the knowledge that he could now answer such questions if he wanted. 'By the way, I'm feeling peckish. Is there any bread?'

She jumped up. 'Bread! I'll give you bread. I'll bring you a proper meal, love. You must be starvin'.'

Once alone, Goodman began to reorientate himself. Sailor and the others would arrive soon. He must decide exactly what he would and would not say to them and to Sara. Now was the time to make up his mind. Did he wish to stay as Alex Goodman, at least while searching for Mary and Lucy, a task which might take quite a while? He weighed up the factors in favour.

His Beetle must have been long stolen or impounded and his home repossessed. He had owed his bank a large sum of money even before they moved house. He assumed that, when his bank had sorted out the mess with the estate agents, the building society and their own loan department, he would have ended up unpleasantly in the red. He could return and clear his name now that he was rich.

Neither he nor his wife had relatives with whom they had kept in touch. They had not had time to make new acquaintances in Dudley but he thought of two good friends in Leominster with whom Mary should still be corresponding. One was Lucy's godmother. He decided to call them at once. Even contemplating this filled him with a delicious anticipation.

Then the thought struck him that, to make any such call, he must use either his real name or a false one. This was the crux of the matter. The bugbear was the law. Could he reclaim his own identity without alerting the police to actions he had taken over the past fifteen months which might brand him as a thief, a murderer, or both? How could he know the answer? If the only way to detect the location of a minefield is to blunder about in it, he mused, then his natural inclination was to avoid the danger altogether. Since there were no great advantages and great potential for trouble to be had in reclaiming his original identity, it surely made sense to stay as he was. Alex Goodman by name and, currently, Andrew Smith in his National Insurance book.

His memories of his late parents were fond and proud. He would never sully the family name if he could avoid it. He had done nothing of which he was ashamed but, should Trevor's death at his hands or his participation in robbery become known, he would prefer that 'Alex Goodman' carry the can.

Sara brought him the telephone and he called the operator. Lucy's godmother was at home and seemed to accept Goodman's plausible reason for enquiring about his 'old girlfriend' Mary and her family.

'I'm sorry,' she said, 'but they all moved up to Birmingham a year back. Maybe more. He had a new job up there. They were all very excited about it. I think it was some Australian beer company and I can only presume they were moved on to Sydney because I've never heard a word from Mary or Lucy ever since and, to be honest, that's most unlike them.' She promised Goodman that, should Mary ever make contact, she would call him at once on Sara's number.

Seeing the crestfallen look on his face, Sara urged him to be optimistic. There could be many reasons why Mary had not made contact with Lucy's godmother.

'Such as?' Goodman asked.

'Look,' Sara could only reply. 'Sailor will soon be here. He'll know what's best.'

Sailor came with Tosh, Columbo and Art. They greeted Goodman like a long-lost brother and passed on good wishes from James and Chemist, who were busy at the coolers and the lab.

Goodman felt proud to be accepted by these people and his confidence, dented by his phone call, began to return.

'Are you really Alex Goodman then?' Tosh joked. 'Or a Welsh poet of renown?'

'I am indeed Alex Goodman. The hospital somehow got that right. But I'm no poet. Nothing so exciting: I was an accountant with a small business in the Borders.'

'An accountant!' Columbo roared. 'Alexo's an accountant. Just what The Family need to keep the books, eh!' He clapped his great hands together with gusto.

Sailor stayed behind when the others departed and Sara left them for an 'out-call'.

'Well, then,' said Sailor, sitting down on the decorated Indian tin chest which served as Goodman's cupboard and seat. 'I have to tell you that Sticks, Mr Winston Silcott, can't be your Tricks. Last night, while you was still in with Jack and Tender, I called my Ol' Bill friend at his home. He said all hell was let loose on the Farm and warned me to keep clear. He'd also come up with the results of checks on Sticks's crime record. It proved, one hundred per cent, that the big boy was two hundred miles away from Brum on the night the badger men done you in. Still, now you got your memory back it don't matter.' He chuckled. 'So then, what's next for Alexo?'

'I've got to find my wife and daughter.'

'Of course. I am happy for you, boy. But how you goin' to start? Ain't no missin' persons bureau in the UK, you know.'

'The police. Maybe you have a contact who could check records back to July last year?'

'Sure, I have. But I must tell you, I wouldn't hold out much hope. Scotland Yard don't have no centralised computer system for missin' persons. District police keep index cards but I done a lot of work tracin' kids for brothers and I can tell you, you got to be patient.'

'Is there no welfare system search unit?'

'Lookin' for the lost? No way. The Family Tracin' Service of the Sally Army does a good job but they got poor facilities. The police would be our most likely bet but what am I goin' to say? They'll ask, "Why are you only askin' now when the disappearance was fifteen months back?" '

'Maybe I should come clean,' Goodman said.

Sailor frowned. 'You do that, boy, and you're openin' a can of worms. How do you know if the law don't have your prints from Trevor's corpse if they found it? Or from your blaggin' jobs with Columbo? Or hidden videos of you doin' wheelies for the Emby job? Once you stick your neck into a police system, they'll drill away until you maybe say the wrong thing. Your story don't hold too much water when you think about it. They may even think *you* done in your missus and kid.'

Goodman's heart sank. He could see Sailor's logic.

'You don't know how much they know about Trevor havin' been in the wood at Kinver. If they make that connection, boy, you're in deep trouble. If they put you on ice that's not goin' to help us find your old lady.'

'Sailor,' Goodman's voice sounded desperate. 'What's your advice?'

'First you mustn't prop your hopes up by ignorin' the facts. You say you heard a scream when they put the sack on your nut?'

'Yes, I'm sure I did. I must have thought it was Mary and tried to escape. One of them must have hit me at that point.'

'Do you know where it happened?'

'Yes.'

'Exactly where?'

'I think so.'

'And their faces?'

'Definitely.' Goodman closed his eyes. 'I can see them now . . . Tricks and the Americans, Trevor, Jake and the badger man Paul Blackledge. I can hear their voices. I could repeat to you just about every word they said. All these months I knew nothing. Now the whole nightmare is sitting in my skull like a video on endless replay.'

Sailor looked at Goodman. 'You're a brave man, Alexo.'

'No, I was stupid. None of this would have happened if I'd minded my own business. I risked Mary and Lucy. How could I have done that to the two most important people in the world? If anything happened to them, it's my fault.'

'You think there's a chance they got involved?'

'I don't want to think that. But the scream . . . it could have been Mary. And why else would she and Lucy have seemingly disappeared from the face of the earth ever since?'

Sailor stood up. He towered above Goodman's bed. 'Alexo. You must be strong. To brood will do no good. I'll start straight away with enquiries, OK?'

Goodman nodded. He did not try to speak. His head was crowding with dark possibilities.

'And two other things. I know how we can find your Tricks, almost for certain . . . Soon as you're up and about.'

He paused, as though not wishing to add anything further, then went on. 'And if you decide on it, I can get Columbo to drive you to the wood. Just to make sure.'

Goodman looked away, but then nodded. The wood. The sett. Sooner or later he must face the truth.

16

October 1985

Sara Carpenter's Gujarati grandmother, Devaki Mistri, had left the village of Morali Bazar and travelled by steamboat to Kenya, where Grandpa was working on the new railways spreading out from Nairobi. Sara was born in India in 1970, but when she was four months old her parents settled in Kenya. Then, when she was three, they took her to England, where she grew up as an English, East African Indian.

To complicate matters further, her parents went back to their home town in India for their first holiday, and died there of a sudden sickness. At five, Sara found herself with an English foster-mother who thought 'Kasee' too difficult to pronounce and renamed her 'Sara'. The little girl was left with few memories of her family except what she culled from diaries, letters and cuttings found in her late parents' family chests.

When Goodman had first told Sara that he was married she had recognised, by the sudden tightening of her soul strings and the sense of being let down, that he attracted her. If she had previously even considered such a thought she would have scoffed at herself. But now, feeling desolate, she took refuge in prayer.

Sara went to the local Gujarati temple, in Highgate, only on the main saints' days and then only when visited by Gujarati friends from Bradford. She had no family to bother about and she made sure her northern friends never suspected the source of her income. None the less she tried to pray twice daily and to fast once a week.

The phone rang and the caller, who had seen her advert in *Escort* magazine, turned nasty when she said she was fully booked for the day. She slammed the phone down on a torrent of abuse and pulled back the curtain which hid her little altar. Taking five small copper *diwa* bowls from the centrally placed silver dish, she filled them with ghee, purified butter, into which she inserted cotton wicks. When she had primed and lit all the *diwa* she knelt and prayed to her chosen deities, Laxmi, the goddess of good fortune, and Saraswati, the goddess of knowledge.

Sara sang the Aati, quite like the Lord's Prayer, in Gujarati, shuffling as she did so towards her right. Then she read a passage from the Mantra of Gaytri, goddess of the universe, and prayed that Gaytri guide her thoughts over the Christian Goodman in ways that would work well for them both.

At school in Tottenham Sara had attended lessons in the Christian faith, but the Divinity master had never forgiven her for her 'insolent' response to one of his questions. Noah's wife, she had suggested, was called Joan of Ark. She thought of Jesus as a good person and could never understand the elder generation of Tottenham Asians who denounced mixed marriage. Goodman, she decided, would make an excellent husband.

Nobody had excited her sexually for years and her job hadn't helped. But she remembered the feel of Goodman's smooth white skin when she had undressed and washed him for Dr Khimji.

She did not exactly pray to Laxmi that Goodman's wife *had* been murdered but the thought lurked not far from her consciousness.

Sailor and Goodman waited their turn in the reception room at Tottenham Police Station but a policewoman, seeing Goodman's bandages and livid facial bruising, took him, with Sailor in close attendance, to a side room.

'Like some tea, love?' she asked Goodman. 'You looked like you was goin' to faint in there.'

He agreed with a wan smile.

'And you?'

Sailor nodded. 'Give me four sugars.'

'What's the problem then?' she asked, placing three pink mugs on the table and opening a notebook.

Sailor told her how, the previous day, he and Goodman had been shopping together in Green Lanes when two large Jamaicans, one with a handgun, had attacked them and knocked Goodman to the ground. They had then stolen all Sailor's cash and disappeared.

'Why didn't you report this at once?'

Sailor gave her a long, rambling but persuasive story about having Goodman's wounds treated and the inadequacies of the National Health Service. He produced one of his five available sets of identity proofs and Goodman fished out his National Insurance form in the name of Andrew Smith.

The policewoman sighed. 'I'm going to have to report this as a major crime. I'll see if I can get someone from the CID to deal with you.'

As Sailor had predicted, the mention of a mugging involving a handgun enhanced the CID interest in their case and a detective constable soon arrived to take a statement. This led to an appointment being made with the C11 'witness albums' department at Scotland Yard because Sailor, who said he knew most 'local' Jamaican faces, swore he had never seen either of the muggers before.

The Tottenham DC ran both men to the Yard in a squad car and a C11 civil servant led them to a booth in the mugshot-index room. For an hour the young woman steered them through a succession of heavy, well-thumbed identity albums of African and Caribbean faces, both frontal and profile.

When Goodman came to the unmistakable face of Tricks he showed no reaction except to blow his nose. When all the albums were exhausted, they thanked the woman and the DC drove them back to Tottenham. He explained that little could be done without an identification and urged them to call him at once if ever they saw either mugger again.

'If you're quick and we're lucky, maybe we'll catch the bastards.'

He dropped them off at a café near Manor House, where Sailor stared hard at Goodman.

'Are you sure it was Tricks?'

'Yes.'

'The face you had your hand on as you blew your nose?'

'Yes. Yes.'

Sailor shook his head, bemused.

'Man,' he muttered, 'this boy is deep shit, I mean deep. Your

Tricks is Vix or Mafia, real name Stafford Douglas. Until about '83, early '84, he was mean but no don. Just small-time mean and small-time money. Guns and weed and girls and a couple of death contracts on his "friends" who got too big for their business boots.

'Then some JA police contact fixed him up with some Yanks with Mob connections who were wantin' to set up crack-wise in Europe. This put Mafia in a different league to most street Yardies. But he's still based partly in Brum and the West Midlands Police hate his guts. Mafia's got good contacts with the Customs boys at Heathrow and Brum Airport. In addition to his JA police crack source, he gets quite a bit of his cannabis from HM Customs at the airports. They take a cut of the proceeds. I'd grade him as mid-range powerful over here but he may be a dark horse. We'll need to look into things for you.'

'Do you know who the two Americans he was with might be?' Goodman's eyes were bright with the vision of success.

'I could maybe find out from Troon's Los Angeles clan. Ah Troon is a very old friend of mine, Korean and makes his bit workin' for the Tongs and the Triads. His clan are split between Seoul and LA. What I know about Mafia, Stafford Douglas, is through Troon. I doubt if even the UK police know half of what brother Mafia is up to 'cos he keeps his act real close to his chest. Even his Brum soldiers probably don't know what he's doin' with the Yanks.'

'So why would he be interested in badger digging?'

'From what you told me, I reckon some of his Yank friends were over here on their crack business with Mafia and he offered them some local fun up in Brum.'

'They called him Tricks, not Mafia.'

'Vix, Mafia, Tricks, whatever! Some of us use half a dozen street-names. It's good security. How about you, Alexo? How many names you got?'

Goodman smiled uncertainly at that.

'Where does he live?'

'Dunno. But I can find out. He may be in JA or the States, or Amsterdam, Bristol or Brum, or right here in the Manor. To some brothers he keeps a low profile and, as Mafia, runs a DJ show called Mafia Town, playin' reggae in the top clubs like the Porsche and the Hummin' Bird in Brum and Steppers in Brixton. To his Yank brothers he calls himself Vix or, you say, Tricks. He's a devious man, and I must tell you Alexo, I don't want no involvement for The Family with him, OK?'

'Whatever you say, Sailor.'

A pause followed. Goodman had learnt enough about Sailor not to interrupt his 'pools of silence'.

'Do you want Mafia topped?' Sailor asked at length.

'Topped?'

'You know my meanin'.'

Goodman did. 'My trouble now is Mary and Lucy. They have disappeared since that day we went walking. I have no proof they were hurt or even seen by the badger men, except for the scream. Could this man Mafia kill innocent women in cold blood?'

'He didn't kill you.'

'That's true but maybe he thought I was dead.'

Sailor nodded. 'Yes, Mafia could kill. He is cold and mean. They say he stashes crack in the home of his own mother but, when she needs money, he gives her nothin'.'

'If he killed Mary, if he touched a hair on their heads, I would say yes, Sailor. I would want him and his people "topped", whatever it cost.'

'OK, my friend.' Sailor smiled but his eyes were cold. 'I suggest first I try to locate Mafia through his associates, his soldiers. Find out all about his scene. Then, if you decide to make a move, at least we'll know where to find him. If you want to look at him, just to make one hundred per cent certain that Mafia and Tricks are the same, then we'll be able to take you to look at him. This you can leave to me.'

Again the pause, the pool of silence.

'Second,' Sailor said. 'You got to face goin' to that wood. I know you don't like this, but until you do you'll know nothin'. There may be clues there. Good ones or maybe bad ones. This you have to do or, man, you'll go mad not knowin' either way what's happened to your little ladies.'

'You will love them too, Sailor, when we find them.'

Sailor tried to smile with him.

Amy and Barry had parted soon after their shared nightmare on the Isle of Wight. Barry had reacted by telling Amy that, much as he adored her, she must choose between him and the Animal

Liberation Front. They were lucky, he said, to be alive. He would never again involve himself in any ALF activity.

Amy, on the other hand, was hardened by her encounter with Blackledge and his badger men. She determined to do everything in her power to fight back at such people. The ALF, she assumed, would be her best hope because many of their activists appeared willing to take risks. The problem, she soon discovered, was the natural ALF tendency to go for the easiest options. They made quick publicity bombing meat freezer trucks, exhuming the remains of aristocrats known to have been keen fox-hunters, planting incendiaries in furriers' and threatening isolated chicken farmers. With such activities they stood little chance of personal risk other than the popular martyrdom of a brief spell in prison. To risk the undercover work necessary to trap badger men involved extreme danger to life and limb and the vast majority of ALF activists were not prepared for this.

Amy was frustrated but not defeated. She heard on the ALF gossip grapevine of a North London cell specialising in fund-raising by unorthodox means, including drugs distribution. She decided that anyone prepared to lead the lethal life of the London street dealer to raise cash for the cause would be the right sort of person to help her crusade. A year after her traumatic experience on the Isle of Wight, Amy was living at 7 Alfoxton Avenue with a mix of squatters including two ALF heroin dealers and a bomb-maker. Their anarchic principles extended to their sleeping arrangements, which irritated Amy since the bomb-maker had halitosis and the dealers were lesbians. However, she put up with their unwelcome attentions for the sake of the end-game and this paid off, for the bomb-maker agreed to join in her plans to destroy individual badger men in their homes in the same way that they killed badgers in theirs. As a deterrent to others, Amy estimated that such action might prove compelling. Anyway it was worth trying and worth the occasional bonk from the bomb-maker with bad breath.

All wearing jeans and jackets, Taff Jones, Clive Mills and Barry Walker, of the St Anne's Crime Squad, were watching the Alfoxton Avenue house – the subject of ongoing day and night observation – from blue Escort B958 LBJ.

'Bingo,' Taff murmured. 'Long-legs and Chemist are back in their mini-van. This time we'll bottle them off.'

Tosh spent less than ten minutes with the ALF people. She found their whole set-up chaotic and could never forget the public support which ALF leaders like Robbie Lee gave to the IRA. She collected the cash that the lesbian dealers owed The Family. They were good regular customers for amphetamine sulphates but, as Tosh knew, they dealt mostly in heroin. She took a further order and left, noting the attractive blonde curled up in the squat's only visible armchair. She wondered if this decorative addition to the low life of number 7 was a lesbian anti-vivisectionist, an aristocrat's daughter turned New Age Traveller or a Special Branch plant.

Tosh failed to spot the watchers. Rear observation from a mini-van is about as efficient as that from a Lancaster bomber with no tail gunner. The blue Escort kept its distance and trailed the mini-van down Green Lanes and into Spring Park Drive beside the West Reservoir.

Tosh and Chemist split up as was their wont after leaving the van and took a circuitous route to the lab, then operating from 19 Peak House within the giant Woodberry Down Estate. Taff and Clive followed Tosh. Barry stuck with Chemist and, when both targets reunited at Peak House, Clive stayed to watch as his colleagues sped back to nearby St Anne's to collect the relevant snooping apparatus. Goodman, arriving on foot from Manor House tube station, was observed only by Clive, who did not recognise him.

Tosh, swearing at Art's habitual sloppiness, decanted chemicals into various containers.

'You come to help, Alex, or just to get in the way like some fiddlin' Taig?' she fired at Goodman as she slammed the door bolts back.

'If you're not too busy, I'd hoped to have a word with you,' he replied meekly.

'Well, Chemist is meant to be in charge this mornin' but he had a bad night so I'm doin' a spell for him.'

'Is there not some new drug that he could try?' Goodman asked.

'*Nil*. Not really. He's had a go at shiatsu, acupuncture, nutritional changes and NHS advice not to smoke, because that'll make him twice as likely to develop full-blown Aids. Also never to sit in the sun since that might bring on the lesions of Karposi's Sarcoma.'

'But smoking helps him bear it all.'

'Tough. Life's not fair, so it's not.'

'What'll happen to him, Tosh?'

'Only tomorrow knows the answer. Maybe there'll be a cure all of a sudden. But personally I would counsel "the quickest way out" when the suffering gets so bad the lad is merely survivin' for the sake of it . . . Euthanasia.'

'They say you've killed people.'

'Indeed, do they now? Who says that?'

'James.'

'Did he tell you I still do?'

'Yes, but he says you kill only those who blacken the face of the earth. That you and The Family stand for the underdog.'

'And the underbitch.' Tosh's expression was deadpan.

'Yes,' said Goodman, 'and the underbitch.'

'Why do you ask, Alex? Do you want somebody killed? Are you an underdog?'

'I came to see you because of my dreams. All this week now my nightmare has kept recurring. It has a classic theme. I see Mary and my little daughter Lucy running through deep woods and looking over their shoulders in terror. Their mouths are wide open, gasping for breath and screaming their fear. Then blackness wells up from behind and overwhelms them. I awake shouting their names.'

'What are your plans, Alex?'

'Tomorrow Columbo is taking me back to the wood, to the badger's hole. There may be clues.'

'If not?'

'I will have to approach Tricks, or Mafia as he apparently calls himself, for information.'

'That, I gather from Sailor, may not be so simple.'

'I may have no option.'

'Have you considered that Tricks and his friends may have killed your wife and daughter? What would you do then?'

'They were there to kill badgers. There would have been no point, no reason why they should have hurt Mary or Lucy.'

Tosh stared at Goodman. 'These badger men are violent bullies and most are hardened criminals. We have them all over Ireland. I dislike the Animal Libbers, who are so approvin' of the IRA, but I bear them no hard feelin's. The badger-baiters are different. I'd have no compunction rubbin' out a badger-baiter who had harmed your family, Alex. There's my answer even though you've not asked the question.'

'Thank you. Of course, I hope it will never come to that. I believe they, my loved ones, are still alive somewhere. But I have tried to prepare myself for the worst; to picture my reactions should the worst have happened, and to know what to do. To know that – as a business contract, of course – The Family, you, would be prepared to help me obtain whatever justice might be called for . . . that is enormously helpful.'

'You should consider the implications fully.'

'I have done. If they have hurt my family I would want them to suffer. I could not go to the police without losing my own freedom in the process. Normally I would have laughed at this. In the old days I was a great supporter of abolishing capital punishment and my father, an ex-army vicar, brought me up believing both in the utter sanctity of human life and in forgiveness. This past week, spent recovering and pondering, has allowed me to concentrate my thoughts. If they killed my family, I will kill them, use my money to have them killed. A better word would be "executed".'

'You say this as a general intention. But have you thought how?' Tosh asked.

'Presumably,' Goodman dissembled, 'you would prefer me to leave the method to your discretion?'

'There are many ways but my rule is ANC, and that's not the African National Congress. It stands for "Apparent Natural Causes". I'm on nobody's hit list, since leaving the UVF, because of ANC . . . And another thing, when vets put dogs to sleep, they do so with as little mess and fuss as possible. To them it is a job for which they are paid, their emotions are not involved and professionalism is all. That is how it is and has always been with me once I know that the dog should be terminated.'

'How can you satisfy yourself on that?' Goodman asked.

'I look at the facts and ask the question: "Would this person have been hanged by the government in the days of capital punishment?" That is the format I would apply to those responsible should you find that your family have been killed.'

'Do you always use the same method?'

'That's my secret, Alex, but I will tell you there are as many ways

208

of having people die without attracting the coroner's alarm as there are shamrocks in South Armagh. Sit yourself down, lad, and listen.'

Tosh adjusted taps and levers, topped up feeder tanks and lit a cigarette. There were, she began, between twenty and thirty professional contract killers in the United Kingdom and a similar number in France. In the USA she had heard estimates of over a hundred, of whom a dozen were women.

'In Britain,' she said, 'I think I'm unique, which is odd because women make excellent assassins. Nobody suspects us. We can be physically close with a man without alertin' him and, if we bulge in the right places, nine-tenths of a man's awareness will be blunted by desire, so we can easily draw him to remote spots without arousin' his suspicions.'

She explained that there was no 'going rate'. Just as prostitutes charge £5 to £5000 for ten minutes of their time, depending upon the wealth of the client, so murder missions are the subject of free market bargaining. Tosh considered herself to be the best in the ANC business and charged ceiling prices accordingly, 'except to friends'.

'There's many ways of killin' without clues, but back in Ireland, and ever since, I've concentrated on four methods: explosives, poisons, suffocation and "suicide".'

Later, when Tosh had finished her lecture on the dark arts of making murder simulate natural death, Goodman remained silent for a long time, playing with his hands. The Ulsterwoman lowered her voice, sounding almost gentle.

'Why, you may be askin' yourself, am I tellin' you these things? It's because I think you are a nice person. You should think about the sordid details of murder before you commission it. For me, I condone the deaths of my targets because they are always truly bad people. Otherwise, I would not be involved, even though I have for many years made a good part of my income as a paid dispatcher. Think well, Alex laddie, before you ask The Family to kill any human being. Once it is done, you can never undo it, but must live with the deed for the rest of your days.'

Goodman gave a weak smile which was intended to show his appreciation for Tosh's thoughtfulness. But, in truth, he was feeling somewhat queasy and was frightened she might spot the fact.

209

'When do you go to the wood?' she asked.

'When Columbo is free. Maybe tomorrow.'

'Well, I will pray for you that the news is not bad but I beg you to arm yourself with pessimism.' She rose and kissed his forehead. He thought it a miracle that anybody so beautiful and so capable of gentleness could have done, might still do, such unspeakable acts as she had just described to him.

'I must go,' she said. 'We are takin' shifts with Leon's boys to locate Mafia by tailing some of his known associates.'

17

October 1985

Korbi Richter spat the fish bone into his napkin. Stafford 'Mafia' Douglas, aka Tricks, found the German's manners in line with his personality: offensive. A shame because Mafia was otherwise enjoying the meal and the experience. That afternoon Richter was to take him to meet the bosses of Redden's Mexican cartel. He'd never been to Central America before. Brixton could have been a million miles away. It was good to relax; he had almost forgotten how.

They were lunching in the top-floor restaurant of one of Mexico City's tallest buildings, the forty-three-storey Latin American Tower with a breathtaking view on a rare smog-free day.

Richter enjoyed imparting knowledge, and appearing erudite, a particularly German trait, but Mafia Douglas was getting bored with his ongoing lecture on the subterranean instability that bedevilled the city, built as it was on a volcanic lake bed. He livened up when Richter unexpectedly asked him if he knew the man at a far corner table.

'The man with the military moustache?'

'Yes. His name is John Ridgway and he works with the FBI. He followed us from the airport. For four years he has been part of an operation coded Caesar, set up to bring down our organisation.'

'FBI?'

'Yes and no. We think Ridgway and some FBI colleagues may have set it up as a personal crusade. At least in part unofficial.'

'How do you know this?'

'We are well established in the intelligence community. Washington is porous, like Mexico City. It leaks its secrets and we make it our business to know where to catch the drips.'

'Do they know about our UK connection?'

'I doubt it. We learnt about Ridgway and Caesar only a month ago and have yet to pin down the extent of their knowledge. When we do, we will implement damage limitation, starting with Ridgway. I have a lady doctor friend in Los Angeles who works with people's minds. Under sedation, her patients invariably tell her what they know.'

'Why's he here?'

'I suspect he is interested in you. How you fit in with the organisation, who you are and why the two of us are in Mexico City. He or his people will keep us under close surveillance.'

'But the meeting this afternoon?'

'We will go by public transport. This they will not expect. Despite the subsidence, the city has an excellent twenty-six-mile subway system, fast, efficient and ideal to elude the likes of Ridgway. Also I have made arrangements to delay him.'

Richter's arrangements consisted of two mean-mouthed officers of Mexico's Gobernación secret police who sat down uninvited at Ridgway's corner table and, after ordering glasses, helped themselves to his wine carafe. JR Ridgway recognised them for who they were and waited. Secret police are the same the world over. An official badge was at length produced and the owner told JR he was suspected of illegally exporting Aztec artefacts of great value dug up by Mexico City subway diggers. They refused to furnish their reasons for such an accusation. When he had finished his meal, he was to accompany them to their headquarters from where he could call his embassy.

JR watched Richter and the black man leave the restaurant. He hoped that Díaz, his local assistant and driver, would be alert but he doubted it.

Two hours later, with no apology, one of the Gobernación men took a phone call and told JR there had been a case of mistaken identity and he was now free to leave. JR telephoned Jed Mason in Washington as soon as he had confirmed that Díaz had not seen Richter leave the restaurant with or without a black companion.

'The Mexican President is crooked,' Jed stormed. 'Their Attorney

212

General is bent. So what do you expect of their security services? Richter must have arranged it.'

'I have still worse news, Jed. Richter knows about Operation Caesar. He told his guest, the black guy whom he calls Tricks, that we have been after him for four years.'

'How do you know this?'

'I paid the waiter to change pepper pots when Richter had sat down. I'd bugged my pot on arrival.'

'Clever boy. So where's the leak?'

'Certainly not the Caesar team.'

'No, I agree. I'll give it some careful thought. What'll you do?'

'There's no way I'm going to find these bastards in Mexico City by chance so I'll head back to LA.'

JR rang off and ordered a stiff whisky. He suspected that Caesar had been compromised by the CIA. Jed had instigated Caesar as an offshoot of a CENTAC operation during which he had first come across Korbi Richter. CENTAC had CIA involvements. That could well be the leak.

Few people, at most perhaps a dozen of America's senior security men, were privy to the inner structures of CENTAC, yet for ten years it had remained the only body in existence capable of attacking the power and corruption of the world's great international drug syndicates.

In 1970 the two main US drug enforcement bodies, then the Bureau of Customs and the Bureau of Narcotics and Dangerous Drugs, were riven with jealousy and internal power struggles. In 1973 they were merged to become the Drug Enforcement Administration. Recognising the unprecedented and growing power of cross-border drug barons, Tony Pohl, boss of Washington's DEA, in 1973 created CENTAC despite opposition from many powerful CIA and DEA directors. Although CENTAC was officially controlled from within the DEA, its actions and its power went beyond those of that organisation. Each operation under its aegis was given a number and called a CENTAC. CENTAC-24, for example, aimed at a Far Eastern drug empire, employed fifty-two enforcement officers, intelligence operatives, FBI analysts and CIA directors in one way or another. The advantages were obvious. Control came from a single source, the CENTAC director, but the resources of all the federal and state facilities were available without the usual delay caused by too many departmental chiefs all wanting their say.

The disadvantage was the danger of leaks, which, as Ridgway acknowledged, could come from a number of sources. The prime suspects in this case must be the CIA and not just because their director William Casey included Albert Redden among the Friends. That was merely incidental to the wider dichotomy, the fact that CIA operatives worked with, lied for and paid bribes to the world's most active criminals in order to achieve their prime CIA aim, the defeat of communism, which meant maintaining good relations even with cocaine-conniving governments.

Many South American governments are implicitly involved in drugs and their narco-trade is often protected by the US Government through the State Department and the CIA. Venezuelan oil, for example, is more important to the USA than the cessation of Venezuelan-sponsored drug activities.

The CIA reacts with aggression in the Washington corridors of power when other 'lesser' agencies such as the FBI, DEA and CENTAC try to bring them to book. In many CIA eyes, almost any crime can be condoned if it furthers the cause of patriotism.

When the great oil-price hikes of the 1970s collapsed, cocaine money (known to bankers as coca-dollars) took over from petrodollars so that, by the mid-1980s, Swiss banks held ten times more money belonging to tiny Caribbean nations with drug connections than funds from Canada, and twice as much as from West Germany.

Intelligence takes precedence over law enforcement so that criminals with diplomatic connections, the Ochoas, Reddens and Noriegas, are left alone for as long as possible and even paid retainers, so that they can continue to pass intelligence to and do dirty work for the CIA, the action arm of the State Department, irrespective of the drug billions these same cocaine barons are generating from the addicts that the US Government has openly pledged to help. International crime can eventually ascend through politics and diplomacy to a level where, having triumphed over all its enemies, the likes of John Ridgway, it then controls even the very agencies designed to suppress it. At that point crime is no longer identifiable as such by those whose job it should be to overcome it.

JR was tired of hearing Reagan rant on about his government's war on drugs. Only by destroying the drugs at their source could such a war be won, but the leaders in drug source countries wanted power and riches, so they often participated in the traffic and made it clear to Washington that they would brook no interference. The CIA went along with this more often than not to maintain intelligence and diplomatic rapport. If other US agencies crossed their path, the CIA could turn lethal.

JR remembered an old DEA friend, Mike Powers, assigned to north Thailand. Powers was too successful for his own good and local Thai dealers had his wife killed as a warning. Powers then turned his considerable talents to unearthing her assassins, but the CIA, cooperating at that time with the relevant Thai drug barons, did all within their power to block and discredit Powers. This despite the fact that, before joining the DEA, he had for years been their most successful agent in Vietnam, won many medals and dined with the CIA's Director.

JR's many CIA friends would always appear shocked when he mentioned examples of CIA support for drug networks but none would deny that they had 'dealings' with dealers. 'What would you do,' they would respond, 'if you had to choose between turning in a crack dealer and leaving him in a position from which he can inform the CIA about anti-American terrorists?'

Redden and Richter, JR knew, dealt in high-level international crime with the fall-back protection of the CIA *and*, he believed, high-level FBI people. This Mexican incident was the first time JR suspected 'on the ground' CIA interference. He replenished his drink and raised his glass high. Caesar would put Redden and Richter away, CIA or no CIA.

In loose-fitting mechanics' overalls and carrying a toolbag between them, Richter and Mafia emerged from the tradesmen's entrance of the Latin American Tower. Richter headed for Calzada San Antonio, between the City Hall and Supreme Court, to enter the Metro system. He waved at the great cathedral ahead of them.

'Today's metropolis is nothing,' he lectured Mafia. 'Just a filthy city of pollution and poverty, a drain on our US resources but only 400 years ago, when the Spaniards arrived, this lake island was the greatest cultural centre in the Americas, the sun city of Tenochtitlán. There were huge pyramids here for sacrifices. At a single ceremony the Aztec priests ripped out 19,000 living hearts to placate the gods.'

Mafia made no comment on Richter's definition of culture.

They were met at a metro station in the Puente de Alvarado by four agents of the MFJP, Mexico's FBI, who escorted them by a works tunnel to a waiting limousine.

'Nobody has followed you,' the senior agent assured Richter. They removed their overalls in the car which took them out of the city to a sweltering plain, the bed of the lake that once protected the island city of Tenochtitlán. They passed through Squat City, a region of countless low-rent apartment blocks and five-storey condominiums built for the never-ending flood of immigrants from rural Mexico and Central America.

After passing the smog-enshrouded bulk of Cerro de la Estrella, they entered a chaotic industrial region and Richter switched from tourist guide to business mode.

'Soon we will enter the new site. You will see why we have taken over this business. Mexico is the ideal alternative to Miami. We do not want all our eggs in one basket, especially one liable to become as hot as Miami after we begin to push for business which the Ochoa cartel consider to be theirs. Colombians and Cubans run their business. We believe in Jamaicans. Your people have shown themselves to be more ruthless than the Latinos. We like that.'

Mafia nodded his appreciation of this high praise.

'*Na ja*,' Richter grunted, moving on. 'We will discuss our overall plan when we arrive but there are two points just for your ears.'

Mafia was not so happy with Richter's first point. He was to bring IRA and/or Loyalist paramilitary arms buyers to Miami the following month to witness the effect of the new HTA fire-storm pack. Many people survive explosive bombs, as all terrorists are well aware. Margaret Thatcher in Britain and Hitler at his Wolf's Lair are but two examples. With HTA there would be no such inefficiency. Every human being and every document would be burnt to a cinder, with no trace element, no tell-tale bomb fragment, left behind.

Although the HTA device already had a market in Pakistan, Redden was looking for other clients and liked the idea of combining two businesses. When, in a month's time, the representatives of the Colombian cartel met up with their intended European partners, the Corsican Ricord group in Miami, there was to be a beautifully executed HTA burning. What better sales pitch than for

216

prospective buyers to witness the 'real thing': the neat immolation of Redden's competitors.

Mafia had no IRA or Loyalist paramilitary contacts but he knew better than to say so. He agreed to find suitable potential HTA buyers. 'And your second point?' he prompted.

Richter nodded. 'We will be arriving soon at our new site, Rodríguez Freezapak. I will introduce you to the two directors. We have no problems with the senior man, Rafael Fonseca. He is pliable and clever. Also, he has the right Mexican contacts, including the head policeman, MFJP Director Manuel Ibarra. But Fonseca's number two, Miguel Duraz, is too ambitious. He dislikes the coming together of our interests. I suspect that, when we first approached Rodríguez, he tried to block us. Very shtumm. Our job for you is simple. Duraz will shortly be sent to Italy to buy technical equipment of a medical nature and, as his European contact, you will naturally look after him during his visit. Once he has finished organising the shipment of this European gear, you will ensure that he vanishes. Then send details for us to pass to the good Mr Fonseca explaining the death of Duraz in some natural accident. Is this clear?'

Mafia said that it was.

'Good. Then Duraz will be replaced at Rodríguez by our own man, who, in the course of time and when he has learnt all that Fonseca has to offer, will have Fonseca himself sent on a mission to Europe. Such is life, *ney?*'

Rodríguez Freezapak, deep in the heart of an industrial complex which smelled as though it would be lethal to live and breathe in for more than an hour, took up an area the size of four football grounds and was entirely surrounded by twelve-foot steel net fencing backed with plywood and topped with high-voltage live wire. The double gates opened after a phone conversation between their chauffeur and an unseen doorkeeper.

Mafia counted more than forty giant freezer trucks parked about the compound before he gave up. There may well have been twice that number. They drove to a single-storey block laid out like an army headquarters with a central corridor and offices off to both sides.

Fonseca and Duraz greeted them with the respect due to the new company owners. There were no Reception signs, Mafia noted;

217

visitors were perhaps a rare event. All around him he heard the hum and rush of the conditioner units which protruded like black incubi from the otherwise monotone grey of the buildings. The overall chemical stench of the city's polluted air was indefinably different here.

After Mexican coffee and sweetmeats Fonseca asked Richter, of whom he seemed afraid, if they would like to look around the site.

'*Natürlich*, but first, Herr Fonseca, I would like to explain why I have brought our European representative, Mr Douglas, here to meet you. The Italian refrigeration gear about which we have corresponded will soon be available at a knock-down price as the factory owners are bankrupt. We suggest that one of you go to Europe early next month to check there is no technical reason we should not use it as a basis for expansion here.'

As Richter had rightly surmised, Duraz was nominated for the job and Mafia expressed himself happy to meet him in London before travelling with him to Turin.

'Expansion is vital,' Richter enthused, 'because our organisation has big plans for the immediate future. The cocaine from all South American countries has to pass through the bottleneck of the northernmost country, Colombia, in order to reach the USA. Thanks to their stranglehold on virtually all South American cocaine, including their own, the Colombian barons control the source of our wealth. The Medellín cartel is by far the most powerful group, with the Ochoa family and Escobar at the forefront, *ney*?'

Everyone nodded. So far all was common knowledge.

'From the Colombian jungle airstrips, never mind what goes by sea, countless tonnes of coca are flown over the Caribbean Sea to the USA. Florida is the natural arrival point so we have our distribution centre there. So does Ochoa and everyone else. The Miami Police Department is fortunately corrupt but there are signs that the US Government intends to stamp on Miami with big boots. OK, this is reason number one for us to set up an alternate distribution point. Look at a map and you see only one other suitable spot, Mexico. For camouflage, a mega-sprawl just like Miami would be best. Many millions of *mensch* in one spot so . . . Mexico City, *ney*?' He flashed his quick, cold smile.

'From here we will distribute to all the major US cities which already receive your South American meat. For us the beauty of your Rodríguez Freezapak system is that, because you have your own illegal cargo for the US medical market, you already have in place your tame Customs and your dummy compartments in all the trucks in addition to your air-cargo containers to Europe. All we have to do is share space. Some individuals might shrink at the idea of such a trade but, Mr Tricks, your Englishman Samuel Butler had it right. He said: "Morality is the custom of your country and the current feeling of your peers. Therefore cannibalism is moral in a cannibal country." Cocaine and frozen human parts, a neat combination, *ney*?'

Mafia, the only person previously ignorant of the nature of Rodríguez Freezapak's speciality product, was impressed by Richter's logic.

'You, Mr Tricks,' Richter continued, 'need not worry about distribution in Europe of the business in human parts since Herr Fonseca already has that well in hand. Today, however, we will discuss how best to arrange the packaging and subsequent separation of the cocaine. Both commodities will leave here in the same containers for the same European destinations, the system we are already processing successfully to the States thanks to the efficiency of Mr Fonseca and Mr Duraz.'

A dark-skinned Asian knocked and entered. He addressed Duraz.

'Rahman is ready to show us the system,' Duraz said, looking at his watch. 'We have to access the refrigeration at certain times.'

'Be patient, my friends,' Richter said. 'I have not finished.'

For another hour he covered the overall plans. Those that affected Mafia involved the considerable increase of cocaine shipments soon to enter the UK from Mexico in addition to the normal Florida-sourced supplies. He foresaw no difficulties in widening his markets. It was a matter of deciding which other UK-based Yardie dons to remove from the scene. When Richter had finished, Fonseca introduced their site guide. 'Rahman, like all our staff, is from Bangladesh. Unemployment is rife in his country, whereas here the pay is good and there are bonus incentives. These are removed if there is any security lapse. Rahman, our surgeons and other specialists are all Muslim Urdu-speaking Biharis, and all were involved in 1971 in the killing of their brother Bengalis in East Pakistan. They collaborated with the invading West Pakistan Army and in nine months helped murder over two million fellow-Bengalis.

When the Indian Army intervened and East Pakistan became independent, Bangladeshi "collaborators" like Rahman were hunted down and executed. They are still wanted men at home but here they are the backbone of Rodríguez.' He placed his arm across the fragile shoulders of the Bihari as though patting a dog.

Rahman spoke good English. First he took them to his own office and showed them a map of the plant.

'The compound is divided in two. The meat packaging and freezing side takes up two-thirds of the whole area. Nobody from the meat side can enter, or see into, our "secure" zone, but once one of the fridge trucks is loaded with meat it is driven to the secure Weigh-in hangar and left there for an hour or two by the driver. At that point our people load the truck's dummy compartment with the cocaine and the human organs destined for the same city as the meat.'

Rahman's pointer stick moved across the diagram.

'The secure zone consists of three main buildings, all of which you will soon see. Our freezer vans collect bodies from nine different points around the city and deliver them to the Arrivals Block. Here they are prepared, washed, pruned of hair, teeth and, if a graded disease is identified, discarded. Then, labelled, they are sent either as bodies ordered in their entirety to the Exit Building or, if they are to be cut up, they go to our Operations Building. In Operations they are prepared for individual orders. A single body may end up, for instance, with kidneys for Chicago, eyes for Topeka and heart for St Paul. All unwanted items from Arrivals and from Operations are crushed, boxed and driven by the collection vans to a contract incinerator business. Any queries?'

Mafia, who had seen many live humans abused and knifed over the years, was beginning to feel uneasy and not looking forward to the factory tour.

'Once Operations have completed the surgery and packaging, the addressed parcels are moved to the Exit Building, where they join the whole-body packs for crating and loading in the Weigh-in hangar. When the driver returns from the meat side of the compound to his truck in the hangar he has no idea that anything has been added to his load.'

The small group proceeded to the Arrivals Block. A guard at the entry door moved aside and they entered a brilliantly lit atrium filled with neat rows of steel trolleys, each bearing a naked body with a yellow label stapled to a kneecap.

'A part of the body seldom recycled,' Duraz explained.

Mafia, despite the cold of the refrigerated room, felt the first stirrings of nausea. The glazed marble eyes of a Latino girl, too young for pubescent hair, stared up at him from the nearest trolley. He noticed a bullet exit hole in her stomach. She had been shot running away from her killer.

'Mr Richter,' he said, 'I do not need to inspect the building to do my part.'

Richter's lip curled. 'I understand. Of course. Fonseca?'

Fonseca asked Duraz to escort Mafia back to the office. When they had gone Fonseca said, 'If your friend is unhappy in Arrivals it is as well he does not come with us to Operations. We have six Bengali surgeons there dissecting some two hundred units each week.'

Outside Mafia loosened his tie, relieved to be out of the charnel-house.

'Who are the end-users of your bodies?' he asked.

Duraz shrugged. 'That's not my business. Obviously organ transplant procedures are highly complex, as indeed is our removal work, so top-level surgical facilities are vital. Many countries have a chronic shortage of organs. The recent progress of medical technology has made transplants commonplace. Hundreds of thousands of rich people can prolong their lives with a transplant. We know of seventeen major facilities in North America employing two or three dozen specialist staff and surgeons of the highest competence, some but not all of whom have been struck off their country's official register. In countries with organ shortages, wealthy people fly abroad to get fixed up. We call them organ-tourists. India is a popular place for this.'

'So most of your spare parts get re-exported from the States?'

'A high ratio, yes, but not the majority. Only a fifth of the 200,000 US annual transplants are recorded in their National Register. The rest, performed by private and often illegal clinics, rely on the purchase of organs wherever they can get them. If they deal with the sales agents of a reputable company, such as ourselves, they avoid the dangers of fly-by-night operators who remove, store and transport under less than perfect conditions. This can be extremely

221

risky for the transplant recipient and gets a bad name for the relevant clinic.'

'And the bodies – who were they?'

Duraz raised his hands skywards. 'Who can say? Ninety per cent are children between five and twelve years from Central and South America and from backgrounds of poverty. The other ten per cent, also from these countries, are assassinated or "disappeared" and then passed to us. Sixty-eight thousand Guatemalans have officially disappeared in the past twenty years and lesser numbers in Salvador, Chile, Uruguay and so on. In Honduras, some of our best sources are the *casas de engorde*, fattening warehouses, where they store kidnapped children. The street catchers are paid 200 lempiras, $300, for a reasonable child. From these holding pools, we can order up what we want when we need. The warehouse keepers also provide children for adoption or prostitution, so not all the inmates will end up in little pieces. If they catch a child destined for us away from a cold room they will chloroform it and transport it live to a fridge facility. At present we get about 300 bodies a month from Central America. They seldom get caught, although foreign journalists have been shown little corpses carelessly left on city dumps with surgery scars, missing eyeballs and kidneys.'

'So it's a one-way export business from South to North America?' Now that he was away from the bodies themselves, Mafia's unease had vanished. He was fascinated.

'Of course the Latino clinics and universities need organs but they are self-sufficient. The city police and paramilitaries who keep the streets clean of beggars and thieves have to round up bands of sewer urchins. Brazil uses its own poor to patch up its rich. The same holds good here in Mexico. We have abduction rings in Zacetecas, Durango and Aguas Calientes states serving our private clinics in Tijuana and Ciudad Juárez. It's all just supply and demand.'

'You make it sound like official policy.'

'Not here in Mexico. No. Not yet. But China earns good foreign currency by selling kidneys and other parts taken from executed prisoners. The Chinese Minister of Justice has decreed that prisoners must be executed in a manner which preserves all organs of value. He said the purpose of allowing sentenced criminals to donate their organs is to "help them fulfil their desire to contribute their love for society". Maybe that's what we at Rodríguez are doing . . . Where are you from?'

'Jamaica. But England just now.'

'Well, the English were pioneers in this trade. Two centuries ago they allowed Tyburn corpses to be dissected by eminent physicians. Within minutes of a hanged person's last kick, the medical vultures would cut away arteries and veins, lungs and bile. Last year a Wimpole Street haematologist was caught making a fortune selling white corpuscles to Holland . . . *Joi Bangla*.'

'What?'

'Listen.' Duraz raised his finger.

From the area of the Arrivals Block, Mafia thought he heard a plaintive song and the thin, unworldly music of some unseen instrument.

'That is Abidur, our storeman and bard. He plays a two-stringed Bengali *dotara*, a mandolin, and sings the songs of their poet Rabindranath Tagore. If there was a Bengali corpse in there, it would sit up and sing along with Abidur.'

For a moment the two men sat and listened to the music from the Dantesque room next door.

'I am learning Bengali,' Duraz told him. '*Joi Bangla* means "Victory to Bengal".'

Mafia quite liked Duraz. He wondered idly how he would dispose of him after their Italian trip. He preferred to concentrate his thoughts on selling arson bombs to IRA terrorists rather than on morgues and human bits. He shivered to echoes of the long-forgotten voodoo of his youth.

18

October 1985

'Could do with some of that sunshine here.' Paul Martin was making conversation. He was the only local Isle of Wight man present in The White Lion pub in Arreton. The five badger diggers were all over from mainland Hampshire for the weekend's sport. The endless terrier gossip had lapsed at the onset of ITN's *Ten O'Clock News*, currently showing Princess Diana soaking up adulation and the sun in Australia.

Five months earlier, sickened by what he saw happening on badger digs, Paul had approached Terry Spamer, long-time RSPCA Special Operations Unit boss and undercover strategist. He had then agreed to undertake the hazardous and unpaid role of supergrass to help Spamer catch diggers at work.

For the police to stand any chance of successful court action against badger diggers, they had to be in on the action and this meant upfront detailed knowledge of planned digs. To follow the diggers by car was virtually impossible since they travelled to remote spots in the early hours, when they could easily spot any RSPCA or police tail.

Most Fridays, visiting diggers and hare coursers from the mainland met at favoured Isle of White pubs such as The White Lion to get pissed on Whitbread's and Gale's ale and brag to one another about their dogs, many of whom were in the bar, and about famous past digs. Paul Martin had learnt to be cautious. He knew that Stephen Clifton, one of the most avid local diggers, was also the professional Huntsman of the Isle of Wight Hunt. Paul had warned

Terry Spamer of the RSPCA not to tie in yet with the Isle of Wight police in case any of them were diggers out of hours and especially not to mention his undercover work. 'Do that and I'm a dead man,' he warned.

'I'd give her one,' a Portsmouth digger exclaimed, craning his neck to view the TV screen behind the bar. The Princess of Wales had appeared in a short, lime-green dress.

'I reckon she's overrated, myself,' Jake, a scaffolder from Bournemouth, offered, 'but I'd not jump over her to get at you.'

Loud guffaws rewarded this rating of the royal attractions.

'I stuck a twelve-bore barrel up a duchess once,' said Alfie from Preston. 'It were on her estate and she'd interrupted a good dig. We saw her off all right but we had to abandon the sport.'

Various anecdotes followed, each more dramatic than the last, on the topic of violent reactions to interference by the public. Jake the scaffolder, well tanked up and not to be outdone, won an eager silence by dropping a cryptic comment into the hubbub. 'We killed three of them,' he announced casually, looking up at the old flintlocks on the pub walls.

'You killed three Joe Public in Bournemouth! Pull the other one, Jake. You – never!'

'No. Not in Bournemouth. I only been down south for a year. This was up near Brum, where I was then. Place called Kinver Wood, full of good brocks. I used to help out ol' Amphets Trev every now and again and one weekend we did a dig for some Yanks. Well, this family appear out of nowhere and the husband gets all snotty. "Don't be so cruel!" he says. "Stop this at once!" Anyway, a big black geezer with these Yanks tells me to search the bushes. They tie up the family, all three of them, and a week later when ol' Trev gets to pay us off, he says, "Don't tell nobody you was in Kinver 'cos we had to do them all in." '

'What happened?' The other diggers were listening eagerly.

'Nowt. Or if it did I never heard about it. Mind you, Trevor disappeared not long afterwards. Never did get any more work from him. Right nutter he was and all.'

A few minutes later, having bought a round for the diggers, Paul headed for the Gents but detoured to the public phone. He called a number from his pocket diary and left a message. Then he returned to the bar.

Next morning Amy called Paul back at his boat builder's office in Wootton. The excitement in her voice was obvious. They had met only once since the day she and Barry had joined Blackledge's Isle of Wight dig and been saved by Paul's quick thinking.

Paul had promised her he would let her know if ever he heard of any further Blackledge activity. She had told him she would not rest until she had the man caught red-handed and put away where he belonged.

'And you're quite certain this was Blackledge he was talking about?' she pressed.

'Well, Jake never mentioned him by name but the place is right . . . Kinver Wood is up Birmingham way. He's always been active up there and Amphets Trev often worked for him.'

'So if the three corpses are still there, and we could put this Jake in the dock as a witness, we could nail Blackledge for murder?'

'It seems possible. That's why I called you.'

'I'm really grateful, Paul. Can you find out where Jake lives?'

'I'll try.'

'Great. Then we can go and visit him. Find out exactly where the wood and the sett are and get Blackledge's address.'

'But this Jake is no saint. He's not going to like your waltzing up out of nowhere and asking pertinent questions. At best he'll give you two fingers. At worst you could be at risk. You, above all people, should know not to muck around with the likes of Jake.'

The following morning Paul called Amy to apologise. He had not been able to get details of Jake's address except that he lived in a rented bedsit in Bournemouth and moonlighted as a freelance scaffolder. 'I can't afford to appear overcurious,' Paul explained. 'He avoided the various innocent ploys I tried to get his address. I'm sorry. If I think of a way I'll let you know soonest.'

Amy thanked Paul and called an ALF acquaintance in Bournemouth whom she knew only by his action-cell name of Ben. From sleepy Bournemouth, Ben had masterminded a poisoned Mars bar hoax the previous year which cost the chocolate company £3 million. She asked him to locate Jake for her and two days later was called by someone called Sylvia, who gave her Jake's full address and a short CV. As always, Amy was impressed by the ALF's nationwide ability to track people down. Although many were punks, anarchists and thugs, there were over 100,000 members, of whom a majority were staid, middle-aged professional people, including a sprinkling of civil servants and clerks with access to useful records and files.

'Be careful,' Sylvia warned her. 'This bastard is speciesism scum of the most dangerous sort.'

Amy thanked her and drove to Bournemouth, where she had to wait all day parked outside Jake's bedsit. When he returned, towards 8 p.m., Amy appeared at his side as he fumbled with his door key.

'The ALF,' she said, 'are planning to kill you. I've come to warn you.'

This tactic worked well, as any badger digger exposed in court can expect threats and hate mail from the ALF. At any rate Jake was worried enough to invite Amy into his foul-smelling pad. A badly skinned fox pelt was partially responsible and piles of unwashed clothing did not help. Amy wasted no time in coming to the point.

'This is £250.' She slapped the notes down on a heap of terrier magazines. 'In return I want information.'

'But the ALF? You said . . .'

'Forget the ALF. I'm nothing to do with them. I just need two items of information.'

'Who're you? Police? RSPCA?'

'Neither.' Amy removed the money and stuffed it back in her briefcase. She did not like handbags and the image that she thought went with them. 'I need to know the location of a badger sett and the address of one of your friends, a dog man.' Then, she added, by way of creating confusion: 'It has to do with stolen goods that have been buried.'

'I've never stolen nowt,' Jake protested.

'Of course you haven't,' she sighed. 'Give me the information and you can forget I was ever here. I'll tell nobody.'

'You're saying you'll give me the 250 smart ones if I tell you where a badger sett is? That's it?'

'Right.'

'Give me the cash first.'

Amy was ready for this. 'I'm happy to do that but let me tell you which sett I'm after. You and others killed a family of three there last year.'

'That's lies! I never killed nobody. Not last year. Not ever!'

227

'Fair enough. You never killed them. But you know where it was.'

'Listen, girl. I don't know who you are or where you're from. All I can tell you is I had nowt to do with it. I was there right enough but I didn't see nobody topped. One of the boys, Trevor, told me later about the killings but I had nowt, I tell you nowt, to do with it.'

'So you can't help?' Amy stood up.

'Wait. I didn't say that. I just said I didn't do it. I could help put you on to a bloke up Brum way who'd answer both your questions. How's that?'

Amy shrugged. 'That'll have to do me, I suppose.'

'Give us the money, then.'

She handed him the notes and Jake counted them laboriously. It was peanuts to her. The Alfoxton Avenue ALF cell was spending that much daily on luxury groceries alone. Their drugs business was booming.

Jake stuffed the money into a pocket and smiled at her crookedly. 'So now I just have to tell you to get the fuck out of here.'

'Do that,' Amy said quietly, 'and you'll find out who my friends really are and you'll wish you hadn't.'

'OK. Listen. I'll draw you a sketch of this bloke's place as I remember it. You'll have to get yourself a proper map, but when you reach Kinver village use this.'

He drew a crude set of directions to a property some two miles from Kinver.

'He lives over here but drives his dogs daily to the woods south of Compton Road, and when ol' Trev drove us to the dig in his van afore the others arrived, we had to drive this bloke back to his place smartish. He said he'd like to join in the fun but Trev knew better.'

'So this man was your local contact, your guide to the setts?'

'Christ! That's what I said, innit? It was him that met up with the bloke what paid Trev and the rest of us. You want to know where the sett is and where Trev's client lives? OK. That's the fella what'll know. I've not seen Trev for months. Don't have a number for him either.'

'This man – he'll talk to me?'

'Don't ask me! Maybe he will. After all, I'm talking to you, ain't I? You can buy most geezers if you pay them enough.'

Back at the commune, and remembering her Isle of Wight

experience at Blackledge's hands, Amy decided not to visit Kinver alone. She waited until the following Wednesday, that being the weekday when 'Oxley', the bomb-maker, slept with her. She had recently attacked him on the topic of his bad breath with the result that he now took Amplex tablets like other people eat Smarties and had become almost bearable in bed.

Oxley was a secretive sort who had named himself after his ALF hero, Sheffield bomb-maker and mini-incendiary pioneer Ian Oxley, who specialised in cigarette packets containing a mix of weedkiller, sugar, petrol and washing-up liquid controlled by a cunning electrical and mechanical circuit.

Oxley was devoted to Amy, but his motto was 'most things in moderation', so he smoked only three cigarettes a day and visited Amy's bedroom only on Wednesdays. He was small but wiry and Amy decided he would provide at least basic protection whereas her other two ALF flatmates, *outré* lesbians given to hysteria, might scream at the first flutter of violence.

'I've often thought we should do more to fight the diggers and baiters,' Oxley echoed Amy's sentiments. 'We spend too much time focused on scientists and furriers who hurt animals for commercial motives, but minimal effort combating the sadists who kill for sheer pleasure. No, I'm delighted to do my bit against these villains of yours.'

'We'll need money.' Amy was quick to spot the right moment. The previous week she had wheedled enough funds from the coffers of the two lesbians to pay off Jake in Bournemouth. She feared that their Kinver target might be more expensive to bribe.

'They give me only just enough for my basic materials,' Oxley told her. 'I've nothing in the kitty at present.'

'Come on. You supply your bombs to over thirty cells in the Home Counties alone. Throw your weight about for once. Crudité is putty in your hands.'

This was true, the younger lesbian had a soft spot for Oxley, for she loved food and he was the only cook at Alfoxton. Oxley soon gave in to Amy's pressure. He invented a sudden rise in the retail cost of weedkiller and Crudité released £500 in cash. Thus armed and travelling in Oxley's shabby delivery van, they drove to Kinver and found without difficulty the house Jake had described. The place smelled of dung and a cacophony of dogs yapped from hidden kennels. Amy had briefed Oxley well.

'Excuse me, sir, madam.' Oxley doffed his tweed cap at the surly character who answered to his knocking. 'We are from the Veterinary Service. To be precise, the Consultative Panel on Badgers and Bovine Tuberculosis for the Hereford & Worcester and Staffordshire district. Can we ask your advice on this immediate area? We will only trespass briefly on your valuable time.'

'Go on, then,' the man growled, offering them neither a cup of tea nor a seat. His wife, a vague shape in the background, looked embarrassed but said nothing.

Amy took over, opening her briefcase and checking some notes. 'We have reports of diseased badgers caught in Brindley's Dingle to the north of Kinver and affecting the Compton Hall herd. Likewise in Bodenham Wood to the south. We need to check this area too, if we may, and would value your advice on any active setts that you know of.'

'Does it have to be today? I'm bloody busy.'

'We have come a long way, sir,' Oxley said quietly, 'and have a large area to cover. The Wombourne police advised us on which properties we should visit and told us you are always helpful.'

'Did they now? Well . . . You got a map?'

Amy hastily produced a 1:10,000 Ordnance Survey sheet covering the Wolverley and Kinver area. 'Do you have somewhere from where we can see the ground?' she asked him.

'Right outside the door'll do,' the man grunted.

They put the map on the roof of Oxley's van. Amy produced a Metropolitan Police badge. She was uncertain whether this was the real thing or a forgery. Following a major ALF raid on the Wickham Laboratories in Hampshire the previous year, she had been given the badge by a boyfriend in the Front who was subsequently jailed.

'We did not wish to alarm your wife, sir' – Amy's voice was now harsh and determined – 'but we are investigating a murder.'

'What?' The man's face had gone ashen. 'You mean this has nothing to do with badgers? Why come here? There's been no murders here. Never, never. That badge is London Police. What you doing up here?'

Amy thought the man might well have a stroke. The veins in his cheeks were suffused and his hands were clutching at Oxley's van's wing mirror as though for support.

'At present you, sir, are not under suspicion. We were called in by the local police because this involves drug dealers participating also in the sale of badgers for dogfights in our London area.'

The man's mind raced. He knew now what this was about.

'Look, I know nothing about drugs and nothing about murders. We do have a brock problem round here and, off the record . . . ?'

Amy nodded.

'Well, everyone does it. The brutes spread TB if you let them run wild so we fill in their setts, pipe slurry down their holes. But you can't get the tractor near enough sometimes, or else stripies come off public land on to the farms and you can't slurry public areas, can you?'

Amy and Oxley said nothing. They had played it right. With luck they wouldn't even need the bribery funds.

'So when these geezers from Brum came along last year with their terriers asking if I had any foxes I wanted rid of, I told them about the main brock setts round here. I know that's what they were after. Not foxes!'

'How far away are these setts?' Amy asked. 'We'll need to see them.'

'Well, I told them about three different setts but they were only interested in something near a road – easy access. I remember that because normally their type likes to keep well away from roads. So I told them about the Valehead sett 'cos that's just off Kingsford Lane. In fact those brocks don't bother us much out here – too far away. But there's no other sett, as I know of, so close by a road.'

'Can you identify it on this map?' Oxley asked.

'I expect so.' He reached for his glasses and peered at the map. 'Hereabouts,' he said. 'About two hundred yards west of the lane. There's a path put in by the Manpower team in 1983 which passes within maybe twenty yards of the sett. See the "K" of Kinver Edge. The sett's about the width of my thumb from the "K" to the lane and just where the lane begins to bend west.'

'Could you take us there? Our van's full of gear.'

With bad grace the man drove them to the sett. The journey took less than ten minutes and the walk into the wood from Kingsford

Lane a mere two minutes. Later, back at the man's home, Amy was blunt. He should not be given time to think.

'We appreciate your cooperation, sir, but we need the names of these men. I believe your assertion that you had nothing to do with their activities and your continued cooperation would indicate that you are not shielding them.'

'Officer,' the man almost pleaded, 'I would love to tell you names but these were rough types. I had no wish to antagonise them. If they had told me their names they would probably have been false. I saw no point in asking. They drove a white Escort van. That's all I know. I just wanted rid of them. It must be well over a year ago now. I can't remember what they looked like.'

Amy could see the man was trying to avoid having to help prepare an Identikit. 'If they ever come again,' she told him, 'please call us at this number immediately.' She wrote the Alfoxton Avenue phone number and the name 'Amy' on the back of a London taxi card. 'Your own number, please?'

He swore viciously as the van disappeared down his drive. He had noted the van's registration. That evening he kept calling Blackledge's number until, six hours after the couple had left, he made contact.

'What's up, mate?' Blackledge sounded annoyed. 'You sound like somebody's shoved a skewer up yer bum.'

'Look, I'd not have bothered you without good cause. You know that. I've just had a visit from a blonde girl, mid-twenties, posh accent, and a bloke. Looked like university types except she showed me a Metropolitan Police badge and she knew all about your visits here last year. She said they're investigating a murder and drug-dealing with badger-baiting thrown in. They wanted to see your dig in the wood, the one beside the road. And they wanted your name.'

'So what did you tell them?' Blackledge snarled.

'Nothing. What do you think? I had to show them the sett, of course.'

'Had to show them? You stupid bastard! You didn't have to show them nothing.'

'They would have taken me in if I hadn't. By showing them, I kept things looking innocent. After all, there's nothing there . . . Is there?'

'Did you get their details? Like which Force?'

The man perked up. 'Their van number.' He read it to Blackledge.

'Was it a marked police van? Describe it.'

'Not marked. No. I assumed they were CID in a Q-car. You know, trying to look normal.'

'What was it then?'

The man described the van.

'You have the brains of an epileptic ape. No police have ever been seen, since the peelers had bloody horses, with cars older than ten years. Yet this bitch turns up in a B-reg Vauxhall and you don't even question her. If they was fuzz, I'm a friggin' gay.'

The man said nothing. It seemed safer.

'So, if they wasn't fuzz, what the fuck were they? Animal Libbers? The League Against Cruel Sports have been known to try infiltratin' digs. The RSPCA wouldn't be so dumb as to impersonate the Ol' Bill. Get their address?'

He eagerly passed on the telephone number at 7 Alfoxton Avenue and the name of Amy.

'That all? You wanker. I can't believe you didn't twig. If she'd been legit, she'd've had a proper printed Met card whether she was CID or uniform. You're an ignorant shite and if you've set the bastards on me, I'll have yer balls for breakfast. I'll give you a chance, mate. If they show up at your place or nosin' at the sett, you let me know at once – like in minutes . . . OK?'

'At once. You can count on it.'

'So, how will you watch the sett?'

'I'll fix it. Don't you worry. I'll fix it at once. Round the clock.'

Blackledge's voice lost a few degrees of frost.

'OK. OK. You do that. And if you come up with the goods, maybe there'll be some more readies in it for you . . . You twat.'

When he heard Blackledge ring off, the man shouted at his wife for a whisky. Bullying her was the best way he knew to restore his ego when he had been harassed. He mopped his brow with a Kleenex. Blackledge was a scary bastard. He rued the day when he had agreed to take money to show him the setts. If anyone ever asked him what the Devil looked like, he would say Blackledge.

He had a hundred and one other things to do without spending all day and all night down in Kinver Wood watching the sett. He telephoned old Mr Noble. Whenever he took the dogs walking he'd run into the old fellow, crippled with arthritis and in his seventies but, summer and winter, day and night, he'd be creeping around the

233

woods after moths, bottling and recording, then releasing them. He spun the collector a fine yarn about nasty poachers killing all the wildlife and about to decimate Kinver Wood. Mr Noble oohed and aahed and promised he would call if he saw anybody suspicious in the woods.

Amy and Oxley made love that night despite the fact that it was Friday. She was grateful to him and even found herself enjoying his attentions. As she lay back with a cigarette, her legs slumped over his chest and stomach, she regretted that their success with the Kinver man had led to a cul-de-sac. No address for Blackledge and no evidence from the sett. They had found several entrances more freshly dug than others but, with an autumn and subsequent summer gone by since Jake's 'murders', it was difficult to be sure which hole to inspect. Short of a major excavation, or knowing the exact spot to dig up, Amy realised she was on to a non-starter. Never one to cry over spilt milk and having done her best, she would just have to hope they had sufficiently frightened Blackledge's badger spy. With a bit of luck, when Blackledge next called on him, he would phone Amy.

19

October–November 1985

Goodman felt sick with foreboding. They had reached the M5–M6 junction. Within thirty minutes they would be in Kinver. That morning, when Sara had asked him why he was borrowing her window-box trowel, he had shrugged, unable even to fudge a response.

The car phone burred, breaking into his gloomy train of thought. Columbo picked it up then passed it to Tosh. 'It's your man,' he said.

Tosh listened for some minutes then said, 'Bye, love,' and replaced the receiver.

'Sailor,' she told them, 'has just heard from Art on the Brixton watch. Says Mafia's got some ugly friends.'

'He turned up yet?' Columbo asked.

'Not a glimpse but we've got somebody there pretty much round the clock so it's just a matter of time. Yardie gossip will soon lead the boys to him.'

The previous night Sailor had followed what promised to be a valuable lead on one Jo-Dog Willetts, a particularly evil-looking character, trailing his Volvo to a basement disco in Brixton. It had taken very little effort to establish that Jo-Dog was Mafia's main man in London. Before long Mafia himself was bound to show up.

When they reached Kinver, Goodman clearly recalled his previous visit in the Beetle. He caught himself turning to catch Lucy's pretty smile and remembered with a sudden pang how she always knew so many useless bits of history about everywhere they went, even

Clacton-on-Sea, and how she would lean forward between Mary and him, with her arms around both of them, when she saw something exciting. Sometimes, apropos of nothing in particular, she would kiss them lightly and say, 'Mum, I love you. Dad, I love you. Kiss little Lizzy B.' This, she told them, was a refrain she'd learnt at school and came from a local place called Hope End, once the home of Elizabeth Barrett Browning. When pressed for greater detail, she would simply shrug and giggle. That was one of the things he had especially loved about her, her easy acceptance of life in general, the good and the bad. Then one of his shoes pressed against Sara's trowel and the cause for this journey sliced into his thoughts like a cold sickle. Surely no human being on earth could have wilfully, knowingly harmed his Lucy.

They munched their way gloomily through Tosh's lunch, then parked in the same Kinver Wood lay-by where Goodman had left the Beetle fifteen months before.

'It must seem an age ago,' Tosh said gently into the silence. 'I don't imagine there is much in common between the likes of us, The Family, and the folks you knew at your home. The country is a place of innocence when seen beside the black heart of most modern cities.'

'I've certainly learnt some urban facts of life,' Goodman agreed, 'that have jolted me out of my cosy, pre-Kinver outlook on life.'

'Shall we drive somewhere for a while?' Tosh suggested as the afternoon dragged slowly by. 'There's an hour till dusk.'

They motored about the countryside to the south of Kinver, listening to the radio until darkness came, when they returned to the car park.

Goodman retraced his old route into the scrubby woods to the east of Valehead Farm. Even by day the differences between high summer and mid-autumn would have confused his memory: in darkness, everything was new, so he stopped frequently to check his map. The straight-line distance to the sett was 400 yards but by curving into the wood, a gentle climb away from and then back towards Kingsford Lane, a dimly perceived series of game paths soon led them after half a mile to the rough-hewn bench on the hilltop.

Columbo, alert in an alien environment, stayed back within the shadows of the bush while the light from a near-full moon bathed

236

the clearing and the bench. As Goodman tried to recall the direction of the sett, Tosh breathed the night air and wondered at the strangeness of this wood that was to her neither town nor country. Sure, you could hear the hoot of owls and the bark of a fox but the night sky radiated with the back glow of lights from huge urban sprawls and motorways from which came also the unceasing hum of distant traffic. She wondered when Kinver Wood itself would succumb to the inevitable bulldozer.

'Let me check around for a while,' Goodman whispered.

The path fell away at a fair gradient towards the lane, verged with head-high bracken, dead and dying. Goodman looked about him as he descended the path and soon spotted the faint gleam of a slashed branch. Impossible to say how old or how recent. A secondary track, no more than a rabbit lane, angled away uphill a few yards to the under side of a stubby tree and Goodman knew he was again at the sett. When Amy had come here a week before she too had found the sett, although on a darker night, but Goodman knew which of the many entrances he sought. Amy had not. He fetched Tosh and Columbo.

'Do you want help?' Tosh asked. 'Labour?'

Goodman shook his head. 'Thanks, but we've only got the one trowel and, well, it's . . . for me.'

Tosh settled herself in the bracken close by, as Goodman began to scrape leaves and twigs from the soil beneath the tree. He switched on the heavy torch which Tosh had brought and, as he dug, inspected each successive trowel-load in its beam. His initial, almost paralysing dread dissipated and a bowl-shaped depression slowly grew as he worked. An unpleasant odour filled his nostrils.

The first foreign body, neither flake of granite nor slither of tree root, that his trowel struck, was the bone of some animal, possibly the fractured shard of a deer scapula. Goodman hurried on. Two more bones appeared, one almost complete and similar to a human digit.

The smell of decomposition made him retch, but his digging grew faster.

Tosh sat up quietly, a handkerchief to her nose, then reached across and studied the smallest of the bones. She said nothing but she knew it belonged to no beast of the forest. Then she heard the hiss of Goodman's breath. He knelt rigid and motionless, staring down at his hands, held out as though in supplication or utter disbelief. He held a single scrap of dark material: a fragment of cloth. Tosh tried to imagine her own feelings if she were Goodman at this moment and if the scrap of cotton shirt, for such it was, belonged not to Goodman's loved one but to Sailor, murdered and rotting in the forest. She could not visualise her reactions, could only guess at them, and her heart, through all the warps and barriers with which she had for so long protected her inner self, went beaming out to Alex in his terrible moment of discovery and darkness. Kneeling, she put her arms around him and said: 'It was many months ago, Alex. They are in heaven now.'

'Mary,' he keened. 'My Mary.' The shirt was blue, patterned with white flowers and containing enough polyester to have slowed the rotting process.

Goodman held the cloth to his lips, then to his cheek. He began to cry, a dry, choking sound, and pressed his forehead against the noisome earth. His sobbing rose to a low wail of anguish. Tosh sat back against the tree and lit a cigarette. She knew all about grief, how best to help and when to let tears run their course.

Goodman's misery was yet tinged with a crumb of hope. No sign of Lucy. He seized the trowel and began again to attack the sett. But Tosh grasped his wrists.

'Wait,' she said. 'Think about this, Alex.'

He looked at her, uncomprehending. 'Lucy,' he muttered. 'She may not be . . .'

'That's true. But we are now sure there is evidence of murder here. I know enough about forensic pathology to ask you to consider carefully what you are doin'. This place is full of clues now but each and every bit of spoil that you disturb lessens the chances of a murder case against whoever did this. Or, failin' that, we could at least obtain vital knowledge of what exactly happened. Maybe even indications of the how and the why of it.'

Tosh spoke with an insistent certainty.

Goodman nodded. 'We must get the police here.'

He shook his head in disbelief as he sat beside her, running the fabric between his fingers.

'Not the police, Alex. Of course they have the resources and the system to find the evidence, charge the guilty and put them away. But you will be in the thick of it and they will check your story under

238

a microscope. The chances of their learnin' about Trevor's death at your hands are too high.'

'I would risk all that to put Mary's killers away for life.'

'To be sure you would. But don't for a minute count upon them going down for life. Or even for ten years. Or at all. You could end up bein' the only one in prison for your troubles.'

'So why are you talking of forensic pathology?'

'I was meanin' a pathologist *of our own* to sift this place for clues, produce a full report for us to act on. The Family can probably achieve justice for you, Alex, more surely than the British law, and without riskin' your own liberty.'

'You know a pathologist?'

Tosh laughed. 'No, but we can always hire or acquire experts. There is nothin' we can't do if we have the funds and, in this case, you've good credit.'

'The only good thing in all this is that my path crossed yours.'

'Maybe it makes up a little for your path havin' first crossed theirs.' Tosh flicked a finger towards the excavated soil. 'So you'd like me to go ahead, then?'

'Please,' Goodman murmured. 'But I thought forensic pathologists worked only for the government. Are they not forbidden to investigate murder on a private basis?'

'Every man,' Tosh said, 'has his price and there are skeletons in every cupboard. Even Christ kept a whip in his toolbox.'

Bob Geldof, pop singer and famine reliever, was the nearest thing to a hero for Tosh. As she handed an order for amphetamines to Oxley, she noticed the long-haired, open-shirted Boomtown Rats singer on the TV at Alfoxton Avenue, roundly condemning the world's betrayal of the starving. Amy, curled up in her armchair, was eating carrots.

'Give them hell,' she shook a carrot at Geldof. 'The bureaucratic wasters.'

Tosh and Amy cheered the blunt-spoken Irish pop star. They chatted a bit, Tosh pleasantly surprised to find somebody in that 'nut-house' imbued with a clear brain and not, like all others she'd met there, blinkered by their own fixations. The phone interrupted them. Amy, in a short nightdress, scattered carrots and took the call. 'Seven,' she said.

It was the man from Kinver, his tone noticeably less rude than before.

'I've traced him for you, the badger man,' he told Amy. 'He lives in Blackburn and I can show you exactly where to find him. I owe him no favours. Like I said, I've never had owt to do with him. I could meet you in Blackburn?'

Amy's heart leapt, her mind racing with images of Blackledge, the tortured badgers, the corkscrew and the tongs.

'Good,' she replied. 'I'll come up with another officer. How about 25 November? We're up in your area again then.'

It was agreed. The man named a Blackburn pub and a time to meet.

'That bastard,' Amy said as she returned to her carrots, 'has been annihilating badgers. You interested in animals . . . ?'

'Tosh. Call me Tosh.'

'I'm Amy.'

'Hi. You say badgers?'

'Yup. That call was all about a bastard who nearly killed me a year back on the Isle of Wight at a badger dig. I'm trying to have him put away.'

'That's curious,' Tosh smiled. 'I'm on to somethin' similar but not on the Isle of Wight. No, I'm not normally into animals. My time's taken up tryin' to cure dumb humans. Hey, I must rush! Nice to have met you. See you again.'

Amy smiled as Tosh left, for she was excited. Once she found Blackledge's house, she would have him listed as an ALF target. She would supervise the bombing herself. Oxley was developing a new generation of highly lethal car bombs. One of the Front's splinter groups, the Animal Rights Militia, had recently blown up the cars of two scientists at the British Industrial Biological Research Association but their gas-cylinder bombs were crude compared with Oxley's new models. That night Amy was especially accommodating to his urges and he promised her a bespoke driver-activated car bomb whenever she wanted.

When the Kinver man had finished his call to Amy, he threw back a double whisky. 'Well?' he asked.

Blackledge, seated opposite him, grunted. 'Not bad. The little bitch seems to have taken the hook. Listen carefully. After you've met up with her at The Swan, here's where to take her . . .'

Once he was satisfied that the man would make no errors, Blackledge drove to Birmingham, to the terraced house whose address Tricks had given him. The West Indian never seemed to use the same RV twice.

Blackledge had hoped to get back home in time to visit the allotments and scrapyard on the border of Rishton and Great Harwood, where he kept his dogs. Some days he liked to give them a good three-hour walk so that they would look their best at shows.

Personally he failed to see what all the fuss was about over the Kinver dig. Nothing had actually gone wrong when all was said and done. Nobody could come back on them now, surely? Not after nigh on a year and a half. But Tricks was no fool and he seemed worried. Blackledge knew he would have no trouble getting the blonde Libber bitch to talk. The thought struck him that Tricks might want his boys to work her over. He determined to prevent them spoiling his fun.

A West Indian, an imposing six foot three, let Blackledge into the house in Moseley Road. Blackledge recognised the man as Dylan, a nightclub owner he had not previously seen with Tricks. He smelled ganja and orange-scented joss-sticks. Two or three pretty black women sat around Tricks in a dark, drab lounge.

'Welcome,' Tricks greeted him, then glanced at the girls, who wandered away. Opening two beer cans, he wasted no time on small talk. To him, Blackledge was trash, a mere runner. None the less he did have contacts and therefore usefulness. Also, he must be fully aware that his own skin was at risk if the Kinver problem ever came to light.

'If this ALF girl was a one-off, no problem,' Tricks said, pacing tiger-like as he spoke. 'But a year back you told me about that clerk who followed your driver Trevor about, then drove him off the last day anybody ever saw him. There's got to be a connection.'

'Tricks. I can sort this,' Blackledge urged. 'Leave the bitch to me and I'll break her. She'll spill whatever she knows, no bother.'

Tricks thought about this. 'OK. She's all yours. But I need to be there. Anythin' to do with the Yanks is number-one big. No mistakes allowed. Where's it to be on the twenty-fifth?'

'There's a place where I stack stuff in the woods. I'll leave you my map. The shed is ringed in red. We'll expect you at four o'clock that afternoon. By then we'll have softened her up.'

In 1884 Sigmund Freud recommended cocaine as a great new cure for syphilis, depression, anaemia and just about any other ailment. In Atlanta, a medicine-maker mixed coca with caffeine to produce Coca-Cola, and all over the world individuals from all walks of life began to abuse their bodies and minds with the processed extract of the coca leaf.

In the public lavatories of the car park beneath Birmingham's Perry Barr Shopping Centre, Tom Hainey, a fourteen-year-old rent boy, slammed a dose of concentrated cocaine into his bloodstream, sat back on the chipped enamel seat and felt himself fly to the roof of the world and beyond. Nobody, not even the richest man on earth, could feel better than he for those few brief moments.

As Tom crashed down from his super-high, his brain reacted in panic and pushed out neuro-blocker chemicals to suppress the sudden mad behaviour of his nerve cells. Now he sloughed deep into depression, craving another rock in order to soar again but rocks cost cash. Luckily it was Friday, the day the Professor shopped at the Centre at 5 p.m., spent a few minutes with Tom, then collected his car from its usual spot for the hour's drive home. Regular as clockwork, unlike most of Tom's customers. The old man had proved a gold-mine, especially the previous Friday.

The Professor arrived on time, glancing nervously all about him. This was unnecessary, since the place was a known bum-boy parlour, as established as any city brothel. He rapped four times on the end cubicle and Tom slipped the latch to let him in. The retired academic undressed except for his socks and spectacles, then sat on the seat to watch Tom do likewise. There was very little space but that did not matter.

Similar goings-on took place in the other cubicles much of the day and night, all year round. Some of the partitions had golfball-sized holes drilled in them at groin height so that strangers in separate cubicles could interrelate without a face-to-face encounter. This was of paramount importance to many respected pillars of the local community for whom exposure would be socially and professionally disastrous.

Sometimes undercover police embarrassed a few such wretched

toilet misusers by arresting them and ensuring the local press learnt their names – a far more effective punishment than any fine or prison sentence.

Leaving Tom £15 in cash, enough for a single 'rush', the Professor hurried off through heavy rain, shielding his shopping bag beneath his calf-length mackintosh. He became aware of Tosh only after she had kept level with him for some moments. Under the cover of her white umbrella and matching the stride of her long legs to the Professor's stubby ones, she passed him an A4-sized black and white print (with which Chemist had pronounced himself technically pleased).

The Professor recognised both the naked bodies in the sordid tableau. Fortunately his heart was strong enough to take the shock and he followed Tosh into a coffee-shop. They drank tea and his spectacles steamed up. His eyes smarted from her smoking but he hung on her every word and relief began to flood over him as he realised she was offering him a way out. She was not from the CID after all.

His name would not be bandied about the club; he would not be ostracised from all the circles he moved in. Nor would his son, who was an eminent banker. His chances of a pleasant and well-earned retirement might yet be realised. For a moment he had stared into the abyss and he knew he would do just about anything to escape plunging into its miserable maw. The woman, God knows who she was – probably a cunning con artist and professional blackmailer – was making him an offer. He listened stunned to the outline of her proposition and his blood pressure began slowly to return to a safer level as he saw there was indeed a way of keeping the awful photograph hidden from the press.

When Tosh mentioned financial inducement, and a handsome amount too, he hardly noticed. Had Tosh been able to read the Professor's thoughts behind the foggy lenses, she would have known no carrot was necessary. The stick was enough. But Tosh was taking no chances. The Professor, after all, was the fruit of three weeks' diligent research and surveillance.

Two weeks earlier Leon had been attached full time to the man they had dubbed the Professor. On 8 November an initially boring shopping trip had led Leon down to the Gents at the Perry Barr Centre and the discovery of the Professor's seamy little secret. Leon had spoken with Tom and a sum of money had changed hands. The rent boy assured Leon that the Professor would be back, good as gold, the next Friday and indeed every Friday.

Chemist had come up from London to supervise the camera work. He found that two deviants' holes were already drilled in the partition of Tom's favoured cubicle but they did not cover all likely angles. So Art drilled three more to ensure all aspects of the action would be properly recorded.

In order to pinpoint a suitable pathologist Tosh and her 'staff' had worked from the phones at the Peckham 'Home', casting a wide net to include all possible active and retired forensic pathologists through 'Ears' Norton and other Metropolitan Police contacts, the Medical Directory and the list of members of the British Association in Forensic Medicine. Since she was ideally after a pathologist living not too far from the prospective work site, her team had concentrated on names with addresses in that general area.

Kinver was covered by the Staffordshire Police but lay at their borders with the West Mercia and West Midlands Forces. Initial checks were made on a number of doctors in and between Birmingham and Manchester. None was found to be in debt and none, according to carefully chatted up colleagues and neighbours, was conducting illicit affairs or business.

Out of twenty-three others, chosen from a wide radius, five were rumoured to be 'naughty' and Tosh unleashed her hounds to locate the skeletons in their respective cupboards. The Professor had come up trumps.

Watching him closely through the haze of her cigarette smoke, Tosh assured him that his name would remain for ever her secret if he did as he was told.

'You do realise, madam, do you not, that what you are asking me is utterly against our code of conduct and would, if discovered, have me jailed and my name blackened by my peers?'

'I do,' Tosh agreed. 'Just as you realise that, if you do not follow my instructions to the letter, you will definitely be up to your ossicles in faeces, to use forensic terminology.'

'A working pathologist would do your job far more quickly and thoroughly than I,' the Professor murmured. 'Someone with constant access to specialist government laboratories.'

'That's your problem, Doc.'

244

'How long since the murder? How was it done? Precisely when? Sandstone or clay burial?'

'We will brief you in full on site,' Tosh replied, her UVF training making her feel uneasy in the busy café.

The following day she accompanied Goodman and Columbo to the Professor's home near Birmingham and, after parking up the road, telephoned his number. He had stipulated that nobody be seen calling on him as in his street Neighbourhood Watch meant just that. He emerged in tweeds with an umbrella and small Globetrotter suitcase, fussed about in his Triumph Herald for five minutes and finally moved away to meet them at the end of the street. He drove at a steady 40mph, which infuriated Columbo, and their convoy took ninety minutes to reach Kinver. Goodman led the way from the car park to the sett and helped the others with the bulky gear.

The night was dark with the threat of rain clouds and live with the conversation of trees creaking and susurrating in the wind. They erected the cotton bell-tent over the sett and under the tree, leaving open the downside flap from which to pass labelled spoil bags out to Columbo who carried them back to the car. There were two headlamps and four adjustable battery-powered lights on a skeletal frame. Goodman kept watch away from the action.

The Professor worked painfully slowly, took numerous photographs and chatted constantly whether or not anybody was listening. Five hours later he announced that his hip was paining him and he could do no more. Bearing in mind the diameter of the hole as now ascertained and the likely depth, he anticipated a further such night's work, possibly two. Nobody argued. Even Tosh could see that the old man was doing his best.

A cheesy, ammoniacal odour clung to the tent and their clothes. They carefully placed the two or three hundred tagged sample bags, some of them 60cm in length, into boxes made up from cardboard slats. A total of nine heavy bags of loose spoil, all labelled with numbers denoting general depth from the surface, filled the boot and back seat of Columbo's BMW, so Tosh joined the Professor for the drive into Handsworth, where they had set up a laboratory in the basement of Chemist's sister's house. Everything that the Professor asked for, they obtained. Most of his work would be done in the laboratory of a not yet retired, long-time friend of his, but the

Professor only carried with him what would fit into his Globetrotter.

The second night's work in the wood turned out to suffice. The Professor confirmed he would need no further spoil, so they filled the hole with earth from nearby before flattening it with boards. Then they spread more earth and leaves as camouflage. The tent and all other evidence of their visits were removed.

As they left the site, Goodman stopped the Professor. The others were on their way to the cars.

'Can you tell me anything yet, Doctor?'

'Nothing, I'm afraid. It will take me weeks. Possibly two months. There has been predation by animals. Foxes are mainly responsible. Matter has been spread far and wide, I suspect.'

'I would be grateful if you could let me know as soon as you have a definitive report. I will give you my London number. If I'm not there you can leave a message.'

The Professor wrote the number in his note-pad and assured Goodman he would make contact as soon as he could.

Kneeling in bracken, not ten feet away, the Kinver man also memorised Goodman's number. The day before, old Mr Noble, the moth-collector, had called with news that the 'dreadful poacher people' had camped by the badger sett. So he had rushed to the site the next morning, spotted the tent and lain in wait from just before dusk. His patience was rewarded when three men and a woman had appeared at 8 p.m., chatted inside the tent and worked, God knows at what, for several hours. Unable to see into the double-lined tent or to overhear the conversation of the silhouetted figures within, he had tried to creep round to the open, downhill side and narrowly avoided blundering into Columbo, who was sitting smoking in the bracken below the tent. After this, he had retired to the uphill side of the tent and only began to hear clear snatches of conversation when the tent was collapsed.

Blackledge compared the London number which the Kinver man gave him with that of the ALF girl Amy and was surprised to find them different. He assumed that the girl used two phones or that the second number was for another member of her activist group. He told the Kinver man to check the sett and the wood around it with care to establish what was going on. He was looking forward to

Amy's visit and to the process of extracting from her the reason for her interest in him and the sett.

20

November 1985

As a police cadet in 1974, Mick Pearce had worked on the case of the 'Black Panther' murder in Staffordshire. He had received a number of Chief Superintendent Commendations and he believed in using his initiative. Four years earlier the black owner of a Walsall nightclub had been viciously stabbed with draper's scissors and Pearce, then an ambitious young detective, had worked long hours in his own time to find and arrest the culprit. When Dudley Crown Court acquitted the man, Pearce left the building with tears in his eyes and an emptiness in his stomach at the injustice of it all. In the summer of 1984 he first crossed the path of Stafford 'Mafia' Douglas, an encounter he would regret for the rest of his career.

Detective Constable Pearce had put away half a dozen of Mafia's cannabis and cocaine couriers but none dared put the finger on their boss. As intelligence officer for the West Midlands Police and concentrating on black organised crime, Mick Pearce knew as much as anybody about Yardies in Brum and many Yardies knew him.

The first time Pearce had met Mafia, the Jamaican had boasted: 'Don't mistake me for a little Villa Road puppy dog, man. I'm international, Pearcey boy. You forget that and you're in trouble.'

Shadowing Mafia in his own time, Pearce used a dilapidated Ford Transit and changed the number-plates every other week. On 25 November Mafia relaxed in his white Mercedes 500SL with Orlando 'Kingston' Williams at the wheel and a minder taking business notes in the passenger seat. The main problem was the IRA. Finding an interested arms buyer had proved a slow and complex business and, with only five days to go to the Miami HTA demo, Mafia was beginning to worry.

Pearce knew Kingston and the minder by sight but could not place the Latino type in the back with Mafia. The Jamaican dealt with local whites, including HM Customs men at Birmingham Airport, as Pearce was well aware. There were also indications of Dutch and North American connections but this was the first Latino that Pearce had spotted doing business with Mafia, which was why he had risked his wife's wrath by staying on Mafia's tail long after he'd planned to go home to take her late-night shopping at Tesco in Five Ways.

The Mercedes had left Birmingham at 4 p.m. in traffic that was heavy all the way north to the outskirts of Leyland, where Kingston found the way to a remote wood called Stanning Folly. Pearce's tail job was no problem except for the final few miles but even then a smattering of other vehicles remained to hide behind.

Pearce was fascinated by Yardies and their crime, and although sickened by their crude violence he was fond of his many Jamaican friends, informers and even some of his Yardie targets, colourful characters all. Never a dull moment on Yardie duty, of that Pearce could be sure.

He knew lads brought up in Kingston slums whose idols were Lee van Cleef and Clint Eastwood screen characters handing out death with big revolvers. These Yardie wannabes obtained their first guns in their early teens, often crude 'bicycle-bar' rifles but leading to deadly semi-automatics like the Glock.

They killed without compunction, often without forethought, and fatal knife fights were common even over mere dominoes arguments. They were arrogant and racist, feeling innately superior even to fellow Caribbean islanders, Trinidadians, Bajans, St Lucians and British-born Jamaicans.

Coming from Kingston, the murder capital of the world, where 99 per cent of all killings were political or drugs-related, it was small wonder their murderous activities carried on in their new homes abroad.

Even the poorest housing estates in England were heaven compared with the West Kingston slums, but you needed a great deal of cash to live it up in England. And that came most easily from drugs. As Mick Pearce explained to his wife, drug-dealing was often the only available escape route from the birth-trap of the Kingston ghettos. Hash or 'cockpit' ganja. Then powder cocaine. Then crack. Increasingly powerful drugs with ever-better profit margins to increase the spiral of violence and the spoils thereof.

Once they have made it out of the ghetto, what to do with their new-found wealth? UK Yardies, illegal immigrants to a man, dream of ending their days back in mansions in JA, but, while in the UK, property is not their number-one priority. After all, they can't drive around and parade their home to other Yardies. Yardies have neither education nor standard professional skills. Bad boys don't go to school, at least not after primary. The aim is to be a big don, a high ranker. That leads to the greatest of all gifts: the respect of their peers.

Conversely the worst insult is 'diss', disrespect, for which they punish the offender. Somebody treads on their toes or stares at them at a function, so they 'crease' him then and there.

They may have killed in JA but when they move to the UK they need to kill again to outrank existing UK dons. They must show their capacity for extreme violence at the drop of a hat.

Mick Pearce knew all this. He understood Yardie psychology, which made him an excellent detective. He listed seven priorities for an upwardly mobile Yardie, all interlinked. Money, drugs, violence, firearms, politics, family – sometimes up to fourteen baby-mothers and twice that number of children – and internationalism, the floating life between JA, the UK, the USA and Canada. Involvement with all these facets of life gave a Yardie status and respect.

Over the fourteen months since Pearce had started to watch him, Mafia had climbed the ranks with inexplicable speed. His beginnings in Handsworth were inauspicious, welding work for Holland & Cheston in South Road, sorting at a Perry Bar egg factory and bicycle assembly at Raleigh Industries in Smethwick. Then he had launched into minor cannabis dealing and reggae, with his own record labels: Tipper Town, Mafia Town, Now Generation, Art and Craft, to name a few. The discs sold well in the UK and JA record shops because he hired quality singers like Amon, Clarke, Sillit and Priest.

By 1985 Mafia's associates included senior dons with double-figure assassinations to their credit. Men like Robert 'Bowyark'

Blackwood aka Rankin' Dred, by repute the deadliest Yardie in Britain.

In his spare time Mafia bought designer wear in Italy and sold it in Seven Sisters Road. The previous week, in Turin, he had combined clothes purchases with the scheduled meeting with Miguel Duraz at the refrigeration equipment factory. Now beside Mafia in the Mercedes, the Mexican was looking forward to watching the old English sport of cockfighting with steel spurs. This was not something Mafia knew about but it had provided a reasonable explanation for their visit to the isolated shack in Stanning Folly.

That morning Blackledge had been to his taxidermist, Brian Jackson at Eaves Farm in Whalley, and collected a magnificent albino boar badger. He was in the best of moods as a result and much looking forward to further acquaintance with the well-shaped, blonde Amy in his shed at Stanning Folly. He kept all manner of odds and ends there, mostly items like badger gear which would look bad if found by the fuzz in his home.

He wished the Jamaican was not involved in the interrogation but he had arranged the timings to give himself a clear hour's start with Amy and that should be ample both to make her talk and to enjoy himself in the process.

He parked well away from the barn and walked the last few hundred yards, pleased to see the Kinver man's Toyota pick-up already there. He entered the building noiselessly and found the man gesticulating at the girl.

'Don't panic. He's often late. It's his way but he'll not let you down. You give him the cash and he'll show you Blackledge's home and the abattoir where he works. Can't do better than that, can I?'

Amy was beginning to feel something was wrong, purely because of the shifty manner of the Kinver man. She was seriously toying with the idea of packing this meeting in altogether and arranging a RV somewhere safer and more public. She wished Oxley was with her. When, hearing a noise, she turned and saw Blackledge with his mocking leer, her heart froze. Too late came the realisation that the Kinver man had deceived her.

'You done well,' said Blackledge as he handed the man a wad of notes. 'The bitch won't bother you again.'

'Thanks. How about the sett? Will you be wanting anything done there?'

'I'll let you know. See you later, then.'

Blackledge's gaze had not left Amy for a second. She felt as a mouse must when cornered by a snake. The Kinver man's car started up and Amy darted for the barn doorway. Blackledge extended his leg and she tripped. He pulled her up by her hair. She shot her fist, fingers extended, at his eyes but he caught her fingers with his free hand and bent them back till she screamed.

'Proper little cat, eh?' He grinned down at her. 'We're goin' to have fun, aren't we?' He dragged her to one of the barn walls where lengths of orange binder twine and tufts of hay littered the floor. He lashed her thumbs and wrists together, threw a length of twine over a high, rusty wall-hook and pulled on the free end until her hands were hauled high and only the balls of her shoes took her weight. He went through the pockets of her jeans and denim blouson, throwing all the contents to the ground. He took the cash and police badge, making no comment.

Then, glancing at his watch, he fetched across a plywood box, up-ended it and, parting her straining legs, sat down with his knees between them.

'We got thirty-five minutes. You can holler but nobody's goin' to hear you.'

He ripped open her shirt. Then he undid her belt and pulled her jeans and pants to below her knees. Amy bit her lips and prayed to whatever God might listen. Her wrists and shoulders screamed their pain at her.

Playing with her body, Blackledge told her exactly what he was going to do with her over the next half hour unless she told him why she was interested in the Kinver sett. Had she been following him even before their Isle of Wight meeting because of her interest in Kinver? Who else was involved with her?

As he spoke he became aroused and rose to unzip his trousers. They both heard the noise of the car halting outside. Blackledge swore and pulled Amy's lower lip down until she opened her mouth. He pushed binder twine between her teeth as a crude gag, and ran to the entrance. As he did so, Mafia appeared with Kingston, who was armed with a semi-automatic rifle. Blackledge, appearing from the shadows, was brought up short.

'Cool it, King,' Mafia, recognising Blackledge, shouted at his henchman. 'Go tell the boy to keep Duraz in the car awhile. Tell the Mexi I'm checkin' all is well with the set-up before lettin' him in.'

Kingston left and Mafia glanced at Amy squirming below the beam.

'She talked yet?' he asked Blackledge.

'She was just about to. You're early.'

'Am I?' Mafia raised his eyebrows. 'My watch must be wrong. Listen, we have to hurry. I have a date with an Irishman. This girl must talk right away. No more messin'.'

Mafia produced a large, black Smith & Wesson revolver from his cotton jacket and pressed the barrel against Amy's temple. He called the gun Satan.

'You seen brains splash about, lady?'

No reply.

'Not a pretty sight. Especially when they're yours. Mr Blackledge here has just asked you some questions. We all want the answers and we have an appointment shortly. I'm goin' to count to six. Then Satan's goin' to put a bullet through your pretty blonde head. OK?'

He pulled back the hammer and moved the barrel to a point immediately under Amy's flaring nostrils. Then he noticed and removed the binder twine.

'Now you can talk, eh?'

Mafia was no beginner at scaring information out of people but Amy screwed her eyes up and repeated to herself the initials ALF, ALF as a mantra. Badgers, she remembered, put up with painfully slow deaths at the hands of these men. Oxley would avenge her. She would not tell them about him or Alfoxton Avenue. She would not . . .

'. . . Six,' said Mafia, then lowered the revolver. 'You think this is a threat I won't carry out?' He went to the open barn door and called out: 'Kingston. Everything's ready for the cockfight. Bring Miguel and the shooting-stick for his comfort.'

When Miguel Duraz, smart in business suit and expensive Italian accoutrements, stood blinking in the comparative gloom of the barn, Kingston pinned his arms from behind and pushed him roughly towards Mafia and the girl.

'What is this?' Duraz gasped. 'What are you doing? Tell this man to release me. Who is this woman?'

253

Mafia ignored him and addressed Amy instead. 'You know why the IRA kneecap people? No? I'll tell you. It's very painful, very difficult to repair and often cripples you for life. One knee is bad. Two and you might as well be dead.'

Blackledge was growing interested in the black man's professionalism. Mafia nodded at him. 'Make her watch,' he said.

Blackledge clamped his hands to Amy's head, using his fingers to force her eyes open.

Mafia held his gun behind one of Duraz's knees and fired. Blood and matter burst through the front of the Mexican's trousers. He groaned and then fainted.

'OK?' Mafia looked at Amy. 'Will you talk to us? Or shall I blow his other kneecap away?'

Amy's reply was to vomit over Blackledge's hand and down her own naked stomach. She nodded her head wildly. Of course she would talk. She would say anything to anyone to stop this nightmare.

Mafia pressed his gun against the back of Duraz's head and fired again.

'He was a nice enough guy,' he told Kingston. 'Take him to the Ribble Estuary via the Longton path I showed you. Weight him well and keep your speed down – at least till you've got rid of Miguel. Be back here in two hours at the latest.'

Pearce, well hidden and sixty yards from the barn, cursed when he saw Kingston and Mafia's minder reverse the Mercedes half into the barn and load something heavy into its boot. They then drove off but he decided to stay and find out whom Mafia was meeting in the barn. He suspected a major drugs deal was in progress. If only he had a mobile radio or a weapon.

As he crept closer, a woman's scream rose and fell, muffled by the thick barn walls. That decided him. He could not stand cruelty to women. He tore into the barn shouting: 'Police! Let her go!'

Blackledge swung away from the girl and Mafia removed his gun from her mouth.

'Pearcey!' he exclaimed. 'You been tailin' me again? This ain't your jurisdiction.' He levelled the revolver at the detective's stomach.

'Shoot the bastard,' Blackledge snarled. 'Who the fuck is he?'

'Babylon,' Mafia said simply. 'Walsall Undercover.'

'The rest of the squad will be here in minutes,' Pearce said with as much confidence as he could muster. 'I came in early when I heard the lass scream. Let her be and I'll make sure it's held in your favour at court.'

Mafia knew no policeman would be stupid enough to interfere in such circumstances without the assurance of imminent reinforcements.

'Come on,' he said to Blackledge. 'Let's git, before the US Cavalry arrives.'

'What about the girl?'

'Forget her. I've got another source for the same knowledge. Come on.' He muzzled his Smith & Wesson against Pearce's cheek. 'You got no witnesses to this, Pearcey. Pity, eh? See you about town, then.'

They left in Blackledge's Escort, heading for the nearby village of Longton to find Kingston and Mafia's car.

Pearce, his eyes still unaccustomed to the gloom, cut Amy down and took her to the nearest restaurant, the motorway services near Charnock Richard. He treated her with gentle respect and, when she showed no signs of wanting to talk about her recent experience, he did not press her. He decided to go as slowly as she wished. She wanted to visit the Ladies.

'Will you be OK?' he asked. 'Do you feel faint still?'

'I'll be fine,' she smiled briefly. 'The sickness has gone. You've been very good to me.'

Amy squeezed his hand. She felt lousy leaving him. He had saved her from God knows what fate. The black man had in a way been even more terrifying than Blackledge. She knew she would have told him everything, including the involvement of Paul Martin, Oxley and Ben in Bournemouth. She also suspected that he would have killed her as soon as she'd told him all she could. Much as she would love to see both Blackledge and the black man locked up for ever, she dare not oppose them in court. They would seek her out and she was no match for their professional evil. She accepted that now. She would not meddle with Blackledge again. And she must not mention the horrific shooting, for the nice detective Pearce would then want her as a witness. So she hurried from the restaurant to the fuel pumps, where she approached a driver for a lift back to London.

Pearce waited ten minutes before asking the restaurant staff to check the toilets. He suspected at once that Amy had absconded through fear of involvement in court proceedings.

Scarpered, he thought, shaking his head. Now I've got nothing on Stafford bloody Douglas ... No drugs, no weapon, no assault witness. He wandered to the phones in order to face the wrath of his wife.

Mafia drove straight to the Humming Bird in Handsworth. A girlfriend of his was a daughter of Lloyd Blake, who managed the three-floored reggae disco. Blake was in his office up above the hall but otherwise the place rattled with emptiness. All the bars were closed. No flashing lights, no star-spangled strobes to dazzle the thousand, bouncing, spaced-out ravers on the huge floor beneath the stage.

Mafia and Blake had worked together many times, but Blake knew nothing of Mafia's US connections. He was and always had been a secretive man.

'Caretaker Ken', Mafia's minder, brought two Irishmen in suits up to the office and Blake wandered away while Mafia discussed the marvels of HTA. The flight to Miami was all laid on: the Irishmen had only to declare the IRA's serious intent to purchase the HTA products and he, Mafia, would arrange the visit for them. They promised him a speedy response from Belfast and left.

Ken then drove Mafia to Ladbrokes on the Handsworth Front Line. Blackledge was there waiting.

'What have you got?' Mafia asked. They shouldered their way through the screen-gazing groups of gamblers to an unoccupied corner.

'An address in Finsbury Park,' Blackledge muttered. 'The owner's a Paki girl and she's got a white lodger. A sick-looking geezer on the dole. My bloke Raymondo says these two can't be right. They couldn't raid an ant's nest, never mind go diggin' in dark woods. So I checked back with my man in Kinver who gave me the number – him that watched them diggin' by night – and he told me there was no mistake. He checked the number over several times, like.'

'We missed out in your barn today,' Mafia said. 'Too bad because that girl knew something. Listen, I got a job out of the country for a while but I'll be back before Christmas. Say, four weeks from now. Find out about the Paki and anyone who visits her place. When I get back, I'll have some soldiers pay a visit and clean them up.'

21

November 1985

Both men sported the same nickname, 'El Gordo', 'Fat Man', in reference to their heavy paunches, so El Gordo the driver greeted the other man with the word for namesake.

'*Tocayo*,' he said, 'I have come for the dirt.'

'I have twelve, including the two from Peru.'

'I have room.'

The driver worked for *los dueños del cupo*, 'those who hold the quota', the leaders of Colombia's Medellín Cartel, the largest and most profitable crime ring in the world. Pablo Escobar, the Ochoa family and Rodríguez Gacha from Bogotá were the *dueños* in November 1985. The South American empire of the Cartel was vast and, like any other complex corporation, suffered from internal crime. Escobar dealt harshly with the suspected and the guilty to deter others.

El Gordo had come to Medellín to collect for trial and execution the latest batch of in-house offenders. Escobar's lieutenants had introduced a new security system to prevent escape from El Gordo's laundry van. Once the prisoners were seated in the rear compartment, a wire loop was passed through a hole punched in the ear lobe of each man and clipped to a central cable which ran the length of the van's fuselage. El Gordo's assistant watched the passengers through a perspex panel in the rear of the cab. If any prisoner moved from his seat, the assistant pressed a button which applied a mild but unpleasant electric shock to all. Continued troublemaking led to the selection of a higher voltage.

El Gordo signed for the twelve doomed men and watched them shuffle in leg irons to the van. The irons were unlocked once the men were seated, cuffed to one another and attached to the power circuit. The van headed out of Medellín on the road to Puerto Triunfo.

Colombia produces 10 per cent of the world's cocaine and the other 90 per cent passes through Colombia from its Peruvian and Bolivian sources *en route* to the USA. Eighty-two per cent of the street value of all Peruvian and Bolivian cocaine is paid to Colombia. A mere US$45,000 million is earned from home-grown cocaine, whereas a massive annual income of $330,000 million is earned from Colombia's share of the Peruvian and Bolivian harvest.

Colombia's non-narcotics export earnings total only $5750 million, a tiny fraction of the $375,000 million from cocaine. Small wonder that all aspects of Colombian life are influenced by the drug. Even the Church has been corrupted. Avianca, the national airline, is heavily involved in drug transport. The government, the military, the local police, with a few valiant exceptions – all are rotten to the core.

El Gordo left the noisome confines of Itagüi in southern Medellín, the mile-high Andean metropolis famous for gold, coffee, orchids and cocaine. Medellín is Colombia's second-biggest city, after Bogotá, but the first in worldwide notoriety. Narco-crime supplies the oil on which Medellín runs. Churches, the centre of life in the seventies, now provide a rendezvous in their echoing emptiness for drug dealers. El Gordo headed out to the airport, on a dog-leg to collect an important prisoner brought in from Bolivia, and passed by two great shanty towns, Comuna Noroccidental and Comuna Nororiental, bordered by open sewage canals and rife with violence, prostitution and poverty. Both communes had been established to soak up the mass of terrified refugees from rural areas during the fifties when La Violencia, a genocidal civil war, killed off 300,000 Colombians.

El Gordo's assistant, Ramón, came from the Medellín slum of Barrio Antioqua. From this hell on earth the Cartel derives most of its most accomplished assassins. Barrio Antioqua has schools that teach how to pick pockets, how to kill and how to be a child prostitute of either sex.

In Europe most people would find considerable difficulty in

locating a paid killer. Not so in Barrio Antioqua, where contract assassins advertise openly. *Trabajito* – 'little job' – experts are two a penny and can be picked up at a dozen or more street corners. Any taxi driver will tell you where to go. To have a family member, a noisy neighbour, or somebody pressing you for payment terminated will cost $100 or thereabouts but a judge with a bodyguard might cost $10,000. You have only to furnish your street assassin with a photo of the victim, an address and some basic information on day-to-day movements. If you are suspicious that your *asesino* is a fake, you can demand a *muerto de prueba*, a test kill, which can involve any chance passer-by.

Ramón, a low-grade killer, specialised in *asesinato de la moto* within the El Poblado district north of the Medellín river. Riding pillion on a motorbike, he would fire split-head bullets at close-range targets in limousines along the mega-rich Las Lomas and Las Diagonales roads, the most secure district of Medellín, lined with fine trees, art galleries and luxurious mansions.

Ramón and his kind ensure that Medellín remains the murder capital of the Americas, with an average of seven killings a day and twenty-five per weekend. Group massacres are popular, especially during church services and funerals.

Beyond the city, El Gordo's laundry van passed through rich pasture-land and fields of grazing horses and, three hours later, left the main Puerto Triunfo road for the village of Dora Dal and the hilltop villa of Pablo Escobar, the Hacienda Nápoles. More than sixty armed guards wearing jeans and bandoliers patrolled the security fences, watch-towers and grounds of the hacienda, and Ramón's written instructions were carefully checked by the gate guard. The prisoners were counted like so many bullocks entering a slaughterhouse, uncuffed and unloaded on to a tennis court, their ear loops still in place.

Escobar kept giraffes, elephants and hippopotami on the estate, as well as his personal selection of adolescent catamites. He owned other estates in Colombia and gave bountifully to the poor of Medellín. Unlike his aristocratic colleagues, the Ochoa family, he came from a modest background and had started life as a gravestone thief. In 1976 he was briefly imprisoned for cocaine smuggling, bribed his release and murdered the policemen who had arrested him. From then on his rise to the summit of the Cartel was rapid and helped by a reputation for ruthlessness.

When the prisoners arrived, Escobar left his blond boyfriend at the swimming pool and, dressed in a bathrobe of gold silk, was driven by jeep to the nearest of the estate's twenty lakes. A sunken concrete arena the size of a squash court and some ten feet deep provided a giant barbecue floored with a glowing bed of charcoal embers. Several guards stood around and a number of invited guests. This was a ceremony repeated intermittently, depending on the number of offenders discovered within the organisation. The prisoners were herded from jeeps, their shoes removed, then forced to the edge of the smoking arena.

Escobar said a few words of 'warning to others' which constituted the prisoners' trial. Then, shoved and clubbed to the edge of the pit by the AR15 guns of the guards, they dropped to the floor of the arena. For ten minutes they danced about screaming. Some fell over or deliberately lay down to escape the agony of the soles of their feet but the respite gained from their thin clothes was brief. Some, lying on the bodies of others, took over twenty minutes to die. The audience clapped. The area around the arena smelled of roast pork.

Escobar and the accountant Rubi were taken later in the day to a private airfield where one of Escobar's DC4s headed north over the Cauca and Magdalena rivers to the beach resort of Santa Marta. Here the two men were met by members of the Noguera clan, lords of the Santa Marta Gold marijuana crop, the finest in the world, who escorted them to the resort of Puerto Galeón. Two key members of the Ochoa family had already arrived as had several other cocaine maestros, including Gonzalo Rodríguez, Carlos Lehder, Luis 'Kojak' García, two Corsican mobsters and the BCCI Medellín drugs supremo Hassan Parvaiz.

The meeting, in an idyllic Caribbean setting, was partly a debriefing session for the Cartel-inspired raid earlier that month on Colombia's Supreme Court. Forty-five members of the M19 guerrilla group took over the Justice building in central Bogotá and, when attacked by the Government's elite anti-terrorist unit, shot and killed Colombia's twelve leading judges dedicated to the policy of extraditing Colombian drug barons to the USA. The attack effectively quashed all chances of a meaningful and lasting extradition agreement, an achievement warmly toasted by all at Santa Marta.

Preliminary discussions sealed an agreement in principle with the Corsicans, who promised that their leaders would meet Escobar and the Ochoas in Miami at the end of the month.

Luis 'Kojak' García, the spitting image of US actor Telly Savalas, had transported drugs for the Ochoas between 1979 and 1982 and then retired. The Ochoas were keen to retrieve his services. So were the Noruegas of Santa Marta. Neither group was aware that Kojak now worked for the US Drug Enforcement Administration. He had spent four highly profitable years running drugs between the Bahamas and Florida with his fleets of aeroplanes and slimline 'cigarette' powerboats. He knew of many landing-strips hidden among the 3000 square miles of Everglades swampland, many of them on the edges of suburban Miami. From cocaine pick-up points like San Andrés in Colombia he would fly his Learjet non-stop to the Everglades, make a low approach and release a cargo pack on skids, with a drogue chute attached, to glissade to a halt in the marshland. Then he would gain height and land openly at Miami International. Early in 1983 Kojak decided to retire from trafficking and a year later he became a DEA informant.

One of Auguste Ricord's Corsicans, present at the Santa Marta meeting, telephoned his SDECE handler, who in turn telephoned Jed Mason. Wheels within wheels. Jed had made the French contact five years earlier when FBI agents were being encouraged to develop foreign links and depend less on CIA support. Jed now knew the date fixed for the Miami meeting, Thursday, 28 November 1985.

On 25 November Jed arrived with JR at the Intercontinental, one of only three of the major hotels in Miami, the so-called Shining City, not hand in hand with drug traffickers. Here the two Operation Caesar agents could be relatively sure their conversations were not being tapped nor their belongings searched as soon as they left their rooms. In Miami, drug revenues were greater than the combined incomes of tourism and all other legitimate business.

Miami, the Indian word for 'sweet water', was founded in 1896. Not yet ninety years old, the city was already mired in corruption.

Traffickers bribed judges, drug barons financed local politicians and civil servants sold information from confidential documents, such as upcoming road and property developments, to the highest bidder. Criminals were defended in court by lawyers who had once been the city's most eminent prosecutors. Many erstwhile top anti-drugs agents now worked as private detectives for Miami-based Colombian mobsters.

At this time Vice President Bush injected huge resources into Miami's law-enforcement units, making them by far the biggest police force in the south-eastern USA. Most narcotics crime centred around Miami's Colombian and Cuban communities wherein strife and internecine jealousies provided fertile ground for the drug agencies to recruit informers.

As soon as Jed received the SDECE tip-off, he contacted his most able Miami informer, a Cuban named Ferno, and told him to identify the venue for the Miami meeting. This had seemed like a tall order since Miami is spread over thirty-four square miles with 400,000 citizens, including 100,000 *marielitos*, the Cuban refugees released in 1980 on Castro's orders from Havana's most severe jails. On their arrival, Miami's murder rate had rocketed. The city morgues could not cope so the Medical Examiner's office had rented refrigerated trucks from Burger King as temporary morgues.

The original 300,000 Miami residents were mostly of European stock, American blacks and Haitians. They had settled throughout Metro Dade county but the more recent arrivals quickly established ghettos. The first wave of Cuban refugees in the 1960s, mostly professional folk, had settled close to the Miami river and the airport between Flagler Street and the Tamiami Trail, which they nicknamed 'Calle Ocho'. This Spanish-speaking district soon became known as Little Havana.

Ferno ignored the Haitian areas of north-east Miami and the Yardie ghetto, to its immediate west, squeezed between Liberty City and Little Haiti. Likewise he wasted no time on Little Vietnam, which makes up the low-life section of eastern Little Havana and borders downtown Miami. This is the front line of the Latinos and the black gangs and no place for a high-grade rendezvous arranged by top-rank Colombians. Ferno had put the word about on the Cuban and Colombian crime fringes, of rich pickings for information about 'the big meet on 28 November'.

'I struck gold in Uncle Charlie's,' Ferno told Jed and JR in their room at the Intercontinental. 'That is a gay place off Calle Ocho where lieutenants for the big Medellín and Cali rings go to relax. They got a nice dance floor, bars and cubicles with male prostitutes.'

'How did you know the guys with the info would be gay?'

'I didn't,' Ferno said simply. 'Yesterday I checked the gossip at Biscayne Boulevard, like between 42nd and 79th, that's the straight-sex zone. The hookers' pimps there knew zilch, so I concentrate next on Uncle Charlie's and right away a Cubano nancy-boy tells me to see Pearl from Perrine.'

'Perrine?' Jed queried.

'Sure. Perrine's down the Dixie Highway, south of Rockdale. All blacks and public housing. Cocaine boys on every corner queuing by the pay phones to fix deals. Every dealer carries a stack of quarters and a beeper. Pearl is a black Cubano gay who works for the Medellín boys through Rubi, their Miami accountant. He talked loose to a boyfriend who works part time at Uncle Charlie's. I paid the boyfriend 2000 greenbacks for this.'

Jed knew Ferno's bill would be hideous. He had probably only paid $500 but was preparing the way for his expenses claim.

'You'll be reimbursed as usual,' Jed murmured.

'Sure. No problem. I was just saying.'

'Why choose a place way out of town and in a black ghetto?'

Ferno shrugged. 'Maybe they figure everybody's stoned out of their minds in Perrine and the police don't worry folk much down there. Any surveillance by the law would stand out. Pearl's rented them the Mansion. That's an old-style place. All wood and two storeys. There's a couple of crack houses at the same address.'

Jed thanked Ferno, who departed, leaving a marked city map and his current contact details.

'Wood?' JR whistled. 'So far all the HTA targets have been concrete.'

'True, but the Caesar tapes stressed they want to show off new mini arson packs to the IRA this time.'

They inspected Ferno's map and found the house not far from Perrine's Richmond Drive. Miami's lay-out made things easy. Numbered streets beginning with 1st Street and progressing consecutively north and south from Flagler Street are designated 'street', 'terrace' or 'lane' and those going consecutively west and east from Miami Avenue are named 'avenue', 'court' or 'place'. Odd house numbers are on the north side of every street and the west side of every avenue.

Ferno had warned Jed against any activity in or around the Mansion after the night of 26 November because Pearl would be using hired hands, including his boyfriend at Uncle Charlie's, to check the place out forty-eight hours before the meeting.

This left a day and a night for Jed to fix up his recording and surveillance hardware. He avoided contact with the Miami FBI office, who would normally provide all such facilities on call. After JR's frustrating experience in Mexico City had pointed to leaks, they had closed ranks. No more information sharing until they identified their spy. To this end Jed contacted an old Washington friend whom he trusted implicitly and whose own contacts in the upper echelons of the FBI were senior enough to be able to identify Redden's godfather or godfathers within the Bureau. Redden's Casey-inspired protection from CIA investigation did not explain his apparent immunity from the FBI.

Jed's Washington contact was a top lawyer whose influence and contacts on Capitol Hill were second to none. He had heard Jed out, questioned him in depth and promised he would do his best, unattributably, to identify Redden's 'FBI umbrellas'.

JR agreed with Jed to keep the details of the Miami meet entirely 'in-house'. Because HTA crime was officially the baby of the ATF, they had previously passed on all HTA information from Caesar to Jed's LA contacts in the ATF. But hostilities between the Seattle Fire Department's investigators and the ATF Bureau had pushed the matter into the public domain, with both sides leaking HTA data to the press whenever it suited them. The first big HTA-ignited blaze, in January 1984, had taken place in Seattle, as had half a dozen other suspected HTA arson events over the months that followed.

'If opportunity arrests are made at this Miami meet by the ATF or any other agency,' Jed offered, 'I can't see them leading to convictions. On the other hand if we let Redden's HTA attack go ahead uninterrupted, we may reap vital video evidence, enough to pin the bastard for good. And if, in the process, we wind up with a few dead bodies, they will all be top-grade narcotics criminals. Dogs eaten by dogs. A double whammy.'

JR nodded. 'I agree. We have a unique chance to record Redden's

264

men setting up an HTA fire. The target is wooden and the charge, judging by the Caesar description of a mini-pack, will be different to the stuff they've used previously. In many ways a smaller charge could be more lethal, involving a weapon far more practical for use by terrorists, special forces, arson insurance fraudsters and God knows who else.'

'So we're agreed then?' Jed looked up. 'We go it alone? Where do we get the surveillance kit? If we have to set up before Pearl's people sweep the crack house, we've got to get moving now.'

'Roberto,' JR said. 'I'll leave his family name out of it. He's FBI but helps the Miami CENTAC boys when he can. He keeps a close mouth and he knows you can trust no one down here. For example, the narcotics officer who in 1981 first established the Miami CENTAC, Raúl Díaz. When he left the Force two years later he joined a private detective agency and now spends his time shooting *down* CENTAC's court cases against narco-crime.'

'This Roberto,' Jed asked, 'he can fix up the Perrine crack house, the Mansion, tonight?'

'Sure. He's never let me down. I'll call him now.'

'And he'll keep everything quiet?'

'If I ask him to . . . And providing nothing gets out of hand.'

Korbi Richter stood behind the roll-bar, shifting his weight from leg to leg and bending at the knees to absorb the shock as the thirty-five-foot Aranald cigarette boat struck the occasional irregularity on the calm, moonlit surface of the Atlantic. At forty knots the sleek speedboat was taking it easy. The three Yamaha, thwart-mounted, 250-horsepower outboards were capable of sixty knots and more. Each engine cost $20,000 and the *clavos*, hidden smuggling compartments, added an additional $80,000 to the overall cost of $400,000. On board with Richter were Arturo the boatman, the nameless Assassin, and John Anderson the HTA scientist.

The US Government, hoist by the petard of Reagan's noisy war-on-drugs PR, was desperate to block cigarette boats from bringing Colombian cocaine to Florida. Twenty-six separate law agencies, federal, state and local, between them fielded over a hundred patrol boats, including the fifteen impressive eighty-knot Blue Thunder boats of the US Customs strike force based from a high-tech surveillance centre in Miami.

Cigarette boat Number 103, taking Richter and the others to Miami while completing a drug run, was one of Redden's Bahamas-based fleet. One thousand kilos of Bolivian cocaine, at a Miami street price of $18 million, shared the hidden storage spaces with the Assassin's weaponry for the Perrine job, a M60 machine-gun with tripod and ammunition, a M70 grenade launcher and a box of grenades. Anderson's HTA kit consisted of four standard ammunition boxes with a good deal of inner space taken up by bubble-wrap protecting the chemicals and detonators.

Crab Cay lay twenty minutes' cruising through pole-marked coral shallows to the north of Redden's anchored houseboat, a sixty-foot Hatteras tuna fisher. At Crab Cay, Number 103's boatman had veered north-west to Memory Rocks in deep water off the Matanilla Shoals. After collecting the floating cocaine bundles to augment the existing contraband in the *clavos*, they headed south-south-west in open sea.

Number 103 carried $50,000 worth of radar-jamming gear and several coats of special fibreglass paint which made the boat virtually undetectable to government radar-surveillance gear. Additionally Redden's men paid Customs officials for copies of their duty schedules, so they would know in advance how best to avoid the Blue Thunder patrols.

Despite all the rhetoric of Reagan and Bush, plus the cash and effort pumped into the war on drugs in Florida, 60 per cent of the tidal wave of cocaine, flooding into the USA by every conceivable method, arrives by small boat along the Florida coastline. The fact that any small boat could be a smuggler and over 125,000 pleasure craft sail about off Miami during the summer months does not help the Customs, whose radar cannot tell a drug boat from a pleasure craft on a family outing.

John Anderson, Redden's HTA scientist, had earlier tried to sleep on board the bucking boat but had given up and now stared out into the silvered darkness. Where had he gone wrong? From a senior CIA chemical engineer with exciting horizons, he had come to this, jumping at the beck and call of cocaine smugglers. Perhaps, he reflected, co-opted rocket scientists of the Third Reich had felt the same way. HTA was *his* brainchild. If only in 1979 he had not succumbed to the first tempting approaches of the Mob, their promises of his own laboratory assistants and unlimited research funds. All of which had since fallen foul of their inability, in 1984, to understand the nature of the huge technical obstacles involved: the need for patience. They had soon run out of this commodity and sold Anderson plus his HTA project like some cheap auction lot to the first bidder, Albert Redden, whom he had come to fear and to hate.

It was typical of Redden that potential buyers were to attend this first field test of the new HTA mini-pack. Of course, Anderson expected success but one should always be *sure* before conducting a public demonstration.

Arturo handed Richter a metal Thermos cup of black Colombian coffee. The boatman was one of nineteen Floridian *peces* employed by Redden for the Lucaya to Miami night runs. Richter recognised the signs of the typical *marielito*, the unattractive skin pigmentation caused by years of malnutrition in Castro's jails.

'*Compadre*,' said Arturo as he offered the Assassin coffee. 'Your health and your future.' He knew the reputation of his fellow-Cuban was second to none among Cubano killers. He had been hired by the Medellín Cartel a fortnight earlier to assassinate a drug trafficker, Barry Seal, then under house arrest at a Salvation Army centre in Baton Rouge. Seal was the government's only witness against Jorge Ochoa, shortly to be extradited to the USA from a Madrid jail. Ochoa was the world's number one drug king and Seal's survival was critical to the prosecution.

Through a friend in the Bahamas named Carlos Lehder, a close associate of the Ochoas, Redden had learnt about the Assassin's contract to kill Seal and, through a front, offered him twice the fee to botch his attack on Seal. Redden's aim was simply to ensure Seal's survival and thus guarantee Ochoa's life-long imprisonment. Since the Assassin was now on his payroll, Redden had sent him with Richter and Anderson to handle the meeting in Perrine. Should anything go wrong with the HTA attack, the Assassin would be waiting outside the Mansion to greet would-be survivors with his M60.

Redden had briefed Richter after receiving a personal call from William Casey with details of the time and location of the Miami meet. Luis 'Kojak' García had informed his CIA case officer about Perrine as soon as he'd returned from the Santa Marta conference. Casey's hero was Reagan and Reagan wanted results in his 'war on drugs'. Politically Casey could not afford to offend Colombia by authorising CIA assassination of the Ochoas, the clan responsible for four-fifths of the Colombian economy. However, it was quite a different matter if Redden's men achieved the downfall of Jorge Ochoa with no apparent CIA connections. Casey would then have his cake and eat it. So the CIA kept well clear of Perrine.

Arturo looked at his gold Rolex Submariner and congratulated himself. Timing was critical on this journey, for he was about to enter Biscayne Bay and the Miami river with its 'flagship patrols', not his normal haunts further down the coast. He knew a dozen inlets and estuaries with shallow approaches where no coastguard would dare follow, especially by night.

After all, a 'coastie' in charge of a million-dollar patrol boat would hardly risk his career by steaming into unknown waters after a single cigarette boat with an unknown cargo. His salary as a coastie would be 100 dollars a day before tax. Arturo earned 30,000 tax-free dollars per run, sometimes more. His open-sea navigation was not too hot, but so what? With two satellite navigation systems on board he had only to read the dials to reach any selected grid coordinate in the Caribbean and meet up with the Colombian mother-ship, a freighter, many miles from any patrolled zone. This was nursery stuff for Arturo.

At 5.30 a.m. he moored close by a dingy Miami river bar, the Santa Barbara, where a limousine and a pick-up truck waited. Two uniformed members of the Miami River Police stood in the shadows of the building. Richter had paid them well. Any unforeseen intervention at this stage was their responsibility. Miami's police were, in 1985, about as difficult to bribe as hungry guard dogs offered hamburgers.

Richter used the mobile telephone in the limousine. He woke Stafford 'Tricks' Douglas in the Fontainebleau Hotel on Miami Beach.

'The HTA set-up by Anderson is scheduled for tonight. You will keep our Irish friends on call from 4 p.m. onwards, *ney?*' He rang off and smiled. He was looking forward to the first active phase of the attack on the Ochoa empire.

The Mansion crack house in Perrine appeared deserted. Pearl, as a known Cartel freelancer, had no worries from local crime and never bothered to secure those rooms at the Mansion not used for cocaine freebasing or storage. Two satellite dishes sprouted from the roof, for secure communications with Pearl's masters in Medellín. All street-side doors and windows were barred and, inside the building, the main, beautifully furnished meeting room with an oval confer-ence table and seating for twenty, occupied the centre of the building, with no windows and surrounded by corridors. The room had been custom-built for a 1983 meeting organised by Carlos Lehder and never used since. Pearl planned on having cleaners and caterers, carefully vetted and supervised, work through 27 Novem-ber, the day before the meet.

On the night of the twenty-sixth the building was empty. Ferno led Jed, JR and their FBI friend Roberto's team through the shadows at the rear of the Mansion. Roberto's men gained entry to the house and, shortly afterwards, to the conference room. Within an hour the place was skilfully wired for remote sound and visual surveillance. Jed and JR did not even enter the building.

On the other side of the street, Ferno had rented two floors of an empty apartment, one of them merely to keep other people out. He led Jed and the others upstairs and JR whistled with admiration on arrival. In the short time available Roberto had set up a complete command post almost as sophisticated as Operation Caesar's HQ in Los Angeles.

Ferno, wandering about with his professional antennae aquiver, came across thirty fifty-five-gallon drums of chemicals in a back-room on the ground floor.

'Ethyl ether,' he told Jed. 'The most efficient solvent for cocaine processing.'

Jed checked out the standard receiving units for the voice-activated recorder bugs secreted in the conference room across the road and for a parabolic mike, capable of picking up conversation over 300 metres away, which was aimed across the road from their apartments to record the words of exterior guards and of conversa-tions between guests as they arrived. The instruments planted within the conference room included wall-mounted spike-mikes and pinhead bugs inserted into chair seats and light fittings. These last were inert receivers which would not be located by any electronic sweep Pearl's people might carry out the next day.

A bank of six TV monitor screens in the command post would be manually activated as soon as Roberto's gadgets team detected activity in the Mansion. The subminiature CCD video cameras were all wall-mounted. Each used an 8mm fixed-focus lens capable of supplying great detail without the need for special optics, thanks to an in-built electronic iris. All the camera's electronics were mounted on printed circuit boards that could be positioned away from the lens and connected only by thin ribbon cables. The active eye of the camera was thus tiny and easily concealed by Roberto's well-practised colleagues. Between the six lenses, with their ninety-two-degree field of view, the entire room was covered.

At 9.15 p.m. they had reason to be thankful for their early arrival when the sound recorders clicked on and alerted the watchers to the arrival of HTA boffin Anderson, and Mafia and his IRA arms buyers, accompanied by three of Richter's local people. Roberto activated the remote switch to the thirteen-volt DC camera batteries. Jed and JR watched fascinated as Anderson inserted two devices into the seats of chairs positioned away from the table and Richter's men meanwhile secreted their own surveillance units about the room. There was a general panic when one of Roberto's bugs was discovered in a light fitting. Jed and JR listened intently to the ensuing argument and were much relieved when a decision was reached by Anderson that the bug did not look recent and was probably an inactive leftover from some previous meeting. Somebody stamped on and shattered the tiny microphone.

The two IRA men watched intrigued as Anderson worked, doubtless picturing themselves at some later date doctoring the British House of Commons in a like manner.

By 11 p.m. the Richter group was clear of the Mansion and, soon after midnight, Jed's team departed from Perrine leaving only Roberto's gadget men behind.

The Colombians and the Corsicans met in Maxim's on the corner of 74th Avenue and South West Eighth Street, a classy public restaurant painted blue outside and entirely without windows. Their bodyguards ate in watchful groups around the outside of the room. The restaurant had been reserved for the evening by a local functionary for the Cartel. Rubi intended to set Auguste Ricord's Corsicans entirely at their ease. Hence the choice of a public eating place complete with pianist and cosy lighting. Rubi made his apologies that neither Escobar nor any member of the Ochoa family had been able to attend. This, he said, was due to the unfortunate US-inspired witch-hunt, following the Cartel-instigated murder the previous week of Colonel Jaime Ramírez, head of the National Police Narcotics Unit and Colombia's great white hope of effective police action against the Cartel.

Rubi himself acted as host, toasting the mutual success of the Cartel and the Corsicans in their European venture. He had the full power of the Cartel *dueños* to sign the agreement on their behalf should approval be reached by all at the imminent meeting. The general mood was convivial by the time the four Corsican leaders and the seven Medellín representatives led their guards outside and drove in convoy to Perrine.

At the Mansion the guards, some in the cars and others in the shadows about the building, nursed sub-machine-guns and watched one another with twitchy trigger fingers. Nobody feared an attack from within the building. Representatives took their seats about the oval table and the conference convened.

Outside factors intervened at this point. A detective of Metro Dade's Vice and Intelligence Narcotics Unit (VINU) from the South Section of the Organized Crime Bureau had, on a random hunch, tailed one of Richter's locals the previous day to the Mansion. Richter's men had spotted the battered VINU Lincoln and phoned a car-dealer friend to check the State's automobile licensing computer. This spat out the information that the Lincoln's licence plate was 'no longer in service', a sure sign of surveillance by VINU men.

In a panic on receiving the car dealer's news about VINU surveillance, Richter's man – unable to locate Richter – called up Anderson and his group, who were operating from a rental van one block away from the Mansion and its protective cluster of limousines.

Anderson, keen not to allow any hitch to this demonstration of his prowess, proof of his long years of dedicated R&D, persuaded the others that there should be no delay. As soon as the conference was in progress and Richter's Assassin was installed in his rooftop position, the HTA devices should be activated.

At one moment JR, chain-smoking contentedly under his earphones and viewing the monitors, could have been surveying any corporate conference. The next, with no warning sound or signal, the HTA devices ignited. He later estimated that the men inside the inner room were roasted alive within twenty seconds, some sooner, and that the guards caught in the outer corridors may have survived up to two minutes after the ignition. He remembered the first sound, like that of great firework rockets shooting skywards. Then came a nightmare cacophony of elemental chaos which he could not describe but which had to do with oxygen consumption, compression, vacuum and all-consuming heat. If there were human screams of horror or pain, they were cut short as the recording bugs melted down, instants only before the video lenses became blurred and the monitor screens blacked out.

Following the flare ignition JR had seen a blinding flash of white and yellow. Possibly phosphorus, but he could not swear to it. Jed agreed afterwards that there had been no visible smoke nor flame – just heat and light like the fireball of a nuclear explosion.

The watchers in the command post craned their necks to the high street window above the monitors and stared at the inferno across the road. Two of the guards' limousines had already roared away. Others were following. Nothing short of a huge incendiary bomb, JR marvelled, napalm or thermite perhaps, could possibly have turned the entire Mansion, within the space of two short minutes, into the roaring vortex of white heat which hurt his eyes and warmed his face even behind plate glass a hundred yards from the heart of the furnace.

The Assassin on the roof had found himself redundant but he waited until the pyre of the Mansion, quickly exhausted of combustible materials, burnt down to a blackened shell. Nobody appeared in the streets to watch the fire. Local residents who had earlier observed the limousines and the men with the Uzis knew better than to show curiosity. Nobody called the police or the fire services, and since the blaze did not spread to other buildings, only the owners of the Mansion crack houses were affected and they were unlikely to complain publicly.

The Ochoas, Escobar and the Corsicans could not suspect each other since both sides had lost their representatives. They put out their spies but obtained no leads on those responsible.

The IRA arms buyers were enormously impressed by HTA as a

potential weapon for their terrorist armoury and expressed their interest via Mafia.

Jed and JR gained no further clues as to HTA's make-up but the film from Roberto's camera, taken from the surveillance apartment, provided a breakthrough in the quest for Redden. This came with the discovery of an excellent series of photographs of the scientist Anderson leaving the building after preparing the HTA devices. He had briefly removed his baseball cap and spectacles to wipe his brow with his handkerchief. Jed faxed the photographs to Washington, whose computers consulted one another's data banks and furnished a startling history of John Anderson, erstwhile CIA specialist officially assumed dead after a fire in the Adirondacks in 1984. Anderson, camping alone, had died in his tent when his camping stove exploded, his inquest record stated. The identity of the charred corpse in the melted nylon sleeping bag had been established by forensic studies of the CIA identity disc found around its neck.

'Probably some lonely deer hunter that Anderson bagged up there,' Jed commented, 'to provide the necessary material for his official death.'

John Fiat Anderson, born in 1934 in Arkansas, the only child of a Danish chemist, had excelled at college and, in 1953, was head-hunted by Sidney Gottlieb, the head of the Chemical Division, a secret unit within the Technical Services Staff (TSS) of the CIA and tasked with the discovery of a 'truth drug'. In those days of US zeal to outwit the communist foe, the USSR was believed to have a drug that could control the human mind. America must obviously counter with its own concoction and decided, among other psychochemical experiments, to concentrate on LSD.

In 1966 Anderson, who had advised the CIA on the use of the drug, was made redundant, along with many of his colleagues, mind control through LSD having proved a spectacular failure. He transferred on contract to naval research programmes, ending up at the US Navy Air Warfare Center at China Lake, where he specialised in chemicals designed to achieve enormous pyrolysation and gasification of materials, achieving maximum 'punch' from a minimal source.

In 1979 the West Coast Mafia's own ongoing HTA project, then called Hi-Heat, lost its prime expert to cancer. The Mob searched within the armed forces to locate and employ a suitable scientist to take over. Having drawn a blank with the US Navy Research Laboratories and the USAF, they tried the Sandia National Laboratories, the Rocket Research Company of Olin and the Weyerhauser Corporation Fire Technology Laboratory all to no avail. By the time some bright Sicilian spark thought of China Lake, the salary offered was sky-high and John Anderson accepted with alacrity.

Now, after six years' slow progress with the Mob and then with Redden, he was growing grey with the frustrations of constant carping about slow results and fluctuating budgets which he could never rely on. If the Miami mini-pack trial went well, he would instantly press Redden for his next major trial, with a 200kg device, on a large non-combustible target. If that was successful the sky was the limit. Miniaturisation. Less HTA materials for the same devastating effect. Just as clumsy, unstable gelignite had led to Semtex, so Anderson's HTA mix would soon become the insurance assessor's nightmare, never mind the devastating new toy of special forces and terrorists alike.

As soon as the Perrine fire was successfully concluded Anderson had telephoned Redden and asked that his next Seattle test fire go ahead immediately. His laboratories were nineteen miles from the city centre and there were countless excellent civilian targets in the Seattle suburbs. Ten months before, Anderson had completed a trial at a carpet store with walls of concrete, steel and brick and some 150 square feet in area, an ideal proving ground. However, the building contained dense combustible materials and nine months passed by before Anderson was ready to destroy a mainly concrete and steel shell with no flammable content to feed on. Nine days earlier, at an electroplating workshop in nearby Tacoma, he had done so with partial success. After minor adjustments, he was now ready for the final trial.

With Redden's immediate approval, following the Perrine event, Anderson planned to go ahead at once with an attack on a major bare-bones Seattle structure. Ideal conditions were naturally an unattended building, so he planned for Saturday night, when there would be no risk of overtime workers. The agreed date was 30 November.

Jed learnt of Anderson's identity early on Friday, 29 November, and with JR's agreement avoided what in normal circumstances would have been their obvious next step, to gain up-to-date information from the National Crime Information Centre (NCIC) giving Anderson's latest known address, his automobile data and details of his family and associates. But whoever was spying on Operation Caesar would quickly learn of Jed's interest in John Anderson and, if acting true to form, would warn Redden off. So Jed called Allen Schweitzer instead. Al owed him one.

The NCIC mainframe computer in the Hoover FBI headquarters was bigger than a football field and contained vast data reservoirs. Over 20 million information items were held, 100,000 accesses were made daily and 68,000 law agencies were on tap. To prevent unauthorised access to this great depository of secrets, the FBI had numerous checks and balances, security codes and encryptions. This effectively kept out most outsiders but 80 per cent of those who abuse the system were themselves former FBI agents, part of the old boy network, who were prepared to access the records of any named US citizen to help out a friend or to earn a fee.

Al Schweitzer, an ex-Silicon Valley corporate investigator attached to Narcotics, had spent years cultivating an army of law-enforcement officers as well as individuals with access to credit bureaux, banks, local government and telephone companies. Schweitzer took down John Anderson's known details and promised Jed whatever he could scrape out of NCIC. Four hours later he called back with an address and two unlisted phone numbers near Seattle. Jed moved fast, phoning a friend at his Washington DC office to prepare a surveillance team in Seattle as he and JR were driven to Miami Airport. He warned his friend to log the surveillance as a standard CISPES task and not to mention Anderson. Within hours Anderson's private address near Seattle was under full-time watch and the scientist was observed being dropped off there by taxi, probably direct from his Miami flight, by dusk on 29 November.

The following day Anderson was collected early by a Toyota pick-up. His moves were then monitored continuously and, when Jed and JR joined the 'Street-AWACS', the main FBI surveillance van, Anderson had met up with his HTA field team and was busy supervising the loading of the Toyota with ten-gallon drums. It was apparent to the watchers that action of some sort was planned for the immediate future.

At 8 p.m. JR checked his street map as the Toyota and a second car drew up in an industrial area of Seattle.

'South Monroe Street,' he breathed. 'A light industry and storage district. Kill the headlamps.'

The Toyota pulled up outside a squat concrete storehouse. Three men in boiler suits pulled six containers shaped like beehives from the rear compartment and carried them into deep shadows. One approached a door in the centre of the building and let himself in with a key. Men and equipment entered and the door closed behind them. Their transport drove off.

Ridgway gave the binoculars back to his driver and looked over his shoulder.

'Do we go in and catch them with the materials now, Jed? Even if the big fish aren't here and it looks like they're not, this is surely our chance to analyse the HTA mix.'

Two technicians and two agents were crammed beside and behind Jed. Further back, red and green lights moved across the face of various consoles, the high-tech guts of the AWACS. Some of the gear was too sensitive to allow smoking, a major drawback for tobacco-addicted watchers.

Jed rubbed his eyes. He was short of sleep.

'It's a nice idea, but I think we'd do better to approach Anderson and offer him a deal. If he tells all he knows about Redden and HTA we've got an open and shut RICO conspiracy case.'

JR nodded. A lovely thought.

'How do they select those HTA burn targets?' Jed wondered aloud. 'They must have scoped out this place with care as they've got keys . . . Unless there's inside help.'

'At random, we reckon,' the AWACS oppo piped up. 'Anywhere with the right sort of structure and preferably no great fire load of its own. The HTA hit ten days ago was an electroplating shop in Tacoma. Nothing much to burn there but steel lathes. Yet the whole place went up like tinder in minutes. Two of the targets have been uninsured or heavily undervalued. None of the owners of HTA arson targets have been suspect or connected. So it seems the arsonists use any suitable properties for their ongoing research and development. To erect and then burn down structures of their own would certainly be less cost-effective . . . What's the plan now, boss?'

'When they've laid their eggs they will want to hightail it,' Jed replied. 'Their Toyota will presumably collect them on call. Make sure they are followed. We stay here and video the fire itself from start to finish, taking care not to attract the attentions of the Seattle Fire Department and Arson Squad when they turn up.'

At 9.30 p.m. the Nikon motor-drive of Jed's photographer began to click as the arson team, including Anderson, exited from the building. The Toyota drew up and within a minute they were gone. The muted intercom in the AWACS wagon announced that Jed's shadows were 'stitched to the Toyota's ass'.

At 9.45 p.m. the building began to emit black and white smoke which billowed out of vents and loose-fitting door frames. Windows and then doors exploded outwards. Flares of intense white heat, not dissimilar to take-off time at Cape Canaveral, shot from the central area of the concrete edifice.

Jed reached for a data sheet which issued from one of the AWACS computers.

'The target is a store called Victory Bumpers,' he read. 'Owned by one Richard Christopherson. No criminal record. Sole use of the premises is the repair and storage of vehicle bumpers . . . non-combustible metal bumpers.'

They watched and listened in awe as the roof fell in and heavy internal roller doors collapsed with a shriek of clashing steel.

The first fire engine arrived soon after 10 p.m., just in time to witness an exploding holocaust of radiated heat as flashover occurred throughout the structure. Pillars of white flame exploded skywards, spawning showers of blazing spark clusters. If there was anybody in the building, they would by now be cinders.

The whole building was quickly devoured by the inferno, melted and charred by successive incandescent-red to carbon-arc-white surges of superheat. Within twenty-eight minutes of ignition, the entire steel-and-concrete erection, with its stored banks of steel and aluminium bumpers, was a burnt-out hulk. Jed was impressed.

The Seattle firemen sat back in their gleaming trucks and watched the fire burn itself out. They had learnt, through the deaths of some of their brethren at previous such fires, not to play around with any conflagration showing HTA symptoms. Their remit was to keep clear, move the public away and stop the blaze from spreading to nearby property. Previous efforts with high-pressure hoses to extinguish HTA fires had had the opposite effect; water merely aggravated the inferno, fanning more intense and higher flames.

Temperatures met by fire-fighters in some of the world's fiercest traditional conflagration-sourced fires have been recorded at 2300°F but HTA produces 5000°F and more. An HTA arson witness reported seeing 'Rods of white-hot energy that consume huge and often empty industrial complexes in minutes, melting steel girders and crumbling concrete to glassy powder'.

A few months earlier Seattle Fire Department had conducted tests in a vain attempt to isolate the ingredients of HTA. Despite thousands of hours' work by experts from all over the USA, they had failed to determine the nature of the accelerants responsible. Thermite was the prime suspect but tests showed that, by itself, thermite could not create such spectacular results. Moreover, it invariably left a tell-tale slag signature which had never yet been found in the ruins of HTA fires.

Forensic analysis of arson debris to trace suspect matter, using the most advanced detection methods, had not been helpful. Speculation that a concoction resembling rocket propellant had achieved an exotic fuel-oxidising cocktail was never verified. Nor had any flammable or combustible material been seen or smelled by any witness at any of the HTA fires.

'The Arson Squad will soon arrive,' Jed warned, 'and they suspect anybody and everybody found watching an arson site.' He looked out at the dark upper windows on both sides of the road. 'Somewhere up there Redden's experts may well be watching and recording the results of their handiwork. A thorough house-to-house search could be worthwhile. What a shame we live in a democracy. Search warrants are a gift to the criminal fraternity.'

The AWACS crew began to pack up. Jed's enthusiasm was infecting the watch team. They knew nothing of Operation Caesar, only that they were helping out an agent rumoured to have been a CENTAC man and that he now looked like a cat with a platter of cream.

JR unpacked a celebratory Camel but saw the sour sideways glance of the AWACS ops officer and put back the cigarette with a sigh.

'Four years it's been, Jed, but now I think we've got the bastards, Redden, Richter and God knows how many more. Anderson will talk. When he sees this video, he'll realise he's facing fifteen years minimum unless he sings like a bird. Will you tell Washington right away? They'll be pretty pissed off if you don't.'

Jed shook his head and kept his voice low. 'The Seattle SAC' – he referred to the local FBI boss – 'knows nothing about Caesar. Only that I requested his surveillance support for a CISPES operation, checking on left-wing troublemakers. I will put in a standard report mentioning chance involvement with the fire. He's unlikely to check my report through with these lads. He'll have a hundred and one other more important things on his mind.'

But Jed did have a problem. JR was right: he *should* report the locating of John Anderson to headquarters, to the FBI office of his Assistant Director of Criminal Investigations and to his own Los Angeles SAC. Neither man would be likely to question his decisions but it was his duty to keep them informed. He should not even be contemplating the 'turning' of an ex-CIA agent gone sour, as Anderson had, without touching base in LA and Washington. His CENTAC years had given him clout and the habit of Lone Rangerism but this would be going too far.

On the other hand when, the previous month, he had told headquarters and the LA SAC about Mexico City, JR had been compromised on arrival and lost Richter as a result. Jed made his decision quickly, as was his habit. He would again speak to John Shaheen, his Washington *éminence grise*, and ask him to make direct contact with Jed's Assistant Director, thereby detouring around potential leakage by the AD's office staff. He would say nothing at all to the LA SAC.

He and JR must now get some sleep, for they were rapidly becoming zombie-like. Once refreshed, they would slip into Anderson's home in Bremerton, near Seattle and go for a RICO, the FBI's most successful weapon against organised criminals like Redden's network. The RICO statutes are a batch of federal laws which permit agents to prosecute the entire criminal organisation benefiting from a particular crime, including arson, rather than just the individual who committed the felony.

With Anderson and the Victory Bumpers HTA arson video together, Jed knew he had Redden and every other criminal ever involved with him caught in a steel-webbed net. He called John Shaheen in Washington.

Clark Clifford, former US Secretary of Defence and the most influential lawyer in the USA, met John Shaheen at a restaurant near McPherson Square. Unlike Shaheen, Clifford was not one of Casey's Friends but he was a long-time business associate of the BCCI Bank's President, Hassan Abedi.

Clifford was Chairman of First American, an inter-state bank worth $11 billion which Abedi had secretly purchased in direct defiance of US regulations. Clifford also served as BCCI's lawyer in the USA, an obvious conflict of interests. Abedi had been paying Clifford huge sums for seven years to front his American operations. Clifford provided him with a respectable, indeed ultra-respectable, face since Clifford was a dominant force in Washington, an adviser to four presidents, senior aide to Harry Truman, a creator of the CIA, Kennedy's own lawyer, Jimmy Carter's counsel and special envoy; the list was impressive.

Clifford was well aware of Abedi's involvement with President Zia and the CIA operations in Afghanistan. Abedi had paid Clifford over $7.8 million for his advice and his contacts. Shaheen, through Jed Mason's unwitting call, had now chanced upon a serious threat to Redden, the BCCI/CIA Afghan operation, and therefore to Clifford. The HTA project was immediately threatened but, should the Washington press catch a whisper, a whole can of Watergate-type worms might be opened, endangering Clifford through his intimate relations with the criminal bank. As Shaheen understood the call from Jed Mason of the FBI, with whom he went back some twenty years, the HTA scientist Anderson was key to the FBI arrest of Redden and a court case likely to blow BCCI right out of the water.

When Clifford left him, Shaheen assessed the situation. They were in trouble, or would be if they didn't act quickly. Anderson must be kept away from the FBI, so Shaheen called Albert Redden at once.

'What are you suggesting, John?' Redden was noncommittal.

'Nothing that you can't work out for yourself, Al. We all of us are doing what's best for the US of A. We both agree that, right now, HTA has great potential as part of the anti-Soviet war effort in

Afghanistan. Like Blowpipe hand-held anti-gunship missiles, it could revolutionise the mujahidin response capacity. Anderson has been the key to its production. I simply feel we should move him out of harm's way immediately.'

'I understand, my friend. You are right. I will look after it. Rest assured.'

Redden rang off and called Korbi Richter on his private line at the Wilshire Boulevard office.

'Korbi, I will be brief. According to your report today, Anderson was 100 per cent successful with the warehouse test.'

'Sure.' Richter was surprised. This was not a matter which Redden would have normally queried. 'He's got there. That was the final test. HTA's home and dry now.'

'So he'll be wanting his pay-off?'

'That's right. Fifteen million dollars and cheap at the price. The HTA field containers are sealable and tamper-proof. Nobody, not even the Pakis, will be able to analyse and reproduce the constituents. The 200kg sets and the mini-packs will be production-line ready in a month or two with or without Anderson.'

'OK. I want you to wipe the guy now, like yesterday, and make it look like one of the Latino mobs did him in. Anderson has become a liability.'

'Why? What's changed?'

'The Op Caesar creeps are on to him.'

'So we move him. Hide him.'

'No.' Redden's tone was steady. 'He's outlived his usefulness. He's a risk to us.'

JR arrived at Anderson's house on the west side of Puget Sound in the small hours. The living room was furnished in black marble with glass and steel furniture and thick white rugs. Weird Chinese puzzles, outsize Rubik cubes and other three-dimensional games graced table tops in lieu of flowers. He found Anderson on the kitchen table facing the ceiling. His hands and ankles were bound to the table legs with curtain cord and his death, JR decided, must have been distressing. He recognised the mark of the Latino groups: the 'Colombian Necktie'.

They had cut a hole in Anderson's neck, immediately below his chin, and forced his tongue through it. He would have choked and suffocated. JR had heard it said that a victim with a strong heart could survive for four or five minutes before finally succumbing. Anderson's eyes protruded frog-like. He seemed to be wearing a red bow-tie. JR's heart was heavy. Redden was again one jump ahead.

Jed later assured JR he had told nobody but his trusted Washington friend of their Anderson plans. They were at a loss to explain the murder. Perhaps a genuine coincidence was involved. Anderson might have been running drugs on the side, for all they knew, and clashed fatally with Colombian traffickers. None the less the two men agreed they would henceforward keep Operation Caesar from all outsiders.

For the moment, their remaining leads were not hopeful. They agreed to lie low for a while and wait for Redden to make a wrong move.

22

December 1985–February 1986

Mafia had grown to admire the two IRA arms buyers. Their hatred for the British was tinged with humour and, like him, they did not let their emotions stand in the way of their end-goal. One, John McIntyre, had turned out to be not an Irishman but an American IRA sympathiser from Boston, believed dead by MI5 and the FBI. The other, Maguire, had spent years under various guises persuading Americans in the arms industry to part with sophisticated weapons and with designs for the IRA to copy. Both men were delighted with the potential of HTA and assured the man they knew as Tricks that they would do their best to persuade the IRA's Army Council to go for it in a big way.

Korbi Richter was pleased with the successful removal of Duraz and with the way Tricks had handled the IRA buyers. He had gone so far as to offer Tricks the chance of big business in what he called troubleshooting for the bank. Redden had, over the past six years, executed a number of 'dirty jobs' for BCCI in exchange for exclusive financial services. Most of the 'dirty tricks' agents he used were Germans but Richter was always on the lookout for suitable personnel. For London-based work he could see a bright future for Tricks since BCCI's operations there were expanding.

Back home in Handsworth, Mafia slipped back into his homely reggae and cannabis image. He had no wish to excite the West Midlands Police or anyone else with suspicions of his growing eminence and scope. Turning to overdue minutiae, he concentrated on the last meeting with Blackledge, which his police nemesis, DC Mick Pearce, had interrupted. In North London Blackledge had since located a flat with the telephone number used by the people observed at the Kinver sett. He called Kingston in Brixton.

'You got two good boys from Manor House way? Scare some information from a coolie girl. Make it like soon.'

He gave Kingston the details of Sara's flat in Keynsham House and the general background to what he wanted.

Sara was worried about Goodman. He had, since finding evidence of his wife's murder, sunk into a deep depression. He telephoned the Professor daily, ate little and spent his time either sitting silently with Tosh's patients in the coolers or reading cowboy stories to Chemist, who was having a bad spell and could hardly manage the laboratory by himself on his worst days.

'Why don't you take a rest, Alex?' Sara cajoled him. 'You're lookin' exhausted.'

'I need to be with people worse off than me,' he replied simply, 'I have nightmares when I sleep and even when I stop to think. I need to know *exactly* what happened in the wood. Then I can decide what to do. If only the Professor would finish his work.'

'You should try yoga, Alex. I could teach you. You are a gentle person but these things are pullin' you towards aggression. With yoga you learn the concept of Ahimsa, non-violence, then you can live again outside your nightmares.'

'I have become my nightmares. You cannot understand. I did what I thought was right in the wood. They were doing unspeakable things to the badgers. I only asked them to stop. But if I had done nothing, Mary and Lucy would now be alive.'

'You did the same for me. Remember? At the building site. It's your nature. You can't blame yourself for what happened. Your little daughter loved all animals, didn't she? Yeah, well she'd have wanted you to stop them, wouldn't she?'

Goodman's lips crinkled with the hint of a smile. 'She did love rabbits.'

'Well then,' Sara touched his back with the palm of her hand. 'Try to remember that we are in the hands of fate. Nobody can blame you.'

'I am sorry, Sara,' said Goodman, looking at his hands and

284

stroking the red outline of the scars on his finger, 'but I can never forgive what these evil men have done to my family. I have no wish to forgive. I have only a living nightmare in my head which will never go away while those who caused it go unpunished. I am sorry.'

Sara yearned in her heart to comfort her lodger with her body. Thinking of him increasingly enabled her to forget the flabby bodies, the bad breath and the abusive language which went with her chosen profession. But she could see there was no room in his mind for anything but despair, guilt and hatred. She busied herself at the cooker with Bombay Mix and garam masala, a dish that normally made him purr.

Detective Constable Clive Mills admired the generation of Jamaicans who had arrived in London from the West Indies in the 1950s. He knew they were as distressed as anyone at the vicious criminality of so many of the British-born Jamaicans of later generations.

'Your typical Yardie,' Clive was fond of saying, 'despises pimping. Too much like hard work. He'll be mostly into crack. Or fraud. Not armed robberies, which involve elbow grease and organisation. Yardies go for extreme violence. Then you get your up and coming junior Yardies who do street robberies with big lock-knives or long-barrelled heavy revolvers. Five or six youths to a pack. Like wolves. Mostly by night. They find their prey at bus stops or down in the tube. Some select their victims in shops, follow them into quiet streets and attack as they get into their cars. A woman with a handbag is easy meat, a straight snatch. Men with briefcases sometimes fight back: they are stabbed and kicked. That's life in Manor House.'

'Seems pretty quiet,' Barry muttered. He and Clive were patrolling their turf in Tottenham. Taff Jones had left the squad for a while, seconded to Broadwater Farm enquiry duties in the aftermath of the Blakelock killing.

'Let's move on,' said Clive. He drove slowly, but not too slowly. Both men had developed an uncanny knack to spot crime. Anything slightly out of place, somehow wrong, registered a red light as they silently watched the everyday throng pass by. From Green Lanes they turned down Woodberry Grove into the heart of the Woodberry Down Estate, if such a place has a heart. It was owned, following the dissolution of the Greater London Council, by the

London Borough of Hackney, which was grossly understaffed and quite unable to keep tabs on who was doing what and where on its property.

The estate lies at the juncture of the jurisdictions of four police forces: Tottenham, Hornsey, Stoke Newington and Holloway. Naturally enough, most duty sergeants use this as a heaven-sent excuse for keeping patrols there to a minimum.

Clive whistled. A Jamaican street girl in her early twenties had dropped her cigarette and bent to pick it up. She wore black thigh boots, a white microskirt and no underwear.

'Shall we caution her?' Clive joked.

'What for? No knickers?'

'Let's go. They've got enough aggro without us.'

Barry and Clive were not on a 'tom patrol', after prostitutes. Their speciality at the time was the detection of illegal drug laboratories. Hours of patient observation of street dealers and the cautious cultivation of informers preceded most successful raids.

They noticed the middle-aged stockbroker-type almost as soon as he appeared – as out of place on the estate as a chicken near a fox's earth and about as vulnerable. He stopped in the shadows of the archway entrance to one of the blocks, withdrew from his holdall the hat, robe and clip-on beard of Santa Claus, and put them on before continuing on his way.

'Weirdo,' muttered Barry.

'Well, he's a lot safer in that get-up than wandering around here in a City suit. That's for sure.'

'What's he up to?' For Barry there had to be an explanation for every citizen's action at all times. If not, something fishy was at hand.

'Forget it, mate. He's not into the weed, that's for sure. Maybe he's got family on the estate less fortunate than himself and he's taking them a stocking full of goodies for tomorrow night.'

'Way out, mate. You'll never make Detective Sergeant. Look at his holdall. Nothing in it now he's got the outfit on. But you're right on one thing: whatever he's into, it's not the hard stuff.'

They moved on up Newnton Close, beside the dark waters of East Reservoir. As they did so, Father Christmas shuffled up the concrete steps of Keynsham House to Sara's flat. It was a year almost to the day since his last visit there.

He was a solicitor by profession and six short months from retirement. He had been the last partner to leave the office of his Walthamstow practice, and at 3 p.m. he had wished his secretary Harriett a Merry Christmas. She would close the office for the holiday break. He had planned his visit to Sara like a covert military operation, aiming to improve on his security of the previous December. For a year he had fed on his fantasies. The Father Christmas outfit was brilliant. Nobody would recognise him and, being extremely nervous, he did feel as though all the world was watching him. He had read somewhere that prostitutes hide cameras behind mirrors and then blackmail you. Well, he could keep on his beard and remove his spectacles. He felt that, like Michael Caine, he was more recognisable with his spectacles on.

He had two whole hours now at his disposal. As far as his wife Beth was concerned he was doing the last-minute Christmas shopping. In fact he had shopped at lunchtime and left the bags in the back of his Anglia parked safely by Walthamstow Town Hall. He would not risk bringing the car anywhere near this depraved area. He congratulated himself. He could even bump into dear Beth and she'd never know it was him. Not that there was any chance of her coming to these parts or even, poor woman, leaving their home. The new Zimmer frame helped her mobility, but only from room to room.

He had met Sara the first time the previous Christmas as he exited from Seven Sisters tube station. He was instantly hooked by her childlike half-smile and the small, pert breasts outlined against her T-shirt. She gave him her price as he sidled up to her. She could see he was scared stiff talking to her in public.

'Anything?' he asked.

'No trouble – but extra, of course.'

He nodded and she gave him her address.

'Press the black button. I'll meet you there in fifteen minutes.' She knew his type. He would not let her down.

When she left, he had gone to a news stand to buy an A–Z, for he had no idea where to find the address she had given him.

Now, on his second visit, he had no need for a map. He had fantasised the route a hundred times and more, for Beth would, perhaps could, no longer enjoy sex with him or anybody else. He argued to himself that she would be understanding if she ever found out but he knew that in fact she would be horrified, disgusted and probably die, for her heart was weak and diseased.

He climbed the stairs. The mixed urine and cat smell was powerful but only served to excite him. He would make the sex last this time and indulge his most primal urges. He knew her price would have risen from £20, but he had saved cash slowly over the months so that Beth would have no suspicions. He was determined to do it twice and so had £100 in notes. He would savour every image so he could replay the memories over the grey months ahead. Christmas, he knew, would be as deadly as ever. Beth and her geriatric parents for four days of inane banalities, mostly on the topic of their dreadful poodle Clarence. His visions of Sara would keep him sane during the festive visit and even its sickly nadir, the oohing and aahing as Clarence's gifts were opened.

Sara loosed the door on its chain. She showed no sign of recognition. He wondered, as she let him in, whether or not to remind her they had met before.

'I've never had a real Father Christmas,' Sara said, giggling as she stroked his whiskers. She lowered her voice politely to discuss the price. 'Twenty hand job, thirty oral, fifty corrective, 69 or any position you want. Half an hour max.'

It came out as a single litany and he latched on to the awesome fact that this magnificent little girl, even more superb than he remembered, would do anything and let him do anything for £50. He rolled the thought around on his tongue. Half an hour of paradise.

He took £50 from the wad tucked into one of his socks, where he had hidden it away from muggers, all but the £20 kept in a pocket to sacrifice if he was attacked. He told her he would probably like a repeat performance for the same price if she kept things 'really slow'. He refrained from mentioning what he had been up to that morning in the office loo with the express purpose of blunting his ardour.

Sara switched on a German porno video which depicted four Teutonic blondes being beasted from behind by a like number of musclebound types. She was gratified that Father Christmas hardly glanced at the heaving heavies, having eyes only for her.

She undressed him slowly, savouring the recently applied under-arm deodorant and aftershave. She bit her lip to stifle her laughter

288

when his erection was snared by the slit in his baggy, pink jockey pants. She had learnt that attempts at humour are seldom appreciated until afterwards.

'What's our name?' she asked as she fondled his scrotum.

'John,' he said.

'That's what I thought.' She smiled up at him and licked his nipples. Had this bloke stuck out for twenty quid she would have accepted but then she would have skipped the frills. With fifty smackers down and every prospect of the same again, she pulled out all the stops, determined to do her lascivious best. With the proceeds of this last minute pre-Christmas windfall, she would buy Alex the blue corduroy shirt and the jade cufflinks. They would enjoy a proper Christmas with all the trimmings.

Under a floorboard beneath her bed she had stashed more than £110,000 in cash from Alex's share in the robbery but she never dreamt of touching his money. He had unknowingly given Sara something she had never before experienced: the knowledge that somebody *trusted* her. Her self-respect was boosted from zero. Alex, a real gent, trusted her. She thought he also lusted after her but she could not be sure. His mind and his heart were still tied to his missing wife and child. Sara understood and was sorry but that could not stop her lying awake and dreaming that one day he would take her away to a land where there was sun and no clients.

'No,' the man was saying, 'please leave it.'

She had begun to remove his red, fur-trimmed hat. She shrugged. If only he knew what he looked like with his false beard, pot belly, eager but miniature dick and that silly hat, he would probably be shocked into a state of terminal flaccidity. Which, she reflected, would be bad for her. She liked to encourage her 'gentlemen' clients to become regulars.

She greased one of her index fingers with Vaseline and played with his anus while running her lips up and down his acorn-like penis. When she sensed his approaching climax she had him lie on his stomach on the bed. For a while she massaged his shoulders to cool him down. Then turning him over, she knelt over him, her feet either side of his head, and teased him with her tongue. She knew that he could see her mouth rising and falling against his crutch, framed by her hanging breasts and, closer to him, her genitalia. It was an image calculated to climax him in less than ten seconds. Her intention was then to massage his back gently for half an hour, after which she could start work earning the second half of the promised fee.

The Jamaicans slipped the lock and entered quietly. Sara was unaware of their presence until she felt Father Christmas go limp in her mouth, then the shock of a sudden pain in her backside. The taller black man had stabbed his middle finger into her and, crooking it, pulled her backwards towards him. He stifled her scream with a sharp slap to the face.

'Shut up, lady.' Nobody could say he wouldn't stand out in a crowd: a white, furry Kangol hat set off his mauve silk suit, pink shirt and black tie. Heavy gold 'cargo' looped his neck, matching the gold flashes on the Chinese collar and epaulettes of his jacket. His 'soldier' looked what he was, a pock-skinned moron well suited to mindless acts of cruelty.

'You goin' to frisk the daddy with the mini dango, Falls?' Kangol nodded towards Father Christmas. Falls looked dismayed. Then Kangol guffawed. 'That's a joke, man.'

Falls relaxed, relieved that he was not expected to touch the fat whitey on the bed. Thereafter Mafia's two Jamaicans ignored the man and concentrated on the girl.

The telephone number obtained by Blackledge, according to Mafia's police contacts, definitely belonged to this flat. Kingston's orders were that they should question whatever inmates they found here and leave only when they knew who had been digging holes in a wood near Birmingham and why.

Kangol ripped off Sara's silver necklace and pocketed it. 'Now you *are* naked,' he purred. She had little doubt as to what would follow. He raped her with quick efficiency, holding her neck with one hand to bend her forwards over her dressing table.

'Hey, you, grandpa. Yes, you on the bed,' Kangol shouted as he withdrew from Sara and tucked himself unwashed into his trousers. 'Don't you wish you had one of these? Black man's magic, eh?'

Father Christmas quaked with fear and kept quiet. He wished above all that he was back with Beth, even with her parents and Clarence. He was sure these men were about to kill him. Falls cleared his throat. Kangol looked at him, hesitated briefly, then nodded. 'OK, she's just coolie scum. You go ahead.'

Falls dropped his silver-plated handgun and his trousers to the floor.

'Here,' he ordered Sara as though speaking to a cur. He pushed her to her knees on the bed and moved her head about to the rhythm he preferred with cruel jerks of her hair. His eyes were fixed, throughout the brutal coupling, on the video and its panorama of bouncing German bottoms.

Kangol rooted about in the cleaning cupboard until he found what he wanted, a steam iron. This he plugged in and switched on.

'Name?'

'Sara.'

'Who live here?'

'Me.'

'And?'

'I do my work here.' She nodded at the bed.

'Who else, girl?' A note of menace emanated from the mauve suit.

'My lodger, Mr Goodman.'

'Your pimp?'

Sara's brain raced. 'Yes.'

'Where him now?'

She shrugged.

'Him been diggin' in Birmingham?'

'Digging?'

'You know. Shovel . . . earth. Shit, sister, don't fuck me with your stuff. I ask, you give me answers straight, OK?'

Sara was frightened. More so than she had believed possible. Her mouth was dry. She forgot the pain in her vagina and her neck, bent too far back when he had raped her. The fear overruled the pain. Yet the fear was all about the pain still to come. She was desperate to cooperate with these men; to tell them anything and immediately. But at the very back of her mind she hoped she would say nothing that might harm Alex.

Falls, having quickly satisfied his lust, had tucked his gun in his trousers and seized her from behind, one hand around a breast, the other clawed into her crutch. She felt the outline of his gun pressed against her buttocks. Kangol was testing the steam iron. The extension cord was too short, so Falls carried her closer to the wall socket. She felt urine run down her thighs.

Falls took his hand from her breast and held her Adam's apple between thumb and finger. Kangol moved the sharp end of the iron close to one of her nipples. She could feel the heat. Falls's fingers tightened against her scream of terror.

'Who from here has been diggin'?' growled Kangol.

'In Brum?' added Falls.

Sara desperately wished that she did know somebody who had been digging in Birmingham. Even if she had, she could not speak as she fought for air. It crossed her mind that these men were more interested in what they were doing than in gaining information.

She felt the searing agony of hot steel against her nipple. Her captive body arched bow-taut and her eyes bulged out. Father Christmas watched as though hypnotised and smelt the burnt flesh.

Falls removed his fingers from her neck. She gasped for breath. Kangol placed the iron on the glass-topped dressing table. He gave the three small rooms a perfunctory search but failed to find anything of interest. He had no wish to dirty his suit, so the floorboard cache beneath Sara's bed was in no danger.

When he came back he pressed the iron again against her blistered nipple. She fainted briefly. Then he let her speak. She told him all she knew about Goodman. He was a Welsh accountant who had lost his wife and daughter in an accident, had killed someone, she did not know who, up north, and fled to London to hide from the police. He had lived ever since off his earnings as a pimp to several girls in the Manor House area. He was good to her and he did not own a shovel. He was an accountant not a gardener.

Why, Kangol asked, prising her lips apart with the tip of the iron, would her telephone number be used by people digging in Birmingham? She wept and shook her head wretchedly. It must have been a wrong number. And badgers? What did she know of badgers? She knew nothing of badgers. Badger was the word some of her clients used to describe her private parts. That was all. Both men smiled. Badger. That was good.

Kangol decided the Asian girl was innocent. He had plenty of experience of people's limits and how to break them down. Whatever Kingston was after, it was not to be found here. The absent whitey, the pimp Goodman, sounded a real wimp. There was a mistake somewhere. He selected a ten-inch green dildo from a shelf of Sara's professional equipment and forced it, between false

292

beard and moustache, into Father Christmas's mouth. Falls laughed dutifully.

'Make a good postcard, eh?' he said.

Kangol ignored him and turned to Sara.

'You never seen us, gal. We was never here, right?'

She nodded eagerly but to no avail. Kangol held her down and Falls slowly ran the steam iron across her unharmed breast. The act was as savage as it was pointless.

'You talk to the pigs and we come back . . . then you're dead pussy.'

For a long while after the two men had left the flat neither Sara nor her client made a move. As Sara's fear receded so the pain came in waves. Somebody had once told her to soak burns in cold water. She limped to the bath. This galvanised Father Christmas, who wrenched the dildo from his mouth and, abandoning his festive regalia, dressed and fled from the room. He was £50 the richer as a result of Kangol's visit. Forty minutes later, back in Walthamstow, his natural decency returned sufficiently for him to call the police and ambulance from a phone box. Then, roll on Christmas with Clarence. Never again would he cheat on Beth.

The Stoke Newington police sent a Metro patrol car to Sara's address but the two officers took the 'scenic route' – Force jargon for a response sufficiently slow to avoid the likelihood of arriving at a still-hot crime scene.

An ambulance team had already disturbed the flat in attending to Sara's most immediate needs. She was in shock. Because of the obvious sadism of her unknown attackers, a fingerprint team was sent for and swabs taken from Sara before she was delivered with great blisters hanging from her chest to the specialist burns unit at Roehampton Hospital.

The scene-of-crime officers who fingerprinted Sara's flat found a great many prints which did not belong to Sara, nor her attackers, nor her clients. They were to be found in all parts of the flat except Sara's room and were presumed to belong to a lodger despite her denial that there was one. The 'lodger's' prints were sent with the others to Scotland Yard's national fingerprint computer Videofile. They did not initially match up with any of the three million criminals' existing prints.

The Videofile, set up in 1975, had proved a great saver of time and salary money. Only the previous year dozens of officers had checked the Yard's entire fingerprint index by hand in the course of the Black Panther murder enquiries. The 'lodger's' prints proved not to be those of any known criminal. However, because they were very faint, and because of the severity of the attack on Sara, they were passed to the forensic laboratories in Lambeth, where sophisticated scanning gear, the most advanced in the world, was used to detect and enhance the faintest of prints.

Ignorant of all this, Sara was worried nonetheless for Goodman's safety in case the Jamaicans should return when he was at home. She warned him to be careful when he visited her in hospital, bringing her flowers and chocolates. Her eyes filled with tears partly because he cared enough to come but mostly because she could see his mind was filled with bitterness and his heart frozen over.

When she told him, 'They are lookin' for you,' his only reply was, 'I shall soon be looking for them.'

The police found nobody in the Keynsham block who had heard or seen anything at the time of the attack on Sara. Even Father Christmas's visit had apparently passed unnoticed. Sara told the police as little as possible and refused vehemently to press charges against anybody for anything. She was scared witless at the memory of Falls and Kangol. The police had seen it all a thousand times before. Bullies escape the law because witnesses are terrified. Such is life in the concrete jungle.

Vaginal swabs taken from Sara were passed for DNA profiling to the computerised Swab Index at the Metropolitan Police Forensic Science Laboratory. Genetic fingerprinting had been used for the first time to prove parentage only two months before and the mood in the DNA laboratory was very gung-ho. However, although the mixed semen traces produced a DNA profile for each of the two assailants, neither matched any profile held in the Index. Matching the DNA profile of hair from the pillow and hairbrush of the 'lodger' excluded from the minds of the police the faint possibility that he might also have been one of Sara's attackers.

Early in February 1986 Art drove Tosh and Goodman to a meeting place selected by the Professor, a beauty spot between the Abbey of Calke and Staunton Harold Reservoir, not far north of Ashby-de-la-

Zouch. They found the pathologist pacing the abbey grounds in a high-collared raincoat and a 1940s trilby. This disguise, intended to prevent recognition should he be seen speaking to the 'dreadful IRA woman', made him look like a Peter Sellers version of a KGB agent. Art stayed behind in the BMW.

'*Dia duit*. God be with you. How'd you get here, Doc? Bicycle?' Tosh greeted him.

He ignored her question. 'I want to get this over quickly. Shall we walk further round the reservoir?'

'If you like. You have nothin' with you?'

'Like what?'

'Well, I thought maybe a report. Your results.'

'You did not ask for a written report.'

Tosh suspected he was apprehensive of providing further material which might later be used to blackmail him.

They walked on either side of the Professor, oblivious of their surroundings. Goodman had decided to pay him £10,000 in cash. This was twice the figure Tosh had mentioned when she had first approached the pathologist in Perry Barr. She had with her the money and the compromising photographs for hand-over pending an informative report from the old man.

'Should I speak plainly?' the Professor addressed Tosh, ignoring Goodman, for it was she who controlled his destiny. This was as well since Goodman was openly nervous, rubbing his hands together and blinking behind his spectacles. Tosh nodded, waving her hand as if to say, 'Get on with it.'

'I warned you it would take time without proper facilities and having to work in secret. I was expecting mere skeletal remains since the bodies had remained *in situ* for fifteen months. As it was, I was pleasantly surprised. Much of the remains were in splendid condition.'

Discretion, it seemed, was not the pathologist's strong point. Tosh was worried, and rightly, for Goodman halted abruptly.

'You are talking about my family, Professor. What do you mean by "splendid condition"? Were they . . . ?'

'Dead?' the Professor snapped. 'Yes, they are both dead. I had assumed you knew this. You asked me to find out the details *behind* their deaths, did you not?'

'So I did, Doc,' Tosh said quietly. 'Listen. Mr Goodman is

naturally upset. This is very difficult for him, as it would be for anyone in his position.' She squeezed Goodman's arm. 'Alex, do you wish for the Professor to carry on?'

For a long minute Goodman stared out over the water. The landscape was as empty as his heart. The last spark of hope had died with the Professor's words. Lucy was gone too.

'Just tell me how they died.' His voice was almost inaudible. 'Who did it? Describe them to me.'

'I am not a magician, Mr Goodman. No pathologist is. We are only as good as the existing evidence. Some corpses, a week or two old, say, are bristling with evidence whereas a forty-year-old mummified corpse might, so to speak, be clueless.' He walked faster as he warmed to his topic. 'What we look for on the most obvious, superficial level is first and foremost what identity can we give to a body. In the case of your wife, for instance, a piece of her shirt was enough, but not all corpses are found with recognisable clothing.'

Tosh could see that the Professor was not one for brief answers. She turned to Goodman.

'Alex. This is a mistake. Why don't you go to the car and wait with Art? The Professor's findin's may be disturbin'. Let me tell you the facts in my own way, OK?'

She stared at him, her green eyes sympathetic but compelling. Goodman nodded. 'I'll be in the car,' he said and turned back. The great man-made lake and the dark outline of the abbey seemed to spin and he heard a roaring in the back of his brain. He knelt, then lay down, at the edge of some scrub and waited while the dizziness passed. Until a moment ago he had nursed just the tiniest hope that little Lucy might somehow still be alive, that the Professor would identify only Mary's remains. He turned over on to his stomach, sick to his soul with the enormity of his grief and his loss.

'I'm sorry if I upset Mr Goodman,' the pathologist said, 'but you must understand the difficulties that I face, have faced, with your task.'

'Go ahead.' Tosh was a good listener. 'Take your time.'

'As I was saying. I needed first to be certain that the body or bodies matched the description you had given me of the two Goodman females. If, for example, one cadaver had turned out to be that of a black male infant, you would have needed of course to rethink your situation. Could you be sure, for instance, that this "burial site" had never been used before by these men?'

'I see your point,' Tosh admitted.

'As it turned out, there *were* only two bodies. One was partly skeletal and its skull, along with some other body parts, must have been predated by foxes. Badgers appear to have avoided reuse of that entrance to their sett.'

'We also reached that conclusion,' Tosh said.

'However, below the depth of fox disturbance, the human remains were in various different stages of decomposition, which allowed me to reach a number of deductions. The first clues I had to look for included indications as to the sex of the bodies. Clothing, hair length and style, jewellery and earrings are no longer the reliable guide to gender that they were when I was a student. But many clues can be obtained from the bones. Male femurs are longer and more massive with the greater sciatic notch of the pelvic bone being deeper and narrower. The male pelvic girdle also stands higher and is more erect than its smoother, flatter female counterpart. The trauma of childbirth, of course, causes changes to the pelvis such as pubic scars from the tearing of tendon insertions.'

Tosh was glad that Goodman was absent.

'Mrs Goodman, if I may so describe her, had as it were lost her skull. A shame, since I could have deduced her sex from certain cranial features. Female skulls are generally smoother, rounder, smaller and less muscled. Supra-orbital ridges are often absent altogether, their palates are smaller and often parabolic rather than U-shaped as with men. I located some of her teeth, fallen from the jawbone. Female teeth are again smaller. The lower, more deeply buried portions of her body had retained elements other than mere bone. One must always remember that, where putrefaction is advanced, the internal pelvic organs may still indicate gender. The uterus is for instance magnificently resistant to decomposition.'

'How comfortin',' Tosh murmured, but the pathologist was not listening.

'Age,' he pressed on as though back in some lecture theatre, 'is more difficult. Teeth help, of course, but that is the odontologist's field. I understand modern dentistry has removed many of the old signposts but much remains to be gleaned, so never miss a tooth. The "arcus senilis" is another age pointer, the grey or white ring round the pupil, since it seldom appears in the under-sixties. Hair colour is often misleading, for one can find grey hair at twenty-five and dark "youthful" hair on seventy-year-old scalps. Skin is a general indicator prior to putrefaction. Its general elasticity and thinness. Senility brings red Campbell de Morgan spots. In skeletal remains one is helped by arterial sclerosis and arthritis. Ossification centres are complete in five-year-old skeletons after which the fusion of epiphyses provides an age calendar until about twenty-five years . . .'

'And all this is of direct relevance in the case of this little girl and her mother?' Tosh had been unable to stop herself interrupting. She had stopped walking to help her irony sink in but she might as well have waved a wand at a monsoon.

'Much of what I am telling you did indeed apply in my approach to *this* case, yes. I think you will understand more given a general grasp of the subject rather than a blow-by-blow technical description of my deductive processes over these past eight weeks. Death is a process, not an event and while the cells of some tissues are still alive, others are dying or dead. The corpse may be partially "alive" for days after the person is dead, especially in temperate climes. If these or any two bodies had been left above the ground then, after a week, I would have expected the state of putrefaction to include swelling and reddening of the face, greenish marbling of the skin, slippage of the epidermis causing large sacs of serous fluid to burst leaving slimy pink surfaces. The brain would by then discolour to a soft pinkish-grey and, within a month, would liquefy. Most of the body hair would have loosened, ready to slide away at the least pressure. Marked gas formation would be present. The face, the penis and the scrotum would have swollen to balloon-like proportions, with protruding eye-globes and tongue. Internal gas pressures are such that women have had macabre post-mortem "deliveries" and body fluids are forced from all orifices. Hence the strange noises that can be heard in unrefrigerated Third World morgues.'

Tosh wondered whether the Professor's report would have been less detailed and more sensitively phrased had Goodman not withdrawn.

'After several weeks, you can expect the red-green skin tinge to deepen dark green or black with heavy maggot infestation and destruction by predators. Skin slippage by this stage will render fingerprinting difficult and the body fat of obese bodies will fill cavities between organs with yellow liquid that makes autopsies unpleasant. Then, several months after death, all softer tissues will have disintegrated, leaving only the solid organs such as the heart and uterus, along with tendons and ligaments, attached to the skeleton. These, too, will slowly fall away so that, in broad terms, the corpse will after a year and a half be a mere skeleton with tendon attachments and, after three years, a collection of bones.'

'You're sayin', are you not, Professor, that after fifteen months the Goodmans were at the bone and tendon stage?'

'I am saying that they would have been, had they been left unburied in a temperate climate. As it was, their body state was very different because they were buried at a depth between seven and four feet, under heavy soil, within minutes of their deaths.'

'So they were partially whole, were they not?'

'Partially, yes. The time-scale of the decomposition process varied greatly between the two bodies, and in the case of Mrs Goodman the head was missing, the upper trunk and arms were skeletalised and part-predated, whereas the lower trunk and legs were moderately intact, especially where protected by thick clothes and boots. You should understand that putrefaction involves tissues becoming moist, gas-ridden and liquefying down to the skeleton whereas mummification, where decomposition is dry, involves skin tanning and tissues turning to a fatty wax called adipocere.' The Professor's hands made kneading motions as though rolling a ball of moist clay.

'The Goodmans were buried before insect eggs were laid so initial maggot infestation was absent. Their grave, part of a well-drained hillside, has remained relatively dry. Most homicides are found in shallow scoops easily accessible to beasts and thus blowflies. The Goodman daughter was well preserved, her face being totally recognisable despite distortion through shrinkage and loss of eyes and lips. Her autopsy was virtually standard such was the lack of putrefactive deterioration. The lack of oxygen had inhibited aerobic organisms.'

A detached fascination was creeping over Tosh the more she heard. 'Then you're sayin' the Goodman girl is even now unaffected by maggots? I find that amazin'.'

The Professor shook his head disapprovingly. 'I did not say no maggots. Certainly no flies had time to lay their eggs before burial and the thick soil cover greatly delayed subsequent infestation but some phorid flies like *Conicera*, the coffin fly, lay surface eggs and their larvae then burrow down to the corpse. In this case I did find specimens of *Coleoptera* and *Diptera* adults at a depth of 55cm but none at work on the girl.'

'But insects destroy evidence,' Tosh interjected. 'They can hardly help your reconstruction of events.'

'Not at all,' the pathologist was incisive. 'They can and often do provide critical chronological evidence. Rationally successive waves of sarcosaprophagous insects are known to colonise the corpse at different periods after death. Many murder cases have been decided entirely on the evidence of maggot types.'

'Where does all this take us now? Could you bear to focus on specifics? God love you.'

'I have painstakingly taken into account all of my findings and built a picture of what must have happened on 28 July 1984, in and around the badger sett in Kinver Wood.'

Tosh attempted to hide her impatience. If she had had a husband or lover even half as pedantic as this man, she would have shoved him long ago into a crematorium, leaving nothing to inspect.

Slowly, and with an alarming series of pistol-crack creaks, the Professor managed to kneel on the wet grass. Taking up twigs and positioning them around a designated replica of the sett, he demonstrated his theory.

'The aggressor or aggressors bound and possibly gagged Mrs Goodman. The daughter, perhaps because she posed no physical threat, was not secured and, if at any stage she was gagged, this was not the case when she died. The mother's right arm was detached and the skeletal remains only partially retrieved. The left arm, also skeletal but still possessing tendon tags, was in place and, interestingly, two of the digits, the fourth and fifth, had been disturbed in a specific but confusing manner inconsistent with animal predation. Both females were savagely beaten or kicked. Mrs Goodman had fractures to her ribs on one side only and heavy "defence" bruising to her thigh and buttocks on the same side. The daughter was kicked on the head, and hairs lie across the bruised area. A second kick or blow has detached the lower maxilla, including the mandible, the palate and upper dental arch, from the rest of the jaw. Yet she was conscious at the moment of death.'

The Professor paused, for the first time seemingly uncertain how to suitably describe his findings.

'The daughter's right hand was clasped vice-like about a tree root in the narrows of the grave, I should say the sett. Her body was head down. There was an amount of earth in her mouth and what you would call her windpipe. The fact that her hand was in a state of *rigor mortis* or, more precisely, cadaveric spasm, would indicate to me that, at the time of her death, her muscles were engaged in violent exertion. The nails of both her hands were broken and split.'

The pathologist began to reposition the twigs. 'Man's inhumanity to man sometimes surprises even me,' he said, shaking his head sadly. 'I am sorry to say that the Goodman girl had been physically attacked from front and rear. She showed perineal tears with substantial ripping between anus and vaginal introitus indicative of rape. Teeth-mark bruising was evident on her neck and chest. The man or men responsible, in no establishable sequence and having bound Mrs Goodman, set about removing rings from the fingers of one, possibly both, of her bound hands. She attempted to struggle and was beaten or kicked. Her daughter was then assaulted, kicked and thrown into the gaping hole. Earth was scooped down on top of her as she tried, upside down, to lever herself from her predicament. Her mother was then pushed into the pit, possibly already dead, stamped on and left with her hands bound behind her, the least buried part of her some 20cm from the surface at the moment the assailants finished pushing soil back into the sett.'

Tosh and the Professor looked at each other, she wondering whether he was ever touched on an emotional level by his findings. She suspected, at that moment, that he was merely desperate to rid himself of everything to do with Kinver and to ensure the Perry Barr photos were destroyed forever. He must, she realised, be fearful lest she renege at this point and keep them from him.

'Thank you. You could not have done more,' said Tosh. '*Maith thu*. Good on you.' She slipped an envelope from the folder that she carried. 'These are the only copies and the negatives. You should set your mind quite at rest. Let it be a wee lesson to you, far though it may be for me to moralise. Mr Goodman has decided to add his thanks in the form of a cash fee which you will find enclosed.'

The Professor took her proffered hand in his uncertain grasp. Then he nodded, already moving backwards towards the Abbey of

Calke in thankful retreat from her presence. She waited awhile, staring out over the lake and wondering how much and how little to tell Alex.

23

February 1986

Mafia Douglas and Kingston Williams, wearing full-length navy-blue raincoats over their dark suits, cradled their firearms against the steady rain. It was 18 February 1986. Kingston hated winters in London and yearned for jasmine-scented dawns trembling with the magic plaint of invisible tree frogs, the Caribbean version of Alpine cowbells.

To squat beneath a rhododendron bush at 7 a.m. in such foul weather was bearable only because of the prospect of an imminent killing. Mafia had said there would be no guards and none of the Nigerians would be armed. But, as always, he needed to be certain. Caution was the secret of his success. Thus their pre-dawn presence in the Lewisham walled garden of the wealthy Nigerian sub-baron. This discipline killing was part of Mafia's increasing workload for the BCCI bank.

Adekunle Abajingin, Ade to his many friends, had made a good living during the early eighties by conning British universities and colleges. He possessed, under false identities, twenty-two National Union of Students cards allowing him places on a great many BA degree courses. This in turn gave him grants from several regional education authorities worth £35,000 a year and left him plenty of time for his other scams involving benefits for housing, unemployment and social security.

Ade was of Nigeria's powerful Yoruba tribe, whose writ held sway in the Ark Club, the Lewisham NCE. In 1985 the seventeen NCEs in Britain, originally christened 'Nigerian Crime Enterprises' by Scotland Yard, netted a total of £8–9 billion in fraud against the British taxpayer.

The National Criminal Intelligence Service was and is able to demonstrate indisputable evidence of this horrendous and direct drain on the nation's welfare system. But to do so in public would be politically incorrect and blatantly racist. Most British citizens are aware of the Sicilian Mafia, the Triads and of Kray-type East End crime. Yet NCEs, the Nigerian fraud gangs, are virtually unknown to the general public, despite being the most successful criminals in the United Kingdom.

Adekunle Abajingin had been accepted as a member of the Lewisham Ark Club NCE early in 1984 and continued his career in welfare fraud under their auspices and utilising their complex fraud facilities. At the Ark Club 'school' he taught 'mule' tricks to young beginners fresh to the intricacies of on-person smuggling. He taught his pupils how the body can effectively conceal over a hundred cocaine-filled condoms. First the prospective mule had to prime his or her gullet by gulping down large grapes covered in honey, then it was best to expel as much air as possible so as to prevent the condoms floating in stomach juices, which are highly corrosive, rather than passing through the digestive system. Bowel-blocking pills were also a must to ensure no lavatory was needed before clearance of all airports.

That autumn, respecting the NCE policy that all members should be ready to switch their operations within the Club to suit ever-changing scenarios, Ade became a cocaine courier between Lagos and New York's John F. Kennedy International Airport. In Lagos he was sent with large sums of cocaine cash to the Apapa branch of BCCI, who were laundering the money through BCCI Caymans into a US dollar account.

Ade and a Yoruba cousin from the bank staff of BCCI's Enugu branch began to develop a clever system of syphoning off cocaine funds in such a way that BCCI Lagos appeared guilty of defrauding the Yoruba NCE.

The baron of the Yoruba NCE complained to the man who had been appointed by Hassan Abedi of BCCI as the bank's chief mover in Nigeria, the Sultan-designate of Nigeria's fifty million Muslims. This man, Alhaji Dasuki, instituted an enquiry which fingered Ade's cousin. In February 1986, in an Enugu cellar, the broken Yoruba confessed to his interrogator across a metal table upon which lay a number of his fingers and toes. At the time Ade was relaxing with his English wife and their two young daughters at home in Esher. He was delighted at the invitation to a business breakfast at the home of the Ark Club's Lewisham sub-baron. He left home at 6.30 a.m. to avoid rush hour on the A3 into London.

At 7.30 a.m. Art woke with a jolt at the wheel of The Family's BMW. This was the eighth night he had spent parked across the road from The Vox in Brixton, watching some of South London's most notorious crack dealers and their chicks coming and going from the underground nightclub. Art noticed the rain had stopped.

'Can I help you?' asked a thin, Italian-looking face pressed against the BMW's fogged-up windows, features taut with suspicion. The man was snappily dressed and his 'suitcase' lurked in his shadow; that is to say, the personal enforcer shaped like a Samsonite who gave him the confidence to speak so cheekily to a Jamaican such as Art in Brixton's heartland.

Art did not open the window. He merely scowled at the man. 'I'm sleepin',' he said. 'How about you?'

'You've been here, or hereabouts, for over six weeks, you or your friends. I assume you are CID. People notice and it gives me a bad name. I own all 9 Brighton Terrace, including the club. We run a respectable business and I object to this open harassment. If your observation activities continue, I shall be sending the Police Commissioner an official complaint.' He stomped off, the suitcase flashing Art a passing glare.

Art changed his mind: the man was eastern Med, not a wop. Most likely a Greek. They owned a good deal of Brixton. His name probably ended in 'akis' or 'opolis'. Sailor would know how to square him but he was in Los Angeles for another three days yet. Art popped open a can of Coke and stretched. Then his mouth opened slightly and his eyes widened. Straight ahead, as the Greek and his heavy disappeared into the covered entrance of 9 Brighton Terrace, a grey Mercedes drew to a halt and Mafia stepped out.

'Bingo, man.' Art made jiving movements of joy and bruised his knee on the gear stick. He dialled the Peckham Home and got an irate James, up half the night with a screaming turkey in one of the coolers.

305

'I've done it, brother. I got the bastard. Right here. I's lookin at him.'

'What the hell is you talkin about, nigra? It's six o'clock and I've had no sleep. You call Col back in two hours when you can make sense.'

'*Wait*, Brother James. I'm talkin about Mafia, Tricks, Stafford Douglas, OK? The big Yardie don. He's come to The Vox. I need help like five minutes ago. Tell Col to get his black ass here faster than you can say Ol' Testament.'

'But you got the wheels, man.' James was waking up.

'He can use the Mini or the Bedford, can't he?'

'He'll be there,' James yielded. 'I'll kick him off his girl Camelia right now. Prise them apart. Praise the Lord.'

'Tell him to take the portable with the battery in case I'm gone when he gets here.'

They rang off. The Mercedes driver, whom Art recognised as Mafia's sidekick, 'Caretaker Ken' Murray, joined his boss and the two men disappeared into the shadows of the heavily secured disco. Ten minutes later a white Transit drew up behind the Mercedes. One man got out but Art could see the silhouettes of four or five others in its rear. Shortly before 8 a.m. the Mercedes and the Transit left Brixton via Coldharbour Lane and headed south-east for Lewisham.

The guests arrived in small groups, all Nigerians and all men, for female NCE members were non-existent. A majority were smartly dressed Yoruba in their mid to late twenties. Almost all had been students in Britain or the USA during the late seventies when Nigeria's oil boom had caused economic prosperity and great hopes for a golden future.

Government ineptitude, coupled with corruption among ministers and civil servants in Lagos, resulted in near national bankruptcy in the early eighties when worldwide oil prices plunged. Nigerian students throughout the English-speaking world found themselves deserted by their sponsor and resorted to drug trafficking or fraud to maintain the good life they had been led to expect. They were accepted into the NCEs in droves, for they were the brightest and most able Nigerians of their generation. Rife corruption back home gave them a perfect home base for their piracy and by 1986, virtually free from police interference, five hundred NCE cells were operating worldwide under the loose control of three tribal, Lagos-based infrastructures.

In their host countries NCE members set up or bought out useful 'front' businesses, including pharmacies from which to submit fraudulent medical insurance claims, janitorial services to obtain confidential personnel records from businesses, and travel agencies to arrange the movements of their heroin and cocaine couriers – sometimes as many as a dozen complete with NCE overseer on a single jumbo flight.

In 1982 Ibo and Yoruba NCE sub-barons had established two schools in London and Birmingham specifically to instruct NCE apprentices in the skills of documentary fraud, the intricacies of the British welfare system and how to milk it. The schools' locations were highly mobile.

NCE members became officials at Petty France to obtain passports, baggage handlers at Heathrow to steal consignments of blank credit cards and birth certificates and, by 1985, they were well established in local government and the Post Office.

The police attempted to form a specialised Nigerian Crime Squad but this idea was abandoned as likely to prove racially provocative. Informers were few and far between because NCEs were tribally based and would-be snouts feared for their families back in Nigeria. As a general rule, and unlike the IRA, NCEs did not punish their own turncoats but hired Yardie enforcers for the task.

The Ark Club sub-baron, who had lived in Lewisham since the sixties and was an original NCE lieutenant in the UK, greeted each of his guests at the front door. Two Pakistani servants and a Goan cook served a mammoth, rice-based, traditional Islamic breakfast and, when all seventeen invitees were present, seats were taken in the sumptuously furnished dining room.

The sub-baron, addressed as Ayeni by all members of the Ark Club ('Ark' stood for the initials of a Yoruba prince, and the club motto was 'Serve to Save') gave a few words of welcome, followed by a reading from the international NCE gospel known as the 'Money Prayer'. 'By the Father within, and all the powers that be, I believe it is the Lord's good will that I enjoy an abundance of money. God is King and, as his heir, I claim joy, peace, health, love and all the money I can use. The voice of God in me screams of wealth in abundance. The Money Prayer will help me achieve divine prosperity. Thanks be to the Father.'

Ayeni, owner of a network of minicabs in various British cities, lowered his outstretched hands and beamed his pleasure at his flock.

'Welcome, brother Arkians. May I ask you to switch off your mobile phones. We want no interruptions. Our Secretary will now read out the Minutes of the last meeting. This meeting will last two hours, after which there will be refreshments. At that time I ask that you leave, as you came, at suitable intervals and quietly. One never know who watches and God helps those who help themselves through cautious ways. We may all . . .' He halted abruptly.

The double doors at the end of the dining room were kicked open. The Goan cook entered, tears streaming from his eyes and blood from his broken nose. He was sobbing and his hands were clasped behind his neck. Two tall Jamaicans, one holding a sub-machine-gun, the other a twelve-bore pump-action shotgun, followed the cook into the room. They wore dark suits and heavy gold jewellery beneath open, ankle-length raincoats. Other track-suited, armed West Indians had stationed themselves in the hall and the garden against interference from any quarter.

Mafia's head honchos, Jeremiah Jones and Dylan, took care of much of his pre-Redden UK business, mostly in the reggae world, but Mafia kept them ignorant of his American connections, including his expanding contract work for BCCI London. Thus, on 18 February in Lewisham, Mafia had hired fringe hoodlums from Brixton under the eagle eye of Kingston Williams. BCCI 'dirty work' originated from their Leadenhall Street headquarters in the City but came to Mafia via Korbi Richter in LA.

'Mr Ayeni,' Mafia addressed the sub-baron with a bow. 'We apologise for interruptin' your meetin' in this fashion but you will all be aware of the importance to your mother country of the BCCI Bank. Nigeria owes its creditor banks $5 billion. All your global creditors except BCCI have withdrawn.' He looked around the dining room at the seated black businessmen and his gaze settled on Adekunle Abajingin. He walked slowly across the pile carpet and settled behind Ade's chair. Ade looked at his hands.

'This man, your trusted colleague, has caused friction and sown mistrust between the BCCI Bank and your country to further his own ends. This cannot be tolerated and what now happens to Mr

308

Abajingin should serve as a lesson to you all and, by word of mouth, to your colleagues who are not with you.' He looked up and Kingston, who loved drama, strode down the centre of the room grasping in front of him his shotgun. He held this against Ade's chin and forced him to rise from his seat. Within the confines of the dining room, the explosion was deafening. One half of Ade's skull disintegrated and the contents transferred as if by magic on to the cream-coloured wall. Two NCE men sitting close by were spattered with cranial matter. Nobody moved in the silence that followed.

Withdrawing his men, Mafia again addressed the sub-baron. 'You carry on now, Mr Ayeni. And, remember, this is not a matter for the police. Good day to you all.'

Mafia often matched his dialogue to the company of the moment, ranging from a nasal transatlantic twang to Brum-laced Jamaican patois.

Art in his BMW and Columbo, who had arrived in the mini-van, both followed Mafia's Mercedes and ignored the Transit. They alternated the lead four or five vehicles behind the Merc. The M1 and M6 traffic was heavy all the way to Birmingham, where 'Caretaker Ken' and Mafia parked outside 151 Dudley Road, half a mile as the crow flies from Winson Green Prison. Cecil 'Music Master' Morris, boss of Birmingham's notorious PCRL pirate radio, was in residence and alone. Mafia took only his .38 Smith and Wesson.

Art parked immediately outside number 151, one of the various 'radio shops' between which Morris constantly switched his transmission gear to outwit the authorities. Columbo stayed further up the street. Art heard shouted abuse and sounds of breaking furniture within minutes of Mafia's entry.

Morris, famous in Handsworth, had for several weeks advertised Mafia's reggae shows to his one million black listeners but Mafia paid no bills, so Morris, foolishly, had refused further adverts. This was overt 'diss' and in Yardie terms deserved immediate punishment. Mafia, however, was in an expansive mood and simply warned Morris with a light pistol whipping that lacerated his cheeks and lips and fractured his jaw.

Columbo called James, who told them to stay with Mafia. Tosh and Leon were on their way to help.

Mafia's work for the day complete, 'Caretaker Ken' drove him to his luxurious home in Elmbank Grove, a cul-de-sac on the fringes of Handsworth golf club. Columbo phoned the address to James, who got Dave 'Ears' Norton to run a check on it. Mafia and his second wife Maureen had purchased the place a month before. Their next-door neighbour, a serving police officer, invited Tosh in for a cuppa when she called on him in the guise of a council statistics officer. He confirmed Mafia's domestic status as his immediate neighbour and The Family, their mission complete, retired home to Peckham in time for Sailor's return from the USA.

A crate of Red Stripe was opened to celebrate the running to ground of Mafia Douglas, but Goodman did not join the general good cheer. To avoid dampening the atmosphere he stayed in the coolers, providing an audience for the desperate rantings of the inmates. This helped ward off the images of Kinver that hovered constantly at the threshold of his mind. For two days and nights after she had told him of the Professor's findings, Tosh had feared for Goodman's sanity. She had stayed with him using all her comforting, persuasive skills, honed by so much practice in the coolers, until the wild desperation had faded from his eyes and an ice-cold silence, riven only by the visions, had settled upon him. Then she had gone to Birmingham and, on returning to tell him that they knew now where Mafia lived, she had noted the glint of steel with which he greeted the news; a look which said 'so now the man is mine and he will find as much mercy from me as he showed to my Lucy'.

Soon before midnight, Columbo left for the lab and Art for a girl in Stoke Newington. James came to Goodman with a mug of coffee. 'Go see my brother,' he growled.

Tosh and Sailor were waiting for him in the big room. The previous day Sara, recovering slowly from her ordeal and the subsequent skin grafts, had issued Goodman with £30,000 in cash from her bedroom: the amount agreed for the tracing of Mafia. Sailor took the money. Where, he asked, did Alex wish to go from here?

'You wanted to know the truth, Alex. Now you do. Maybe you feel alone and helpless. But, I tell you, don't think this. *We* are your new family. We love you as our brother in sufferin'. We have need of your abilities. We have work for your talents. This place is your home. Don't feel lost and alone. You are not!'

310

Goodman rose from the arm of his chair and faced away from them so that they could not see his face, read the bare emotions run riot or watch the tears of gratitude soften the determined hatred which clouded his thoughts.

'Thank you both. I owe you everything,' he said simply. 'I can think of no better home than here, no better family now mine has gone.'

Sailor nodded. 'What now, Alex?'

Goodman looked up. His eyes were not those of the gentle Leominster accountant.

'I must have them. Every one of them . . . I will see them in Hell.'

'Them?'

'There were eight men at the sett,' Goodman spoke softly. 'I hold four to be responsible. The rest were minions. The whole of the Third Reich were not punished at Nuremberg. By *them* I mean the two Americans and their British acolytes, Mafia and Blackledge. We could execute Mafia tomorrow but then I would never find the others. He is my only key to their identities. Sailor, you always know the best way. You have agreed to deal with me on a business basis. I ask you to help me force or fool Mafia into leading me to the other three.'

'Do you still discount the police?' Tosh asked. 'Maybe, in the long run, they would be your best path to justice.'

'Do you believe that?' Goodman levelled his gaze to Tosh.

She shrugged. 'It would be nice to think so, in the best of all possible worlds, but Oscar was right when he said, "The good end happily and the bad unhappily: that is what fiction means." I think, Alex, that these men are evil and that they will thrive. You will in all likelihood find they have important policemen in their pockets and they will suffer for what they did to your family and, more recently, to Sara, only if *you* have the will to act as their judge and their executioner. I believe this as God is my witness.'

'We will not be able to force a man like Mafia to tell us about the others.' Sailor was unequivocal. 'But if we could pay him enough money, more than he could hope to gain from them, then he would surely sell them at the drop of a coin.'

'Sounds good,' said Goodman.

Sailor laughed. 'No. Not good. You still have plenty dosh left and, as part of The Family, you will receive your share from our ventures

311

because you share our work. But to buy Mafia from the Americans, we talk big, big, money. They are his US cocaine link. We can be certain of that. Mafia will risk crossing their sort for nothing less than a hundred grand.'

'So we can't force him or buy him,' Tosh summarised. 'How do we fool him?'

Sailor inspected his fingernails, clasped about the bowl of his coffee mug. 'I will do some homework,' he said. 'Then we'll talk again.'

At the Metropolitan Police Forensic Science Laboratories in Lambeth a keen young Assistant Scientific Officer took the latest batch of STMs to the office of the Higher Scientific Officer on duty. STMs, so labelled by some long-gone archivist, stood for 'Still Traceable Murderers'. In practice they involved last-ditch attempts to match up fingerprints by evolving technology which previous generations of detecting machines had failed to identify. Items from still-open murder cases were held when thought likely to have come in contact with the finger or palm prints of the guilty party but where such prints had previously not been detected.

Twenty-seven cases of unsolved murders between 1982 and 1985 were contained in the young civil servant's file, each considered worthy of reinvestigation by the most recent print detection device, a £65,000 argon-ion-laser using 38,000 watts of power and capable of detecting and highlighting latent prints previously invisible to man.

One of the twenty-seven cases was represented by a pair of black leather boots worn by a corpse found in a wood in October 1985. The case officer had noted that the body had been dragged into its final resting-place 'by the boots' and fingers or palms or even gloves should have left marks, if only as latent prints, on the leather. There was a question over whether suicide, misadventure or murder was behind this drug-abuse case but, with no public pressure involved, the matter had received back-burner treatment all along.

Two weeks later, rightly pleased with themselves, Forensic were able to match two clear fingerprints, contaminated by oily dust, against the Yard's AFIS (Automated Fingerprint Identification System) index. The two prints matched exactly those of the missing 'lodger' at the Keynsham House sado-rape the previous Christmas.

Phone lines were soon buzzing between the relevant offices in Lambeth and Derby – in which region Goodman had disposed of Trevor's remains.

24

January–December 1986

'The CIA are worried about BCCI,' Jed told JR when they met in JR's LA home. 'They know they are playing with fire in cooperating with Abedi, but so far the liaison has paid handsomely. BCCI have been, still are, very useful to the Agency all over the world. But now there are ominous signs of the whole banking empire collapsing in a heap of rattling skeletons and extreme embarrassment for anybody found to have been in bed with them. The Pakistanis have lost nearly $500 million this last quarter through bad options trading alone.'

'So why don't the CIA skedaddle while they can?'

'Because in a dozen countries BCCI is still their sole source of information and their most influential fandangler. They lose Abedi's goodwill and they miss out on a great many perks.'

'Well,' JR snorted, 'they can't have it both ways.'

'That's just the point.' Jed smiled. 'I think with our help that they can. All they need is good intelligence. An insider within BCCI HQ reporting, via us of course, on when best to get clear of BCCI, to withdraw all traces of their presence. Not too soon because BCCI are still so useful to the Agency. But not too late either! I think we now have the perfect man for the job . . . the Brit you told me about last year' – Jed slapped a thin file on the table – 'has come in from the cold. Alex Goodman, whatever his true identity, has been traced by MI5 . . . Read it.'

The report was succinct. Early MI5 attempts to trace Goodman in response to JR's request had paddled about in thin air. The man was an elusive chimera. Then, two weeks ago, MI5 routine electronic enquiries had received a response from the Department of Health and Social Security computers. An inhabitant of the London Borough of Hackney, giving the name Alexander Goodman, had made an approach to the DHSS on behalf of 'an Asian dependant, recently assaulted, receiving skin graft treatment and suffering from shock'. The applicant was asking for help to apply for a new flat for the Asian girl, who, he said, might otherwise be attacked again. The appeal had been refused but logged, resulting in the DHSS computer response to MI5.

An MI5 agent was soon sniffing at the Finsbury Park address Goodman had given. A teenage Pakistani girl lived there and, the postman assured the MI5 agent, a white male lodger was often in and out. Further enquiries with the local police revealed an ongoing CID search for the lodger as a murder suspect.

'Murder!' Jed exclaimed. 'I don't believe it. What murder?'

No details were given, but MI5, at Jed's urgent request, spoke to their police counterparts at the highest levels and 'registered' Goodman as frozen from further police action in the interests of national security. Thanks to the ongoing effectiveness of the Reagan–Thatcher *entente cordiale*, such holding actions were possible. The Goodman data, complete with records of his NHS application, his fingerprints and details of the open case on the overdosed corpse, were all passed to Jason's department at Century House. The NDIU (National Drugs Intelligence Unit) database was flagged so that any outside agency, or indeed internal enquirer, was warned to leave the Goodman file well alone. To all intents it had ceased to exist.

'So long as we want,' Jed assured JR, 'we can keep the UK law off Goodman's back.'

'I see he's moved from Birmingham. Maybe he's given up his search for his identity. With the death of the guy he locked up, he must have run out of leads towards the black fella who took his wallet and documents.'

Jed shrugged and passed over a second folder. 'This arrived today and results from my request to MI5 for more data on the man.'

JR whistled. 'This is good stuff.' He extricated an A4-sized photograph. 'It's Goodman all right. Put on a bit of weight and looks less skull-like, but there's no mistake.'

315

'Look here.' Jed's finger indicated a line of print he had highlighted.

'Accountant!' JR murmured. 'The guy must have regained his memory. At Fambridge he didn't even know his profession. Hey, Jed. This is perfect. The man is exactly right.'

'Certainly seems that way,' Jed agreed. 'I should mention MI5 have checked the accountant side and there is no record of his ever being registered. This doesn't worry them too much as they say anyone in the UK can call themselves an accountant without formal qualifications or membership of a professional body. There are all sorts of accountants, from chartered to turf. Many, in industry rather than professional firms, are never formally qualified. Did this guy mention a Pakistani girl at all?'

'No. I don't think so but he could have met her after he moved from Birmingham. Just a landlady maybe.'

'MI5 are suggesting she's a hooker and he's some sort of pimp. He's been seen in bad company by neighbours.'

'Bad company?'

'Local traffickers. Not the sort of people we'd want him with if we get him a high-grade snoop job at BCCI.'

'No problem.' JR was confident. 'He's probably having to consort with traffickers and the like to survive but, given a choice of better things, a return to white-collar work, I am sure he'll take it and shake off the low life.'

Jed nodded. 'So we are agreed then. We use the CIA need for a private eye to insert "our man" Goodman into BCCI's nerve-centre. This I can do, without reference to any outside agency. I have the right contact at the middle-management level of the bank.'

'Why don't the Agency use their own people? They must have the Bank laced with informants.'

'They have,' Jed explained. 'But none on the fourth and fifth floors of Leadenhall Street where it all happens. Casey could install whoever he wants in most places with Abedi's blessing but not where Abedi's own secrets are stored.'

'Like what?'

'Like Redden's secret accounts. Like Noriega's and Abu Nidal's. But, above all, the worrisome reality of BCCI's spiralling debts, the possibility that the whole rotten edifice may collapse at any moment and reveal God knows how many CIA-condoned crimes worldwide.

London is the place where this will happen. Abedi knows that. So does Casey. Goodman will serve two masters.'

'And your contact can get Goodman into the right slot?'

'Life isn't that simple! My contact, Mahmoud, represents a small group of young, clear-minded, visionary individuals. Their faith in BCCI's mission is solid and they do not subscribe to the activities of Abedi's cabal. Not all is evil in BCCI – even at the senior-management level there are executives that can be trusted. Mahmoud will identify the right one for us and get Goodman his backing.'

'So, Goodman's entrance into the world of BCCI would be sponsored by people at the top?'

'Yes, the degree of our success would depend on how strongly Goodman is supported and by whom. If Mahmoud can identify the right person on the fourth floor, Goodman could be shown to be working for Abedi himself. On the one hand Goodman can play the role of disinterested internal informant for Abedi, and on the other report to you if and when he manages to trace the Redden numbered accounts. As a bonus we will be in receipt of a true picture of BCCI's financial viability as a bank, which, without disclosing our source, we can pass to Casey's people and earn priceless brownie points with the Agency. That is,' Jed grunted, 'so long as Goodman hasn't forgotten his basic accountancy.'

'Who will pay Goodman?' JR asked.

'BCCI will! He'll be working for them, won't he?'

'And if Goodman discovers that Redden is the very man he is himself seeking for his own private vendetta?'

'You are the only person who can make that connection for him. You told me he did not know the identities of the people he sought.'

'Sure, but if he has reclaimed his memory he may well recognise Redden.'

'The chances of him seeing Redden at the bank, and I doubt Redden ever physically goes there, are surely remote.'

'Yeah, that's probably true. So where do we go from here?'

'First we, you, approach Goodman to ensure he's willing and available. Next I sound out, separately, the CIA and my contact Mahmoud. We must give him time to insert Goodman *with* the blessing of someone from the very top. Someone we can trust yet

317

who has the confidence of Abedi himself. Then we insert our mole, sit back and wait.'

Nobody knows much about their nearest neighbours on the huge Woodberry Down Estate, never mind the people in the block across the walkway. There are drug dealers all over the place, of every ethnic mix. In the Bernwood block a deaf pensioner died in bed and his wife, equally deaf, kept him there for two years. She continued to draw a married couple's pension and to 'look after him'. There was a period, neighbours remembered afterwards, when there had been a dreadful odour from the flat but then the old couple had never been known for their personal cleanliness. The body was eventually found by accident by a visiting gas official. On Woodberry Down you could get away with murder and a great many other things too, but not if you made enemies. Then you'd be snitched on and the law would come visiting.

The Family took pains to alienate nobody, not even the stray cats. They could move out in hours if they were compromised but they hoped this would not happen, for the Peak House laboratory was perfectly situated. As well as plenty of ventilation it had an excellent warning system in the event of raids by police or rival gangs.

Goodman was settling into his new job as The Family's financial adviser. His mind was actively involved in improving output and efficiency. 'Sort of sales manager,' was how Sailor had described the job. 'We use your skills to raise profits and you use the business to get close to Mafia.'

The new job was the result of Sailor's homework on how best to fool Mafia into identifying the Americans.

'He's a secretive man,' Sailor had told Goodman, 'suspicious even of his own mother. His soldiers are mean, I mean real mean. Even if you was from Mandeville, Jamaica, like Mafia, I would tell you there's no way you're goin' to fool this don. Seein' as you're white and couth, you don't stand no chance.'

Goodman had kept his silence.

'Unless,' Sailor added, 'you make yourself useful. There's two ways you can be of value to Mafia. He's a clever bastard. He's into a lot bigger stuff than we thought at first, includin' two activities here in London where we could work to get you noticed by him. Number one is his contract work for other crime syndicates, dodgy

318

companies, even banks. We got a list of them. Trouble is, that involves nasty stuff. Not your line, Alexo!'

'And his other activity?' Goodman asked.

'Charlie Girl, coke, cocaine. He's big. Cannabis too, and amphetamines on the side, likely enough. Tosh, she agrees with me. That's your best bet to get anywhere near Mafia: get a name in the drugs line yourself.'

Goodman nodded. He could see the logic.

'So,' Sailor smiled. 'The Family, we done taken a vote. All the brothers and sister Tosh are happy to offer you sales manager of our lab. OK?'

Goodman punched his fist against Sailor's as Columbo had taught him. He knew Sailor's way was best. He felt the tears pricking. It was good to belong and to feel needed.

'At first you'll have to learn the amphets business and get to know the streets. Be wise. Then we can work out the best way to branch into coke and do business with Jo-Dog Willetts, Mafia's lieutenant. This is a long-term thing, Alexo. You'll need to be cool.'

'I'll see it through.'

'We may be talkin' years not months.'

'I know. I have nothing to lose.'

Chemist was a good instructor. He was up and about, benefiting from a remission, and sometimes seemed genuinely cheerful as though he had forgotten his illness. He cooked spiced curry-goat or jerk-pork dishes and other Caribbean favourites in the Peak House flat's security lobby, for no open flame was allowed in the lab. Two half-section oil drums housed home-made speakers which blasted out reggae at all hours. The bass sounds of Stylistic playing *Satta Massagana* repeated endlessly. Chemist seldom left the confines of the lab but he dressed meticulously in tailor-made suits with silk shirts, flash ties and Italian shoes. Heavy gold 'cargo' flashed from his neck and wrists. He liked to look his best and the lobby was his shebeen. The centrefold of a Sunday magazine, a green Mercedes coupé with a naked black girl in a lynx coat, was sellotaped above the Baby Belling cooker and a mini-fridge full of Red Stripe 6-packs.

'So you're goin' to double our profits overnight then, Alexo?' Chemist greeted Goodman's 'Plan for Business', the result of his first three months' study of The Family's existing drugs operations.

'Triple them.'

'How long before I can get me this Merc?'

'With the chick included?' Art quipped.

'Of course, or I get them under the Trade Descriptions Act.'

'I've made out a new order system for the gear.' Goodman sat down with them at the dominoes table in the lobby. 'By doubling up on all bulk orders we save five per cent.'

'But where do we store the extra barrels, man?' Art complained. 'We've no room to move as it is.'

'Aw, come on, Art. Don't make problems,' said Chemist, rolling his eyes. 'Alexo's goin' to make us all millionaires. You sit there like an x-head with a permagrin, stickin' your screwdriver in Alexo's spokes, and we goin' nowhere fast.' Chemist ran his delicate fingers down his gold neck chains. 'How you plannin', Alex?'

'For a start,' Goodman explained, 'we need more outlets with less chance of aggro. That means market research to identify blind spots where the more pugilistic outfits are not yet in contention. James is looking at that. Then there are a number of individual freelancers known to Sara, mainly taxi drivers and street girls, who we can be sure are not police informers and who have no gang connections. We can do good business with them. You, Chemist, must never know to whom we sell.'

'But I do!'

'I know. But from now on that must stop. You sleep here and, if we are raided, you will end up under police interrogation or, worse, nailed to the floor by some outfit keen to learn our customer list. What you don't know, you can't tell.'

'True, man. This is true.' Chemist approved the logic.

'Also, we are losing potential growth by not retailing our products ourselves. We should recruit our own dealers right down to street level. A minimum number with maximum security and using a cut-out between us and them.'

'Where to recruit?' Art queried.

'Leon seems to know a lot of likely lads. We need to modernise. Pagers between our buyers and our dealer-controller and certainly an end to Tosh's lethal practice of marching into a buyer's premises with the goods and back out again with the cash. We need to keep the drugs and the money as two separate transactions or somebody's going to end up with Her Majesty in no time. I'm surprised you haven't already.'

320

'We're lucky cats,' Chemist explained.

'Luck runs out,' Goodman said firmly, 'and another good business practice which I learnt in the hotel trade is to be permanently open. Clients need to know that, with us, they can make contact with an order and then expect speedy delivery right round the clock. That means you, Chemist, being on call twenty-four hours a day and not doing your normal trick with the answering machine every time you take a nap.'

'When I get sick, Alexo, I need the sleep.'

Goodman knew this was no whinge. 'Then we need somebody else here at all such times. And another thing. We are providing a product which is too high a quality for too cheap a price. We must gradually dilute the mix and raise the price. Not so as we lose existing clients but to bring us in line with going street prices. Lastly, diversification. It would make commercial sense to widen the product range.'

Art waggled his index finger, circled with three or four gold rings, at Goodman. 'The Family don't sell crack nor joy. That's on principle.'

'Joy?' This was not part of Goodman's recently acquired vocabulary.

'Heroin,' Art translated. 'Brother James don't mind kif, cannabis, or lightning' – he waved his hand towards the amphetamines lab – 'but he draws the line at Peep, PCP, and temmies.'

'Why?' Goodman asked.

Art, helped by Chemist, mouthed the litanies of James.

'Joy makes a man like a zombie, the walkin' dead. Nerves snap, minds fill with snakes and spiders bigger than mopheads, boils and yellow abscesses stain your best suits, your teeth get black and sticky, the pains eat you up and you twitch like a doll. Chase H the dragon and you get eat by Scat the tiger.'

'I see,' said Goodman. 'But temazepam is not as addictive as heroin. Nor is PCP.'

'Brother James,' Chemist explained, 'has a pretty niece called Betty as got hooked on temazies last year. She had one leg amputated where she'd been injectin' the arteries and now she's gone blind followin' her practice of injectin' gel temaz into the corners of her eyes.'

321

'He don't like 1-Phenylcyclohexyl-piperidine hydrochloride neither,' Chemist added, 'or angel dust, PCP, as you illiterates call it, because it causes young folk to die of hypothermia at raves. That's in the US. PCP ain't hit the UK yet.'

'The Family,' Art summarised, 'don't sell no addictive stuff. Amen.'

'But if I'm to make progress with Jo-Dog and Mafia, I need us to deal in cannabis and crack.' Goodman knew both his colleagues were fully aware of his own overall aims.

'Bush is no problem,' said Art, meaning cannabis. 'We could do a sideline in bush. Mafia's boys have all their crack supplies sewn up, so, even if Brother James approved, which he don't, us doin' crack wouldn't help you.'

'For an ounce of cocaine' – Goodman checked his new office notebook – 'we could be getting £800. Heroin likewise. But our amphets and Ecstasy are currently averaging only £80 an ounce. If we branch into cannabis that's a mere £50 an ounce.'

'You seen what heroin does to the cooler birds,' Art commented.

Goodman knew there was no argument to this. Profits and his personal quest did not warrant expansion into the killer drugs.

'Dilution,' he said, 'is the first answer to improved margins and we should start at once.'

Chemist sniffed derisively. 'The Family is Rolls-Royce. We don't adulterate our products. Never have. We have a name.'

'Rolls-Royce near enough went bust,' Goodman said. 'Sailor and James want to see bigger yield from the lab. Having a name won't help. Family products are thirty per cent pure at present. Average tablets on the street are fifteen per cent pure. We can afford a lot more additive.'

'What do you favour?' Chemist asked.

'What are the choices?' Goodman rejoined.

Chemist ticked off his fingers as he enumerated the standard bulking agents. 'Lactose, glucose, mannitol, caffeine, chalk dust, starch, talcum powder, quinine and boric acid. Plenty of choice. I've seen dried mushroom powder mushed into pills and dog-worming tablets sold as Ecstasy.'

'Sounds good,' Goodman commented. 'Lots of scope. Why don't you draw up a list of technical suggestions that you favour and I'll work out the maths.'

322

It was agreed. On the basis that one hundred per cent additive increase halved the purity but doubled the weight, The Family profits should soon take a lurch for the better under Goodman's steerage. He also began to learn about the physics of the lab.

There are over a thousand compounds involved in hallucinogenic amphetamines. The milder versions are derived from such natural product oils as nutmeg, dill, crocus, parsley and saffron, whereas the powerful varieties such as DOM and PMA are purely synthetic. The Family lab was producing two kilograms of amphetamine sulphate per week at a street value of £2000 per kilo. One of the main synthetic ingredients was benzyl methyl ketone (BMK), which The Family had been forming by processing phenylacetic acid, ammonium formate and acetic formate which they purchased in cash from a chemical company.

At first glance The Family's laboratory had given Goodman the impression of a Heath Robinson cartoon, with bubbling retorts and curly glass tubes parading in banks on long metal workbenches. A central bath-tub slobbered and breathed to the rhythm of a small water pump that cooled the entire system. The pungent stench of chemicals cloyed with the sickly-sweet smell of the finished product. But some hours of work with a calculator soon persuaded Goodman that the sky could be the limit given a change in some of The Family's practices. By the summer of 1986 he had, through an introduction by Sara, initiated a flourishing two-way business with an Asian-owned laboratory. The manager Sonny Guha, once Sara's pimp, had previously owned a popular hair salon in the Bonnington Hotel in Bloomsbury. With a couple of bouncers, he now ran a three-storey Victorian squat called 'The House' opposite the TGWU headquarters in Green Lanes, near Manor House tube station.

Guha and his friends held orgies in the near-derelict building, once a fine house with a hallway and high-ceilinged rooms. Sex and heroin upstairs and amphetamines down in the dingy basement. Guha's products dovetailed nicely with The Family's and cannabis from Amsterdam was often on offer at reduced prices attractive to Goodman for onward sale. Guha and Goodman were as chalk and cheese but from the outset they seemed to enjoy each other's company. Guha loved to hear himself talk and Goodman was a good listener, especially on the subject of drug trafficking. Until he could work out a drugs offer attractive to Mafia's people and put The Family lab into a sufficiently powerful position from which to make such an offer, his end-goal would remain a distant prospect.

Since the attack on Sara and subsequent enquiries at Keynsham as to the whereabouts of her lodger, Goodman seldom stayed there. He slept either at the lab or in the Peckham Home. His attempts to have the authorities move Sara to another flat had failed, and since she was happy enough at Keynsham, arguing that there was no logic for another attack on her, he had let the matter lie. Thanks to skilled skin-graft surgery the burn scars on Sara's breasts were inoffensive and easily hidden by a bra. At sixteen she had blossomed into a singularly attractive girl, lissom and nubile, which enabled her to haunt better-class streets and treble her takings. This in turn gave her the funds to advertise in *What's On In London* under the rubric 'Massage' and to build up a clientele of regular customers who frequently forked out £100 in cash for half an hour.

With more time on her hands she began to renovate her flat. Her only regret was her attachment to Goodman. He was under her skin but he did not know it. She dreamed of security, of being his wife. For he was the gentlest man she had ever met and he had trusted her from the beginning. Sometimes, perhaps once every four or five weeks, he would call her, always shy as though he was not worthy of her, and ask her out to dine with him. She lived for those evenings. They conversed easily and the silences between them were comfortable and natural. Afterwards, in the taxi, she would ask him in for coffee and he always smiled gratefully as he declined. She felt she could read him like a book. He was thinking of her age and of his. But mostly he was attached by honour to his own poor murdered wife. Perhaps he had sworn chastity until he had avenged her. She determined to keep herself free until the day when he was ready.

In August 1986 Sonny Guha had payment troubles with the Animal Liberation Front drug ring at 7 Alfoxton Avenue. They were not worth a raid or a fire-bombing, so he tipped off the local Crime Squad at St Anne's and mentioned the fact to Goodman, on whose recommendation he had first done business with the Alfoxton crew. 'Serve them right,' Goodman responded. The Family, after repeated similar non-payment, had ceased all dealings with Alfoxton several months previously. But when Tosh heard of Guha's action, she drove straight round, on the pretext of a friendly visit, and quietly warned Amy, whom she liked and respected, that a police raid was likely. Amy, for reasons of her own, did not pass the warning on to the others. Oxley had long since left the squat but disciples of his must have taken over because when Taff Jones and his squad pounced, they came away with large quantities of drugs and a major bomb-making factory.

'Any time you want a job in Peckham,' Tosh told Amy, 'let me know.' They exchanged contact details before Amy disappeared to a nearby ALF commune engaged in targeting the Rentokil company's vans by spraying hydrofluoric acid on gear-shifts and steering wheels.

As Goodman slowly moved closer to achieving the trafficking status necessary to make tempting business overtures to Jo-Dog Willetts, The Family's narcotics activities under his direction gradually increased in scope and variety, but, during the winter of 1986, he took over an Ecstasy lab at Wigan House in Warwick Grove, Clapton, and unknowingly made his first bad mistake.

Two powerful gangs ranged the area: the Singh clan, which included Sonny Guha, who operated The House in Green Lanes; and the Clapton Mob, whose fiefdom was wide and stretched south almost to Hackney. When the Claptons learnt that some 'Fins'y Park darkies' had muscled in on Wigan House, on their very doorstep, they staked out the place.

Luck played Goodman an evil hand, for the Clapton watchers picked up his associate Sonny Guha and followed him from Wigan House to Peak House, where he discussed deliveries, then back to The House in Green Lanes. The Claptons soon established that all three addresses were thriving amphetamine laboratories with Peak House at the centre of the web.

First they gained credit with the law by exposing the Wigan House lab, which was shortly afterwards raided and closed. Then sixteen Claptons moved in on Green Lanes. The two in-house bouncers, a Jamaican and a blond Cockney, held them off with a single sawn-off shotgun, but the sash windows, unshuttered, were smashed and firebombs exploded in two downstairs rooms. Guha was called and watched helplessly from the neighbour's hedge. He heard two Claptons beside the caravan which had long since been abandoned in the garden of The House.

'Come on then,' said one of them. 'Let's get goin' to Peak afore they get the word that we've done Green Lanes.'

Guha moved fast, calling Goodman on his mobile. Goodman was at Peak House.

'You're sure they're coming here?' Goodman sounded bemused.

Guha's tone was answer enough to dispel any idea that this was a joke. 'They're leaving now. You've only got minutes.'

Goodman woke Chemist, just back from a spell in hospital and feeling low, and Columbo, snoring on his camp-bed in the lobby. Then he phoned the Peckham Home and Sailor said he would call the Koreans, the Troons, at once. 'If the Claptons manage to break in,' Sailor warned, 'just get out through the corridor shaft like I showed you. Don't worry about the amphets gear.'

'It's insured?' Goodman's sense of humour was still intact.

'I'll be right there.' Sailor rang off. He would take thirty minutes, Goodman reckoned. Midnight was long gone and the roads would be traffic-free.

Goodman checked the security of the lab's only entrance. The three small windows were forty feet up and well barred. Even the letter-box flap was held in place by a sliding bolt to prevent petrol bombs.

But the Claptons had done their homework and were aware of such details. Four of their people used the communal fire-escape to the roof of Peak House, from where they dropped CS gas canisters down the generous venting system Chemist had installed for the laboratory. Petrol from a jerrycan then sloshed down the twin pipes, followed by an incendiary device which, despite striking the wire-mesh grill, ignited the petrol with a muffled explosion that briefly stunned the two men in the lobby and blew out a laboratory window.

'There's several geezers out here,' said Columbo, who had recovered first and squinted through the spyhole of the steel door. 'They're stacked with artillery and they got a ram.' He retched into the wet tea towel about his lower face and squeezed his eyes tight against the pain of the gas. Spluttering and cursing, they dragged clear the unconscious Chemist, who had been in the laboratory, blinded by the gas, when the fireball ignited. His hair and eyebrows

326

were singed, his spectacles smashed and his forehead swollen from a heavy fall against the workbench.

Columbo managed to slide out the wall panel above the gas water-heater in the tiny washroom off the lobby. They heard or felt heavy vibrations as the Claptons' ram thudded into the breeze-block partition to the side of the entrance door.

'You go first,' Columbo coughed. 'I'll lift him up to you.'

But the shaft was narrow, a mere twenty-two inches square, part of the original construction of the Peak House block and unmodified by The Family since nobody had thought of the need to manhandle limp bodies along it.

Goodman was finding breathing difficult. His eyes were agony and his nose streamed. He could smell burning cables from an electrical fire and acrid fumes from chemicals spilled on to the hot plates when the retorts had smashed in the explosion. They could not tell whether a fire had started. The fireball, Goodman hoped, might have removed all oxygen in the lab long enough to extinguish any flames. None the less they were slowly asphyxiating from the chemical fumes. Even Columbo's prodigious strength was not enough to drag Chemist's body into the shaft.

'You'll have to leave him,' wheezed Goodman, his voice giving out. Columbo wrapped his cloth about Chemist's face before abandoning him. The fumes should be less lethal at floor level. No point in three dead bodies. The two men wriggled along the dark metal shaft, fighting for air. At one point the venting angled upwards at some twenty degrees for a stretch but then returned to the horizontal and, after fifteen yards, Goodman felt the four wing-nuts of the panel cut into the shaft by Chemist when The Family first moved in. They gulped in the fresh air, then dropped five feet on to the concrete floor of the landing. Close by they heard the baying of the pack as the breeze-block wall crumbled under the impact of the ram. Soon afterwards the unmistakable boom of a shotgun echoed off the stained concrete walls of the stairwell.

'Poor ol' Chemist,' Columbo muttered. They squatted on the floor. The 'fresh air' was in fact a mixture of lingering CS gas impregnated in their clothes and the green slime of urine that veneered the concrete.

'They'll find the panel,' Goodman whispered. 'Then they'll come here.'

327

'How long till Sailor or the Troons arrive?' Columbo croaked.

'Could be too long.'

'We'd better hide . . . I know the ol' lady in number 19 up the corridor.'

They crept along yards of stinking concrete. The shouting of the Clapton yobs faded, then rose again and seemed to approach along their escape route. They ran the last stretch to the door of flat 19 and Columbo shouted through the letter-box. Fingers fumbled with bolts and the door opened warily. A scruffy couple of whites with a wide-eyed, thumb-sucking child gazed at them. They seemed happy enough once they had verified Columbo's identity. They had heard the shouting and felt the thud of the ram but they asked no questions. People on the estate always closed their eyes to trouble. The police were seldom called. Number 19, a temporary squat for this common-law family, was the local clearing house for stolen clothes, electrical goods and car radios.

Columbo gave the squatters £10 and asked for tea. One at a time they used the flat's filthy basin to wash their eyes and faces. After an hour Columbo reckoned it safe to emerge. They returned to the laboratory. Sailor and the Troons must have come and gone, taking Chemist with them. The police had not been called but, apart from a pool of blood where Chemist had lain, smashed glass and the stench of chemical fumes, everything was pretty much as usual.

Goodman stuffed the lobby carpet into the gaping hole beside the door and they called a minicab belonging to Art's brother.

Back at the Peckham Home, the normal Family sparkle was absent as they mourned Chemist, whose chest had been the close-range target of a shotgun, killed no doubt as he lay unconscious. The only consolation was the knowledge that his was a pleasanter passing than the slow wasting of Aids.

On the night after the Claptons' raid, Goodman returned to Sara's flat in the late evening. She knew at once, though nobody had called, that something was badly wrong, for Alex seemed more alone and vulnerable than at any time since the Professor's findings. After they had silently drunk tea in the kitchen, she led him by the hand into his bedroom. Her own room, she feared, might spark offensive associations. They kissed, gently at first and she felt the tears run down his cheeks to his chin. His chest heaved against her breasts but he made no sound in his sorrow. At some point the spark of desire awoke and the kissing kindled their loins. Their lovemaking was explosive yet gentle and lasted through the night. She had never known such carnal pleasures. It was as though she had been a virgin in all but the mechanical sense. The depth and frequency of her orgasms were another world compared with the rare and superficial sexual pleasures of her past. Sara knew she was desperately in love with Alex but she recognised his inability to respond in kind while his vendetta remained the focus of his existence.

Goodman moved back into Sara's flat. As far as he was concerned she was a beautiful friend whom he trusted and with whom he now enjoyed a wonderful cohabitation. Otherwise his energies were fully taken up in resurrecting The Family business, his launch pad, hopefully, into Mafia's confidence.

In September 1986 a Tupperware saleslady cruised Keynsham House and chatted to several of Sara's neighbours. Over a chummy cup of tea a lonely widow, while apologising for not needing plastic dishes, was fulsome in her advice as to which neighbours might be ripe for a Tupperware visit. As she ticked off her fellow-residents on her fingers, she came to Sara and gave a knowing look.

'Men,' she said, wrinkling one nostril. 'All times of the day and night. Not for Tupperware parties, neither, I can tell you. But you could try her, I suppose. No harm in tryin'. She's got a lodger and all, a shy gent – quite different, you know. Maybe he'd like somethin'.'

'Up there now, are they?' Tupperware asked.

'What? The Indian girl? Nah, she's out.' The widow hoisted up her fat-rolls and trundled to the window, where she squinted out with an expert eye.

'I think you're in luck,' she grimaced against the strong sunlight. 'He's in.'

They discussed other potential Tupperware targets and, with profuse thanks, the saleslady moved on. Goodman was bleary-eyed when he opened the door, for he had done the night shift at the Peckham coolers. A practised hand at giving the polite brush-off to persistent Jehovah's Witnesses back in Leominster, he would not let the sales lady in, answer her questionnaire or agree to a free sample offer.

The woman came away with a series of photos taken by a hidden camera in her samples case but no personal information. Jason, her MI5 boss, passed the best photograph to his CIA contact in Grosvenor Square and, three days later, JR Ridgway arrived openly at Sara's flat and let himself in with a skeleton key.

Goodman, returning at midday from a local search for a new laboratory, was startled by 'Hi, Alex,' from his room as he lit the gas hob in the kitchen. He recognised but did not immediately place JR. The last time they had met, the American had looked dishevelled and unshaven.

They exchanged pleasantries over tea and JR learnt Goodman's sorry tale. He wasted no time in coming to the point, for Goodman had said the Indian girl might return shortly. He and Jed Mason had agonised on how best to attract Goodman to the BCCI job. The man was an accountant and would surely leap at the offer of a highly paid London accountancy position with car, pension and all the trimmings. Such an opportunity would be beyond his wildest dreams and infinitely preferable to his current pimping activities for the Indian girl.

But Goodman did not leap; he merely blinked owlishly. He thanked JR politely for thinking of him and asked how he could best make contact after considering the offer.

They agreed to meet the next morning and, when JR had left, Goodman took the tube to South London. At the Peckham Home he spoke with Sailor, James and Tosh. They listened carefully to Goodman's summary of JR's offer. For a while, when Goodman had finished, Sailor was silent, deep in thought. Then he asked Tosh to fetch the file on Mafia Douglas.

He nodded as he studied it. 'This is good.' He sounded excited. 'As I thought, BCCI is one of the organisations Mafia does contract work for. Dirty jobs. Not your line, Alex, but a possibility, OK?'

'There would be no harm in seeing how things work out,' Goodman agreed. 'I'm not doing very well with the narcotics approach, that's for sure.'

'Don't be hard on yourself,' said Tosh. 'You've just had bad luck, that's all. You were doin' fine till the Claptons messed us up.'

They tossed the matter back and forth into the small hours and it was at length agreed that Goodman would say yes to JR and whatever American law agency he represented. If something came of this and he found himself on the inside of BCCI, he could locate their 'dirty tricks' department, the unit that often employed Mafia, and try to become useful to it. If this succeeded, then maybe he could approach Mafia from a far stronger position than would be possible were he merely to stay involved in a minor drugs racket. To say no, on the other hand, would, they all agreed, be to look a gift-horse in the mouth. If nothing came of the job, he would carry on with the current 'narcotics approach'.

When JR met him the next morning he agreed to take on the BCCI job.

Ten days later JR called on Goodman again and this time took him to meet a powerful middle-management executive of BCCI, a Pakistani he introduced simply as Mahmoud. Jed had first met Mahmoud at the New York apartment of the late Javed, where Mahmoud was lodging while acquiring his MBA degree at Pace University, as part of a BCCI graduate-training scheme.

Jed and Javed had shown Mahmoud irrefutable proof of BCCI fraud and hypocrisy in the Third World. Mahmoud had unwillingly become a 'sleeper' within the bank, reporting useful information to Jed from time to time. He was to be Goodman's key contact and his first priority was to locate and suborn an inner-core London executive close to Abedi in order to insert Goodman, a non-Asian accountant, into the Leadenhall Street nerve-centre of the greatest criminal enterprise in history.

Mahmoud's own access to the most senior tiers of BCCI in the City, the supremos of the fourth and fifth floors, was limited. His knowledge of their weak points and susceptibilities, however, was not. He responded to Jed with confidence. 'Give me two or three weeks,' he said, smiling. 'I will position Mr Goodman where nobody will question his presence.'

331

25

December 1986–April 1990

As Goodman understood JR's proposal, all he was required to do, once employed in the innermost sanctums of BCCI, was to trace the accounts of an American citizen and mobster named Albert Redden and, while so doing, keep an eye open for evidence of CIA collusion in BCCI affairs. The brief was wide open, with no set deadline.

Jed Mason meanwhile moved ahead with organising Goodman's high-level insertion into the bank's epicentre in the City of London. His agent, Mahmoud, had targeted Ib'n Hassan Burney, one of a handful of BCCI top executives known to be honest.

Burney's presence at the heart of BCCI's murky web was difficult to comprehend for Mahmoud, who told Jed: 'It's like finding St Francis of Assisi on Stalin's staff.' Burney was regarded as Abedi's closest friend and adviser, and the two men behaved like brothers. Burney revered Abedi and possessed blind faith in his leadership abilities. They had been friends for forty years, during which time Abedi had kept Burney well clear of his 'non-banking' activities.

For some months Burney had openly denounced a group of fellow Abedi disciples who had turned corrupt and whose influence had spread cancer-like through BCCI. They appeared unstoppable even by Abedi himself. Burney could not contemplate, let alone accept, that the mire of BCCI fraud and financial crime was inspired by Hassan Abedi.

Mahmoud believed Burney to be a man of quiet influence who would go to any lengths to preserve his integrity and that of his four fine sons. He further guessed that Burney would be willing to abet and uphold the organs of the law in identifying and eradicating the sources of evil within the bank in the hope that a purge of key wrongdoers might yet cleanse and save Abedi's brainchild.

Jed got the FBI to check out Burney in their own records, and the executive's selection was quickly approved.

Two weeks after Mahmoud's first meeting with Burney, the latter was admitted to London's Cromwell Hospital with acute coronary problems. During a meeting at his bedside Burney reacted with shock and anger to Mahmoud's revelations about the diseased state of the bank. 'This is unbelievable,' he whispered. 'We established the bank in order to bridge the financial differences between the Third World and the advanced economies and to give the under-developed countries the chance to be self-reliant. You cannot imagine how many families in how many countries *rely* on the very existence and growth of BCCI. Such a vital mission and worthy vision must not be allowed to wither due to an unscrupulous cabal of selfish men.'

For a while Burney had difficulty speaking. Then, grasping Mahmoud's wrist, he went on: 'I am too ill to be effective now. I would be outmanoeuvred as soon as I entered the ring. I rely on you and your people to rid BCCI of these parasites. How can I help you?'

When Mahmoud told him of Goodman the old man closed his eyes. His heart had betrayed him but his brain was still sharp and his love for BCCI as strong as ever. He gave Mahmoud the name of a senior Pakistani in the Foreign Exchange Department, a man of rare integrity and loyal to Burney. 'As for the insertion of your Goodman, this can only be done through the office of Mr Abedi himself, whom you should approach through his deputy, Swaleh Naqvi. I will alert Naqvi to expect you.'

Mahmoud did not see Burney again. A few days later he called Jed to say: 'Hassan Burney is dead. He was a great man, God rest his soul. Don't be alarmed. He showed me the way forward with Goodman. Leave it to me.'

Mahmoud met Naqvi, BCCI's second in command, at the latter's home in Finchley. Naqvi had greatly respected Hassan Burney, his own Area Chief in the days before the fall of Dacca, and was therefore prepared to give Mahmoud a sympathetic hearing.

Mahmoud played on rumours of tension between Naqvi and the Chief Accountant of BCCI, Masihur 'Masi' Rahman. 'Sir,' he began softly, 'I approach you, as you know, with the blessing of the late Burney Sahib. I will be brief. The external auditors and Masi Rahman are playing a game which requires your immediate focus. May I put to you the plan I placed before Burney Sahib and which, but for his untimely death, *he* would have placed before you?'

Naqvi nodded and began polishing his spectacles.

'In order to discover what is going on without alerting Masi we should immediately plant our man in the Accounts Department. Personnel have recently placed an advertisement in the *Financial Times*, so the timing is good. But Masi will never take on a stranger without first checking him with care, especially, with due respect, sir, if the man has your support.'

Naqvi chuckled. 'You are right. However, if I were to ask Mr Abedi to appoint Goodman as his *personal* "Special Projects Officer", Masi would have to accept his presence without question. I must meet the man.'

The following day Mahmoud took Goodman to the Leadenhall Street office. He briefed him in the luxuriously appointed Executive Dining Room on the second floor, where they were joined for lunch by Naqvi.

'Abedi will see you now,' announced Naqvi without preamble as they finished their meal. Mahmoud was as surprised as Goodman. They followed Naqvi to Abedi's office on the fourth floor. Deep-pile carpets, plaster of Paris moulding and heavy Victorian furniture set the scene for their hurried meeting with the head of BCCI.

Abedi stared at the Englishman, transfixing him with his great liquid eyes, the eyes of a hypnotist, a manipulator of men. It was clear that he had already agreed with Naqvi to appoint Goodman as his personal spy within the Leadenhall labyrinth. 'I must go to an urgent meeting now,' Abedi muttered. 'Perhaps, Mr Mahmoud, you will see me tomorrow to discuss Mr Goodman's role in our special team?'

Naqvi stayed behind. Outside the office Mahmoud grasped Goodman's hand. 'Welcome aboard, friend. He has accepted you. Your position, with his personal backing, is unassailable.'

'But tomorrow?' Goodman asked.

'Leave that to me.' Mahmoud's tone was soothing. 'That will be merely to dot the i's.'

They met again after Mahmoud's meeting with Abedi. The

Pakistani was exuberant when he came away from the great man. 'Everything is settled. Abedi is now fully aware of your dual role, as Naqvi's man keeping an in-house eye on Masi Rahman and, as of today, he also knows that I work for the Americans and, indirectly, for the CIA. Jed Mason briefed Casey's office to expect Abedi's call to check me out. From then on he accepted my proposals of your status and your role. The Agency, I told him, was worried that BCCI is beginning to crumble. Too many wolves are out for our blood, especially in Washington. The Agency fear that if and when we fall, they will be dragged down with us. They have covertly associated with us for so long and in so many countries that they are loath to disown us until the last moment. What they need to be sure of knowing is *exactly* when that moment will be. That will be your job. *One* of your jobs. Monitoring the warning signs and, when the external auditors show signs of touching the termination button, letting Jed know.'

'Abedi accepts all this?' Goodman was incredulous.

Mahmoud nodded. 'Abedi never has time to listen to mundane data. He wants the overall picture, however gloomy. He asked me: "So the CIA want me to allow their plant in the form of a London accountant, probably an MI5 man, free range here so he can keep a finger on BCCI's pulse and scream warnings to Washington?" Then he asked me why the CIA Director, William Casey, had not approached him in person. "Are we not still friends?" he asked. I told him that Casey was in poor health at present. He seemed to accept that. I told him further that those in the Agency who had approached us were not all of Casey's camp. That their star, however, was in the ascendant at Langley. I admitted that I had in fact been asked to approach Mr Burney, not him.

'Abedi then asked me: "This Englishman, what is his background?" "An accountant, sir," I told him, "who has worked for the Agency many times. Trustworthy and efficient. He will report only to me. If he should attempt to circumvent me and go direct to Washington, I will insist on his removal. I will report only to Mr Naqvi and you, sir."

' "What do *you* feel about all this?" Abedi then asked me. I told him: "Well, sir, the Agency are going to plant somebody on us . . . Better the devil you know." He liked that. He called Naqvi while I was there. Gave it the final seal of approval. Then he dismissed me.'

335

Goodman raised his bushy eyebrows. 'Looks like I'd better polish up on my creative accountancy! And with an overnight crash course.'

'Don't worry,' Mahmoud laughed. 'They say it's like riding a bike. You never forget the basics.'

Taff Jones and Clive Mills were returning home late from a court case when they were called to a suspected break-in. They cornered three hefty burglars in a bedroom. Taff caressed one with a garden shovel and Clive tackled another on the bed, which collapsed. The third surrendered, having wet himself watching Taff and Clive in action. This sort of police work stirred the adrenalin but Taff preferred the intellectual challenge of pitting his wits against the devious cunning of drug traffickers.

Taff's area Crime Squad were miffed that gang warfare had closed down Peak House. They had spent hours observing the laboratory and had been almost ready to pounce. Now they had to start all over again. Frequent attempts to tail the Peak House group had ended in failure. However, Art had been traced to his girlfriend's place in Stoke Newington and, in January 1987, one of Taff's men observed Art calling at a chemical retailing company in Croydon. Taff had made enquiries with the local force, who spoke to a manager at the retailers after showing him a covert photo of Art.

Yes, Taff was assured, the man had been keen to pay cash, provided he could collect the ephedrine within two days, but he had been unwilling to provide a contact address or supply a written order. With this information Taff was quite certain Art's gang, the Peak House crew, were back at work in a new lab and Art was at once subjected to a 'semi full-time' watch.

The Peak House lab had always concentrated on amphetamine sulphate as their main line but the Claptons' raid had caused Goodman to contemplate the current market for other drugs. The Family had readily agreed with his advice that the new Sandridge Court lab should diversify to include methylamphetamine production. Art was sent out to locate supply sources of bulk ephedrine, a key methylamphetamine constituent, unaware that its suppliers, like those of BMK, were often monitored by the National Drugs Intelligence Unit.

Sonny Guha had taken on a new partner, down from Bradford

and previously a 'blagger', an armed robber. Like the majority of blaggers that year he had turned to narcotics under pressure from intense police focus on their kind. He was horrified to find Guha and The Family operating without 'counter-surveillance'.

Accordingly, two of Guha's colleagues were tasked to list, like train-spotters, all vehicles used by Taff and his colleagues from the St Anne's Crime Squad. This was not difficult because Taff's Peugeot and the other squad cars were parked in side-streets near the police station and driven on a regular basis between the station and their users' homes. In addition, Guha's observation team were equipped with mobile phones and his car with a radio scanner from Dixons, to pick up the bandwidths used by the local police.

These high-tech counter-surveillance activities never quite caught on with The Family, however, and by the end of January Taff had pinpointed Art's ephedrine delivery point as Sandridge Court.

Goodman started work at 100 Leadenhall Street, a stone's throw from the Bank of England, at the end of February. With Mahmoud's guidance, he quickly settled into his job. Mahmoud had prepared three separate BCCI offices in different parts of London for Goodman's use. In each there were briefed contacts who taught him the file and data-access processes he would need to act as Abedi's private spy and to commence his complex searches on behalf of Jed Mason. Mahmoud impressed on him that he should trust nobody but the named contacts and at all times be aware of the deep schisms, the factionalism, within the bank.

To muddy the waters about Goodman's identity, Mahmoud's people primed the highly efficient BCCI grapevine, with its links to Karachi, with various rumours. Goodman was an expert creative accountant sent in from on high to interface with the outside auditors from Price Waterhouse and to set false trails. Then again, he was the President's own man, on secret business. BCCI employees were discouraged from asking questions about persons on 'special assignments', especially when they were executive-sanctioned.

Mahmoud's aim was to keep Goodman's profile so low that it was all but non-existent. Curious English employees were kept well away from him. His name was not entered in the constantly updated staff directory. Each hierarchy within the bank's Byzantine structure was to remain ignorant, should Goodman's presence be noted, of his status and exact function.

The layout at the City headquarters was bright, clean and efficient. Hassan Abedi was often present and, a stickler for smart turnout, he – like all other top executives – worked in an open-plan office on the VIP fourth floor. His visitors, among them potentates from all over the world, were therefore seen and inspected from beneath lowered eyelids by all the denizens of the fourth floor.

Burney's office had been on the seventh floor and his colleagues were three other senior executives: Messrs Gillani, Kazimi and Pirbhai. An International Credit and Investment Company Holdings (ICIC) colleague of Kazimi, one Wazir Hussein Jafree, had been instructed to pay £80,000 annually to the Swiss bank of Goodman's choice. This was done by numbered account through BCCI Luxemburg and thence BCP Geneva. Goodman was thus only a number even to his paymaster Jafree.

ICIC was a secret bank within a bank, with its major machinery in the Cayman Islands, where BCCI deposited billions of dollars of laundered monies. All ICIC banking entities were a working part of BCCI, but their accounts were held elsewhere, so the bank's auditors could never obtain a complete picture of the myriad and complex frauds being perpetrated under their noses.

Mahmoud, at a weekly debriefing with Goodman, pinpointed where, in his own opinion, the source of the rot lay. 'You will be aware that the entire auditing profession is made up of individuals who are not sharp enough to detect irregularities or, if they do, they can be easily fobbed off with some "rational" explanation. In a crooked organisation internal audits are for PR only. They are not meant to be productive in elucidating facts. The boss of our Central Audit, Saleem Siddiqi, must have a lot to answer for. It's extraordinary that such massive frauds have apparently never been noticed by our auditors.'

The existence within the bank of 'strange' unidentifiable persons like Goodman, Mahmoud added, would – if indeed they were even noticed in the general BCCI mayhem – tend to minimise internal scams through fear of detection, on the KGB principle of everyone watching everyone else. To this end he had instigated further rumours that would soon be passed from tongue to tongue and altered beyond recognition *en route* like refracted light beams. 'The new man, an accountant as grey as old wallpaper, indeed almost invisible, is looking into the Central Credit Division, well known for its mysterious persons and assignments subject to nobody's scrutiny.' Or: 'He is on assignment from the CCD.' Or then again: 'He is checking on everyone in the Protocol Department, even its boss, Mr Basheer Siddiqi himself.'

Mahmoud had described the Protocol Department to Goodman as an aberration with no parallel in any other bank. Its hand-picked staff selected escorts for visiting Arab clients and accompanied them to casinos and brothels. This was a no-go area for ordinary bank staff. Unlimited funds were available to Protocol, for Basheer Siddiqi was one of the President's most trusted executives.

Mahmoud's weekly meetings with Goodman took place in the West End, well away from the popular City haunts of his BCCI colleagues. 'The obscurity of your work,' he told him, 'providing you make no ripples, should keep you clear of interference. Secrecy is sufficiently ingrained as a way of life with BCCI to keep you flitting about between a series of permanently blind spots. We will make you the man who never was.'

Goodman's natural ability with figures and systems had not deserted him. He soon found himself fascinated with his Herculean task. He was entering a mathematical labyrinth beset with many a cunning false trail, cul-de-sac and spiralling circles to nowhere. But this was his *métier* as well as the way to his enemies.

Sara never questioned his commitment. They coupled often and with passion. Goodman watched her nakedness in awe. He found himself able to talk with her about their lovemaking in a way he would never have contemplated with Mary. He treated Sara's 'business life' as just that; not something of which he was jealous nor even an intrusion into his thoughts when they made love.

'You should double your fee,' he advised her, 'and halve your clientele. A girl of your beauty should not need to walk the streets. You would survive perfectly well on phone responses to your magazine advertisements.'

She listened to him and soon found that he was right. She spent the extra free time primping the flat and shopping for the exotic dinners she loved to cook for him. He now wore smart City clothes to work but, at least within sight of the estate, a dowdy Oxfam raincoat toned his appearance down to blend with the scenery.

Some three months after Goodman joined BCCI, Sara prepared a special candlelit dinner but then funked the announcement she had intended to make. When Alex nudged her afterwards in bed, she squeezed her thighs together and giggled, 'You can't: *Poosavanam*.' He ignored her and renewed his advances.

Sara sat up. 'I want to,' she blurted out, 'but you have made me pregnant.'

He kissed her with spontaneous joy. He should have suspected. He could picture his Lucy when she was a baby. Perhaps Sara's child, his child, their child, would be a girl. Sara could see the wonder and the pleasure in Alex's open features and she was filled with joy. She wept her happiness with her face and arm across his chest. She did everything to please him. She had secretly and slowly improved her diction, diluted her accent, just for Alex.

'What is *Poosavanam*?' he asked.

'Hindus,' she said through her tears, 'forbid intercourse from the second month of pregnancy until two months after childbirth. That way we can be sure of a son. If you were Hindu you'd value a son for only he can offer *pinda* for you to prevent your soul floatin' in limbo after your death. That's *Poosavanam*. But I know you would prefer a daughter, Alex.'

As always he was touched at her perspicacity. 'You will keep the child?' he asked gently.

'Do you want me to?'

'Very much.' He kissed her neck.

They said nothing about marriage. He wondered about her thoughts on the issue, both personal and religious. He was very fond of her and physically besotted but, wedded to his quest, he could not think of a new wife while still haunted by unresolved guilt for the murder of his first love.

Sara yearned each day and every night to smother Alex with her love but she feared she might drive him away. She recognised the mental stresses that plagued him: her ally was her youth, her looks and her patience. Tosh agreed to be guardian to the child and The Family held a party to celebrate Sara's announcement.

Their joy was short-lived, for the Crime Squad raided the new Sandridge Court laboratory later that week and arrested Leon. Art,

340

whose carelessness had led Taff Jones and his men – through the ephedrine purchases – to locate the lab, narrowly escaped the police net but it would be many months before The Family were back in the amphetamine business. The jailed Leon discovered that he was claustrophobic and, desperate to curtail his sentence, led the police to 'Alexo' at Sara's flat. The 'lodger', the missing murder suspect, was arrested. But within hours the Crime Squad let him go on discovering he had been flagged by 'another agency' – a euphemism for MI5.

In February 1988 Hassan Abedi, at his retirement home in Karachi, suffered a massive heart attack and his deputy, Swaleh Naqvi, took over BCCI's reins. The arrangement with Goodman remained inviolate. Nobody seemed to know the extent of Abedi's ongoing 'behind the scenes' influence, so nobody rocked the boat.

Goodman took great care to thread his way between the warring factions within BCCI and not to be seen colluding with either. Abedi's personal charisma had kept the lid on such friction but his illness now allowed the protagonists full scope.

Abedi and Naqvi were originally Indian immigrants to Pakistan, Urdu-speaking Shi'ite Muslims, and their faction, the so-called technocrats, felt responsible for the bank's success because of their skill and experience. Their opponents, the Gulf faction, were mostly Sunni Muslims from Pakistan's Punjab region, led by one Zafar Iqbal and championed by the bank's chief shareholder, billionaire Sheikh Zayed of Abu Dhabi. These two BCCI groupings did not speak to each other socially nor even, at annual conferences, stay in the same hotels.

Naqvi's succession led to an increase in the number of dirty jobs which the bank contracted out to Mafia Douglas via Korbi Richter. Mahmoud warned Goodman about the beating up of an ex-bank manager who had been blackmailing Swaleh Naqvi. There was no proof that Naqvi was himself instigating outside contract work such as this and Mahmoud believed that a senior executive, known internally as The Godfather, was responsible. Goodman's break-through into the 'dirty jobs' network, when it came, was due to some enquiries he had instituted into BCCI dealings with Romania on behalf of the CIA. This work, which he had carried out for a Mr

Shaikh, had, in the event, yielded little of value, but, in the course of it, Goodman twice met Shaikh's boss, Jo-Dog Willetts.

By the end of 1989 Goodman was living an increasingly pleasurable existence with Sara and their little daughter, Jyoti Lucy. In Sara's eyes they were married. But although Goodman was a doting father, the driving force of his life remained his remorseless hunt for his invisible enemies.

Goodman followed up leads to all parts of the BCCI empire but found little trace of CIA collusion and no trace at all of the secret accounts of Albert Redden. The fact that Jed Mason could not supply the names of the accounts, let alone their numbers, did not help. There were thirty 'laundry countries' such as Liechtenstein where money could be buried so deeply with so many legal fronts – fiduciaries, attorneys, corporations between depositor and cash – that identification of the original owner soon became almost impossible.

Since Jed Mason was not paying for Goodman's services, he could afford to be patient and hope that sooner or later his English mole would make a breakthrough.

Goodman was fascinated by the extraordinary world of BCCI. He stole documents, photocopied secret minutes and built up a 'blackmail library' against a rainy day, which Sara hid in her bedroom.

The breathtaking scale of BCCI fraud which Goodman unearthed by himself had somehow escaped the notice of Price Waterhouse and their 300 dedicated auditors for two years. The bank was a huge hall of mirrors in which magicians transformed deposits, largely from Third World countries, to the pockets of oil-rich sheikhs.

Billions of dollars were manufactured out of thin air to conceal holes in balance sheets. There were false loans of several hundred million dollars, customers who did not exist, money that went round in circles then vanished before reappearing under a different ownership.

Goodman obtained and smuggled out filed evidence of corruption against chief executives Swaleh Naqvi, Imtiaz Ahmed, Saleem Siddiqi and many others. Mahmoud also warned him about The Godfather, who kept a shotgun with which he had killed people opposed to him back in Lahore.

Many of the accounts which Goodman tried to follow up

vanished into a voracious sink-hole at BCCI Paris, and others, along with a sackful of bad loans, were transferred to a special cell in Grand Cayman known as 'The Dustbin'. Some of Goodman's most enlightening discoveries were the result of translating hand-written Urdu notes between corrupt executives. One of Mahmoud's three clerks, from the Cannon Street branch, helped Goodman with translations.

By late 1989 Goodman had narrowed down his hunt for the Redden accounts and for CIA-related activities to the secretive BCCI futures trading company Capcom, which was an even more complex financial machine than BCCI itself. Through Capcom documents he obtained proof that BCCI's US bank, First American, was intricately linked with covert CIA operations. Goodman foresaw months of further plodding research ahead and by early 1990 he was uncertain whether BCCI would survive that long. In March that year he sent his first warning to Jed that Price Waterhouse, no longer emasculated by bribed auditors, was threatening the bank with disclosure of fraud.

The general public, including thousands of people whose life savings were banked with BCCI, were blissfully unaware that anything was wrong. In the House of Lords, Labour peer Lord Callaghan stated: 'In my judgement BCCI managers are of the highest integrity and the bank's philosophy is honourable.' At this time BCCI London accounts included those of Saddam Hussein, who had salted some $5 billion out of Iraq, General Noriega: $2 billion from Panama, and Khun Sa, warlord of the Golden Triangle's heroin fortunes: well over $3 billion from Asia.

The following month Goodman was summoned to a meeting on the Embankment. Shaikh, muffled against the cold, said with reverence: 'The Boss wants to meet you.'

'Jo-Dog Willetts?'

'No,' said Shaikh. 'His boss. Mr Douglas. He will be here shortly.'

Goodman's stomach lurched. Suddenly success! He steeled himself to hide the rage he had nurtured for so long against Mafia Douglas, the killer of his wife and daughter. He must show only the correct emotions. Mafia would expect him to be a typical City accountant, bent like the rest of BCCI and willing to sell himself for the right money.

If he had expected an obvious villain, he was disappointed.

Mafia's features suggested an alert intelligence and bonhomie. Goodman took the proffered hand. They sat on a bench beside the river. Mafia's trench coat and fedora would not have been out of place in *Casablanca*.

For a full minute Mafia remained silent. Goodman felt bound to speak. 'I am sorry nothing came of my Romania connection . . .'

'Don't worry, man.' Mafia's voice was rich and mellifluous. 'Them that pays us have not complained. I called you because they now have another job for us. This one is urgent and very big. You are my best chance because of your knowledge of the City. You know, Lloyd's an' all. They want a passenger ship sunk, but no lives lost, by 30 April.'

'But I know nothing about ships,' Goodman blurted.

'Hold it. Hold it, man.' Mafia's voice had lost its warmth.

Goodman regretted his instinctive response. He would never gain this man's confidence by being negative.

'You need go nowhere near this ship. You just find a suitable contact quick, get the ship sunk on time and I pay you big money.'

A dozen queries sprang to Goodman's mind but he merely nodded. Do this job well and he would soon be on chatting terms with Mafia.

'Shaikh will give you details. OK?'

Again Goodman nodded. This time with feigned enthusiasm. 'What is my cut?' he remembered to ask.

'Successful and you get £50,000 in cash.'

They shook hands. When Mafia left, Shaikh gave Goodman a shiny folder.

'Any questions and you call me.' He shivered and disappeared towards Trafalgar Square.

Goodman spent the weekend imbibing the file's contents and deciding on his best course of action. He did not call JR, who would only be perplexed, for he was after all a lawman and Goodman was about to break the law in a big way. Certainly JR would be in no position to advise or help him. If he were to mess up this job, Goodman might lose Mafia altogether.

That evening he met up with Sailor and Tosh in Peckham. Sailor was out of his depth but Tosh, having digested the problem, announced that she knew the right guy to handle the sinking.

'Lundquist,' she muttered. 'Egil Lundquist of Snaptun in Denmark. He was with Schramm's mercenaries. Retired now but knows every criminal in Copenhagen, so he does.'

'But,' Goodman complained. 'The *Scandinavian Star* operates from Oslo, Norway.'

'Alex,' Tosh sounded scathing, 'I've read in ten minutes what you took a weekend to soak up. Thank the Lord you have Sailor and me to do the thinkin' for you! Frederikshavn, the vessel's southern port of call, is the north tip of Denmark, right across the Skagerrak from Oslo and as regular a ferry run as Dover to Calais.'

'So what do you propose?'

'Why, we pay Egil to find us a marine arsonist – not a saboteur, because an explosion would sink the ship fast and kill folk. What you need is a slow but steady fire.' She looked hard at the specifications of the *Scandinavian Star* and her routing. 'She is Lloyd's-class, insured with all safety features, sixteen fire doors, distress systems, life-rafts and a well-trained crew of a hundred. Within two minutes of the fire catchin', the skipper will inform all ships in the Skagerrak. Within ten minutes she'll be surrounded by boats wantin' to help. So, like I say, it's a good arsonist you'll be needin' and Egil will find you the right fella as soon as you name the right fee for the job.'

Tosh was as good as her word. At noon the next day she called Goodman to confirm that the ship would be torched well before Mafia's key date of 30 April. 'But we need to establish why we're doin' it.'

They met that evening and Goodman tapped the file. 'If it's not in here, they don't want me to know. As far as they're concerned, I don't *need* to know.'

'Alex, my dear little man,' Tosh tutted. 'You are hopeless. Never enter anythin' blind. There's always somethin' you can deduce, surely to God.'

She scanned the file thoroughly and, cracking her knuckles like firewood, lectured Goodman. She had conferred with a City friend and reached the conclusion that the most likely motive for the sinking, that of insurance, was not that of Mafia's client. Rather, she thought, especially given a closing date at the end of the month, it had to do with tonners.

'Tonners?' Goodman was nonplussed.

345

'That's what I said. Tonners. Two people, probably mega-rich, mega-bored individuals fed up with Monaco and Atlantic City gamin' rooms, take a wager with each other on how many jumbo jets, or ships of a certain tonnage, will be claimed against over a twelve-month period. To all intents and purposes they could lay the bet through Ladbrokes but they don't. For many years they used to place tonner bets through Lloyd's of London. But in 1906 The Marine Gambling Act stated: "any person gamblin' on loss by marine perils shall be guilty of an offence". None the less people continued with the practice and Lloyd's permitted "tonner policies" to be placed despite the 1906 Act. The main broker of these policies, a lad called Christopher Moran, was finally expelled by the Lloyd's Committee and the activity officially stopped early in the eighties. After that tonners became the preserve of millionaire gamblin' addicts mostly in the US, Japan and Hong Kong. It's a macabre marine version of Russian Roulette.'

'How does . . . ?' Goodman interjected.

'Wait,' Tosh said. 'My research did not stop there. There are two other factors possibly involved. One of the best-known tonner men is a BCCI client of long standin' and, as we know, these jobs Mafia is givin' you stem from BCCI itself. The client in question is a personal friend of Hassan Abedi and of his shippin' muckers the Gokal family. There is every possibility that you will be helpin' this fella towards achievin' whatever minimum claim figure of tonnage he has wagered by a closin' date of 1 May 1990.'

'And the other factor?'

'It may merely be a coincidence, though I'm no great believer in them. You see, the ship was sold to the Danish Vognmandsruten company by Sea Escape of Miami last week and the insurance arrangements are even now undergoin' changes. Most of it will end up at Lloyd's and a lot of the reinsurance boys there are crooked as bent pennies. Say someone involved with the current changes has decided on a big tonner bet coupled with hull reinsurance activities, they could be after a double whammy. These lads don't have to be millionaires, they just play about with the funds of the Lloyd's Names, the ultimate suckers.'

Goodman looked surprised. 'I was brought up to think of the City of London, especially Lloyd's, as the last preserve of true gentlemen.'

'You've got to be jokin',' Tosh scoffed. 'Some folk say Lloyd's started in a coffee house and will end in a percolator. Others say their funny new buildin' has the intestines on the outside and the arseholes on the inside. Listen, Alex, Egil will do the job. You just sit back and wait.'

On 7 April, watching breakfast television with Jyoti on his lap, Goodman was stunned by the news. The ferry *Scandinavian Star*, according to the commentator, had sent out a distress call at 12.30 a.m., owing to a fire on board. The skipper had abandoned ship twenty minutes later and a rescue vessel was alongside in a calm sea within forty minutes. One hundred and fifty people were missing. Goodman, desperate, called Tosh, who in turn contacted Egil. That afternoon he called back, unable to say what had gone wrong but, twenty-four hours later, Tosh relayed his eventual explanation to Goodman. Egil's contract arsonist, a professional, had been instructed to ensure there were no deaths. To this end he had used only slow combustible materials in four separate sites, leaving plenty of free access to the decks.

Unfortunately a number of fire doors failed to function, the Portuguese and Filipino crew were ineffective and deadly prussic acid fumes spread quickly from burning plastic laminate. The toxic gases rushed along ventilation shafts and killed escaping passengers on gangways. They lay there in heaps, later to be consumed by flames. Many children and the arsonist himself were included in the final death toll of 158.

'You cannot blame yourself, Alex.' Tosh told him. 'These things happen. You did not intend anyone's death.'

'No, I didn't. But I am responsible. So is Mafia.' His resolve was not dented. When he received his fat fee for his part in the destruction of the *Scandinavian Star*, hull value $24 million, he gave it all to Tosh for drug rehabilitation charities of her choice.

The sense of normality, of perspective, which home life with Sara and Jyoti had begun to give back to Goodman, now evaporated, leaving his stark, self-imposed mission unbalanced by gentler impulses. Sara, unaware of the tragedy for which he rightly blamed himself, could only guess at who or what had forced him back into his shell. He no longer showed signs of responding to her love. She could only hope that she was not herself somehow the cause.

347

26

Summer 1990–August 1991

Sara and Goodman agreed that, when the time came, they would send Jyoti to the best of schools, no expense spared, and began to invest in a suitable education fund from Goodman's Swiss account.

'You don't need clients any more, Sara,' he told her one Sunday morning. Over the months he had found himself growing possessive towards her. Once, when he had pointed to bruises on her arm, she had merely shrugged.

'It comes with the trade. Some guys only get their kicks by bein' brutish.'

She was, Goodman assured her, ravishingly attractive and could be earning good money as a model.

'You're wrong,' she said, looking wistful. 'Look at any fashion magazine. Asian features are not in vogue. Besides I would hardly ever be at home. You would have to take little Jyoti to the office. BCCI would just love that! Oh dear, are you beginning to dislike the idea of livin' with a prostitute?'

'Don't use that word, Sara. You're not a prostitute, I . . .' He found he could not say it. Three simple words. I love you. They were increasingly on the tip of his tongue. But he feared them. He loved Mary and Lucy. He loved Jyoti. But to admit to being in love with the beautiful Sara would be some form of betrayal to Mary, who was dead because of his rashness and who, after five long years, had still not received posthumous justice. To openly avow his love for Sara would shift his life's driving aim from the payment of his debt to Mary and Lucy. He must not, could not, succumb to this temptation. When the ghosts were laid, when he brought the four evil men to meet their Judge, then he could overwhelm Sara with the love which he already felt but must not show. None the less she should not, merely to assert her independence, have to lie with other, often brutal, men risking injury and, increasingly, disease.

'I am a prostitute and you have known that ever since we met. What's up with you, Alex? You gettin' too grand to live with a tart? Travellin' about the City with toffs in a white-leather Merc is turnin' your head.'

'You're wrong, Sara.' He removed his spectacles so that she could see the love he could not admit beaming through his eyes. 'I've not changed. But our daughter will soon be at school and you know how everyone gets to hear everything about other parents. The word soon spreads. They would tease her. Little children are cruel and hateful to each other, especially if you hand them the ammunition.'

Sara took clients because of her pride. She knew no other means of earning her way, of being independent. She never spent Alex's money and always protested at the many gifts he lavished on her. Goodman understood her rationale and could find no way of questioning it which did not risk damaging her fragile confidence. It would be easy to highlight the dichotomy of her existence. She was, after all, pursuing the most despised of professions to maintain her self-esteem by avoiding what she saw as the degradation of the dole or reliance on Goodman's income. She could not see how maddeningly perverse this outlook increasingly appeared to Goodman.

His allusion to little Jyoti's future well-being struck home. Not immediately but, little by little, Sara began to think of other career options. She started, in the winter of 1990, to baby-sit at a modest fee for working mothers on the estate and, whenever her young charges were in her flat, she took in no sex clients. Goodman was delighted and did not press the matter further. In a way he felt hypocritical, for the *Scandinavian Star* tragedy lay heavily on his conscience. On the plus side he had, through the success of that mission, achieved the long-awaited breakthrough. Mafia now summoned him in person with instructions for new work, much of which, Goodman suspected, was unrelated to BCCI. Most of the contracts involved white-collar fraud, the collation of information about businessmen, the destruction or theft of documents and the obtaining of information through electronic hacking.

After a successful arson job relating to documents and tapes which the West Midlands Police sought in attempting to charge Mafia for drugs offences, Goodman was for the first time asked to socialise, at The Vox in Brixton, with Mafia and his friends. He was the only white man present and he remained deferential. There was no opportunity to chat privately with Mafia, to nurture a non-business relationship. But it was a start, and Goodman was greatly encouraged.

Then, towards the end of March 1991, an awkward situation developed. Mafia proposed another tonner-claim job, this time a bulk carrier called *Mineral Diamond*. Again the claim was to be instigated before the last day of April and Goodman assumed the client was therefore the same tonner gambler as had targeted the *Scandinavian Star* the previous spring. He studied the proposal with care. His first reaction was instant rejection but that might undo all the hard-won progress in his relationship with Mafia. Perhaps this claim could be set up without danger to human life. He studied the file.

The *Mineral Diamond*, Goodman read, was a British-registered bulk carrier scheduled to carry a full load, 135,000 tonnes, of hematite iron ores, a non-hazardous material, from Dampier in Western Australia to the Netherlands. She would have to be sabotaged, owing to Mafia's time limits, during this voyage and Goodman could see no way of avoiding a risk to her crew of twenty-five Indians unless the attack took place in port. One of his London arsonists could perhaps nip over to Rotterdam. He remembered Jed's briefing to watch for BCCI files referring to HTA, some new form of thermite that even consumed steel. Perhaps he could get his hands on some.

He studied the previous history of damage to bulk carriers, presuming such high-tech steel monsters of the deep were fairly immune from mishap. He was surprised. Since their appearance on the world's oceans in 1975, 248 had been lost, including large bulk carriers twice the size of the *Queen Elizabeth II*. One example was the *Gallant Dragon*, which, when scuttled owing to hull cracks, sank in under ten seconds.

The speed at which these leviathans could disappear below the surface, even when in port, dampened Goodman's hopes for a death-free solution. By law a ship's radio officer must be able to reach his station from his cabin in under sixty seconds. Not much good if the ship went down in thirty. Most bulk carrier losses involved what insurers call 'glug-glugs' – total loss of ship and crew.

Unless Goodman could obtain some HTA, he saw little chance of a fire blazing away on the all-steel *Mineral Diamond*. A controlled explosive device timed to detonate in mid-ocean might be a more practical solution. Goodman turned again to Tosh, who knew ex-Special Forces demolitionists who, given a diagram of a ship's structure, could quickly identify the key brackets to cut with controlled blasts timed to activate in mid-ocean or on a given date. But, after consultation with her contacts, Tosh advised Goodman there was no way of doing the job without extreme risk to the crew.

When Goodman regretted he could not take on the job, Mafia did not conceal his displeasure.

'Why not?' he growled. 'What's so different about this ship?'

'My people are all busy. You gave me too little warning. I am very sorry. If I could just have an extra month, there'd be no problem at all. This is a highly specialist job if it is to succeed and the best people simply aren't available.' Goodman said this safe in the knowledge that postponement was not an option.

Mafia was annoyed but accepted Goodman's excuse and turned elsewhere. In the event he must have worked something out because the *Mineral Diamond* sank in the Indian Ocean 1500 miles west of Fremantle on 20 April. No trace of ship or crew was found, no distress signal received and the insurance claim was logged before 1 May.

Goodman was lucky. Two days before the *Mineral Diamond* disappeared, the West Midlands Police charged Mafia at Birmingham Crown Court with crack offences. He countered by producing a tape recording which put his arch-enemy DC Mick Pearce in a less than comely light. The tape was played to the jury, who, after a three-week sitting, found Mafia not guilty and criminal investigations were instigated against Pearce and eleven other officers. Pearce's career was damaged irreparably after he was heard on tape telling the accused that he could take him at gunpoint to the top of a well-known local tower block and see if he could fly.

When the dust died down the West Midlands Police instituted a clamp-down on Mafia's Birmingham activities, at one point confiscating some of his cars and freezing his known liquid assets.

This caused him no pain at all except in Birmingham, so he spent more time based in London. Goodman, despite his negative response to the tonner work, began to hear from and meet Mafia more often. His workload for the trafficker gradually increased.

In June Goodman asked one of his clerks for copies of files from an account named Saspor Quality. This took a week to obtain because the files were boxed and stored at a warehouse in Gillender Street, East London, and logged there under a false name unconnected with BCCI. The Saspor files were, in media terminology, dynamite. Goodman had settled on them as a result of his ongoing search for CIA collusion with nefarious BCCI activities, in this case the tie-up between Casey's Friends and the supply of trigger mechanisms for fuel-air atom bombs to the Israelis and, in 1989, their acquisition for Saddam Hussein.

By studying box-file numbers Goodman deduced that at least 150 other box-files relating to the Capcom company within BCCI – and its worldwide dealings with the CIA – were secretly stashed in London warehouses. The auditors Price Waterhouse had finally given up on BCCI and Goodman anticipated that the Fraud Squad, on leaked advice from a shocked auditor, was about to close in on the bank. He removed all the compromising documents from his three BCCI desks and hid them in Sara's flat. He guessed that the Saspor and other CIA box-files had been sent off premises by the Capcom executives for the same reason.

He called Jed and suggested they meet in London. Jed was too busy but JR came over within the week and took away the Saspor papers.

'Gold dust,' he whispered. 'You've hit the jackpot, Al.' He laughed as he punched the air with a clenched fist. 'I always told you it would take time. Now listen. You have got to get all the box-files with contiguous numbers to these Saspor items. You say the bank close-down is imminent?'

Goodman nodded. 'Any time now. The air is buzzing at the bank. A lot of very worried people. The Fraud Squad have been "secretly" approaching folk with the result that all our UK branches are humming with hideous rumours. I would predict an Armageddon in a few weeks at most. The Fraud Squad, with Price Waterhouse advice, have already had panic sessions with the Bank of England.

The top execs will soon start throwing themselves from windows, or they would do if they were Japs instead of Pakistanis.'

'OK.' JR tapped the box-file. 'You got to be real quick. Careful but quick. We want all the rest of this CIA stuff. You've located a rich seam just in time. Now go for the mother lode, before the shaft collapses.'

Goodman did his best but somehow, in his haste, he triggered off warning bells in high places. The supervisors at both the warehouse addresses, which his clerk had obtained through a girlfriend in BCCI Archives, now told him he could sign out further files only with written permission from Sushma Puri, the director of Capcom. He dared not apply for this, so he decided to have Tosh's friends break into both warehouses. But events moved faster than he had anticipated. At lunchtime on Friday, 5 July bailiffs arrived at BCCI's Leadenhall Street offices and all employees were forced to leave the building. Notices were posted at the entrance to the effect that the bank had been closed by the Bank of England. BCCI banks in sixty other countries were closed simultaneously and $20 billion in assets were frozen.

'Is it too late to get the Capcom files?' JR asked anxiously when he heard the news.

'Maybe not,' Goodman replied. 'We're going in early next week.'

But they were too late. A week before the close-down Capcom directors secretly shredded the contents of a hundred boxes of Capcom data at one site and on 10 July, the day before Goodman's planned raid, the Gillender Street store, owned by Hays Business Services, was targeted by arsonists.

A specific document storage area on the second mezzanine floor was set alight. Great heat was involved, spalling concrete and producing highly toxic fumes. Two firemen died fighting the blaze. The five box-files which had been stored beside the two Saspor Quality containers were destroyed. Goodman was also warned by Mahmoud that Capcom directors were interrogating Archives staff to pinpoint who had furnished details of the storage sites to non-Capcom staff.

'If they finger you,' Mahmoud warned Goodman, 'things could become very hot. There are a lot of angry people about right now.'

Goodman never returned to BCCI. Art dropped him off at The Vox and he told Jo-Dog Willetts that he had left BCCI owing to the

Bank of England closure but that he was, of course, still available to Mafia for business as usual.

Mafia sent for him three weeks after the warehouse fire and they met at Steppers Winebar in Brixton, a stone's throw from The Vox and a favoured Yardie haunt.

An Alsatian bitch growled from beneath a table as Goodman sat down and something clicked in his mind. The juxtaposition of a snarling dog and the close proximity of Mafia. For a moment, had a weapon been to hand, he would have killed the Jamaican then and there.

After praising Goodman's continuing good work, Mafia's mood became grave. BCCI's predicament was being made even worse by nosy journalists around the world. One such, Anson Ng, writing for the *Financial Times*, had just been dealt with in Guatemala. The job Mafia had for Goodman was to dispatch Danny Casalaro, a freelance currently researching for a BCCI article on the East Coast of the USA. To avoid any possible comeback on the bank, Mafia stressed, the killing had to look like a natural death.

He had no contacts, no muscle in the States, Goodman protested. But while he had no intention of killing anyone, he had learnt to show willing. So he agreed to do the job if Casalaro could be lured to London with a faked phone call promising big revelations about BCCI.

Goodman heard no more until, on 10 August, Casalaro's body was found floating in his own blood in a bath-tub, an apparent suicide. Mafia told him the Americans had used LA Yardies for the job, to avoid the likely delay of importing Europeans. Goodman detected no hard feelings and breathed a sigh of relief. Within days he was summoned again to The Vox and given a complex new assignment which, he was certain, had nothing to do with BCCI and was directly concerned with Mafia's personal problems with the UK police. At the end of the briefing the two men, with one or more of Mafia's goons never far away, moved to Steppers for a drink. Goodman steered clear of any fragile topics knowing that he must treat Mafia with kid gloves and advance with extreme caution. One false move or a single misplaced query could ruin all his hard-won progress. And he was progressing. Success was in sight.

That evening he took Sara to the film *Robin Hood* because she raved about Kevin Costner. Then dinner at the Savoy Grill. Sara was overcome with excitement.

'Fancy me . . . Me! At the Savoy Grill . . . D'you think they know? People say, "once a whore, always a whore" and "can tell 'em a mile off".'

'Nonsense, Sara.' Goodman held her hand under the table. 'Nobody's looking at us and, if they were, it would be in envy of my luck. You're the prettiest, smartest lady by far and I want you to enjoy yourself.'

'Oh, I am. I am. Kevin was dishy. You are even dishier and I'm the luckiest girl alive. But what's this all about? Why the celebration?'

'Does there have to be a reason?' he smiled gently.

'Of course,' she giggled. 'Everything you do has a reason.'

'Is that an accusation that I'm a calculating old sod?'

'Yes!'

They laughed together happily and ordered *crème brûlée* to end a perfect meal. They felt at peace with the world.

'It's true,' he admitted. 'There *are* grounds to celebrate. I've received a complex task from Mafia today that's going to be the make or break. He's becoming more and more trusting. By the end of the year I should know who the Americans are. Then I can do what must be done as quickly as possible so that you and I, Sara, can get on with our lives.' He had almost added 'my love'. This happened a lot these days. He held back from such endearing terms with increasing difficulty. As they left the Savoy, avoiding scaffolding beside the Embankment, they passed beneath a ladder.

'Oops,' Sara gave a small scream. 'Quickly! Kiss me to ward off the dark shadow. That's what the Irish girls at school used to say.'

They kissed but someone somewhere failed to notice and a small, cold breeze from the Thames curled around them.

Most of Amy's old ALF friends had left the group owing to 'entrapment', Amy's term for marriage, or, worse, because they had changed their minds about ALF policy. Too much violence, they said. Death threats, car bombs and blowing up universities were not, they suggested, crucial or even beneficial to the long-term goal of helping animals. Amy knew better and she stayed loyal. There were hard lines on her face now and puckered skin on her thighs but she still found no difficulty filling her bed with a succession of young

355

and eager ALF groupies. About one in four satisfied the hormonal overdose with which she had been born. She had grown impatient, a touch narrow-minded and, out of bed, was generally referred to by her ALF brethren as an 'opinionated misogynist'. She constantly railed at group leaders that the movement was heading in all the wrong directions but was consistently vague as to what she considered the right ones. None the less she was valued as a sound planner of campaigns and a brave, aggressive raider.

In August 1991, on her twice-yearly visit to a hair salon, doing her summer switch from long to short and pink to green, she thumbed through tattered magazines and found herself staring at the 1 June issue of *Today*. Pictures of badgers and convicted diggers flanked a large photograph of Paul Martin posing beside a sett on the Isle of Wight, all under a banner headline: 'Exclusive: The RSPCA Spy Who Put Two Brutal Animal Killers Behind Bars.'

Amy had never ceased to provoke ALF members to concentrate their activities more against badger diggers and less against local butchers. Despite her forcefulness she had little success because 99 per cent of the ALF were scared stiff of the diggers. So, when she read about Paul and remembered how he had saved her and Barry years before, she decided to call him. She phoned his old work number and, to her delight, he answered right away and remembered her at once. Few men didn't. She was effusive in her praise. When he thanked her, she detected a flat note in his voice and, with crowbar-like persistence, levered from him an admission that things were far from well. Stephen Clifton, the Huntsman of the Isle of Wight Hunt, and James Butcher, a heavily built local bully-boy and Hunt terrier man, had asked Paul out on a badger dig. Frightened to refuse, he had gone along but first tipped off the police and RSPCA. Despite fear for his wife, a young local nurse, and their two toddlers, Paul had soon afterwards agreed to become an informer for the RSPCA.

Over the months that followed he had lived a nightmare existence. The RSPCA had been trying to catch Clifton since 1982 but, as a popular professional huntsman on private land, he had the perfect cover to indulge his illegal badger-killing activities.

On one occasion, on Paul's tip-off, twenty police officers and six RSPCA men were in position around a sett when Clifton spotted one and told Paul to shoot the man. 'I fired to one side of the RSPCA bloke and thanked God it was me, not one of the others, looking down the sights,' he told Amy.

As the cat-and-mouse attempt to net Clifton continued, the months of fear took their toll on Paul's family. There were tears and doubts but Paul was resolute. After one gory dig, he broke down and wept bitterly but told his wife Sally he would rather die than let the bastards get away. Then, in March 1990, the RSPCA had at last managed to spring a successful trap. Paul was arrested with the others and the media naturally branded him as a digger. For months the ALF subjected his family to abuse and threats. At work he and his wife were shunned by friends and colleagues. He could not let on that he was innocent for fear that the fragile RSPCA court case would be lost.

When Paul appeared in court and Clifton's men for the first time realised who had shopped them, they were furious and subjected Paul and his family to death threats.

Since the trial Paul and his wife had lived in a state of continued fear. The police had installed a direct phone link and erected floodlights around their Newport terraced house but Paul had narrowly avoided attempts to force him off the road and to trap him on the way to and from his boat-building workplace. Only a week ago the RSPCA had warned him to keep a low profile on the August Bank Holiday weekend as one of their mainland moles had heard of a group of diggers planning to 'get the Isle of Wight bastard'.

Paul had received numerous threats during the year since the court case and at first his family had locked themselves at home scuttling out only for work, school and shopping. But that was no good for their marriage nor for the children and Paul was unwilling to disrupt the long anticipated camping weekend they'd planned for the coming Bank Holiday.

'Listen,' Amy said. 'You did me a big favour and I would love to do something for you. You have your holiday. I'll bring some friends I know and provide a hidden escort. Your wife and kids needn't know. You can call me here just before the weekend to tell me details of your movements.'

Paul protested but she could hear the relief in his voice. She assured him the pleasure was hers. Then she called Tosh and, as she'd thought, received an enthusiastic response.

'Surely to goodness. Of course we'll help out. Great excuse to escape London and get a holiday tan. How many of us do you need?'

Later, when Tosh asked for volunteers for a weekend on the Isle of Wight, Goodman's ears pricked up at the mention of diggers. He said he'd like to go too.

'Not your scene, Alexo,' Art squealed. 'Could get rough. Maybe break your specs.' His ribbing was good-natured but James intervened.

'Shut your black mouth, Arthur,' he growled. 'Our Alex may be a black belt at kung fu for all you know.'

Four Family members, including Goodman, with Amy and two Koreans from the Troon clan took the Southampton ferry on Friday, 23 August. They spent an enjoyable Saturday on Shanklin's Welcome Beach in radio contact with whoever was on shift with binoculars watching over the happy Martin family. Paul's two tents were pitched in the beautiful grounds of Ninham Farm and his children were obviously having the time of their lives.

When Goodman's shift came, the contented family scene reminded him of long-ago weekends in the Herefordshire hills with Mary and Lucy. He was hidden in a hedgerow of Landguard Manor wearing, for the very first time since the night at Fambridge on the River Crouch, his old Barbour jacket. Sara had joked that if he was to play Boy Scouts for Tosh, he ought to wear camouflage and look the part. She had fished the long-forgotten waxed jacket out of a tin chest along with an equally worn cloth cap.

Idly prodding his pockets for a Kleenex, Goodman came across a scrap of folded paper. He glanced at it and grunted, memories flooding back. The note was a page torn from an AA book from Trevor's van on which were scribbled various notes and two phone numbers.

Finding his reading glasses he noticed the numbers were prefixed with 0101 for North America. He supposed JR must have forgotten that he'd made notes on the reverse side when he wrote down his home contact details and gave the sheet to Goodman. He was about to look at JR's notes when a movement to his immediate right and a couple of hundred yards away down the hedge line caused him to shrink automatically into the hide as he reached for the binoculars.

Goodman saw four men crouching in the undergrowth, two with binoculars and one with a shotgun. He felt a bolt of shock pass through him and tighten his chest. The nearest man's profile was that of the ox-like chief digger in Kinver Wood, the man called Paul who had figured in a thousand of Goodman's recurring nightmares.

Goodman's mind raced. He must alert The Family at once. The Martin family were at risk. The grounds of Ninham Farm were live with happy campers taking post-breakfast naps. A peaceful scene into which Goodman failed to see how the Martin family's enemies could intrude. None the less he crept to the back of the hide and called Tosh two miles away in Shanklin. She promised to have everybody back at the hide in thirty minutes.

Paul Blackledge's eyes hardened as he stared at the tents. The bastard Martin was clearing up dishes using a bucket filled from the Ninham camp taps. It would not be impossible to get the man away from his family right away on some pretext but more sensible to wait for nightfall. What with Bank Holiday Monday the next day the island pubs and restaurants would be full. He knew this from the island's diggers whom Paul Martin had shopped to the police. They had kept the man running scared for the year since the court case but they could not do him in, break his legs, slash his clever-dick features, themselves, since the law would home straight in on them. So they had put the word out to mainland diggers to do it for them at a time when they had cast-iron alibis.

Blackledge had enjoyed a good few digs on the island and when he heard about the grass Martin he had joined up with five other hard men to do the job. Some had full-time employment but they had all agreed on the Bank Holiday. Clifton had warned them of the tight police security at the Martins' home and, on discovering that the Martins had made a Bank Holiday booking at Ninham, had suggested this as the best time to act.

Blackledge had another good reason for gutting Martin and that was a court case the previous year following his own arrest with four friends at a Shropshire dig. They had almost certainly been shopped but they never caught the culprit. Blackledge's dogs had been confiscated and the driving love of his life taken away from him. He hated informers. As far as he was concerned Martin should suffer the ultimate penalty. A mere leg-breaking session was far too lenient for his sort.

Blackledge motioned to the others. They headed back to their van and spent the day at their hotel drinking and discussing the details of the coming snatch. They would hold a trial, a mock hanging, and so on. Drink and their natural disgust at grasses led them to a barbaric decision: they would, after the bone-breaking, peg Martin out on the beach and sit around with a beer crate as the tide washed over the sod. That would serve chilling notice on other RSPCA plants across the country.

They planned to leave the hotel at 9 p.m. and, at 8 p.m., the five of them were watching television and belching away their room-service chicken-in-a-basket when the phone rang. Blackledge took the call.

'Yeah, love,' he said. 'Come right up.'

He smirked as he replaced the receiver.

'Irish-sounding maid,' he informed the others, 'coming up to turn down our beds.'

They were still sounding off suggestions as to how the maid could be put to better use when the doorbell rang. Jo, a Welsh miner with a beer belly, opened the door. Struck between the eyes by the end of a broomstick, he thudded to the floor. One of the Troons led the way, a small man with a mean reputation in Soho.

Ginger, a fifteen-stone, pock-faced bully well known on the Midland terrier circuit, cocked and brought his twelve-bore to bear on the broomstick-wielding Art but his nose was smashed by a snap kick from the Korean.

The gun clattered to the floor. Goodman, keen to participate, fell on it and bruised both knees.

Blackledge, snarling with rage, lashed out at Amy and knocked her to the floor. One of his steel-capped army boots caught Art's knee but Goodman brought the shotgun's barrel up from the floor and thrust it into the big man's groin.

Blackledge subsided with a groan and Goodman rammed the barrel into his chest. As his finger tightened on the trigger, Tosh screamed in his ear.

'Stop. Alex. Don't shoot.'

He looked at her and snapped out of the grip of blind rage. 'He killed them,' he whispered almost too softly to be heard. 'He was at Kinver.'

Within minutes of their entry The Family had the badger men

secured to one another and to the furnishings. Blackledge writhed about and a snoring gurgle sounded from Ginger's broken nose.

Tosh beckoned to Goodman. Together they helped the bruised Amy to a nearby room that they had booked at vastly inflated Bank Holiday prices.

'What,' she asked Goodman, 'was all that about? As the Lord is my witness, you would have killed that man. I've never seen such a look on your face. Do you know him?'

He told her.

'Amazin'!' Tosh sat on the bed and the soft evening light glowed through the flame of her hair. Goodman had grown deeply attached to her as a caring friend, a sympathetic ear, and a goddess of implausible talents.

'What shall I do?' He was, she could see, in an agony of indecision. 'I want the man dead for what he has done. But I still have no fix on the Americans. What if Mafia pegs it before I can get their details from him? This bastard' – he nodded towards Blackledge's room – 'must know who and where they are too. He would give me a second line on them.'

'Good thinkin', Alex,' she grinned. 'It must be my coachin' of you. So are you glad now that I interrupted your natural impulses back there? Listen, laddie. We'll find out who he is and where he's from. I'm now goin' back in there to put the fear of the Lord into those fellas so they'll leave Amy's friend Paul and his family well alone. You look after little Amy here and be sure to keep out of sight of your nemesis.'

Goodman thought about that. A small voice at the back of his mind told him he had seen a spark of recognition in Blackledge's eyes the second before the gun's muzzle had made contact. But he could not be sure. It was unlikely after so long.

Other inmates in neighbouring rooms must have called the management. Tosh assured the duty manager that all was well. Then, leaving Blackledge and his men with a death warning to keep away from the Martins, she and the others left quickly in case the police had been called.

27

September 1991–January 1992

Goodman found Mafia both arrogant and entirely selfish. He used his own daughters to run drugs from Jamaica to the UK and he left to their fate eight of his couriers imprisoned in the early nineties after being caught carrying his cocaine. Adept at maintaining false fronts himself, he was rapier fast at detecting deceit in others. Goodman soon learnt this and trod with extreme care.

His new task for Mafia was to hack into the police HOLMES (Home Office Large Major Enquiry System) computer for the double purpose of keeping the Jamaican one jump ahead of the police as well as knowing how best to hurt rival cocaine gangs. Somewhere deep within the HOLMES system nestled the Operation Dalehouse data bank, which Mafia was especially keen to monitor because it covered Brixton and the rest of South London's Four Area policing district. Its data concerned drug-related violence and firearms used by crack dealers, especially Yardie illegals.

Operation Dalehouse was the brainchild of a tough Scotland Yard Detective Superintendent, John Jones, who in 1990 had alerted his bosses to the arrival of the Jamaican crack gangs and set up a 'Yardie Squad' based at Parchmore Road Police Station in Croydon, South London. The station had good access to Brixton yet was far enough away to discourage efficient criminal surveillance of the Squad's car fleet. This was an important factor because the undercover officers of Britain's front-line drug fighters are, for budgetary reasons, often expected to use their own private cars for surveillance. They are likely to keep the same vehicle for several years, which risks their personal safety and jeopardises their operations. Of the 28,000 police officers in London only a total of 108 were assigned to the area drug squads. Despite this paucity of manpower and thanks mainly to Jamaican informants plus the HOLMES computer system, Operation Dalehouse had made 260 successful arrests for 370 offences including four murders and 22 attempted murders. None the less 'the Bosses' at Scotland Yard were about to close down the 'Yardie Squad' owing to the pressure of political correctness.

Officers on drug squads were increasingly being wounded by gunfire. The most obvious answer was to arm them but this would result in black dealers being shot, which would spark riots. Only white dealers could be shot without heavy repercussions and they were a tiny minority in Brixton.

In New York drug agents were not allowed to work on cocaine cases unless wearing bulletproof vests and carrying sub-machine-guns. In London unarmed drug squad men told the press with mock bravado: 'It's no problem. We block their bullets with our truncheons.'

The 'Yardie Squad' concentrated on black crime among the Afro-Caribbeans of Stoke Newington and Brixton because that was where the effects of the crack dealers' activities were worst. Nearly all local murders were of blacks by blacks. A quarter of all murders in London were of black people. Black citizens would have rightly complained if no police action harassed the dealers who preyed on their children. None the less the tabloid media were not interested in stories of blacks preying on blacks as these made poor copy compared with editorials hammering at 'the drug-squad fascists yet again handcuffing poor black men who are only involved in drugs because of the oppressive nature of British society'.

Mafia mobsters were arrested from time to time in Britain without the police being called anti-Italian yet through the early nineties the Press screamed out the complaints of civil libertarians that Yardie Squad operations were racially divisive. This persuaded Scotland Yard's brightest and best to close down their most successful drugs unit. Those who suffered most from this decision were thousands of good, often black, citizens in the inner-city crack areas.

Yardie crack networks expanded in the USA from 1985 onwards.

New York's chief drug-fighter, Bob Stutman, came to London in 1989 and lectured Home Secretary Douglas Hurd and his police chiefs. He warned Britain's police to ready themselves because crack flooding into North America had lowered the street value there. London crack prices were now twice those in New York and international dealers were heading to England to reap the benefits. By 1990 Jamaicans were arriving in droves. British-born Jamaican teenagers gawped at these romantic new arrivals, aping their clothing styles, their firearm habits and their propensity for mindless violence.

At first the drug squad men tried to deal with Yardies as they would white criminals, thinking in terms of name, birth date, address, job, previous record and so on. But by 1990 they had realised that Yardies have none of these. A Yardie is his street-name and his mobile-phone number. He has one street-name and numerous aliases. He may have a dozen passports and just as many birth dates and surnames. By early 1992 Operation Dalehouse, having sussed this out, was making inroads into Yardie crime. Mafia was astute enough to recognise the unique power he could obtain by tapping the Dalehouse font of information.

Goodman discovered to his chagrin that the HOLMES set-up was tamper-proof against computer buffs accessing the data bank by electronic means. So he resorted to corruption of a civilian member of the HOLMES Computer Team identified by Columbo as susceptible to bribery. The data bank was constantly updated but Goodman's informant was only able, or willing, to access HOLMES once every two or three weeks. Mafia briefed Goodman with specific enquiries and their meetings in Brixton, usually at The Vox or Steppers, became regular events. Sara often found Goodman moody and disconsolate after his Brixton visits but, in the first week of January 1992, he called her from a Brixton phone box sounding jubilant.

'Almost there,' he purred. 'Let's have dinner.'

'Where? The Ritz?' she joked.

'Yes. Why not. I'll make the booking.'

'You're jokin', Alex.'

'No. I'm not. See you there at eight o'clock.'

When they met he was sparkling with optimism. Mafia, he told her, had fixed a highly profitable crack deal based on information from HOLMES. In the knowledge that his main rival for the deal was sought by Dalehouse on a murder charge, he had shopped the man to the Four Area Drug Squad and, as the sole remaining bidder for a major Amsterdam cocaine consignment, he had achieved a major saving. As a result he was now treating Goodman almost as an equal and had entertained him to an afternoon's carousal on champagne and orange juice. Goodman had gently flattered him about his foreign contacts, his international status and his ability to twist the American dons around his little finger.

'Which,' Goodman had asked Mafia, 'is your favourite US city?' An innocent enough question.

Mafia had waxed lyrical about Los Angeles, the abundance and beauty of its chicks, the voracious appetite of its crack-heads. He stayed only at the best, the most exclusive hotels. The Westwood Marquis was probably his favourite and very handy too for meetings with Korbi Richter, the right-hand man to Albert Redden. His voice took on a noticeable note of reverence as he mentioned Redden's name and, as Goodman knew well, Mafia was not given to easy reverence. Goodman's BCCI brief for JR and Jed included tracing hidden accounts of an American mobster named Albert Redden but why Mafia should be involved with this man was not clear.

Starry-eyed at the trappings of the Ritz, Sara was not concentrating. 'Who are Richter and Redden?' she asked. 'Anything to do with the Kinver Americans?'

'I don't know.' Goodman tapped his white damask napkin against the table. 'Maybe, maybe not. But the point is I've got Mafia's confidence. Now, each time I score a winner with HOLMES, I'll prod a little bit further until he talks about animal sports in general and, in due course, badger digging. Flattery is the key. Wanting to hear all about his amazing experiences. The difficult bit will be, of course, getting the addresses once I've got the names. But after today I know I can do it. I just need to keep his trust and to build up my brownie points.'

Sara said nothing. Life had taught her never to stack her hopes up in advance of an event. That way led only to disappointment.

Seven crack addicts lounged about the dingy basement of The Vox.

Mafia watched their behaviour, listened to their talk and congratulated himself on never becoming a cocaine user, never thinking of crack as a passport to heaven. He knew the ultimate consequences of crack addiction. Cocaine breaks down the body's ability to reconstruct itself. The veins and arteries of long-term users split and they haemorrhage to death, their bodies rotting through lack of cell regeneration. Those who absorb cocaine through their nostrils can end up with ulcerated, perforated noses. This prevents sniffing the drug, so the desperate addict switches to inserting cocaine powder into his rectum, penile urethra or, in the case of a woman, her vagina.

Mafia stayed clear of drugs in order to keep one jump ahead of his rivals. Especially dons like Jah-T, Jamaica's top Yardie, who was shortly to arrive at the nightclub to do big business with him. Crack was no magical mystery. Cocaine and crack were identical except that crack could be smoked and therefore reached the brain with maximum speed and efficiency. The five men and two baby-mothers at The Vox inhaled it through small glass pipes. Lighters flickered and white smoke billowed, filling the basement with the acrid tang of cocaine. The crystal rocks glowed white-hot and all was well with the world.

Each smoker experienced for a minute a taste of ecstasy, a mile-high rush like the best sex they had ever had. Then, for the next ten to twenty minutes they would gradually float back to earth. Unless they lit up another £60 crystal, a miserable comedown would set in, inducing paranoia and aggression. Some men would never smoke crack with other males, even friends, because they knew they would get lethally violent during the downer.

Jah-T entered the club with two of his men in black leather jackets. He and Mafia touched fists and the barman brought their drinks. Jah-T, or Mark Coke as he was known throughout Jamaica, was one of Kingston's most feared dons, as was his father, 'Jim Brown' Coke, before him. He had specified The Vox as his chosen venue for their meeting. He now picked a corner seat from which he could survey the whole room. The management had assured him of no police surveillance even though the club was a favourite 'pig's listening post'.

Mafia was careful to show Jah-T the respect he would be expecting. Each man knew the other's status in the international

Yardie hierarchy. Jah-T wished to set up a crack operation in London and Mafia had sent him word that he would happily become his loyal London deputy since he, Jah-T, would need all his own close lieutenants back in Tivoli, Jamaica, where murderous pressure from political opponents was on the increase.

Mafia, well briefed by Goodman from HOLMES, carefully let slip to Jah-T nuggets of information which revealed him to be unusually well informed. He gave a rundown of some of his UK-based dealer networks, careful to point out that each was controlled by mobile phone: one for heroin, three for crack and three for snowballs – a popular mix of crack and heroin. The risk of police infiltration, Mafia stressed, was greatly minimised by his rule of taking orders only by such means.

'I've got crack clients from all over,' Mafia boasted, 'but I still do well with weed. We call it "Brixton bush" and whites come here even from Scotland. They don't know what they're gettin' with the crack, so we mix it down to only 5 per cent pure. Great profit.'

'UK's havin' a recession,' Jah-T commented. 'Ain't that affectin' your business?'

'No, don. Not at all. Cocaine's no longer a champagne drug over here. People take it to parties like they used to take a bottle of wine. A middle-class white man often spends £250 a day on crack and I got a great market to City yuppie coke-heads earnin' £70,000 a year and spendin' £15,000 of that for my crack. They may have survived thirty years OK without mobile phones and crack but now they can't do without.'

'Aw right, man.' Jah-T came to the point. 'Since you're talkin' sterlin', I will do the same. For £2,000 of JA coke I get £15,000 on the street Stateside after conversion to crack. How you compare?'

Mafia did some rapid calculation. 'For your £2,000, I'd give you £30,000 after my cut.'

'Sound good, star.' Jah-T stared hard at Mafia for a silent moment then spoke in a low voice. 'If we do business, I set the terms. Seen?'

Mafia nodded as humbly as he could manage.

'And I want a little bonus,' Jah-T added softly.

'Like?'

'Like your information. Where you get it from?'

'I got a source.' Mafia was pleased.

'Police?'

367

Mafia shrugged. 'He's on the inside but not police. What he don't know is not worth the tellin'. If we get together, I'll make him available to you.'

Jah-T's eyes gleamed. Intelligence was power. His enemies were everywhere.

'That would be a deal I stick with.'

'You want to meet this man, no problem. I'll have my boys fetch him. One hour . . . He'll be here. For myself, I have to meet an artillery supplier down from Birmingham. He'll be here soon but you go ahead and talk to the white man. See what he's worth.'

Mafia phoned Goodman's mobile and caught him at Sara's flat. 'Come right over. There's a big man here wants to ask you a few questions about our deal. I want you to impress him. Right?'

Goodman arrived at 10.30 p.m. as The Vox began to fill up. Door security was tight but the bouncers knew his face and let him in. Mafia met him in the upper hallway.

'Look, Alex. This guy is Jah-T. He is *the* don of Tivoli. Anybody cross him and they in big trouble. I want you to make him realise there ain't nothin' you don't know about the South London crack scene. Who's up tight with who and who's grassin' to the Ol' Bill and who's on the lookout to chop which rival firm. Got it? You do a good job with Jah-T, boy, and we're in business, big-time caboosh.'

'Will you be staying, Mr Douglas?'

'I'll introduce you and I'll stay nearby but I've a meetin' with some people from Brum. Don't you worry. You'll do fine. If you don't know all the answers, use your imagination!'

They descended in the steel-shuttered lift, Goodman flinching as always at the attack on his senses – the blast of reggae and the stench of mixed drugs – as he arrived in the basement club.

Blackledge carried a tattered, black suitcase. The bouncers at The Vox insisted on checking out the contents but Blackledge merely repeated, 'Tricks, Stafford Douglas, is here. He won't want nobody bloody stickin' their noses in his business. Fetch him.'

Mafia's man Kingston appeared and escorted Blackledge downstairs. Nothing was said; the heavy thud of a ragamuffin bass discouraged conversation. Blackledge stayed close to the tall and muscular Kingston, who thrust a way through the sweating throng. Yardies have been known to kill for the sin of a careless dancer stepping on their shoes. A high percentage of those present, Blackledge knew, would be carrying side-arms, and even if they weren't under the paranoiac influence of some narcotic, he had no wish to cross swords with a local aggro-merchant since this was not his turf. Most of the black males present, though less stocky, were taller than Blackledge. Kingston broke out of the crowd, heading for a secluded corner which allowed a relatively private conversation.

Blackledge suddenly came to a halt. Directly ahead of him two men sat in earnest conversation. One was a heavy-jowled, black man wearing a fortune in gold neck chains. The other was unmistakably the white bastard who had haunted his mind ever since the incident in the Isle of Wight hotel, the man who had all but emasculated him with the shotgun barrel. Blackledge roared an obscenity and charged forwards.

Materialising as if by magic, Jah-T's guards seized Blackledge, and Goodman, looking up, instantly recognised him. He did not hesitate. Sliding from his chair, he melted into the surge of the crowd, threaded his way to the exit and, even as he heard the DJ calling for silence, climbed the stairs and smiled at the bouncers. Once outside, he took to his heels, realising that if he dawdled his escape was liable to be short-lived.

Jah-T was unimpressed by Mafia's explanations of Goodman's sudden disappearance, and himself left the club. Mafia did not get Jah-T's business then or ever since, two weeks later, back in Kingston, Jah-T was murdered.

Once Jah-T had gone, Blackledge sat down with Mafia. 'You know who that white guy was?' he said, his mouth within inches of the other man's ear so as to combat the rhythmic drumbeat of The Abyssinians.

'Sure. He's my man. Does a good job here and there.'

'You're jokin', Tricks. You got to be jokin'. That bloke's poison.' He described the Isle of Wight event, omitting his own discomfiture at Goodman's hands.

'I know who he is. When he looked at me from that chair, he recognised me and he was wettin' himself with fear. I seen that face and that fear before and it's come to me at last where I seen it. You and me was with your Yank friends after the brocks up Kinver way a

369

few years back when he comes burstin' out the bush tellin' us to stop.'

Mafia shook his head in disbelief.

'You sure?'

'Hundred per cent. I don't forget a face.'

'You're sayin' that Mr Alex Goodman, the accountant, has been chasin' after us for nigh on five or six years? But why?'

Blackledge was briefly silent. He knew the answer but decided not to elaborate.

'I've been diggin' stripies since my schooldays and I've met some weirdos over the years. Animal Lib types. Like I say, weirdos.'

'You're sayin' he's a nutcase?'

Blackledge shrugged. 'It's possible.'

Mafia could not accept this. 'I've worked with him real close. If anythin', the man is brilliant.'

'OK. So he's a psycho, Jekyll and Hyde. Lots of your geniuses are round the twist in certain ways. It's a known fact.'

'You reckon he's a loner. Not Judas. Not RSPCA. What about those females that turned up soon after he did?'

Blackledge's eyes slid up to the blue smoke swirl hanging over the dance floor. 'Coincidence probably. We had no reason for thinkin' they were with him. Plenty of people walk about those woods. Listen. I can get my Streatham friends to call on him. Give us his address.'

'We need to find out his motives. Check he really is a loner.'

'Right. Right. You know my shack up Stanning Folly – where we was workin' on Goodman's little blonde bit when the fuzz came. I could have him took there.'

'Good,' Mafia agreed. 'Let me know as soon as you're ready and I'll join you up there.'

With Blackledge gone, Mafia lit a cigarette and started to think back methodically. One thing worried him. Perhaps Goodman, whoever he was, had been seeking the Americans on behalf of some law agency before he appeared in Kinver. Perhaps his personal sensibilities overruled his common sense and his mission when he saw the badgers. If so he, Mafia, had made a serious error mentioning the names of Richter and Redden. And yet it was surely too far-fetched to think that any man, even a nutter, could still be hunting for them all these years later without even knowing their

370

names. None the less Mafia decided against mentioning the Goodman matter to either Redden or Richter until he could squeeze the truth out of the accountant.

Goodman had fled to the Peckham Home. That evening The Family, apart from Art, discussed the débâcle in The Vox. Since the closing of their last laboratory they had held a referendum and, as a result, now concentrated all their efforts on drug-withdrawal supervision. Four new improvised cubicles had been added by converting erstwhile Family bedrooms. Art was on duty but the occasional gurgling scream penetrated the door of the lounge.

Goodman, they all agreed, must move at once from Sara's flat. And, Columbo added, Sara and Jyoti should also come for at least a week or two. But knowing how cramped the Home now was, Goodman steadfastly refused their offer.

'For a long while I've been intending to rent somewhere bigger but Sara's expanding babysitting work depends on friends and clients on the estate so we've never made the move. Now I have an incentive. I will set things in motion at once. We have the means, thanks to BCCI.'

'I don't like it,' James protested. 'You are part of the Family and you're in big danger. Why you not stay here while you fixin' your new place? You got to think of your missus and the little girl, you know.'

After much airing of opinions with nobody wishing to be left out, Sailor laid down the law. Goodman had the impression he was set on his course of action all along but he let the others say their bit to encourage the general illusion that The Family was democratic in all things. The offer of Peckham would be left open but, if Sara wished to stay at the Keynsham flat until she found a new place, The Family would provide protection. Tosh was first to be detailed as bodyguard at Keynsham.

That evening, after an hour of gentle classical music from Sara's tape deck, Tosh begged for 'somethin' with a lilt'. Goodman surprised her by producing a cassette of songs by Clannad. She took her shoes and tights off, propped her lovely legs on a pouffe and lay back in the flat's solitary armchair.

'Only a Philistine can enjoy the sound and meaning of Clannad without bare feet,' she informed Goodman. He forgot his troubles

371

for a moment as he watched his gorgeous guard in her green tank top, black miniskirt and flame-red pony-tail. He loved Sara but he was male and Tosh was surely sent by God to enslave every man she met.

They heard a sudden sound from the street below: the grating slam of a Transit van's sliding door. Goodman moved to the kitchen window and glanced down. All was peaceful. Nothing unusual.

The doorbell rang. In the old days at this hour, Goodman would have expected one of Sara's clients but, since she had left the paid-sex scene, there were few callers after 8 p.m., so he was instantly alarmed. He looked across at Tosh but her long eyelashes were closed and the silhouette of her breasts appeared almost motionless. He went to the door. The visitor, a single male, was too close to be identifiable through the peep-hole.

'Who is it?' he asked.

'Police.' The accent was Midlands – or Lancashire maybe. 'We're making enquiries into the death of Mrs Woolidge, your next-door neighbour.'

If the caller had said he was from the gas or electricity company, Goodman would have been more careful. And if the accent had been West Indian, he would have woken Tosh. As it was, he opened the door a fraction, keeping his foot firmly against it. His subconscious desire not to offend the police stopped him fitting the door chain.

Blackledge's man, Grant, weighed sixteen stone and the initial shock of his charge against the door sent Goodman flying back-wards. Clutching a stubby automatic in his right fist, Grant ordered the dazed Goodman into the living room. Blackledge had briefed him that there was likely to be only the target, a weak-looking wimp, and a Pakistani girl in the flat. The wimp had obviously done well for himself: although small the place was well furnished. The music was conveniently loud. Then Grant saw Tosh. Definitely not the Pakistani, but Christ, what a looker! She was unwinding herself from her chair as he entered.

'Stay put, lady,' he growled, more to impress than to threaten her. He did not rate females higher than flies when summing up aggro potential.

He gestured with his gun and both inmates raised their hands. Like Blackledge had said – easy.

'OK, mate,' he addressed Goodman. 'Put your shoes on. You're coming with me.'

The side door of a bedroom opened and a naked Asian girl appeared drying her long hair with a towel. Her body rated ten points on Grant's Richter Scale. His thoughts were interrupted by movement from the red-haired girl. More a whirr than a movement. Her first barefoot kick, toes curled back, sent the gun flying from his numbed fingers and her second, with the same foot, turned his world into instant agony as his testicles were crushed against the base of his scrotum. The damage would be permanent, the pain would last for days. He writhed on the carpet, trying to scream.

Goodman and Sara stood and stared as Tosh secured their visitor with her tights to the steel grating of the gas fire.

'Turn the music up, will you, Alex lad . . . Sara, you timed your entry to perfection if I may say so, even if you didn't plan it.' She looked at Goodman. 'Know him?'

'Never seen him but his accent's the same as the man in The Vox.'

'The fella you balled on the Isle of Wight?'

Goodman nodded and Tosh smiled. 'How very lucky. You've been wantin' to know all about him and now this kind gentleman will be after tellin' us.' She looked out of the window. 'Keep an eye on the driver of that van. He's lookin' up here. Maybe he heard a noise. He could get impatient and come on up. Sara, I think, as you're a nice girl, you'd better be leavin' the room for a while.'

Tosh lit the gas fire and the backs of her prisoner's hands began to blister, the pain eventually registering above that from his testicles.

'Turn it off,' he croaked. She did. In less than five minutes they knew why Grant had come and, in seven, the Lancashire address of Paul Blackledge.

Tosh brought the van driver up to the flat at gunpoint and bade him remove Grant, still bound and bent forward in pain, to the rear of the van. Once there she knocked out the driver with the gun butt and lashed the two men together. After carefully wiping her prints from the gun, she placed it in the glove compartment and left the van in a street not far from St Anne's Police Station. On her way back to Sara's flat she called the duty officer from a phone box using her broadest Belfast brogue. Two armed IRA men, she announced, were awaiting arrest close by. She described their van's location.

Back with Goodman, she laid down the law. There was no way he

373

or his family could stay another hour in the flat. They would be attacked again and next time their assailants might not prove as ineffective as Grant.

They spent the night in Peckham in the only unoccupied cooler, Sara and Jyoti on the bed, Goodman on the floor. He could not sleep. Everything had turned sour at the final fence and within an ace of success.

The answer came not in a sudden flash of inspiration but due entirely to luck and the coldness of the cooler floor. He pulled up the Barbour, which Sara had laid over him on top of two thin blankets before she climbed into the bed.

He remembered then the detached page he had found in the Barbour. He sat bolt upright and, shielding Sara with his body, turned on the bedside light.

On one side of the paper were JR's Los Angeles contact numbers but Goodman fumbled feverishly for his spectacles and studied the other side, where JR had scribbled notes during that distant van journey to Erdington.

The two names stood out like pillars of fire, the same two individuals that Mafia had already unwittingly identified as the Kinver Americans. 'Goodman is probably after Redden and Richter. Otherwise why should he turn up at Fambridge?' This note and half a dozen others, all with question marks, were scrawled haphazardly, presumably to record JR's thoughts on the events at Fambridge for his subsequent consideration.

The American spook has held out on me all this time, Goodman thought. But, then again, perhaps he never made the connection between me and the Americans after he lost these notes.

As the realisation dawned on him he forgot the cold. This was it then! He could deal with Mafia and Blackledge any time, now that he could get the Americans' details straight from JR. Working out the time in Los Angeles, he crept to the living room. As he passed the open door of the 'duty nurse', still Art, he noticed blonde curls and white shoulders clasped by a black arm. He smiled. All was well with the world.

An answerphone responded at the LA number. Goodman did not recognise the voice. This was not the number he had normally used to contact JR and Jed on BCCI matters. That, he assumed, had been a secure official line.

'This is Alex Goodman for JR,' he told the machine. 'I need to speak to you or, better, see you urgently.' He left the Peckham number.

He crept back to his room but could not sleep. By breakfast time he had decided on the best course. Sara had brought to Peckham all their cash and the boxes of documents secreted out of his BCCI offices between 1987 and 1991. He could not even begin to estimate the full extent of the lethal damage these papers might inflict, especially in the USA, France and Saudi Arabia, should he release them to the media and to opposition parties, but he was aware of their likely power as a blackmail tool.

His initial rationale in copying and collecting the documents had been vague. Should Jed Mason or the BCCI authorities turn nasty at any point, he would have a trump card up his sleeve. Even in his teens, when first working for the Browns, he had kept carbon copies of their more dubious accounting practices. Not that he'd ever done anything with the evidence. It was just an umbrella against a rainy day.

He selected six of the documents as bait, including references to VIPs such as Washington power-broker Clark Clifford.

JR called him at teatime.

'Howdy, Alex. All well in li'l ol' London town?'

'Is this line secure?' Goodman asked.

'Sure it is. You go ahead with whatever you've got.'

Goodman carefully read out his selected excerpts, giving dates and minimal reference data.

'Wow, I won't ask where you got that stuff,' JR said. 'Maybe we can meet.'

'Listen, JR.' Goodman's voice was level. 'This is something different to our earlier agreement. I'm not wanting money.'

'Say no more,' JR intercepted. 'This line is secure but maybe not secure secure. I'll see you in the usual place, usual time, on Friday.'

'Can you make it sooner?' Goodman urged.

'This is real important, then?'

'I do have a problem. Time is not on my side.'

'OK. OK. Thursday.'

Some forty hours later they met at the Heathrow Penta hotel for breakfast and JR looked at Goodman's sample documents. He whistled.

'This could be gunpowder. I just don't believe that some of these Ivy League guys could be involved in this muck.'

'That's nothing,' Goodman assured him. 'I have boxes full of reference to that sort of activity.'

'So what are you after?'

Goodman passed JR the page from the AA book.

'Those two names,' he said. 'Redden and Richter. Names which you could have given me way back and saved me a great deal of trouble. Why didn't you?'

JR had the grace to look uncomfortable. '*Qui s'excuse, s'accuse*,' he said. 'We, Jed and I, knew that you would be wiped out, crushed like a beetle, if you even sniffed at these guys' heels. We would have done you no favour at all to point you at them.'

'So you used me to help you with BCCI because I was English, an accountant and in need of money – or so you thought. If you'd put me on to Redden and Richter you'd have lost my services. Are you telling me that didn't enter into your thought processes?'

'If I did, you'd not believe me. I can only repeat that, if I had given you access to either of these guys back then, we wouldn't be talking right now. You'd have been dead meat way back.'

'Well. Whatever. I'm no longer asking. I'm telling you: if you want the documents, you must first lead me to Redden. Then Richter. As soon as I have met up with them both, you get the papers.'

'I'll check with Jed but I can't see any problem. So long as you realise you'll be out on your own. We couldn't be seen to be helping you. Vigilantism is frowned on in California same as it is over here.'

'One thing,' Goodman asked. 'They do both live Stateside, don't they? I need to know right away because where I go, my family goes too, and we none of us have passports.'

'Sure. One or other of them is pretty much always in Los Angeles.'

JR flew out within hours and Sailor's people applied to Nigerian friends for fake passports for the Goodmans. The key to the Keynsham flat was given back to Sailor, who took Goodman to see Lee, the London head of the Korean Troon clan. Ah Troon, Lee's brother, was clan head in Los Angeles.

Two days later JR called back. The deal was on. When would he arrive in LA? Would Goodman like help with transport or accommodation?

'Thanks but no,' Goodman replied. 'I'm not sure how long it'll take me to get ready but I'll call you when I'm there.'

The Los Angeles Troon clan promised their London kin they would look after Goodman like a brother. Sailor thanked Lee and assured Goodman he could be in no better hands.

No one could tell how long the Goodmans would be away.

'When you are ready,' Sailor said simply, 'The Family will be waitin' to welcome you back.'

They drove to Heathrow in the old Bedford with Columbo at the wheel and James beside him, back-seat driving all the way. Tosh and Art cuddled the four-year-old Jyoti on the back seat to keep her mind off the imminent reality of her first flight. Columbo had reduced all the BCCI documents in a copier and kept the originals at the Home. The Goodmans now had passports and travellers cheques in a new name selected by Tosh.

'Ah Troon will meet you at the airport,' she instructed Goodman. 'I will be prayin' for you. Tell me one thing, Alex. Is your aim clear in your mind?'

Goodman smiled. 'I will not come back until both Americans have paid the price for their evil. Then Mafia and Blackledge. Afterwards I will marry Sara, educate Jyoti, maybe increase the family and, if you're still wanting my help, I'll be at your disposal to help cool your turkeys.'

'Neatly wrapped up,' Tosh smiled. 'I hope things turn out as simple. Don't make a move out there without the Troons behind you.'

They embraced and said their goodbyes. Sara cried and so did Columbo. Nobody noticed Kingston, for he had merged with the crowds of waving relatives. Mafia's men had followed the Goodmans from the Keynsham flat to Peckham. Their plans to seize Goodman there would now have to be cancelled.

'They are definitely on the LA flight,' Kingston confirmed on his mobile.

Mafia could delay no longer. He called Korbi Richter and gave him a heavily sanitised version of who Goodman was, why he was a threat and how he had learnt Richter's identity. His explanation was complex, involved BCCI and absolved Mafia himself from any blame in compromising the Americans. The Goodmans, he advised, should disappear from circulation, and the sooner the better. He passed on their flight number.

28

January 1992

Ah Troon led the Los Angeles branch of the clan, one of three to have grown slowly in influence since their arrival in the US from Seoul in the 1960s. The Chicago and Miami Troons were identical in their set-up except that Ah was allied to a powerful LA Triad.

The Triad boy/girl, 432, who met the Goodmans at LA International was chatty and handled his/her Lincoln Continental with suicidal verve. Jyoti hooted with pleasure as they wove their way loose of the airport traffic.

'You were christened "432"?' Sara ventured.

'No way, dear lady,' 432's laughter shrilled. 'Many Triads have numbers. Ours originated in Guangzhou. The Shaio Ling Circle was made up of 432 disciples, so all our soldiers have that number except our thinkers and planners, who are 415, after the number of stripes on the robe of our great philosopher Kung Ming. Our leader is 489 and so on.'

'I see,' said Sara. 'Very sensible.'

432 took them to the heart of the 'Chinese Beverly Hills', Monterey Park, where the spoken tongues are Mandarin and Cantonese. Ah Troon met them at his office along Atlantic Boulevard, some eight miles east of downtown LA. He welcomed them with open arms and non-stop dialogue, apologising for not having been at the airport owing to work pressure. They must see the city, especially by night. 'Go up in helicopter, please. It is wonder of world. Every colour lighting. Flicker ... Flicker ... Like hell maybe. Very beautiful.'

Jyoti, playing perilously with Ah's inkwell, gazed at the small but chubby Troon with the tinkling, alien voice, her mouth hanging open in wonder.

'Oh, Mr Goodman, sir. You are so welcome.' Ah patted his paunch with joy as though praising a proffered plate of delicacies. 'I know your London. No sun, drizzle, drizzle. My poor brother Lee, his skin is all white from years in Thames fog. Property also no good there due to silly Green Belt. No Green Belt here. To the west is plug-hole sea, which we pollute. City sewer, last year statistics, 12.5 million used condoms wash back on Hyperion Beach. Oh, yes. This Utopia for kiddies. Beach boys, too big muscles. Surfer girls, too big tits. All body surfing on sea of condoms.' Again the jelly rumble of mirth.

'So' – he held up a heavily silvered finger to ward off interruption – 'estate agents no good west. The sea. OK we push, push east San Gabriel. Big land rush. Some silly boys say no more urban spread. Say we bring smog, crime, noise, erosion, too little water, traffic. OK, so what? Who wants Mojave sand? You give me four, five years, we push the Angel City all the way to Llano. And now . . .' – he blinked as though bitten by a sudden thought – 'you go to Llano. 432 take you. When you have rest and food and bathing I visit to make big plans. Troons give you Mr Goodman, Mrs Goodman, very whacking success.'

After a frenetic round of handshaking and a single bow, Ah left them to resume their death-defying journey with 432. After some eighty miles across the bleak San Gabriel mountains they reached Antelope Valley in the high Mojave. The town of Llano was still cut off from urban LA by a single horizon of scrub and mesquite, but close inspection sadly bore out the prophecies of Ah, for countless small stakes marked out the still empty desert in testimony to its imminent conversion to concrete and tarmac.

432 pressed a dash-mounted button to open a set of tall steel gates somewhere in suburban Llano. The sudden verdant green inside the hacienda's ten-foot-high adobe walls came as a welcome surprise. The air was cool from artificial streams that flowed down rock-tiered water gardens. Exotic bird sounds suggested a hidden aviary and a clutch of Filipino maids in short black skirts smiled their welcome. Goodman fought to retain his document case as the Filipinos descended on the luggage.

'Enjoy,' 432 instructed them. 'Tomorrow early I'll be back with the boss.'

They found their quarters stuffed with little comforts and, on Goodman's bed, a note from Ah wishing them peace, good sleep and the 'hospitality of the Troons' for as long as they might stay. They swam and ate and slept and played in a happy daze, for they had never before holidayed outside England. All too soon 432 was back with Ah, who joined Goodman beside a fountain, set high on the uphill side of the property, from where they could inspect the wide and varied landscape through a four-foot-long pillar-mounted telescope.

'First I show you lovely scenery. Yes? Then business.' He bade Goodman squint through the scope and helped him aim it. 'This city, Llano del Rio, once socialist centre of States, now only for capitalist like me. That way . . . The too big sheds there, that is Air Force Plant 42 for Stealth bombers and other secret bomb-planes. Can kill everybody, everywhere. Now, look there . . . When Shuttle plane comes back from space trips we watch him land on Rogers Lake. Dry lake. Now look, scrub scrub bush called yucca or Joshua. They very, very old. You know, like dinosaurs. Maybe oldest trees in world. My Caterpillars wipe them away. Then I put grass for golf all the way and sell to big Jap Nissan man. Here is coffee.'

432 spread out a map of Los Angeles as a maid filled cups of delicate German china.

'There' – Ah's chubby finger prodded the map – 'is Downtown. This is Llano. Lee Troon tell me you goin' to ask FBI man where your number one enemies live. When they tell you this, we Troons make plan to keep you safe whatever you gonna do. I have two hundred good guys but quality of plan more important than number of men. I go Hong Kong in five days for one week, so you try to fix action before then. Hokay?'

'I can arrange to meet my FBI contacts now and here,' Goodman offered. 'Would that suit you?'

'Oh, yes. Very good.'

432 handed Goodman a telephone shaped like a shiny black phallus. Seeing Goodman's hesitating hand, Ah guffawed. 'We have yellow ones too,' he explained, 'but they smaller.'

JR, sounding bright and eager, confirmed that Jed Mason was

381

now also in town so they could all meet up that morning. Llano would be fine.

The agents arrived in a nondescript grey Chevy sedan with a nondescript grey driver and 432 met them at the hacienda's steel gates with a trained sniffer dog. Ah was paranoid about explosives because of some incident in his past. 432 was busy watching the dog check out the Chevy's trunk when a dusty VW Golf slowed to a halt in a side road off the roaring two-lane pandemonium of Llano's Pearblossom Highway. The Golf's two passengers observed the Chevy, which they had followed from JR's Bradbury home, disappear into the high-walled residence. Some ten minutes later, using a miniature Zeiss monocular, the watchers chuckled with pleasure as Jed, JR and Goodman settled down beside Ah's fountain in the coolest part of the garden.

'Set up the monopod,' said one of the watchers. 'We're in luck. Richter will be pleased, *Gott sei dank*.' They focused the sound-sourcing instrument with precision until the conversation half a mile away was fed loud and clear to the built-in tape.

Goodman found JR as cheerful and straightforward as ever, fussing over his spreading waistline as he plundered the Troons' cookie bowl and inhaled his Camel with shameless pleasure. Jed Mason, whom Goodman had not met before, was altogether of a more serious disposition but a trace of a twinkle in his eye did appear from time to time when JR ribbed him. His voice, never raised, was strong and reassuring, giving Goodman confidence despite the oft-repeated avowals of both agents that they could not in any way be seen to help his personal quest.

'Let's get this straight, Alex,' JR summarised. 'We get to show you where you can find both these creeps, Redden and Richter. Then, once you've verified their identity, you give us all your documents. These, you're saying, include proof that the CIA and the White House, through the Reagan and Bush administrations, knew all about the BCCI drugs and weapons deals, terrorist and spy activities and its massive frauds. Yet they did nothing.'

Goodman nodded. 'It's all there.'

'And clear pointers as to who in the US and UK administrations hushed up the scandals and thereby protected BCCI? Evidence of where the missing billions of Capcom dollars, officially unaccountable, have gone?'

'Yes,' Goodman agreed.

'And Clark Clifford?' Jed murmured. 'Evidence of his implication in corrupt bank dealings?'

'Irrefutable, I would say,' Goodman concurred. 'Tell me, who exactly are you after? Redden and Richter and the CIA?'

'Yup. Each and every son of a bitch' – Jed's voice was even – 'who steps out of line and preys on the innocent. Redden and Richter are no different in most respects to a thousand other mob bosses and I have a dozen or more of them in my sights at any one time. Where these two differ is the level of protection they have from the law agencies. When JR and I started to get too close, we were pulled off the trail. At that point we went solo, using people like yourself from outside the Bureau. And yeah, we are on the CIA's back too. And that is official. The Bureau for too long, especially under Hoover, relied on the Agency for foreign intelligence and we grew to distrust them. Certain individuals have become a law unto themselves and that's wrong.'

'There have been instances,' JR added, 'of the CIA stepping way out of line. The knowledge that we, the Bureau, keep an eye on their arrogant asses is just about the only curb on their excesses that exists. There's always a possibility that any secret police – you could say even the Bureau – become a menace to free institutions by abusing their power. When that happens somebody needs to pounce on the guilty parties. Their ex-boss, William Casey, looks like coming badly out of all this, however patriotic his motives, but of course he died four years back so he won't be too worried whatever we come up with.'

JR munched thoughtfully on a cookie and then continued. 'Take, for instance, the data you say you've got on HTA. Zia in Pakistan was surely an HTA end-user but he died three years ago and anyone we now arrest for involvement in the early HTA arson is likely to get off scot-free due to the statute of limitations – the elapse of time since the crime. Too bad! We get who we can when we do. No point losing any sleep over those that slip through the net.'

They talked for two hours. Goodman was fascinated to learn the details of their six-year hunt for Redden and his men.

'Don't worry about names,' JR smiled. 'Theirs or ours, for that matter. What we tell you is what you need to know, enough for your purposes. One day you may be grateful for our reticence. Whatever their real names, here are their photos.'

The photographs of two clean-shaven, short-haired men in suits, looked recent. The back of each picture was stamped 'Los Angeles – 1990 – Caesar'. Redden's features included archetypal Prussian high cheeks, Roman beak and firm chin: a handsome man exuding confidence. Richter, Goodman reflected, could almost be Redden's younger brother but for a Slavic tilt to his eyes and a heaviness of the jowls. Goodman thought, but could not be one hundred per cent certain, that he was looking at the same two Americans who, then in dark glasses, he had watched eight years earlier in the Kinver woods.

'Both men should be in town right now according to our Caesar tapes,' JR commented. 'But we can no longer rely on these as we think Redden is aware of most, if not all, of our tapping facilities and he may be feeding us bogus information.'

'So where will I find them?' Goodman pressed.

'Hold your horses,' Jed countered. 'What guarantee do we have, once we've told you their location, that we will get your documents? If, for instance, you run into trouble when you confront Redden you may never re-emerge. In which case, how do we get the papers?'

'Thanks,' Goodman exclaimed. 'But I don't intend to enter Redden's den unprotected. I will show him evidence that I have details of his secret BCCI accounts in Capcom and elsewhere. He would not dare touch me for fear that my disappearance would trigger this information being sent to the US Justice Department, FBI and IRS.'

Goodman did not mention to Jed his carefully laid plans arranged with Ah Troon nor his actual intentions towards Redden and Richter. Neither JR nor Jed would thank him for prior knowledge of mayhem and murder on their patch.

'I ask you to trust me,' he said, looking in turn at the two law agents. 'The best I can suggest is that I drive immediately from my meeting with Redden to any site you nominate, at which point I will hand you all the documents. While I am with Redden, my car – provided by Ah Troon, who owns this place – will wait outside for me. The suitcase with the documents will be on board.'

'That's not exactly a guarantee!' protested Jed.

'It's the best I can offer. I ask you to trust me.'

JR and Jed looked at each other, then back at Goodman. They

both believed him to be an honest man. There was anyway no alternative. Jed nodded.

'We'll go along with that. We will wait for you at this intersection.' He produced a much-used foldaway city map and indicated a crossroads on Wilshire Boulevard not far west of the San Diego Freeway. 'Redden's office is right here on Wilshire. As far as we know the nerve-centre, including Redden's personal suite, is on the fourth floor. When will you make your move?'

'Soon,' Goodman said. 'I'll give you the timing once I'm ready. Nothing will go wrong.' He felt elated and capable of anything. Six years had passed but his resolve had never faltered. And now, at last, he was home and dry with the last two addresses of the four guilty men. The rest would be easy. He did not stop to consider if he was capable of killing a human being. One thing at a time.

Kari Lasova was born in Moscow in 1946, the daughter of a brilliant surgeon whom the Soviets had captured in Berlin during the last week of the war. Professor Lasov had worked for Heinrich Himmler in Dachau and specialised in aviation medicine tests. Patients were immersed in ice-cold water in different types of clothing to see how long they took to die. Others were crushed or 'inflated' to death in pressure chambers to test preparations for high-altitude flights. Lasov's subsequent work in Moscow had utilised prisoners brought to his laboratories from the Siberian gulags. He was kept under house arrest by the Soviets when not working but his daughters, both encouraged to follow in his specialist footsteps, were given the best schooling the State had to offer.

Kari graduated with honours from Leningrad in 1968 and was soon involved in the then hectic race to beat the CIA in finding the ultimate truth drug. Since 1947 both the world powers had spent millions of dollars or roubles on programmes of research into drugs through which individual minds could be controlled. In 1972 Kari was posted to the Sychyovka Special Psychiatric Hospital, where there was an abundance of prisoners, a few genuinely mad but most merely dying slowly from the effects of the drugs and the inhuman treatment doled out by the warders.

In 1976 she risked her career by writing to the KGB Chairman, Yuri Andropov, detailing unspeakable practices in the hospital. She never received a response. Kari grew embittered. Her father had been humiliated and died in penury during the 1970s. She knew that her own potential was being squandered through lack of opportunity and research funds. That same year she accepted the rare offer of a transfer to the Carbo-Servia, the forensic ward of Cuba's Havana Psychiatric Hospital, where she witnessed even more repulsive scenes than at Sychyovka and her skills were all but redundant. She fled via Miami to Buenos Aires, where German cousins found her a research assistant's job with the military government.

Aware of the limitless scope for an aggressive self-seeker in the world beyond Marxism, Kari slept around with the high and mighty. Her favourite haunt was the basement bar and restaurant of the Plaza Hotel, where the intellectual élite of Argentina gossiped away their lunch hours and their evenings. In the late seventies all was well in Argentina. 'So long as our beef bulls don't turn homosexual,' according to a popular Buenos Aires saying, 'the Argentinian economy will flourish.'

Kari knew what she was looking for and did not take long to seduce an aggressive Army Intelligence colonel with a wealthy background. They enjoyed passionate weekends, an hour's flight from Buenos Aires in the beautiful Uruguayan beach resort of Punta del Esta. The colonel loathed the Peronist urban guerrillas and, on learning of Kari's skills, found her a well-paid post with an Intelligence unit specialising in interrogation 'without a trace'. She now became actively involved in torture. 'The first time with violence is like the first time with love,' she said to her colonel. She found it increasingly easy to bury her qualms and stifle the stirrings of her conscience.

She balanced her interrogations with psychology and experimented with family groups. Even though aware that only one family member had the information she was after, she would question them as a unit, all naked and all forced to watch acts of degradation performed on their nearest and dearest. She learnt how much more vulnerable a person was in such circumstances.

In 1980, three years after the World Psychiatric Association adopted the Declaration of Hawaii, Kari moved from Argentina when her colonel was killed by guerrillas, to supervise the 'confessions' of Uruguayan political prisoners. The Declaration states that 'no psychiatrist must ever use his or her professional abilities to

386

violate the dignity or human rights of any individual'. For two years she worked under Uruguayan psychologists Dr Britos and Major Maciel at Uruguay's notorious Libertad Prison, where she pioneered work on prisoners with the drug Flughenazine.

Head-hunted by the Chilean Secret Police in 1982, Kari was given a laboratory and modest budget of her own in Santiago. Out of work hours she enjoyed leading the good life until the mid-eighties, when Pinochet's fall from political power prompted her to accept an offer from a West German chemical manufacturer helping Saddam Hussein with an ambitious chemical-warfare project. Her work in Baghdad for the chemical sub-unit of the AMAM Secret Police culminated with successful nerve-gas massacres of Kurds in 1988. Once again restless, she felt her talents cramped in Iraq and flew to New York. But orthodox psychiatry did not attract her, so she applied to the CIA. Their researchers learnt of her background and she was blacked.

In 1990 she moved to Los Angeles and met up with an Argentinian widow who introduced her to the wonderful life of high-grade, part-time hookers. 'Film stars, top producers and corporate supremos,' she was assured, 'all pay fortunes for attractive, mature escorts with class.'

'My darling Kari,' her friend enthused, 'you are just built for the life. Right age. Fantastic figure. Fab fun for any guy with a brain. These Hollywood caballeros have monster egos. Come, *esta noche*, to the Peninsula Hotel in Beverly Hills. Six-thirty is best. Then you take your pick. *Madonna mía*! The money is unbelievable and the fun time is like you were back in your teens.'

Korbi Richter picked Kari up that summer at the notorious Monkey Bar and they entwined limbs with enthusiasm for a month. Their temperaments were too similar for them to last long as lovers but Richter spoke to Redden about that old CIA dream, the achievement of power over men's minds.

Redden's attempts to carve out chunks of the Medellín cocaine business had fallen by the wayside in the late eighties but Kari Lasova's mind-bending work offered the possibility of new and subtle ways to take over the Medellín Cartel. No violent drug war, just the sublimation of its top brass.

So Kari was given the laboratory, staff and budget of her dreams, with plenty of low-life Angelenos from Skid Row volunteering their veins for a few dollars. Her staff transported these pathetic volunteers sedated to and from the laboratory. Some stayed a month. Some died. Nobody knew or cared.

In early March 1992 Richter called Kari to his office. Redden was away in the Bahamas, where he based himself increasingly for his deep-sea fishing jaunts.

'We have our first business customer for you – an Englishman,' Richter told her. 'He will come tomorrow, *Ich glaube*. Can you be ready?'

'Ready?'

'*Ja*. We need answers from this man. Answers he will not wish to give, *ney*?'

Kari hesitated. In terms of her ability to control the minds of the hobos and addicts on whom she experimented, she was pleased with her slow but sure advances over the past eighteen months. But she knew there was no great breakthrough just around the corner. She had learnt from previous sponsors of her work never to admit to slow progress nor yet to promise the earth. She had hoped Richter and Redden would have no specific need for her mind-bending skills for several months if not years. She had grown confident that they were accepting her project as a long-term investment.

'This guy is special?' she parried Richter's question.

'Very special. He has critical information in his possession which may be capable of inflicting great damage on us. He has, *wahrscheinlich*, searched for us for six years but we cannot discover why nor what is his end-game. So we need to keep our options open. Not to alienate him irreparably before we know all the answers. The best course would be for you to enter his mind and place us in control without causing him physical damage. He has documents. We must obtain them from him before he shows them to a third party.'

'I understand. But you must appreciate my limitations. Before, when I asked you to listen, you said always you have too much work.'

'I am not so busy now, Kari. Explain.'

'For years I tried all the drugs known to the KGB and CIA. You have heard of scopolamine, the "truth drug". That was always a myth. It never worked. Nor did the lie-detector. Any effect they may have had was purely psychological, to help cow the patient by the mere threat of their application.' Kari lit a long cigarette, then continued.

'Of all the truth drugs I have found the barbiturates sodium amytal and sodium pentothal the best to numb a patient's higher reasoning abilities while making him keen to be communicative. But too much of these amobarbitals leads quickly to sedation and slurred speech. To counter that, I inject also methylphenidate. The secret is the exactly correct dosage and timing, which differs from patient to patient. Once they are disinhibited yet receptive they are ripe for narco-analysis, the exploration of their mental state.'

'So you can expect truthful answers at that point?'

'Not at all.' Kari sounded impatient. 'You make simplistic the most complex machine in existence: the human mind. Narco-suggestion is the stage when I can suggest that the patient says or does things. If the patient's attitude towards me is favourable, I can achieve remarkable success at this stage. But I have to alter the initial attitude if there is present in a patient any resistance or hostility, any desire not to reveal information. This, I imagine, will be the case with your imminent visitor?'

Richter was curt. '*Natürlich*.'

'Give me three days with him. Is this possible?'

'Why so long?'

'Long! You joke, Korbi. I have a Skid Row whore on the fifth floor who is now ready to do my bidding eight months after I started work on her. No-one has touched her physically for six months yet she breaks into a sweat of fear if a plate falls. If any emotion is evoked, she wets herself. If I let her out I can guarantee she will never again enjoy a lover's caress. Yet she is as "sane" as you or I. My work eats deep into my patients' minds, their nervous systems, their actual chemical structures. My method combines different treatments to devastating effect. I use pain and threats of pain in conjunction with offers to eliminate further pain. I may say, "I will inject your artery here with this long needle. The pain will be exquisite. The effect may render you insane. Talk to me a little and we can avoid the needle and the pain." '

'Now you're talking old-fashioned thumb-screw therapy, *ney*?' Richter was scornful.

'Of course' – she refused to rise – 'but as one ingredient only. Others, all available in my lab, include electronic sound and laser

389

beams, horror on film, isolation in time and space, leading to the very lip of the precipice that is sanity. When my patient is teetering on this cliff edge, only then is he or she ripe for my serum cocktails and narco-analysis. Six months ago I would need two weeks minimum to reach this point. Now I can stand every chance of success if you give your man to me for just three days and nights. He will talk yet there will be no signs nor memories of ill treatment.'

'Three whole days,' Richter muttered. 'Surely simple hypnosis would be *schneller*.'

'The finest hypnotist in the world can operate only on a willing patient.'

'OK.' Richter's smile was paper thin. 'You'd better get ready for your first non-Skid Row patient.'

When Kari had left, Richter phoned the high-speed Hatteras tuna boat on which Redden lived when in the Bahamas. But Redden had already left for a week's visit to Medellín, so Richter made up his own mind on how to deal with the Goodman problem.

First he would gauge the extent of the threat once Kari had sucked Goodman dry of information. He already knew from the Llano tapes that Goodman had shown the Op Caesar shits sample papers to excite them. Now they would be slobbering for the rest.

Richter's path was clear. Use the two Caesar agents as bait to obtain the documents, then eliminate them.

As 432 raced west along Wilshire Boulevard, Goodman carefully rehearsed Ah Troon's instructions. 432 passed the car phone back over his shoulder. 'The boss,' he said. Goodman listened carefully. Ah Troon confirmed that his men had 'gently' incapacitated Jed's and JR's technician in the Op Caesar room. Now the Troons could monitor every word from Redden's office.

'Any sign of trouble, Mr Goodman, and you say the word "Katya". Talk very, very clear. Katya. Then, after maybe fifteen minutes, my people will be with you. Maybe me too. Hokay?'

'And if there's no trouble?'

'Then you come straight out and enter my very white Cadillac car. Good?'

Goodman slammed the door of the Lincoln and walked with as much confidence as he could muster into the office block.

At the reception desk notice-board in the atrium Goodman noted a number of known corporate names resident in the building but nothing indicating the presence of Albert Redden.

He dialled the house phone number he had been given by Redden's secretary the previous day. He had said he was from the Internal Revenue Service investigating tax anomalies. He was told to take a particular lift to the fourth floor and was met there by an attractive black girl. 'You have met Mr Redden before?' she asked. 'No? Oh. You will like him. We all do.'

He was led down a corridor which changed colour constantly in response to some hidden rheostat. He noted the deep-pile carpeting and the many side doors, none labelled or even numbered. Soft classical music by German composers sounded from discreet speakers. The door at the end of the corridor swung open at the girl's touch and Goodman found himself confronted by Richter; the same hard, ageless face from which he had flinched in countless nocturnal replays of Kinver. He was pleased at the absence of redeeming features in the man he had come to kill.

Richter, without introducing himself, indicated a high-backed black leather chair, one of eight around a low teak table in the centre of the spacious office. Heavy white curtains covered the window side of the room. Hidden spotlights highlighted at least a dozen black and white photographs, all action scenes of deep-sea fishing. Over the monster desk, Goodman recognised Redden, posing in front of a busy marina, with a scuba harpoon and one arm around the bare shoulders of a smiling blond teenage boy.

'You know Mr Redden?' Richter's voice was impersonal.

'I have dealt with his tax affairs before, yes.' There was a moment of silence. 'Will he be long? I have a busy morning.' Goodman gestured with the leather file that he held.

'Mr Alex Goodman.' Richter's eyes bored into him. 'You are not from the IRS. You have come here for reasons connected with an FBI enquiry into the affairs of Mr Redden and myself and I intend to learn exactly what those reasons are. I too am busy and I hate to waste time. Mr Redden is not in Los Angeles at present so you will have to make do with me.'

Goodman's resolve crumbled. He had come prepared to maintain his IRS façade long enough to attract both Redden and Richter into the same room, produce a silenced gun, which Ah Troon had taught him to use, and put an end to the matter. Suddenly everything had

391

gone wrong. JR and Jed had assured him that both men were in Los Angeles. Richter must be lying. He must bluff it out. Not panic.

'I assume you are trying to protect your Mr Redden from this enquiry but I suggest you take me to his office at once. Any attempt to frustrate this enquiry can only do Mr Redden and your corporation harm.'

'Good try, Goodman. But this is Mr Redden's office, as you have already noted, and I will waste no time, with my inferior talents, continuing our conversation.' He stood as a side door opened and Kari Lasova appeared in a business suit but nonetheless leaking sex at the seams. She sat between them and regarded Goodman with clinical interest.

'Professor Lasova,' said Richter quietly, 'will be looking after you for the next few days. At any time you wish to tell us about your situation appertaining to Mr Redden and myself, you should indicate accordingly to save yourself continued treatment. The Professor is a professional, possibly the world's best in her specific field. Would you like to talk now?'

Goodman's mind raced. Redden's absence had thrown all his plans. His immediate temptation was to grab at the gun in his coat pocket but even as he considered this, for him an alien act, he decided instead to talk his way to summoning the Troons.

'I feel as though I have walked into a madhouse with yourself as Dante and the Professor as *Katya*, the she-devil. If this is some joke, please come clean at once, because, as I said before, none of this will look good on my report.'

Goodman prayed he could keep up his bluster for the fifteen minutes estimated by Ah Troon. But Richter or Lasova must have pressed some button, for a Latino girl dressed like a nurse entered with a tray of bottles and syringes. The Professor pierced the foil lid of a bottle with a long, narrow hypodermic needle. 'The thiopental, please,' she addressed Richter. 'Everything else is in the laboratory.' He opened a floor safe behind Redden's desk and gave Lasova a box.

Goodman began to talk. 'OK. OK. There will be no need for that. Of course I will tell you every detail of my interest in Mr Redden . . .' He began to ramble on about the CIA and BCCI and Redden's accounts in various money-laundering countries. He mentioned a few key names he knew would ring bells. Fifteen minutes became for ever but Richter waved Lasova off when she lifted the syringe in readiness.

'Let him talk a while,' he said. 'I will separate reality from invention.' He took a call from a flashing telephone on Redden's desk. 'You say Mason has to go back to Washington tomorrow? I see . . . OK . . . Never mind how long we take here. You go ahead now. You'll find Mason and Ridgway at the intersection waiting for Goodman. Call me when it's done.'

'How long do we wait?' JR asked. 'Exactly what is Goodman up to with Redden?'

'That's immaterial,' Jed sighed. 'What matters is he gets it over with quick and clean. Mex is on duty in the Caesar shack. I told him to call if there is any sign of trouble at Redden's. But Goodman seemed confident and his Korean friends didn't look like they would mess around.'

'Couldn't Pedro patch the conversation in Redden's office straight through to us?'

'Nope. Apparently not. Not without every CB bandit in town listening in and half the LAPD. Look, stop worrying. How come you sit there smoking like there was 'bacco blight and yet you're still yak-yakking like a hot roost chicken? Just cool it. He'll be here sooner or later with the papers.'

They were parked forty yards back from the intersection with Wilshire. Noon was edging by and the street was empty but for a bag lady checking dustbins. Two motorcyclists approached. JR watched them in the central mirror. He saw the way they checked street numbers. Probably message delivery. They halted ten yards back, consulting lists on a clipboard. One, clutching an LA street map, came to Jed's window on the driver's side of the Chevrolet.

'Howdy,' he said. 'We're looking for 2026 Sunset.'

As JR noted the unusual design of the man's helmet, the thought came to him that it was not a helmet at all but a gas mask. His right hand shot across to his left hip but his fingers failed to grasp the handle of the .38. Gas hissed out from a pipe mounted on the motorcyclist's helmet, possibly a Tabun derivative, and both occupants of the Chevrolet were dead within moments.

The motorcyclists, verifying that the bag lady had noticed

nothing, let themselves into the Lincoln and dumped their motor-cycle gear, along with both bodies, behind the front seats. They lowered all windows and set the air-conditioner on full blast. Once their gas meter registered 'safe' they removed their masks and donned the dead men's hats, dark glasses and jackets. Further down the street, two sedans with tinted windows cruised to a halt and their occupants settled back to wait.

As Mafia's men in London, so the little-known Renkers Posse, a sub-clan of a New York Yardie gang, contracted efficiently for Richter in LA. The Yardie word 'renkers' comes from the smell of old urine on the pavement, a term as basic as the ruthlessness of the gang members.

The jet-black SWAT vans drew up noiselessly outside the Wilshire Boulevard office block and eighteen men, all athletes of small stature, swarmed into the reception area. Each man had studied photographs of the building, plans of its telephone and emergency systems and details of the fourth- and fifth-floor layouts. They were well rehearsed. Three minutes before the arrival of the vans, two Asians with FBI SWAT credentials had shown their badges to the building's security manager.

'The trouble is confined to the fourth and fifth floors only. Threatened suicide with an automatic weapon,' one told him.

Four men had cut all telephone and electronic output from the Redden premises and prevented all movement within its corridors, lifts and stairwells. All staff queries were parried with: 'Stay calm. Stay in your office. Armed suicide attempt.'

Ah Troon and three of his SWAT men burst into Redden's office. Goodman was still talking, still unharmed.

'We must be quick,' Ah told Goodman. 'What you need? Is this Redden?'

'This is Redden's main man. He says Redden is abroad.' Goodman turned to Richter. 'Tell me where I will find Redden and these men will not harm either of you.' He meant it. *He* intended to do the harm.

As Richter moved to sit down, he activated a pressure pad in the arm of the chair. But nobody in the building responded. Richter counted himself a good judge of his fellow men. In Goodman he saw what he knew to be a weakness, a man born unable to kill his fellow

394

humans. His brain raced. By now, he knew, the car trap would be in place. He had not yet stood the Renkers men down. Once Goodman left the building, he was bound to take the vital documents straight to Mason and Ridgway.

'I cannot tell you Mr Redden's whereabouts. He is on a boat. He is always moving.'

Ah grimaced at Goodman. 'What you do, do quick. In four minutes we go.'

Goodman, given no scope for indecision, closed in on the thiopental and filled a hypodermic. 'Hold them down,' he ordered Ah's men. He plunged the needle into the main forearm vein of the Lasova woman and forced the yellow liquid out of the syringe. She began to scream but a Troon filled her mouth with cotton swabs from the tray.

Goodman turned next to Richter, managing, after several inaccurate jabs, to inject the arteries in both his forearms, using two hypodermics already primed by Lasova. In each case he stopped in mid-plunge, leaving the syringes hanging from Richter's arms by their needles.

'The full amount may be deadly,' he told Richter. 'I don't know. The uncertainty is maybe killing you. Where does Redden live?' The German's eyes were tight with hatred. He remained silent. Something in Goodman snapped. His face close to Richter's, he snarled: 'You killed my wife and my little daughter. You took away all that I lived for and you never cared. You care for nobody. I will find Redden without you.'

He already knew that he could do so. With the help of Redden's fishing picture and documents from the floor safe.

'Watch your professor. She is dying.' Goodman emptied the remnants of both hypodermics into Richter's bloodstream and then refilled one with thiopental. 'Now you will join her.' This man, Goodman reminded himself, was responsible for thousands of young people slowly killing themselves with needles. He had murdered Mary and Lucy. Goodman forced the thiopental into him. 'This is long-overdue judgement,' he told the German. 'This is for my family.'

Richter's eyes and forehead veins bulged out. He seemed to be straining to talk, desperately seeking to tell Goodman something, but the effort was fruitless against the effects of the massive flow of the drug coursing through his system.

'I am ready,' Goodman told Ah. He unhooked from the wall the photograph of Redden and the blond boy and, kneeling to observe the floor safe, withdrew a pile of files from one corner. The rest of the safe was filled with cash and handguns which the Koreans proceeded to remove. Ah approached the low table where Richter lay.

'Give me my gun,' he called to Goodman. 'Three may keep a secret if two of them are dead.'

As Goodman followed Ah's men to the elevator, he thought he heard the silencer-muffled sound of two shots.

Ah joined him. 'Just to make sure,' he said in answer to Goodman's raised eyebrows. The SWAT team exited from the office block as speedily as it had entered. Back on the fourth and fifth floors, nobody yet dared move from their offices. Ah's white stretch Cadillac drew up at the block's main entrance. Three Asian 'SWAT men' in their all-black combat fatigues, ammunition belts and neck radios climbed into the central seat. Acid-proof goggles hung around their necks under Kevlar helmets and body armour plumped out their chests. One carried a 9mm SIG pistol, one a pump-action shotgun and the third a Heckler & Koch MP5 sub-machine-gun.

The driver powered the heavy car away as the last door slammed.

'There may be shooting but you not worry,' Ah warned Goodman. 'This my very special health and beauty limo. Hess & Eisenhardt Armouring Co. in Cincinnati make good job. Seven-point-six-two armour-piercing round hit door or floor or roof . . . Ping, ping . . . Fuck off, bullet. All armour plate,' he giggled happily. 'And the windows from your England. Cost £10,000 for window glass, 50mm thick of Pilkington Triplex polyvinylbutryl, polyur-ethane, polycarbonate. Lots of poly poly and no shatter from bullet. Jolly fine.'

Goodman at once began reading fast through the files from Redden's safe. He whistled aloud. 'These belonged to J. Edgar Hoover,' he told Ah excitedly. 'FBI boss. Very hot stuff. JR will love them.'

They came to an intersection and the tyres squealed as the heavy Cadillac veered into Westside. Ah screamed at his driver in Korean and the car slammed to a halt. Binoculars were handed back and the

Cadillac's sun-roof slid open above the heads of the three 'SWAT men', who cocked their weapons.

'Ha! Nobody on those mo'bikes,' Ah mouthed. 'I'm not liking this. Not at all. I think maybe this is stinking.'

'That is Jed's car,' Goodman observed. 'He came to Llano in it. Do you have my case ready for the hand-over?'

Ah did not reply. His binoculars were now trained on the two sedans further down the street. 'One's got an advert from a South Central car dealer,' he murmured. 'This no good.' He yelled suddenly at the driver, who jammed the Cadillac into reverse and executed a bootlegger turn.

The Renkers men in the sedans and the FBI car reacted as one. Black smoke spat from screaming rubber.

'They are very much after your briefcase.' Ah spoke rapidly to Goodman. 'Take papers out and throw empty case from window. Distract, distract.'

Goodman did as he was told and, looking backwards, saw the second sedan halt to retrieve the bouncing case. He flinched and ducked low as the rear window and trunk were struck by a fusillade of bullets from sub-machine-guns. They were now in loose traffic and Ah shook his head when his armed 'SWAT men' turned enquiringly.

The Cadillac, despite its armed bulk, powered forward and, expertly driven, soon appeared to lose the pursuing vehicles. The driver chose a confusing route back to Ah's Monterey Park office.

'Your FBI friends both very dead, Mr Goodman,' Ah said without emotion. 'What you do now?'

'Can you get my papers back to Sailor?'

'Very easy. Not a problem.'

'Who were they?' Goodman was bewildered.

'Ki?' Ah addressed his driver.

'South Central black men. Maybe Crips boys working for Wilshire white men.'

Ah nodded. 'Redden pays black gangs for such work. Plenty fire-power for good price. But black men no match for Korean. Hokay. What you want now, Mr Goodman? We have kill your number one enemy. All now very good for you?'

'You have been wonderful, Mr Troon. I can't thank you enough.

397

But the man who we injected was not the big man, Albert Redden. He is on a boat in the Bahamas and I need to find him now.'

'You go Bahamas?'

'I think so, but first I need to identify exactly where his boat is. The photo I took from his office must be fairly recent because his face has not aged when compared with this up-to-date photo that Jed Mason gave me. Behind Redden and the boy is a crowded marina. Could you possibly identify its location? I will also go through the paperwork from the safe for clues.'

'Very good.' Ah seemed to relish the idea of the detective work. 'Top Troons are in Miami. Troons can do anything. Give me two, three days.' He spoke in rapid Korean to his men then turned back to Goodman. 'It is possible Wilshire badmen trace us by my car. If they want your papers very bad, they maybe come after you. We think they know all about you since moment you arrive from England, so you must change your name for safety before you go Bahama. We fix passport and visa, no problems.'

'That's very kind but . . .'

Ah waved his hand. 'Not kind. Sailor very good friend to London Troons. Nothing bad must come to you, Sailor's brother. My men say you and your women not very safe in Llano. We move you to better house. I have sent my men to take away all FBI tapes from recording room in Wilshire. Nobody know you go to Bahama. FBI men dead. German man and blonde doctor bitch very dead.'

Goodman found Sara and Jyoti were already at the new Troon safe house, Jyoti complaining about the loss of pool, fountain and gardens.

'It won't be for long, my love,' Sara assured her. 'We'll soon be goin' on another flyin' bird to a lovely island with white sand an' lots of swimmin' in the sun. A place called Bahama.'

'Where are we? Where is this house?' Goodman asked the Korean maid. The safe house consisted of a luxurious basement with ping-pong and pool tables, fruit machines and a large TV screen. Jyoti soon forgot the lack of a garden, for there were no windows.

'This is Alhambra suburb,' the Korean girl informed them. 'Right across San Bernardino Freeway from Monterey Park. Many Chinese, Koreans, Viets. All work in garment trade. Many film stars from Hollywood and San Marino come to eat our scrummy food. We have more than four hundred restaurants here.'

The maid told them to press a button any time and she would come at once. Left to themselves, the Goodmans considered the future. Although JR had been a shadowy, little-known acquaintance, his very existence had served as a reassuring prop to Goodman, who was genuinely sad that the agent was almost certainly dead, along with his colleague Jed Mason. But there was nothing Goodman could do about it. Richter was also dead but Los Angeles was no longer safe. Nor was London. If Ah could locate Redden's marina hide-out in the Bahamas, Goodman proposed to go there and, after dealing with Redden, stay there for as long as Sailor advised before returning to London. Sara was happy with this. Her world centred exclusively around Jyoti, who had grown into a bubbly little extrovert with the delicate beauty often found in Anglo-Indian girls and the God-given happiness of her mother. Sara was teaching her to read and write and she knew nothing of her father's perilous existence.

Goodman's thoughts allowed him little sleep on their first night at the Alhambra safe house. He felt drained, satisfied at the outcome of the meeting with Richter yet unable to face up to what he had done. It shocked him to think about the vengeful violence which had gripped him in Redden's office. For seven years he had intended to kill, without questioning his own ability to do so. The reality of *having killed* nonetheless horrified him. He suffered wide mood changes. From horror he found his mind switching to elation. He had done it. He had avenged his family. One down, three to go. He could do anything. God was behind him. He would see it all through and be resolute for Mary's sake. For Lucy. This was more difficult now that Sara and Jyoti were a part of his life. He wanted to stay alive because there was now a valid reason for his survival. Although he did not admit it to himself, his growing contentment at life with his new family was gnawing little by little at his sense of commitment.

Henri Staaten was a dwarf and the personal loyal secretary to Albert Redden in Los Angeles. He telephoned the Bahamas on the secure line with the news of the SWAT visit. As always, he kept his report succinct and objective.

'You say SWAT men killed Korbi and Kari?' Redden's voice sounded tight. 'Are you sure?'

'Nobody in the building saw anyone, after the tax inspector arrived, except the SWAT team. Security swear to it.'

'Tax inspector?'

'Just IRS.'

'Was he expected?'

'Yes. Mr Richter had apparently agreed to see him and had told Security and the secretaries to let him straight up.'

'So why are you worried about these Koreans if you personally suspect that Korbi and Kari injected then shot each other and died by suicide pact?'

'Because the Renkers Negro, Edwards, has always proved reliable and, as you know, has done a number of jobs for us this last year.'

'Exactly what is he saying then?'

'Apparently Mr Richter called him three days back with instructions to eradicate two law agents and ambush anybody handing over documents to them. Mr Richter wanted these documents. The ambush went wrong but Edwards has traced the vehicle which escaped to the boss of a Korean mob in Monterey. Security also commented that, despite visors and helmets, the entire SWAT team looked like Asians. That's not usual for FBI SWAT teams.'

'No. Of course.' There was a pause, then Redden sounded decisive. 'I will fax you all instructions regarding the funeral arrangements. Tell Edwards to follow up his instructions from the late Mr Richter. He should locate the documents from the Koreans and hand them to you. Let me know when you have them.'

That night 432 drove the Cadillac from the Monterey Park office to the Alhambra safe house. A Korean photographer took flash pictures of the Goodmans for their new passports. Two shadow men from the Renkers gang reported this to gang leader Delroy Edwards, who instituted a close watch on the Alhambra apartment. The Korean maid was seen doing 'heavy shopping' and looking furtive each time she locked and unlocked the apartment's complex door security. Edwards told Staaten that his boys would 'go in tomorrow night'.

29

January–June 1992

Five members of the Bounty Hunters gang had raped Suzy Tiva in a Wilmington Avenue side-street when she was twelve. The previous year she had lost her virginity to a drunken stepbrother. She was a tattooed, chain-smoking *chola* girl from a broken home in LA's South Gate barrios. Now fifteen, she had seen it all. Bite scars marked her breasts and a livid purple crater on one cheek bore witness to the chunk of flesh torn away by a gang rival's teeth. Seven per cent of the 150,000 gang members in metropolitan LA are female. Most look sexy and feminine but many carry guns and have blown opponents' brains out as handily as any macho male.

Two years earlier Suzy had served a corrective year in Camarillo's Ventura School, where she had befriended the sister of a Renkers gangster. After Ventura she became an honorary member of the Renkers, sleeping with several and graduating to gang status in jobs where a non-black female could open doors or at least deflect suspicion. She had been briefed for such work that evening.

Like other street-tough *chola* girls, Suzy had developed a convincingly intimidating manner. She looked frightening and knew it. Her current boyfriend outside the Renkers was an 'OG', an 'Original Gangster' and feared warlord from the Crips Gang network of South Central LA.

At 10.02 a.m. on Friday, 9 January 1992, Suzy walked out of the Great Western Bank in Mission Hills wearing an orange 'pussy-pelmet' micro-skirt and blue-tinted butterfly glasses. She stopped briefly to inspect the contents of her handbag and, in response to this all-clear signal, a green Lexus sedan drew up beside the bank. Two armed Jamaicans ran inside, fired warning shots at the staff and took $162,000 from the safes. Suzy had just earned herself an easy $5000. She climbed into a nearby Buick Regal and drove off. No cop had ever stopped her on suspicion of under-age driving, for nobody would have guessed she was only fifteen.

She switched on the cassette player and beat out the gangsta-rap rhythm against the gear-shift. The lead rapper, Easy-E from the group NWA (Niggers with Attitude), went for the authentic 'sound of the ghetto': police sirens, screaming family arguments and gunshots echoing off the concrete flanks of high-rises.

The police arrived at the bank ten minutes too late. This was not surprising, since all 3600 banks in LA had been robbed at least once in the past ten years.

LA's Clockwork Orange world of murderous street gangs is a multiethnic one. Its more than four hundred gangs include 236 black and Latino and 84 Asian 'sets', controlling great chunks of the inner city and seemingly impervious to the temporary inconvenience of police raids. Salvadoreans kill Chicanos for narco-turf. 'Lord of the Flies' Cambodian boat-children murder their elders and chance passersby for a dollar. But the highest-profile groupings are the two hostile mega-gangs, the Bloods and the Crips, often distinguished by the colour – red or blue – of their clothing. Both gangs originated in 1972 in ghetto high schools.

Californian schools were first integrated in the 1940s and white groups like the Spookhunters terrorised blacks, who reacted by forming black gangs. The arrival of crack from Colombian cocaine in the early eighties escalated all forms of inter-gang violence. The three most violent black gangs in LA were working in 1992 on a truce to end twenty years of bloodshed but were finding it hard to attend meetings for fear of being shot *en route*. The Renkers, being Jamaican not American, ignored the truce and continued to kill with abandon. They were headquartered deep in the gangland jungles of the Crenshaw district; vicious men and women with sleek German cars, Motorola mobile phones and fast reactions.

Two groups travelled to Monterey Park at 10 p.m., each consisting of six Renkers foot-soldiers. Only experienced killers were allowed into the élite 'jugular' groups with their all-black track suits, Reeboks and bandannas. They travelled in two Mitsubishi vans, each armed with a prototype M60E4 machine-gun and Mark 19 grenade launcher from Saco Defense in Maine. The men carried a mix of laser-beam-aim, steel-ball-firing, pump-action shotguns and short-stock AK47 rifles.

The Renkers' leader, Delroy 'Uzi' Edwards, who had murdered fourteen men while in his teens, favoured the AK47 over more sophisticated modern weapons. 'It isn't just a gun,' he would say to apprentice Renkers. 'It's a legend. It works in jungle mud or desert sand. I've dug one from a swamp and it worked. You can depend on them. Vietnam GIs used to dump their M16s and take AKs off corpses. Seventy million have been sold. They've left a long blood trail and so will we.'

The Renkers' vans detoured to Artesia Boulevard to pick up Suzy Tiva, in LAPD uniform and carrying a birdcage. Then north-east to Monterey Park and Alhambra. Suzy left the others and rang the bell of the Troon safe house. Inside, the Korean maid glanced at the closed-circuit system, saw the policewoman, and called Ah's emergency number.

'Police calling,' she said.

'How many?'

'Looks like a single woman with a bird box.'

'A bird box?'

'Yeah.'

'Could be a trick. Maybe they've traced the SWAT raid to us. Better be careful. Hide the English folk before you go see the police.'

'OK.'

She hung up and checked the alarm buzzer in her pocket. Six numbered buttons on its dial each activated different responses at a single pressure. Back down in the basement she led the Goodmans to a cunningly contrived fire-proof priest's hole revealed by swivelling the jacuzzi.

'Police come here,' the maid explained. 'Only few minutes. Then I come back. Let you out. Till then you make no noise.' She put her finger to her lips and smiled at the wide-eyed Jyoti. Then she swung the pool assembly back over the entrance to the well-lit cubby hole which included a TV screen monitoring activity in the rest of the apartment. They watched the maid open the front door after peering through its peep-hole.

Jyoti screamed and clutched at Sara as the policewoman clubbed the maid across the nose with her truncheon and, when she fell, struck her again as she lay senseless.

Eight armed men in black slipped into the hallway. Then four more. They began to search every corner of the apartment.

The Troon on duty at Ah's house saw the number four button flash on his console and called Ah. This button indicated the need for emergency action. Within eight minutes the Troon quick-response team was rushed to the safe house and began to close in on the Renkers men.

Inside the apartment the Goodmans listened to footsteps move about the bathroom inches above their heads. At one point Goodman heard the same metallic click of the jacuzzi unit as had accompanied the maid's initial opening of their hidey-hole. He drew in his breath and clasped Sara and Jyoti in readiness for the worst.

'Look,' Sara whispered, staring at the screen. The basement search had ended abruptly and the black ninja-like figures returned to the hallway in response to some unseen command.

Outside, the Renkers' vans had attempted to escape the Troon ambush but the Koreans' cars had closed in on the block and sown all escape routes with Stinger Spikes – lattices of plastic teeth strewn across roadways. For once, outgunned and away from their home ground, the Renkers were forced to fade away on foot or risk a wipe-out. Ah's rapid response had saved the Goodmans and, once the last of the Renkers men had gone, two Troons came to release the Goodmans from the hide.

Goodman was briefed by Ah the next morning. Although the Miami Troons had not yet located Redden or his boat, they had learnt enough about his recent movements to head Goodman in the right direction, the island of Grand Bahama, less than half an hour's flight from Miami. The marina in the photograph had been identified as The Running Mon, which specialised in deep-sea fishing from the southern coast of Freeport, the capital of Grand Bahama. A signature found in a corner of the photograph had been identified as that of Sonny Martin, owner of the marina.

Enquiries about anyone using the name of Albert Redden had, unsurprisingly, met dead ends and the boat in Redden's photo did not reveal any clues as to its identity. However, Ah confirmed that the craft was a Hatteras thirty-foot Sports Fisherman cabin cruiser, powered by three inboard engines and with sleeping space for a crew of eight. Checks run on the thousands of these craft registered in Florida were negative when set against the name of Redden but such cruisers were designed with reasonably shallow draught and Redden would be able to tie up at any waterway, canal or marina anywhere on the island. Freeport, Miami had advised, was criss-crossed with artificial canals, mostly ten feet deep.

The Troons had made discreet enquiries in Freeport with a Mrs Thurston from the Tenant & Cooper Estate Agency. She was reputed to know everything about everybody. But she had never heard of any Mr Redden renting or buying property on Grand Bahama.

'You're out on own, my friend,' Ah apologised. 'I can do no more Mr Sherlock work but we keep big eye on you. Not forget Troon is your angel, hokay? Not forget also this very dangerous place. Most periculous. Many hundred of acre of bush and long road with no people. Bad boys catch you there and Troon cannot help. Miami Troon give you new papers, fix all transport and contact in Bahama. How long you think to stay Freeport?'

'Hopefully I can trace Redden from the existing information in a month or two. For safety, I'd better say three. Three months?'

'Very good. I fix place with fine maid for your family for three months. Of course, no cost. For love of Sailor.'

Goodman called his Geneva bank to arrange a personal account in Freeport and settled back with Sara to browse through a mass of Bahamian tourist information and the less flattering *History of the Bahamas* – all brought by the Troons.

Ah assured them his home was impregnable in the unlikely event of further trouble but advised them to stay inside until his arrangements for their move were ready in a day or two.

'I can see why Redden spends so much time there,' Sara said before reading aloud from a brochure: 'the most desirable country in the world for an expatriate in terms of personal freedom, space and lack of bureaucracy. You are left totally alone. There are no inspectors.' 'He must love that. Plus the fact that the population is less than 90,000 but over a million tourists visit annually. Lots of strange faces and boats to hide among. Three hundred days a year of balmy sunshine, the best deep-sea fishin' access anywhere, yet so close to Miami you can see the Palm Beach lights by night.'

'This book,' Goodman chipped in, 'describes the islands as "a sunny place for shady people with 29 isles, 661 cays and 2,400 'rocks'. There are many isolated hides for fugitives from the law. Raiders have trained here for attacks on Cuba and Haiti. Narcotics from South American freighters are collected by Bahamians, stored and hidden by Bahamians and boated to the US by Bahamians ... To encourage an ongoing all-season flotilla of pleasure craft between Freeport and the mainland, the island's Immigration authorities check entry papers rarely and then only at main entry ports." Ideal for the likes of Redden.'

At Miami International Airport the Goodmans were met by Lu Troon, one of four Miami brothers tasked by Ah to speed them on their way to Freeport. He gave them new passports and visas. Lu often travelled to the Bahamas for meetings in Nassau.

'You all fly Eastern Airlines to Freeport,' he told Goodman. 'A thirty-five-minute flight, in two hours. This is address of apartment there. We have chosen because you will escape notice of locals. You just tourist family. Island authorities not know you exist. Keep nose clean. Your visas all indefinite but you must do no work. Work visa not possible. Apartment owned by us, maid paid by us. Also boatman Devaux paid to look after you. Phone number here. OK?'

At Freeport International Airport Goodman soon spotted the Bahamian maid, who, as agreed, held a card reading 'Tate Ornithology'. She introduced herself as 'Mary'.

'And your family name?' Goodman asked.

The maid laughed as though he was joking and set about finding a luggage trolley. She fitted everyone and all the bags into her Mazda saloon. Bahamian patois English was not so far off the Jamaican version but Americanised.

'Lovely,' Jyoti kept repeating. Sara held her up. The roads were all bounded by well-mown verges and divided into central reservations planted with mahogany trees and flowering tabebour. Five minutes from the airport they passed by a number of hotels and office blocks, all of tasteful design and separated by lawns with bright flower-beds. Locals cruised in smart cars. Tourists with pink legs and shorts browsed side stalls of conch shells and basketry. Nobody was in a hurry. Balmy breezes caressed the tropical heat. Perfection.

They parked by a big apartment block with cheerful yellow doors.

'Jensen Court,' Mary announced. 'Leave your stuff for Johnny. Let him do the work.'

Her laughter was musical and infectious. Goodman could tell Jyoti would love her.

'McDonald's,' Mary informed them, 'is just round the corner and there's a pool if you like to swim. The big pink building with pillars up the street is the Port Authority. They're like local government. They built all of Freeport over the past twenty years. The big boss is Mr Jack Hayward. They call him Union Jack. He's the chairman of your English football team Wolverhampton Wanderers.'

She fiddled with a big bunch of keys and let them into an air-conditioned apartment. 'All yours,' she announced. 'Enjoy.'

A well-built black Bahamian in his late twenties appeared from the kitchen and shook their hands.

'I'm Johnny Devaux. Mary and me . . . We look after you . . . Anythin' you want, you holler. First you make yourselves at home. Then I show you about town. OK?'

He went off to collect their bags.

'Mr Troon say we must make you look like snowbirds,' Mary said eyeing the Goodmans critically. 'So we got to get you out of those European things and into some local batik gear. There's plenty of good-priced stores in the market. You have a cool drink and unpack.'

By the end of the day Devaux had driven them about Freeport and some of the surrounding areas, Mary had taken them shopping in Goombay Park and, over tea, given them a thorough briefing on the locality.

'Snowbirds,' she explained, 'are the winter tourists. They're mostly Canadians and Americans. Also Europeans and, rarely, Asians. They flock in for the winter when it's not too hot. October till April mostly. Lots of them fall in love with our island. They come as tourists and then stay over. Some I know have been livin' here ten years and more without the authorities catching up with them.'

Devaux returned and helped himself to a beer from the fridge.

'Mr Troon,' he said, 'has told Mary and me that you is here to find Mr Albert Redden. I have start to look for him.' He produced from a chest of drawers the photograph of Redden at The Running Mon marina. 'Sonny Martin, the owner, won't talk but I have a friend on the staff at the Mon who remembers this guy and his boat. We've been doin' a spot of nosin' about but there's hundreds, maybe thousands, of boats like this Mr Redden's a-comin' and a-goin' all year. He could be any place around the island and that's assumin' he's here at all. If he is, we'll find him sooner or later. I got a good spy network.'

Johnny came from the west end of the island, the village of Eight Mile Rock, and, like most islanders with boating skills, he had participated in the drug-running boom of the mid-eighties and knew the island's myriad cays and hidden coves as well as the next man. He was candid. 'Cocaine has been good business.'

In the late sixties, with the islands still under British rule, marijuana from Jamaica would stop off in the Bahamas for onward shipment to Florida. In 1979 cocaine took over. A chance police check of a light aircraft that year revealed a cargo worth $2 billion, the biggest police seizure ever. Marijuana was still landed but demand had faded to the extent that, on deserted Black Rock islet, the police discovered a six-foot-high wall of the drug that extended for over a mile.

'Yank pilots,' Devaux told them, 'collect the drugs – say 1000lb of coke per flight – from desert strips on the Guajira tip of Colombia. They get 30,000 bucks for each 900-mile round trip. I used to take a cigarette boat out for Nick Stewart and other local boys, collect the load from an outlying strip or, with a satellite fix, from floating sea bundles – wherever the Yanks dropped them.'

In Colombia drug suppliers killed one another throughout the eighties and, on the Florida mainland, the dealers did likewise. The so-called Cocaine Wars. Competition was intense. But the middlemen in the Bahamas co-existed happily as there was more than enough business to keep everyone happy. Sir Lynden Pindling, the first post-independence Prime Minister, was himself being investigated by the Privy Council for allegedly receiving undeclared 'gifts' of over $1 million from dubious sources. But Pindling had won black Bahamians their independence from colonial rule and could do no wrong. He became the longest-serving leader in the Commonwealth.

'Have you always lived here?' Goodman asked Devaux.

The Bahamian was silent for a while, then shrugged.

'My pa used to make a good livin' in Nassau but he fell out with a big "obeah" man in the pay of Colombians. That's like voodoo but different. Obeah made him go mad so they locked him up in Fox Hill, in the mental block, with forty others. They killed each other sometimes and they ate their own dirt. Downwind of the prison you could smell their shit for miles. They clean it up now but my pa died there and my auntie brought us here to start up fresh, you understand.'

Goodman decided to avoid further personal questions. 'What about touring the island?' he asked. 'How safe is it?'

'Safe?' Devaux grunted. 'Twice as safe as anywhere in the UK. No tourist has ever been troubled here except for occasional thievery. There's been a few housewives gently raped 'cos that don't mean so much over here. My ol' drugs boss Nick Stewart, he in the nick now not for his coke business but for rapin' his sixteen-year-ol' cousin so thorough they had to remove her uterus. But for tourists Freeport is a genuine paradise.'

'No exceptions?'

'Of course, my friend. Life is full of exceptions. Number one. Don't go muckin' about lookin' wealthy in the villages up west end nor out on the eastern golf courses. There's been a couple of muggin's out at the lonely holes. Also watch Pinders Point. There's bars in the bush out there like the Harbor Lights Inn. They do big deals there and don't like snowbirds nosin' about.'

While Devaux and his friends searched for Redden, Goodman had time on his hands and made the most of it. In London he had grown accustomed to watching his back, jumping at the sound of the doorbell and generally learning to live with fear. Now, suddenly, he was free from such shadows.

'Can we stay here for ever, Daddy?' Jyoti asked one day, licking a brandy-flavoured Bahama Mama ice-cream from beneath a Foreign Legion kepi.

'Can we?' echoed Sara.

'Why not?' Goodman found himself saying.

He lay awake that night. They were naked on the sheets. Sara turned heads wherever she went and Goodman marvelled that she loved only him, craved his physical attentions and whimpered her

409

pleasure during their frequent lovemaking. Her years of prostitution meant nothing to either of them, for she summarised that whole experience as having to do with 'economics and mechanics, not emotions'.

'I never felt really naughty,' she told Goodman, 'until your body first touched mine.'

Goodman's focus had veered from the past to the present. Whole days and nights passed by without a thought of Mary and Lucy. The guilt feelings that this would normally have caused were absent. He assured himself that this interlude in paradise was not in any way an abandonment of his mission. After all, at last he had successfully, and against great odds, dealt with Richter. He had earned this time of self-indulgence. Sara and Jyoti had been patient for so long that the least he could do, while Devaux followed the Redden trail, was to lavish his attention on them.

As May flamed into June the snowbirds melted away and the apartments all around emptied of their sun-pink French Canadians.

'Why the sudden migraine?' Sara asked Mary, the maid.

'She means, why have the snowbirds gone?' Goodman explained. 'She thinks a migraine is when all the birds get a headache and fly south.'

'Sod off,' said Sara, and stuck out her tongue.

'Very soon it will be hot and humid,' Mary advised. 'Better back in Quebec. Next month there'll be nobody on the snowbird beaches. But Williams Beach will still be packed with us locals.'

In May, as they explored further east beyond Barbary Beach, they discovered white sandy coves and bays, fringed by casuarina and palm, which stretched away to the horizon without a soul in sight. They swam and played naked, luxuriating in the long, carefree days of cloudless sky, savouring, when they lay back, the sun and the silence.

Towards the end of the month Devaux announced he would need $500. A boatman friend living by the Casuarina Bridge on the Grand Lucaya Waterway had recognised Redden's photograph and seen his boat pass his bungalow south of the bridge two days before. For $2000 he would quickly locate the boat and her owner. Devaux had told him $500 or no deal.

Goodman handed over the cash. To his surprise the sudden

confirmation, after so long, that Redden was on Grand Bahama and attainable did not enthuse him as had his previous discovery of Redden's Wilshire Boulevard address. On the contrary, he found himself depressed and in a quandary. Life was now precious and immensely enjoyable. For weeks he had hardly given Redden, or indeed his whole rationale for being in Grand Bahama, a thought. His entire *raison d'être*, born of hatred and obsession for revenge, had evaporated without his noticing. The weeks of balmy idyll had filled his mind and his heart with a new and all-consuming love. The ghosts of Mary and Lucy no longer haunted his subconscious.

Yet, perhaps through some character flaw, he could not brush aside his hunt for the killers at this moment of successful detective work; the fruit of so many years of risk and dedication. He decided on a compromise. He would continue to track down Redden and his UK colleagues. But, this done, he would try to provide the relevant police forces with sufficient evidence to charge all three with murder.

He said nothing of his deliberations to Sara. Life just now was too perfect to mar with any jarring reference to the past. Indeed their Shangri-La existence was so precious he wished it would go on for ever, but he realised its texture was as fragile as a pre-dawn dream.

In the second week of June, on returning from a morning's outing to the bush caves of Margrolie Point, Sara noticed an angry-looking mole on Goodman's shoulder. He agreed to have it looked at by a doctor since it itched but, that afternoon, Devaux came to the apartment and all talk of moles was usurped by more important matters.

'Your Mr Redden's boat was moored last night by Observation Hill at the north end of the Grand Lucaya Waterway.'

'Is he on board?' Goodman's mouth was dry.

'My friend couldn't tell . . . Says he was only paid to find the boat.'

'How long will the boat be there?'

Devaux gave an eloquent shrug. 'The only way to be sure to catch them on site is to go there now.'

Goodman sighed. He lacked zeal for the chase. But he told Sara, who hid her disappointment. All these weeks she had sensed she was winning Goodman over. She had exulted at every sign of his growing love and the draining away of the cancer of his hatred. The

411

discovery of Redden's boat was like an ice-cold douche on her hopes.

'All right, love,' she murmured, reaching for Goodman's hand. 'Be careful. Come back soon.'

He kissed them both, gave Mary a hug and followed Devaux to his car. Devaux briefed him as they drove east from Freeport, the roadside houses becoming ever less frequent until the road was lined only with forest.

'Five-sixths of Grand Bahama is bush,' Devaux said. 'Head that way' – he pointed down the line of the car's shadow – 'a bit north of east, and you can keep goin' some seventy mile without seein' nor hearin' anythin' but the wind and the trees. You can kill a man round here and nobody's goin' to find the bits. They won't even bother to try.'

Goodman stared out at the thousands of acres of forest and waterways, wondering why there were so few takers for paradise.

'Your man Redden,' Devaux went on. 'If he's a big guy, like from the Mob, this is a great place for him. The best climate in the world, the best sea fishin'. No hassle from the police, even them as isn't bent, 'cos they got plenty of work in town and never come out here. Nobody knows who rents some of the isolated houses in these parts. Nobody sees when they come and when they go. Or who they are.'

Near a well-built bungalow, Devaux halted the car. 'Wait here,' he said. 'This is my friend who seen Redden's boat.'

He disappeared round the back of the house clutching a Property Locator map of the island. He was back in ten minutes looking pleased with himself.

'He says the boat is up a side canal close by Observation Hill.' Devaux tapped the northern tip of the Grand Lucaya Waterway on his map. 'There's five Latino types on board. My friend thinks two of them were the same guys he seen a month back in one of the houses just east of Pine Bay. Maybe Redden got a base there too. I know that place well. Bit trouble back in '87. I work then for a lieutenant of Mr Reynoso, big drug boss.'

They drove north and then west through the forest to the edge of the Dover Sound canal complex, cut into the land where the Lucaya Waterway debouched on to Little Bahama Bank. The forest fell away to miles of saltwater swash: low scrub subject to flooding at high water. Goodman was dazzled by the glare of the blue-green sea

412

after the gloom of the forest. Devaux parked in low scrub and when he killed the engine the silence was stirred only by the sway of the dwarf palm fronds. Nothing moved on the roads or the forest-girt canal. The sea and the beaches were empty save for brine-pocked piles marking a channel through the coral shallows of Crab Cay.

'It's like life after the bomb,' Goodman said.

'Yeah,' Devaux chuckled. 'Not too many folk in these parts. That's why Redden likes it. Can you hear anythin'?'

Goodman listened intently and soon picked up the vibrations of drum beats bouncing from the surface of the canal.

'Music from his on-board stereo,' Devaux explained. 'They're moored in Explorer's Bay, so we'll get a clear view from Observation Hill.'

Devaux moved quietly and too fast for Goodman's comfort. Within minutes his shirt was dark with sweat. They walked through low brush towards the coastline and soon came to a wider tarmac tract signed Essex Road that curved up a gentle ramp and crested, thirty feet above the rest of the low-lying land mass, on a slag-heap formed twenty years before by bulldozers using canal spoil. Devaux's hand pressed down on Goodman's shoulder.

'Keep low now we're up here. They may have someone on deck.'

They lay in the dirt and Devaux passed Goodman the binoculars. The superstructure of the fishing vessel glinted in the sun. Explorer's Bay was half a mile to the south but every detail of the Hatteras was clearly visible through the powerful binoculars.

Over the next hour, taking it in turns to watch and to doze, Goodman saw no movement on board or indeed anywhere at all across the wide land and seascapes.

Black ants the size of mosquitoes scurried about and fought one another. The late-afternoon sun beat down and the old wound on Goodman's head throbbed, reminding him of why he was there.

He wished he was back with the 'girls', as he liked to call Sara and Jyoti, on one of their favourite beaches singing old rhymes and sharing jokes. BCCI and Kinver, the Troons and even The Family had seemed as far away as the moon over the past few glorious weeks and he wanted nothing to change.

Devaux prodded him from his daydreams. A white car had arrived along the rough canal-side track which, on the map, bore the grand-sounding name Maplestead Court. Three men with shopping bags followed Albert Redden up the gangplank. Once on board, Redden was brought a drink and a newspaper. He sat on a high-backed fisherman's seat and Goodman studied his face with care. In the moments before Redden donned a pair of hooded sunglasses, Goodman recognised him beyond any shadow of doubt.

'It's him?' Devaux sounded eager.

Goodman, almost reluctantly, agreed. 'Yes. That's Redden. He killed my wife and my daughter.'

Devaux said nothing. He was pleased to learn this. He and Mary knew better than to enquire but they had often argued as to Goodman's status. He was quite different from other lodgers the Troons had sent to the Jensen Court apartment; patently not a gangster nor yet a policeman and his search for a mobster like Redden had made no sense to either of them.

Now Devaux understood and felt considerable empathy for the gentle Welshman.

'What now?' he asked.

'Let's get back to town and we can make plans.' Goodman's throat was parched from the heat. 'Are you free tonight, Johnny? Do you have friends?'

'For you, any time.' Devaux grinned. He scented action in the wind. 'And yes, I have many friends.'

'Good. I need time for thought. I need to speak to Sara. I will call you at your home at 8 p.m. OK?'

After Jyoti had been read her bedtime story, Goodman opened his mind to Sara.

'We have found Redden. Tonight is best. Surprise will be easy. We could see no guard on the boat nor on the land. Redden obviously thinks his presence on the island is uncompromised. He feels free of enemies. There are five of his men on the boat, possibly armed, but with Devaux and his mates, I could get to Redden with ease.'

'How long will Redden's boat be there?' Sara was wondering how best to encourage postponement without appearing to.

'We have no way of knowing. Devaux's friend says the Hatteras only arrived two or three days ago. Redden obviously keeps on the move. At his next mooring he may have reinforcements, may be bang in the middle of a crowded marina or anchored off some other island. I can't risk waiting. Either we go in tonight or we risk missing him altogether.'

'So what's the plan?' Sara's heart was in her mouth.

'When I saw Redden through the binoculars today, I waited for the bile of hatred to rise in my gut as it did when I first faced Richter. But instead I found an emptiness. His was just another face. I have lost the stomach for it all, Sara, and I think I know why. For eight years I have been driven on as self-styled judge and executioner, blind to all but my vendetta. You were always there but my heart was coated in arsenic and proof against your love. Somehow the benign influence of this place has melted that poison and allowed me to realise what a wonderful and precious love we have together. I want to do nothing that might risk losing you and Jyoti.'

Sara knelt between his knees, laid her head on his lap and listened, still not daring to hope. At that moment Goodman made up his mind and leapt off his fence.

'I've been blind, Sara. But not now. I no longer want to dwell on the past and harbour hatred. I just want us to be together for ever, preferably right here. In short, I've reached two decisions since seeing Redden. Firstly I have no plan for tonight nor for any night. I want to forget him for ever. And second, I want to marry you as soon as possible, to make us legally man and wife so nobody can take you away . . . That is, if you were to agree! Will you marry me, Sara?'

Sara wept tears of relief, wonder and gratitude, even though, in her eyes, they were already married spiritually.

Johnny Devaux took the news as amiably as he greeted every twist and turn of life.

In the morning Goodman called Sailor and explained his volte-face. He heard Sailor tell the other members of The Family and the background whoops of merriment that followed.

'Tosh says she'll be bridesmaid. You are to have a proper wedding only when you come back to Peckham. And, Alex, don't worry none about the Troons. You stay there just as long as it takes you to fix yourself up. I'll square Lu Troon right away so nobody'll think you're hangin' around under false pretences. When you've made up your mind about the future you just give me another call. Right?'

Sara spoke to them all and received their congratulations. Later in the day Goodman explained his decision to Mary and Devaux, who agreed to help the couple find a smaller apartment in the block for $1200 a month and a job for Goodman. All the major international accountants had local branches but Devaux said he would be better doing *sub rosa* cash accountancy jobs for West End acquaintances of Devaux, as he had no work permit.

As they watched Jyoti play alone beside the apartment's pool that evening, Goodman took Sara's hand and asked her, 'How about a little sister for Jyoti?'

Just then, and for a few more days, the world smelled of roses.

30

June 1992

Black Brixton is like a village where everybody knows who is doing what and why. On Saturday, 27 June 1992 the Jamaican community grumbled, spat and flexed its claws because *their* local green, Brockwell Park, swarmed with lesbians and gays; that branch of humanity considered by most West Indians as the scum of the earth. Over 100,000 mainly white perverts were soiling Brixton's grassy sanctum, under the close protection of the Met.

Dykes and queens, chuffers and oscars, all in determinedly shocking gear from genital-clinging Lycra cat-suits to dayglo T-shirts proclaiming 'Sodomy is Best', spent the morning on a 'flaunt' march from Charing Cross to Hyde Park, then trekked to Brixton for the annual festival. They called it 'Gay Pride Day'. 'Our anger becomes energy for our joy,' they chanted on the buses which brought them to London from all over Europe. On the Underground from Victoria to Brixton they whooped, blew their pink whistles and catcalled, certain for once that their very numbers would keep them safe from 'straight bully-boys'. Lesbians, some carrying babies, exchanged long wet kisses while gay men in G-strings jiggled about on one another's laps. Members of the public kept their eyes averted or smiled nervously to show they 'didn't mind'.

By 11 p.m., after the Gay Pride fireworks had whizzed up briefly from the park, thousands of randy revellers headed for gay dives, discos, pubs and clubs all over London, places like Village Soho, Crews next to Stringfellows, Heaven, Comptons, Bang and Boy.

Tosh, dressed in blue butterfly drag, a blue that emphasised her wild, flaming hair, followed the four 'boys' from the park to The Fridge, one of London's biggest gay clubs and conveniently close to the heart of Brixton. She had fielded amorous approaches from various dykes on the march and at the festival but she enjoyed the break from work back in the coolers. The gay scene seemed pretty harmless and Tosh was even tempted to have a go in the park's mud-wrestling tent organised by The Mud Club. The lads with Hussein had all stripped off and rolled about in slimy clinches with dozens of others in the pool of 'environmentally friendly' ooze.

It was not a difficult job for Tosh since Hussein and friends were wrapped up in one another's charms and the entire day had anyway been a sweaty crush of colourfully clad bodies. Her task, for which The Family had been paid a healthy bonus on top of the standard cooler fee, was to observe Hussein closely for one week and inform her client, De Moni, at once if he showed any sign of reversion to heroin.

De Moni, a Turk, was rich, fat and owned Kensington news agencies that catered for Middle Eastern expatriates. Quite where or when he had come across Hussein was immaterial to Tosh. He had taken the virile twenty-eight-year-old Kurd to his home, made love to him and, for a year or more, had been his self-appointed guardian. Hussein shamelessly abused De Moni's generosity by frequenting gay bars and spending a fortune on drugs. De Moni had the previous Christmas threatened to evict his protégé unless he kicked the heroin habit. For a month Hussein had disappeared but, missing his money source, returned and reluctantly agreed to a heroin withdrawal course at the Home.

Tosh felt sorry for Hussein, an Iraqi Kurd whose parents had been killed in Saddam Hussein's poison-gas attacks on Halabja and who himself had been imprisoned and horribly tortured. Having fled Iraq on his release, he arrived in London, where he turned increasingly to drugs to fight off his memories. The Medical Foundation for the Care of Victims of Torture did their best to counsel Hussein but the psychological wounds were deep, as Tosh had soon discovered in the cooler.

At least Hussein seemed to be enjoying Gay Pride Day and, as yet, Tosh was sure, he had purchased no drugs.

There were 1100 gay people in The Fridge, swaying, blotched by coloured laser beams and mesmerised by their own importance on

418

Gay Pride Day. Hussein pushed his way, his crotch being fondled *en passant* by several wide-eyed wallflowers, to the washrooms. Tosh kept close by and did not hesitate at the door. After all, each sex was either sex in The Fridge that day. She saw Hussein swallow the white amytal tablets marked 'Lilly'. Tosh was relieved. Not heroin. Many homosexuals, she knew, took white or blue 'Angels' purely to relax the relevant muscles before an active night.

She followed him back upstairs to the heaving, groping cauldron of sweating skin, leather and Lycra. In a while her target group left The Fridge and sat outside along the pavement with beer cans and roll-ups. Tosh squatted close by with a Coke, relishing the cool night air after the stuffy disco.

At home in Belfast her family and friends had called gays 'lezzies and queers'. They probably still did. To her it was all an accident of birth, like having red hair, green eyes and overactive hormones. She was lucky with Sailor. He played her like the most fragile and complex of beautiful instruments. He could elicit the most sensational, explosive music.

She noticed that Hussein's focus was wavering between the blond teenager with the Eton accent and neat buttocks and Eric, the iron-pumping, beach-boy type from Wimbledon. The fourth man, a stocky Latino, had eyes only for the blond. Perhaps Hussein would take them all back to De Moni's Kensington penthouse in order to tease and titillate his guardian. Tosh knew he was quite capable of such ingratitude. She wondered, as she listened to the four gays, what a visiting Martian would make of their banter.

'There's something wildly exciting about *al fresco* screwing in the trees behind Jack Straw's Castle on the Heath,' the blond youth commented.

'Quickest way to HIV, that is,' grunted Eric.

'Not at all.' The blond made no attempt to hide his cultured tones. 'I know all the signs and avoid the poor unfortunates. The rash in their armpits and crotches. The itch when they get excited, swollen necks, stomach pains, heavy sweats, missing teeth.'

'I think I'd do myself in if I ever came up poz,' said Eric.

'What a waste,' Hussein murmured. 'You never know when they'll be getting a cure. Look . . . Couple of years back you die from PCP pneumonia. Now we got Pentamidine, no problem. And AZT

419

keeps your t-cell count up, keeps you going years sometimes. I tell you. Soon they'll have a full cure. No point in suicide.'

'Bollocks,' said Eric. 'AZT's a load of rubbish. Kills more boys than it saves.'

They finished the beer, began to feel cool and agreed to tank up in a nearby pub.

'Place called Steppers is just round the corner,' Eric suggested. 'There's blacks there but Tony Stepper, the boss, he don't allow nobody to muck customers about. We look all right. I know him. We was at Teddington Secondary together way back. He was the only black out of 900 little white bastards. That takes nuts, I tell you.'

They sauntered along Brixton Road, arms linked, and Eric led them up Rushcroft Road, a short cut to Steppers. Five black youths closed about them from the shadows, humming, 'Battyboys. Battyboys. We kill Battyboys.' Four carried baseball bats and one punched the air, clenched fist gleaming with knuckledusters.

'We got nothin' against you,' Eric said. 'Leave over, mates.'

'We ain't your mates,' one of the blacks spat in disgust. 'Battyboys ain't welcome in Brixton.'

The four gays closed together like a Wild West wagon-train as their aggressors drew nearer.

'OK, boys. Take off or I'll call the cops, so I will.' Tosh had appeared from a side-street in her butterfly suit and brandishing a mobile phone. One of the blacks, guffawing his disbelief, moved towards her, his teeth flashing in the gloom.

'Look what we got here, brothers. I think it's a genuine female. But I'm goin' to investigate its bits to make sure. Nothin' is what it seems round here today.' He tapped his baseball bat against the seam of his trousers, then, snake-quick, lashed it past Tosh's head, aiming to miss by a fraction.

A six-inch pen-gun appeared in Tosh's hand, a Pains Wessex miniflare tube with a screw-on collar adapted to fire .22 rounds. The sharp crack of the bullet's detonation was followed by a startled grunt and the rattle of the baseball bat on the road. The small leaden bullet had lodged in the youth's thigh. He fell, cursing and clasping his leg.

'We are all in the gutter,' Tosh remarked, 'but some of us are lookin' at the stars. Oscar said that.' She smiled at the other blacks.

'Go ahead. Make my day. Clint Eastwood said that, and even if his .44 Magnum was bigger than my poxy artillery, I suggest you lot fuck off right now.'

She was taking a considerable risk and knew it, for a frighteningly high percentage of street-wise blacks in drugs-active areas carry side-arms and by shooting one, she was risking lethal retaliation. Something about her steely air of confidence must have staved off further trouble, for the youths kept their distance.

'I should beat it while you can,' she suggested to the four gays. 'And I think I'll come with you. There's some safety in numbers.'

They edged away from the confrontation and, three minutes' fast walk later, reached Steppers.

'Here, that was awfully decent of you,' said the blond youth, holding out his hand. 'I'm Tony.'

'Tosh,' said Tosh. 'Nice to meet you.'

'My friends here . . . Malo, Hussein and Eric. Why don't you join us for a drink?'

'Delighted, I'm sure.' Tosh found their handshakes limp and warm.

The owners of Steppers, Tony Stepper, and his white wife Louise, wanted no trouble. They served up good music, friendly service and soft drinks to local folk and they didn't like anyone making trouble. Tony came down heavily on those who did and, despite having his hand nearly severed by a machete, had won a reputation as being tough but fair. Now Britain's wickedest Yardies, gang leaders like Rankin' Dred, still used the place frequently but they kept their feuds and drugs off the Steppers' turf.

Tony's mother cooked for Steppers and her friends were older Jamaicans who detested the attitude of the Yardies. Tony himself hated their unpredictable moods, their prickly big-boy egos and their slippery hair-triggered fingers. He'd come to London aged eight and done well. By the age of seventeen he had played for Fulham and Chelsea Youth Football Teams. A horrific paraffin accident had spoiled his football chances so he had moved on to DJ and club work. Yardie troubles and the removal of his alcohol licence led him to change the Steppers style from reggae to European pop and he encouraged a multi-ethnic clientele. The badmen still came to Steppers but they confined their more antisocial activities to The Vox and other such dives.

421

At a small round table on the upper floor, four Yardies played dominoes for stakes of £10 a pass. The atmosphere was tense.

'Who are they?' Louise asked Tony, who looked puzzled as he ran a muscular black hand through his dreadlocks.

'I've seen them somewhere, but I can't exactly place them.'

The players cursed and shot hostile looks at one another. Each man would slam his domino down as violently as he could and taunt the next player to 'Follow that.' Loss of esteem to a Yardie in any public place meant serious embarrassment; even at a game of dominoes. Many ghetto shootings had been caused by lesser sparks.

Kingston Williams was winning the game but kept from crowing too openly, for he knew Jo-Dog Willetts could explode with volcanic unpredictability if he felt diss from any quarter. Kingston looked over his shoulder towards the nearest loudspeaker stack. 'Rewind,' he growled at the DJ, wanting an encore of a powerful Jah Shaka number.

Tony Stepper appeared by their table.

'Respect. Yessir,' he said lifting his hand, his eyes steady, his presence a gentle warning to keep the peace.

'Cool, brother,' Kingston murmured.

Jo-Dog scowled as he slammed down a domino and his partner Kenyatta took a deep slug of his Martell and Babycham to steady his nerves.

The game soon finished and money changed hands; great wads of cash, for they had played for over an hour. They ordered beer and Jo-Dog spoke business. Mafia, now resident in Jamaica, had phoned earlier. It seemed somebody in the organisation was squealing to the Brixton Drugs Squad, who were in touch with the Jamaican police about the network's mules. Mafia wanted an immediate witch-hunt.

'The Vox, brother,' Kingston suggested. 'One of the doormen. Them listen as we are talk. I say one of them boys is guilty.'

'No, man!' Jo-Dog disagreed. 'Chin, Junior and George at The Vox all good boys. No way are them goin' to sell us to the Ol' Bill. We goin' to have to look into this. Maybe set a trap is best.'

Mafia was also planning a major raid on their Brixton rivals. He wanted an arsenal ready by September, when he would be in London on a visit. But their normal arms supplier, Paul Blackledge,

422

had recently been shot close up by a twelve-bore and was temporarily out of business.

'Mafia wants a laser sight for his .38 and a dozen heavy pistols for the brothers.'

'No problem.' Kingston spread his enormous hands. 'Got me a white man in Chelsea just took in 400 Makarov nine-mills from Estonia and a crate of Desert E Magnums from the States. All better prices than what Blackledge offer . . . Hey, man. Take a squint at that chick.'

Kingston was watching a group of five whites approaching the bar past their table. Tosh, at the rear, met Kingston's gaze square on, her green eyes boring through him as if to say: 'You may be a six-foot-four black ram but don't get any ideas with me!'

Jo-Dog's eyes swivelled in time to catch a frontal glimpse of Tosh; not a sight to easily forget. He stiffened and leant across to Kingston. 'She are the bitch that Mafia fancied, remember? She moved with that bank boy who did BCCI work for us . . . Ah, Goodman. You hear this, man. Mafia's Yankee bosses will pay big caboosh for news of this.'

'Nice one, star,' Kingston enthused. 'But Goodman stole all them bank papers and done a runner. Mafia told the Yanks at the time.'

'Sure he did.' Jo-Dog was impatient. 'But they never did find the boy. He could be back here by now. Come, man, we got to make a call to Mafia.'

But Mafia was unobtainable and Kingston saw his chance for kudos. With his own soldier Delroy in a black BMW, he shadowed Tosh when Hussein gallantly hired her a taxi back to Peckham.

The Home was well secured but Kingston and Delroy steamrollered their entry, shooting the locks out. Kingston moved fast down the corridor and bolted all the coolers. James was inside one with a tray of food. Columbo and Art were out. Tosh had joined Sailor in the main room watching snooker on TV. Her shoes were kicked on to the carpet and she was perched on his lap with an arm around his neck when Mafia's men burst in, Kingston's Uzi covering them convincingly.

'Who are you?' Kingston screamed.

'I'm Sailor. Welcome to our home, brother. May I ask who you are?'

'Don't get clever, nigger.' Delroy was aching to distinguish himself. He produced a barbed Javan knife.

'My friend's a handy man with his blade,' said Kingston. 'When he withdraw it, them barbs rip your skin to pieces. Your lady got nine body holes and Delroy would be delirious if I was to tell him to use his little blade on all of them.'

Tosh stayed docile under the black eye of Kingston's sub-machine-gun. She watched for her chance but it failed to materialise. She and Sailor were forced to sit on separate chairs and their arms were lashed behind their backs.

'What I want is easy for you, girl. Your friend Goodman. Where is he?'

Tosh stared at the big black man with disdain, but Sailor said: 'Goodman's in America with his family. We know nothin' more.'

Delroy slashed sideways with his knife and removed one of Sailor's ears. He held it up to Tosh. 'Your man's not so pretty now, eh! I think you better tell my don what he's askin' for. Or your man's gonna lose more bits.'

Delroy, needing information some months before from one John Dyson, a recalcitrant Jamaican shopkeeper, had blown the head off Dyson's twelve-year-old daughter to encourage the father to talk or 'lose your other kids in the same way'. He looked over at Kingston. Did he have *carte blanche*? Kingston nodded and drew up an armchair from which to interrogate and watch while Delroy plugged Sailor's mouth. His method was straightforward. Sailor would suffer and Tosh would talk.

'The man here makes you real happy, yeah?' Delroy leered. 'His hands, his dick, his tongue. They're all goin' to go. One by one, till you tell my boss here what he want to know. Last week I took a steam iron to a Nigerian girl who sidetracked some coke she'd been carryin'. She had a great batty till I ironed it into the biggest blister you ever seen. Everybody sings when Delroy operates.'

Delroy was unfortunate. He moved in close to Tosh and she kicked out as best she could. Her concentration was total and the ball of her foot struck his windpipe at more than forty miles per hour. An immediate tracheotomy might have saved his life but, as it was, he quickly choked to death.

Tosh had kicked herself off balance and careered backwards still lashed to the chair.

'Not just a pretty chicken.' Kingston left her where she had landed and kept a generous distance. 'Delroy was mean but I work faster.' He laid down his Uzi well away from Tosh, picked up Delroy's knife and cut off three of Sailor's fingers. Tosh could only scream obscenities at him. He sawed through Sailor's thumb and threw it on to Tosh's shirt front.

'You evil bastard.' She gritted her teeth. 'Goodman is on Grand Bahama. That's all I know.'

'What's he doin' there?'

'He's on holiday. That's the only reason people go there.'

'Where on Grand Bahama?'

'An apartment block called Jensen Court. I have no number but any fool could find him there.'

Kingston believed her. He put the barrel of his Uzi to Sailor's head and blew his brains out. 'You, bitch, can die slowly for what you done to Delroy,' he told Tosh. Still keeping his distance from her, he aimed carefully at her lower belly and fired a single shot. Her legs convulsed and she groaned in agony. Kingston removed the weapons and then dragged out the body of Delroy, who looked like he was sleeping.

Some twenty minutes later, Columbo, carrying a hamburger and chips for James, returned to find the door locks awry and rushed straight to the main room. Tosh was no longer groaning, but he detected a weak pulse under her ear, to his enormous relief. When feverishly seeking The Family's medical book, he found James locked in a cooler. Aware that Sailor was dead, together they tried to save Tosh. Her eyes flickered open. James cried openly. His beloved brother was gone and now Tosh, who had become like a daughter to him, was dying before him. She spoke to him through her eyes. The pain had receded and the clouds were gathering but she forced a whisper. 'I had to tell them . . . Alex . . . Bahamas.'

James touched his finger to her lips. He knew there would be no point in a doctor and no time for a priest.

'Bible,' James called out. Columbo fetched it and read through the Lord's Prayer and the Absolution as they held Tosh's hands.

'Bury us together,' were her last clear words. Her face relaxed and she seemed at peace as the spirit left her.

In his grief, James was still practical. 'We must warn Brother

Alex. Call Lee Troon, Col. He will know how to find him and Sara and the little girl.'

The Troons arranged for a cremation. Sailor had long since given James his wishes in the event of his death. He wanted no police or legal involvement with his passing. The Family's business was now James's responsibility.

Art returned from a holiday in Bristol and called the many folk who had reason to love Sailor and Tosh. The memorial service was a beautiful affair, with a moving speech by James.

Lee Troon called Ah Troon, who called his brother Lu in Miami. But nobody answered at the Jensen Court apartment, for, with the Goodmans in another flat, Mary and Devaux visited only weekly for mail and messages. A Miami Troon was dispatched to warn the Goodmans. He was twenty-four hours too late.

31

July 1992

The bed of the Atlantic rises three and a half miles at the Tropic of Cancer to prick the ocean's surface and form Grand Bahama. The island's highest point is only forty feet above sea level. Indeed the loftiest Everest across the 700-mile front of all the Bahamian isles is a hillock of 200 feet. Islanders rightly fear the hurricanes, for they cause monstrous waves and winds which gust to over 200mph and pose an annual threat from July until November.

On Sunday, 28 July 1992 the Goodmans packed the panniers of their hired scooters early, dressed an excited little Jyoti in her white cotton jumpsuit and escaped from Freeport while most Bahamians were still snoring. Johnny Devaux, who often accompanied them to point out the wonders of the sea and the forest, promised to join them later. Sara had planned the day starting with family prayers in their favourite wilderness chapel, then a nature walk at the Lucaya caves and a rendezvous with Devaux for a high-tea barbecue on their favourite beach.

They followed Midshipman Road to the Garden of the Groves, a mile or so west of the Grand Lucaya Waterway. Four waterfalls plunge into a lake amid twelve acres of exotic plants, trees and shrubs. Flamingos preen in the hanging gardens and the tiny rock chapel overlooking the lake needs no incense, for the breeze from the waterfalls brings the perfume of a thousand tropical flowers to the nostrils of the faithful.

They sat on a hard wooden pew and prayed their separate prayers. Afterwards they waited a while beneath a great banyan tree and listened to the play of the falling water. Sara had recently been teaching Jyoti the values of listening in silence and Goodman would propound on this advice, whenever Jyoti became impatient, with the Welsh Borders adage 'God gave ye two big ears but only one little tongue.'

They shared a papaya and continued east beyond the Casuarina Bridge to some caves once inhabited by pre-Columbian Lucayans. Jyoti loved the little caves, not sufficiently big or dark to make her thoroughly scared but weird enough to hint at a world of tantalising mystery. Goodman gripped her tiny wrist on the narrow walkways. One cave had been 'closed' by conservationists to protect nesting bats but two others descended to blue pools filled with darting cave fish and amphibious centipedes. The odour of bats' dung and feathery jungle fronds creeping over wet rock walls helped fire Jyoti's imagination. 'Indiana,' she said, 'has been here. Daddy says he's a Welshman too.'

'Uncle Johnny Devaux,' Sara whispered, 'says this is an entrance to the longest known underwater cave system *in the world*.'

'Ooh,' said Jyoti.

They tramped from the caves along rough wooden walkways which led south over a clear-water creek flowing down to the sea. By lying flat on the boards and keeping still, they could spot snappers, crabs and barracudas down among the mangrove roots. Fifty yards from the sea this region of mud and mangrove gave way to sand dunes and a thin band of casuarina planted all along the beach to root the sand against the destructive forces of hurricanes.

'What's over there?' Jyoti asked.

'Where?' said Goodman.

'If we just keep going where the wind comes from?'

'That's east. Devaux says there's sixty miles of jungle out there and three little villages. The furthest one is MacLean's Town, where there's 300 people. All of them are black except one Englishman, who's white, and an Alsatian dog that's black and brown.'

They hid the scooters in the brush because Devaux had said snowbirds often had things stolen from their cars. It took ten minutes to reach the beach because the picnic and snorkelling things were bulky and because they had no reason to hurry. As soon as they had climbed the loose sand of the eight-foot-high dune, the noise of

428

the sea closed about them, muted but busy, eternal yet plaintive, the hidden whispering, perhaps, of the long-dead Lucayans.

Goodman could see for miles in either direction, but nothing moved over the long, white beach. Only, way out on the ocean's rim and above the first blue-black horizon, he could just make out the dancing white horses of a coral reef. Four miles out, and to the west, the sun gleamed on the walls of Gold Rock Island.

The little family enjoyed their picnic on the dune beneath the casuarinas. Afterwards, when they had spread out a rug on which to sunbathe, Sara put a plaster over the angry-looking mole on Goodman's shoulder. 'It's not lookin' any better, my love,' she said, frowning. 'I really think you should have someone see it.'

'It's not been as itchy this week.' Goodman did not want anything to spoil this perfect day. 'I'm sure it's best to wait for Johnny to find a specialist. He's promised to look. Anyway it's only a mole.'

A fat pelican plopped noisily into the sea and helped Goodman change the subject.

'We'll leave the stuff here,' Goodman said. 'There's no one about.'

They ambled hand in hand along the dune, past a hidey-hole for Jyoti which they had dug together on a previous visit and camouflaged with beach grasses, then on down the inland side of the dune to the rich foliage of the mangrove creek.

'Look at all those sandpipers and that great big frigate bird,' said Goodman. 'Last week I saw an osprey. Yet when you walk in the woods there's very little bird noise. I shouldn't be surprised if insidious pollution from Florida isn't already affecting things in these islands.' He ran a finger over the old scar on his head. 'I'm truly happy with our life as it is, you know that. But what I'd love to do more than anything, once we've settled down, is to get a job preserving, helping to save, the animal kingdom.'

Sara, holding her sunglasses down, glanced at him. 'Alex, that's what you were doin' in Kinver when you first saw the badger men! I don't believe in obeah . . . omens, but . . .'

'I know, but I've never actually saved a single creature. I'd like to join a movement. Perhaps get a job with an international group as their Bahamas rep. It's not a job where you have to be an expert. You just need the right attitude.'

'What's brought this on all of a sudden?' Sara looked perplexed.

'I suppose my swims with Jyoti at the Freeport UNEXSO underwater centre, with those dolphins, and along the coral banks.' He sighed at the memory. 'You should have come. It was another world. Unbelievable. Twenty-foot-high coral heads and delicate fringe reefs of scarlet, purple and rose. Finger coral, brain coral, star coral and staghorn coral. Sea gardens of pink gorgonians, yellow sea-fans, sponges, urchins and stars. Nobody could see it all and come away an unbeliever.'

'And all that's being threatened?' Sara sounded doubtful.

'Little by little. Yes. Because it's so fragile. The UNEXSO guys have studied sea life for more than twenty years and they say the signs are bad. They mentioned sea rays that weigh up to 5500lb but are developing horrendous warts and ulcers. They showed us huge swarms of sergeant-major fish, made us listen above water to the pig sounds of the grunt fish and almost touch superb little weirdos like porgies, parrots and yellow goats. Then they explained why the whole life-cycle of the coral, on which these fish depend, is endangered by man-made nutrients, the foul muck pouring east from Florida. And, of course, from other cities close to other coral.'

'Well, if you feel badly enough about it, go ahead. But you'd be better off back in London than here. Just about every big green group has its headquarters there ... Alex, are you bein' serious about all this? You've only just made one big decision. Shouldn't we sort of consolidate for a while? Mary's fixed us up with everythin' here. Our life is now so beautiful.'

Goodman reached for Sara's hand. 'Nothing's as beautiful as you, my darling. Nothing and no one, and you're quite right: we shouldn't rush. I'm happier than I've ever been. But having an aim bigger than spending the rest of my days fiddling with a calculator can't be a bad thing.'

'That's true but why the hurry?'

'I suppose I'm not getting any younger and all this' – he waved at the beach and the sea and the sandpipers – 'is being attacked by invisible pollutants right now.'

'So what can you hope to do about all this?'

'Conservationists *have* caused government policy to change. That's a start. Every individual who strives to fight pollution must help in a tiny way.'

Sara was nodding. 'But I still hope you don't rush things. I wasn't

430

goin' to tell you until I had the hospital confirmation but I know anyway. Jyoti's got a little brother or sister on the way. I'd love him or her to be Bahamian. This place has made us so happy.'

Goodman hugged her to him and shouted his joy so loud that the sandpipers lifted away in a squawking flock and Jyoti looked up in alarm from the conch she was investigating. He gazed over Sara's naked shoulder to the west of the gliding sun, where the future lay, but the light was blinding and he saw only the face of Albert Redden.

'I am sorry to hear of your partner's death. This very sad.' The Russian, Vukov, shook his head theatrically to stress his sincerity.

'Richter was not my partner.' Redden's face was expressionless. 'I have no partner. Any governing body has to have an odd number and three is too big.'

'But he was also from Germany?'

'He was my countryman, yes, and my long-time friend but, *leider*, he is gone and life continues.'

Vukov was head of Redden's newest acquisition, a Russian crime organisation centred in Moscow. Redden had asked Vukov to Freeport to learn more about his new lieutenant off his home ground. He had taken the Russian, in his Hatteras, out over the shallows to the cold, deep waters beyond; the dark kingdom of the greatest game fish on earth, barracuda, shark, kingfish, tuna and blue marlin of up to 850lb.

'Only at this season,' he had told Vukov, 'do we find passing jack, the greatest Bahamian delicacy, for its movements about the oceans are guided by the phases of the moon.'

After two days of unusually successful sport, they had returned to the luxurious house that Redden's local staff had currently rented for him.

Krug was brought to celebrate their relationship. Not partnership, Vukov reminded himself. Tactfully he suggested a further toast, this one to: 'the greatest country of Western Europe, Germany, may she prosper! Cheers.'

'*Prost*.' Redden raised his glass. 'Having twice failed to conquer our neighbours by military might, we will succeed with the economic alternative, of that I am confident. We lost before because of military insistence on literal obedience. I support a discipline where sensible men obey not the order given by their superiors but

431

rather the order which their superiors would have given if they knew what they were talking about . . . Now let us toast Mother Russia, the greatest power in the East.'

Both men laughed and clinked glasses.

'The end of the Cold War between our countries,' Redden pontificated, 'has brought us great opportunities, which we will be discussing, but there are also new dangers. Germany will pay dearly for unification and you, Russia, face what the Britishers call a can of worms. "Freedom," in the words of Czechoslovakia's President Havel last month, "has released an explosion of every imaginable evil." Freedom of speech and privatisation has led of course to less, not more, food in the bellies of the people.'

'That is correct, Mr Redden,' Vukov nodded violently. 'With the Cold War, the people knew where they were and our armies controlled the nuclear deterrent. But now tens of thousands of mass-kill warheads, biological and chemical also, sit without guard. If ninety-five per cent are destroyed by SALT, there is still more than enough to wipe out the world. You know, even now, we have many square kilometres of stacked explosives which you Germans left in 1944. Last week in Vladivostok one dump exploded killing hundreds. Think of the risks of the *nuclear* leftover.'

'Where were you in the war, Mr Vukov?'

'I was in Leningrad. I was a small child and can remember only a little.'

'You are lucky.' Redden gazed out at the forest that surrounded the villa. 'I was brought up in Dresden, a cultural city of baroque magnificence. On 13 February 1945, when I was aged fifteen, my father walked me home from a costume carnival. I was William Tell. My sister was the Lorelei. That night, Shrove Tuesday, the sirens sounded. Our city was crowded with hungry refugees, fleeing from your Red Army. Eight hundred Britisher bombers dropped 3000 tonnes of explosive including 650,000 petrol fire-bombs. Pilots could see the fire from 250 kilometres away. We huddled in a church crypt but, up above, the temperature reached 1000 degrees Centigrade. Telegraph poles snapped in two. As the hot air rose, fresh oxygen-rich gales were sucked in from outer fires with the sound of a roaring waterfall. This fire tornado ate the oxygen. A hundred and thirty-five thousand of us Dresdeners died within five hours – twice the human death count of Hiroshima.'

'And your family, Mr Redden?'

'I was lucky. I blundered through smoke, after losing my father, and came by way of the cellars to the Elbe. A sick woman was wearing wet sheets. I tore them off her and crawled to the water over many blackened corpses. Trees were burning and flaming phosphorus dripped like rain. The dying and the drowning were screaming and choking. The city hospital was itself on fire. The next two days the American bombers came and their fighters machine-gunned the crowded roads. They were efficient. It was the greatest fire-storm ever.'

'But your father? Your sister?'

'My father lived. The SS "Department of Death" bulldozed tens of thousands of bodies into mass graves and burnt thousands more on great pyres. A week later I searched with my father in the cellars. We found my sister and our cousins there still squatting upright together. The fumes had killed them. Nowadays, of course, we can be even more efficient at arson. Tell me, how is your progress in Moscow at finding HTA buyers?'

'Not so good. Our government scientists are trying to sell off their own bomb materials anywhere and cheap. They have a neutron bomb so little as a cricket ball but able to destroy everything within one kilometre of the blast. In Urals they have factories making red mercury, three hundred times more strong than TNT. I have no success with your HTA.'

'So, Mr Vukov' – Redden's tone was clipped – 'tell me, where do you feel our business may progress, where may we advance, inside your territory?'

Vukov was ready, indeed anxious, to impress Redden with the results of his work to date.

'I have given you already my report on the most positive areas where we advance our profit with dramatic success. Most good is drugs smuggling, vice and intimidation.'

'I look forward to reading that report. And on other less straightforward fronts?'

'We control fifteen per cent of all caviar export out of Siberia. I have 300 workers including packaging and transport work. Eighty peasant fishermen supply us instead of government buyers. Of course, this is poaching but Fisheries Protection Unit of Colonel

Butyaev is too few and Volga is so big. My men hear his helicopters come, so they hide in reeds.'

'It will be pleasant to view your financial results,' Redden commented.

'Again the pay is in rouble, not foreign currency, but big money coming from all our Siberian contract work. I have seventy, maybe eighty, projects. For instance, now that region bosses of state-owned industry have big incentive payments they pay me to cut output of rivals. My team arrange anything. Mines disruption, striking even. In Usinsk Region we blow oil pipes. Cause big fracture and thousands of tonnes of oil leak onto tundra, into rivers. The oil workers not get pay like before so they don't care. They don't check radar any more. Also my black-market military buyers get very, very good kit next year. Already machine-gun, night sight, pistol, bazooka – all at fantastic price for the West. And, like I say, next year we also get tank and helicopter and field gun. Big opportunity there.'

'You told me there was video potential.'

'Yes, yes. Moscow is best. But we look at many other towns. People want food so they rent their children. We find pretty ones and train them for the films. Use animals too. With the children. Also films of bears dancing on hot metal, fighting big timber wolves. After the fight referee pull out bears' teeth and claws. We make thousands of dollars from specialist tourists in Ismailovo Park, East Moscow, with the big dog fights. Rottweiler. Pit bull. You ask for me to bring example. Tomorrow I show you very good bear video. We have discover undercover Moscow RSPCA inspector, so we film *him* in pit with three starving bears. We give him penknife first. This very, very good film. One video I think maybe sell for $50 in New York.'

Redden's face relaxed. 'I will tell you a strange story, Mr Vukov. I have a collection of videos of animal fights from all over the world. Some eight years ago, Richter and I witnessed a badger dig in Britain. On the video, which I still have, you can see a man run out of the bushes telling the diggers to stop their sport. They thought he was, *vielleicht*, an undercover inspector like your Moscow man. Anyhow the years went by and yesterday my people tell me this same man has arrived here in Grand Bahama . . . to kill me!'

'Yesterday?' Vukov repeated.

'It is amazing, *ney*? I believe the man received a knock on his head from the diggers and this so deranged him he has doggedly sought out those involved with the sport on that afternoon eight years ago. Of course my men are even now searching the island.' Redden switched back to business. 'So, tomorrow we will look at reports and videos, discuss detailed cooperation for the future, and I will see you back to the airport. Then you have a week to enjoy the Big Apfel.'

When Vukov had gone, Redden took a call from Los Angeles. The background checks on Alex Goodman via the Friends' CIA contacts had come up red-hot. The Briton was thought to possess embarrassing documents stolen from the BCCI bank in London and had almost certainly been involved in Richter's death. This being so, the chances of his possessing the stolen Hoover papers were high. Would Redden like help with manpower on the island? Goodman must be caught alive because the documents were to be retrieved 'for all our sakes'.

'*Kein problem*,' Redden assured the Friends. 'I have my men searching the town now. We know the identity of his Bahamian contacts. The airport and harbour are covered. I am looking forward to meeting this man who has hunted me for so long. This is a small island. We will find him.'

'Perhaps this is all a dream.' Sara joined Goodman at the waterside, where the wavelets lapped the high-tide mark at the base of their picnic dune. 'Somebody sprinkled Lucayan stardust over us in the night. I hope it stays with us for ever.'

They swam lazily. Jyoti slept in the shade of a bath towel awning they had erected. Goodman no longer noticed the scar tissue on Sara's breasts. In shallow water they came together and their legs entwined. Sara's back rested on the smooth white sand and the swell moved them both with soft insistence. Her lips parted with her pleasure and her fingers expertly added to his.

Later, as they came gently apart, she reminded Goodman that Hindus would be shocked. 'I have been pregnant now for eight weeks so you should not enter, nor even desire me. That goes for the next nine months too.'

Alex blew a mouthful of seawater at her. 'Nine months!' he laughed. 'You'd have to chop it off.'

They scooped a hollow in the slope of the dune and built a barbecue with stones from nearby. Soon the nose-wrinkling smell of frying sausage and bacon accompanied the curl of blue smoke, which rose almost vertically, disturbed only by the puff of an occasional zephyr.

Goodman propped himself on an elbow and tapped a booklet Sara had brought in the hamper. 'This fire,' he said, 'signifies our marriage. It is the sacred fire of Homa. According to your custom we should drop five pats of butter into the embers as oblations to the Gods. You, my pretty bride, seated on my left, touch my right shoulder as the butter flares high. At this point I say the words "O beloved, I am *amah* and you are *saa*, which, joined together, give the sound *sa'am*. I am Sa'amaveda and you are Rigveda. I am like the sun and you are like Prithivi, the Earth. Let us love and admire one another and protect each other. Let us see, hear and live a hundred autumns."'

After the food they fell asleep and the sun slid away around the great curve of white sand towards Freeport. No birds sang in the casuarina fronds about the beach. Only lizards and long, black chicken snakes basked in the baking heat. Sara awoke and sat up, her knees touching her chin. She glanced at the others. The only movement she could see in all the world was the rise and fall of the taut skin above their navels. His, a constant rhythm and streaked with black hair, Jyoti's smooth and fluttering like the wings of a butterfly.

The sound, a high-pitched drone, came out of the heat shimmer of the glittering sea, audible for several moments before Sara actively considered its source and scanned the glare for movement. When she first spotted the boats they were moving together, two black specks hovering in the western haze perhaps five miles away. For three or four minutes she watched idly as one boat peeled away, disappearing into the dark line of the coast, perhaps to make a landing. The other craft grew larger until it developed an outline. Then she remembered they were naked.

'Alex,' she called. 'Wake up. There's a boat.'

'What is it?' Goodman mumbled.

'They might see us. Put your things on.'

The crew of the boat must have spotted the smoke of their fire or the bright colours of their towels. Like all islanders, the boatmen

436

were probably curious, not expecting snowbirds so far east. Sara felt a touch annoyed at this shattering of their peaceful world. The invasive boat, closing at forty knots, grew rapidly larger. The outlines of the five crewmen were now clearly silhouetted.

The thirty-foot cigarette boat skimmed arrow-quick towards the family as though intent on ramming their dune. Their annoyance became alarm then fear. The sea was eighteen inches deep for a distance of over thirty yards from their camp and the boat's driver slammed down the throttles of his three powerful outboards at the last moment before the propellers dug into the sand.

'Run, run.' Goodman screamed. 'Run for the bush. I've got Jyoti.' He had seen their Latin faces and their guns. Redden! Somehow he must have discovered. Act now. Think later. He held Jyoti, shrieking in terror, by her waist and, as their beach things scattered in cascading sand, he grabbed for the long-handled barbecue fork.

The slope of the eight-foot dune seemed a formidable hill but they were over it in seconds as the wash from the boat's violent halt burst against the shore and four of the crew leaped into the shallows, clutching guns.

'Spread out.'

Goodman heard the shout as he crested the dune and made for the foxhole hide they had played in during previous visits. Sara was already there. She grabbed Jyoti from him and stifled her screams. Goodman forced his way into a thorny bush some ten yards away, squatting low as he gulped for air.

Only one of the Latinos followed their tracks up the dune. Their spoor led direct to the foxhole. Goodman's brain seemed to engage neutral. A hare must feel like this, he thought, as a dog approaches to eat her leverets.

In the shade of the dune casuarinas Goodman – whose pupils were reasonably adjusted because he had been sleeping – could see more clearly than the boatman, who, for the last hour, had scanned the shimmering surface of the sea.

Jyoti saw the man and the gun five yards away and Sara failed to mask her yelp of fear. Unable to make out the source of the sudden sound and finger jerking against hair-trigger, the gunman squeezed a burst of soft-nosed Uzi bullets into the dark outline of the foxhole. Goodman, moving faster than ever in his life, was still a second too late. As he attacked, the gunman turned back instinctively towards him. The barbecue fork's twin prongs punctured the man's eyeballs and pierced his brain.

The sound of shouting from close by kept Goodman from instantly rushing to the foxhole. Instead he grasped the dead man's sub-machine-gun and located a two-way lever marked 'S' and 'A'. Was this the safety-catch? Goodman had never fired a gun before. Was 'S' for 'Shoot' or 'Safe'? He decided the dead man had left the mechanism ready to fire, so he ignored the lever and retreated into thick undergrowth.

'Don't forget, they said to get him alive,' a voice shouted from the beach.

'Sod that,' growled another voice. 'Carlo has already got the bastard by the sound of it.'

Two thick-set men appeared through the trees, gun barrels swinging from side to side like snakes' heads. A third man joined them from the barbecue site. Goodman waited until the three were grouped in a tight huddle about Jyoti's crumpled corpse. Then he pressed the trigger and held it down until the gun coughed to a halt. He had aimed at waist level but the bullets struck high. The three Latinos died without a sound, collapsing in a loose sprawl about and on top of Jyoti.

Then Goodman screamed, a naked howl of outrage and anguish. He heard the noise of an outboard crackle to life on the beach, exchanged the Uzi for one of the dead men's guns and rushed down into the shallows. The fifth Latino, unarmed, was attempting in vain to free the boat's prow. Goodman ignored his upflung hands and emptied thirty bullets into his trunk at close range.

Jyoti seemed even smaller in death. Goodman tore the bodies of Redden's men off the foxhole and fell on Sara where she lay. She could be alive. He prayed desperately. She must be alive. If there was a God in heaven she would be alive.

Two bullets had entered her chest and one had passed through her windpipe. Half an hour later, when Devaux with two hampers came whistling through the bushes by way of the creek footbridge, Goodman had not moved. He sat by the side of the foxhole, his head nodding slowly back and forth as he grieved. But for the soundless movements of his mouth, his trance was catatonic and Devaux had to slap him hard across the face.

'Alex! Alex! Wake yourself!'

Goodman slowly turned and gazed up at Devaux.

'They have killed them,' he breathed. 'How could I have let Redden go? If I had killed him when first we found him, none of this could have happened. Johnny, will you help me?'

Devaux had buried many bodies over the past decade. As a general rule he preferred to drive out into the brush in the interior of the island and leave the corpses to the birds and insects. The alternative, sinking them out at sea, involved unnecessary effort and Devaux, like all islanders, was allergic to excess manual labour. Thousands of acres of dwarf palm brush existed, never trodden by man, and just waiting for wasted bodies.

Devaux understood at once that Goodman was consumed by grief and by rage. He was not thinking straight. As quickly as he could, Devaux drew from him a clear picture of events.

'Wait here,' he instructed and loped off to the beach. He quickly established that the cigarette boat, exactly the model which he personally craved to own, was undamaged. Hearing electronic clatter, he picked up the dangling VHF transceiver and listened in to the staccato verbal traffic. Ten minutes later he was back with Goodman.

'Listen, Alex, and listen good. Time ain't on our side, boy. You got a wasp nest stirred up all over the island. I counted five separate radio call-signs and an American dude tellin' 'em all their business. These guys had obviously not called their Control back before you killed them. Their Control seems to think they've gone out of radio range 'cos they were checkin' all the south-east coast. One other boat patrol is workin' the southern marinas further west and the main canal. There's more up north and in cars. Sounds to me like your boy Redden is controllin' the hunt from his Hatteras back where we done visit him or near enough up thataway.'

'Will you take me up there, Johnny, in your car? To the Hatteras? To Redden?'

'Hold it ... Easy.' Devaux clasped Goodman's shoulders. 'There's two of us and an army of these guys. We got to use brain, not speed. OK? Listen. Number one, we hide Sara and the little girl until we can come back and bury them proper. The other five we drag into the bush here, and tomorrow I'll drive them in my truck up to the East End bush for lizard food. Then I'll deal with your gear and the scooters.'

439

Goodman nodded. He was grateful that Devaux was setting the course. One thing he knew. He must separate his two conflicting emotions. Now was the time to throttle Redden with his own hands. Later he could give way to his consuming grief.

'Good.' Devaux was non-stop talk, determined to leave Goodman no time for morbid thoughts. 'We'll be safer on the water in this boat. She can outrun anythin' around. But, my car, if we go in her, she'll be overtook by just about every other car on the island. We'll take all these shooters and walk the last bit to the Hatteras. All right? You happy with ol' Johnny's plan?'

Goodman murmured his assent. He did not look back after they had arranged the bodies against discovery and predation.

The tide was on the turn and the cigarette boat proved difficult, even with Devaux's considerable strength, to prise clear of the sand. The late-afternoon heat was still oppressive and both men were relieved when the three Mercury outboards roared to life. Devaux swung the wheel to head west. They kept their speed to thirty knots and carefully scanned the water ahead for other boats. Within ten minutes Devaux was pointing over the windscreen. 'The canal mouth,' he shouted. 'Check the weapons. They may have somebody at the entrance.'

'There's a boat to the west of the mouth,' Goodman yelled. Devaux squinted along the coastline and his mouth pursed in a silent whistle.

'Yowie, Alex. We got ourselves a race to the canal.' He yanked at the throttles and Goodman's fists tightened around the steel safety bar.

The other craft appeared simultaneously to alter course and surge forward at a new angle.

'Check the radio.'

Goodman pressed one of the headphones against his ear and heard repeated calls. 'Two Charlie. Two Charlie. Do you read? Come in, Two Charlie.'

'Alex, can you make like a Latino?' Devaux asked.

Goodman nodded and clicked the pressel on the speaker. 'Two Charlie. OK. Radio trouble. We check big canal now. Out.'

'Two Charlie,' came the instant response. 'Negative. Proceed back to Xanadu. *We* check canal. Over.'

Goodman looked at Devaux for guidance.

'Too bad!' Devaux's chin thrust forward. The throttles were flat down and the canal mouth was a fast-approaching blur. The other boat, which had decelerated during the radio call, now surged ahead again but too late. Devaux reached the canal at fifty knots and 300 yards in the lead. His confused backwash slowed the other boat to a comparative crawl. The boom of their own Mercurys now crashed back from the concrete banks of the canal.

They decelerated to some twenty knots and passed by the rusty stumps where once a bridge had been planned to take Midshipman Road traffic over the canal. A thousand yards further north, and with no warning, a blue cigarette boat shot out of a hidden embayment in the canal wall. Bullets crackled over Goodman's head and shattered the windscreen. Devaux's reaction was immediate. 'Jump,' he screamed at Goodman. They tumbled backwards into their wash and, surfacing, swam to the far bank twenty yards away. As they dragged themselves on to the bank their attackers narrowly avoided collision with the runaway boat. Weapons at the ready, Redden's men rode the madly bucking canal waters and scanned the waves for targets.

Thick undergrowth reached to within four yards of the bank. Devaux snaked his way up and into the brush, followed by Goodman. Neither was now armed.

'They goin' to hunt for us. They'll get all the others down here by radio as soon as they find we're not drowned.' Devaux's breath was coming in gasps but his brain was still in top gear. 'We got to split up. I'll lead them a dance. Set some false trails. Give you a chance. You know my number but don't call for at least twenty-four hours. Good luck, man.'

'How long to Redden's boat from here . . . Walking?'

'Just follow the bank north but keep in the bush in case they put watchers out. They don't know we found the Hatteras, so they can't be sure where you're headin', but be careful. Keep on the west bank as far as the Casuarina Bridge; that's maybe six miles. Walk slow. The bush is hot as hell. After the bridge, cross east and follow the route we took in the car. You ain't in no good position to attack anybody, Alex, but if I can get help in time I'll be waitin' for you at Doverstown View Point, Observation Hill – that's the slag-heap we watched the Hatteras from. So check there before you do anythin' stupid.'

Devaux slipped away and Goodman found an animal trail winding mostly north. The air in the brush was deathly still and stifling. After twenty minutes he came to a part-overgrown tarmac space around a derelict hotel. Somebody had vandalised the nine-storey concrete hulk. Fire appliances, doors, shutters and lights, all were ripped out and a battered van had been abandoned in the reception hall.

Goodman froze at the sound of gravel crunching. Cars were pulling up outside the hotel. Dozens of turkey-neck vultures rose from the roof, screaming at the intrusion, and Goodman slipped out of the far side of the building, past a cracked swimming pool empty but for another wrecked car. After negotiating more bush and swimming across a branch canal, he entered thick scrub cut from time to time by long-deserted driveways. The ground was littered with sharp rocks of Miami oolite, a limestone carbonate.

Remembering Devaux's warning, Goodman took his time to avoid dehydration from the oppressive heat. Sweat drenched him nonetheless. Once the hotel was well behind him he heard no further human sounds. Flies hummed and stung, as did the ants whenever he sat down to rest. A large hairy spider once ran over his ankle but there were no mosquitoes.

As he grew tired so the terrain seemed to deteriorate. He tripped over roots and, inspecting his foot for damage, smelled the foul stench of stinking pea. Mary had warned him and Sara of danger from touching foliage in the island forests. 'Shrubs,' she had said, 'called touch-me-not have hairs that sting, poison wood is every-where and will give you an itchy rash for days and the manchineel tree has deadly fruit and poison sap that will blister your skin like acid.'

Since Goodman had no idea what any of these trees looked like, he stumbled on through the thick bush hoping for the best. Two cars were parked close to the approach to the Casuarina Bridge, the only road crossing over the canal, so Goodman gave the place a wide berth and swam the canal a mile to the north, drinking the salt water greedily, for his throat was parched. He had seen a film advising against the practice but it tasted fine.

For two hours he wandered, lost, between a maze of branching canals and lonely plots until at last he found the Grand Bahama Highway and dragged himself along the route suggested by Devaux towards the northern end of the canal. Four cars passed by and each returned soon afterwards. Goodman hid at the sound of every approaching motor.

The shadows slowly lengthened and the cicadas set up their pre-dusk chakker. Goodman felt faint with thirst and knew he must drink fresh water and rest before finding the Hatteras. A side-road led him to an isolated farm on the edge of the northern swash-lands. No dog barked but cattle bellowed from a ramshackle shed and, as Goodman watched, an old bus clattered past with six or seven cattle workers returning home.

The sun dipped below the rim of the forest as Goodman peered into the cowshed. A solitary Haitian was milking a hundred Holstein cows. Goodman pictured ice-cool milk. He moved to the adjoining building, a warehouse with crates of bottled fruit juice. Empty milk-bottle crates were stashed along one wall. Milk and juice. Goodman remembered that one of the Browns' main suppliers, back in Leominster, had used his milk-bottling machinery to mix fruit concentrates with sugar whenever there was no milk in the system. At the end of the warehouse Goodman came to a single door to the farm office, where a young white man in shorts worked at a desk with a telephone held to his ear. His accent was clearly French.

'No, I'm alone except for Jackson, who's milking. My brother Frederick is in town with the lovely Natalie. It's been bad for days now, the generators. Something to do with the cooler cut-off and it's very hot out here as you can imagine . . . Yes. Good. I look forward to it. See you soon after 10.30 p.m. Two hours' time.'

Goodman clasped his hands in the praying mode to indicate non-aggression and appeared at the side of the Frenchman's desk.

'Good evening,' he said, but the sound from his parched throat came out like a croak.

Twenty-four-year-old Louis Ossude ran the only cattle farm on the island. He supplied a growing fraction of Freeport's dairy requirements and worked like a slave. He was often bothered by lost tourists during the season but seldom in July and never so late in the evening. This one looked sunburnt and very dishevelled.

'Hallo. How can I help you?'

'I'd be very grateful for a drink and just a short rest.' As he spoke he saw the movement of lights against the glass of the office

443

window. A car approaching along the gravel drive. Goodman ducked instinctively and hissed at the Frenchman. 'Please, can you hide me? Men are trying to kill me. Criminals from Colombia.'

The young farmer's mouth split into a wide grin. 'You are English?'

'Welsh.'

'Same difference. You are James Bond, I think. Of course you may hide here. Go back into the warehouse. You will find plenty to drink. Plastic tops, so you won't need a bottle opener . . . My name is Louis.' They shook hands and Goodman, crouching low, disappeared into the warehouse. He heard muted conversation between the visitors and Louis. After ten minutes the Frenchman came to fetch him, proffering a refrigerator-cooled orange juice.

'Your friends have gone. Big limo with shiny hubs and tinted windows,' he said. 'They looked bad types to me. Latinos and not local. All taxis have GB plates, duty-paid cars have blue and yellow plates and rented cars, like theirs, have white SD plates. I told them no Europeans or locals have been out this way for days except my family and the staff. They said they were CID and that a dangerous mugger was known to be about. *C'est complètement absurde. Des bêtises.* The only policeman who has ever come out here is Big Charles and he has an old Chevy with a blue light.'

'Do you think they saw me?'

'I cannot say but they seemed content. Tell me. Are you a dangerous Welsh mugger? I have to say you have a deceitfully harmless look about you!'

'I am not a criminal but I am in trouble if those people catch me.'

'Look. I have been mugged out here twice. You look OK to me. Let me give you a lift to town. To the police, if you like. I will be maybe an hour then I must take my foreman there anyway and see some friends for a drink. OK?'

'You are very kind but I'd prefer just to rest here a while. I'll go when you go if that's all right.'

Louis shrugged. 'Sure. *Ça va*, but it's a long, hot walk to town. You know France?'

'I wish I did.' Goodman accepted two further bottles of Sundance orange juice with gratitude.

'My family come from Gien on the Loire. We have farmed there for years. *Comme le jour et la nuit*, chalk and cheese to this place, I tell you. Here we had to haul up every tree, every root. The land is salty from flood. All the crops' – he waved at the darkness outside – 'that is Floridian alfalfa. All the hay comes compressed from Idaho.' He rubbed thumb and forefinger together and kissed the air. 'Very expensive.'

Goodman could sense the Frenchman would like to have conversed over a beer or a milk. It must be a lonely existence. But he craved for sleep; even if only for a half hour's catnap.

'*Bien!*' Louis noted Goodman's wilting eyelids. 'You sleep in here – in case they come back. I will go finish my business.'

In what seemed like a moment, Goodman found himself being gently shaken awake.

'Sorry, friend, but I have to lock up now.' Louis held out his hand. 'I wish you good luck whatever your problem. Maybe we'll meet up.' He joined his Haitian foreman and drove off in his Chevy.

The smell of the cattle lingered in Goodman's nostrils and the night was deathly quiet as he trudged west to Observation Hill. Devaux was not there. Goodman stared out at the starlit ocean. He could hear Sara's voice whisper the words of the Paraskara: 'Let us see, hear and live a hundred autumns, O beloved.' He saw their faces clearly, his wives' and his daughters', and his hatred was as pure, as undiluted as his love for them had been. He turned, his weariness forgotten, and headed for the canal and the Hatteras anchored there, past the hills of oolite.

445

32

July 1992

Goodman felt the blood on his fingers. He had scratched the mole on his shoulder without thinking as he lay in the scrub overlooking the Hatteras. He remembered the concern in Sara's eyes when she had first touched the growth.

Devaux was nowhere to be seen. Goodman had wandered about the hillocks of Observation Hill and down to the sea mouth of the canal. Waiting impatiently beneath the spread of a royal coconut palm, he had contemplated sneaking aboard the boat by himself but he had retained enough perspective to appreciate the pointlessness of confronting Redden and his staff unarmed. He was bent on a mission of justice not suicide. But what if Redden's men had found Devaux? Then he could wait here for ever for all the good it would do him. Not long before midnight he heard the resonant drone of outboard engines approaching from the south. The sound grew to a roar, as of heavy bombers overhead, then ceased abruptly and the echoes of shouts came to Goodman from beyond the oolite mounds.

He rose and stretched away his stiffness. Now was the time to move in, armed or not, while noise and commotion surrounded the Hatteras.

He walked fast, bending down whenever the quarter moon raced clear of the scudding clouds. The superstructure of the tuna boat served as a homing guide and enabled Goodman to approach the mooring unobserved, using the scant available cover to reach the very banks of Redden's cove, Discovery Bay. On his belly he crawled to within thirty yards of the boat but still could not quite pick up the heated conversation between the four or five silhouetted figures on board. He took his shoes off, eased his body into the warm canal waters and swam quietly into the darkness between the bank and the bulk of the Hatteras. Two cigarette boats, glinting their sleek menace, were moored alongside the bigger craft. The conversation on board was now clearly audible.

'We have the Goodmans' maid.' The speaker, Goodman guessed, was a Latino, for his accent was that of the men at the picnic beach. 'She know nothing but she show us the new place they move into. She say they will come back there soon. She think maybe they go camping for tonight only.'

'So?' The voice was guttural. Redden maybe.

'So we left Rico there. In their new flat.'

'And you say the men had searched everywhere, *den ganzen Insel*, every hotel, restaurant, pension?'

Silence. Goodman had hold of a mooring rope. The water dripped from his hair and he pocketed his spectacles. He had no specific plan.

'The more time he has' – Redden again – 'the greater the chance that we lose him. You must find him tonight. I will double the reward for you all. Cover everywhere. Jonas, you know the local boys. Get word out. Fifty thousand dollars for the man who brings Goodman in. *Geh jetzt.*'

'And you, sir?'

'I will remain with the radio here. Keep in permanent contact.'

'Who shall stay with you? With respect, Ko is only cook. I should leave two of the men with you.'

'I said go, Jonas. I will look after myself, *ney*?'

Goodman ducked low as the cigarette boat crews re-embarked. For a while their wash crashed back and forth between the banks dunking Goodman. His mind raced. There would never be a better time. Only one cook on the boat with Redden. He tore off his shirt, replaced his spectacles after shaking them dry, and crept aboard the Hatteras while the subsiding sounds of the swell and the fading boom of outboards masked the pad of his bare feet on the decking.

What would Tosh do in his position? Go for the line of least resistance. Deceive. Separate your moves. Act only from power. If only she was here now. Or Devaux, for that matter. The soles of his feet were dry now. He squeezed and rolled up the bottoms of his

447

sodden trousers. At the base of the small open gangway, a choice of routes, fore or aft? He smelt toast. The galley. The companionway walls were lined with framed sport-fishing photographs and great six-inch fish hooks pinned to teak plaques with, beneath each one, a printed label with the dimensions of the leviathan hooked by its barb. Goodman forced one such hook from its fastening and advanced silently to the galley.

The cook was thumbing through a motor magazine, one of many on a tiny shelf beside the galley's work surface.

'Ko, come up. And bring *kaffee*.' Redden's voice sounded through an intercom speaker and Goodman, *à la* Tosh, acted at once. Before the cook could close the magazine, he kicked his face as though it were a football back at school in Herefordshire. His foot slammed into the base of Ko's nose. The reward for this attempt at karate was a stabbing pain as though at least four of his toes had been ripped off. However, the ageing Filipino cook dropped back on his bed as though poleaxed. Tosh would have been proud of him.

For two minutes Goodman, on the galley floor, rocked about, holding his foot, until the pain subsided. Then he lashed the cook's hands behind his back using the plastic-coated line on which the galley dishcloths were drying.

He found a bread knife with a serrated blade and placed it on a tea tray. Then he boiled water and filled a mug and a milk jug. The tray clinked as he approached the stateroom. The door was held open on a spring clasp. Redden, in smart white shorts and shirt, was bending over a radio console. An unusually well-preserved physique for a man in his sixties, Goodman noted; lean and well-muscled.

Redden, from the corner of his eye, saw the outline of a man with a tray as expected. During the brief seconds it took his brain to register the slight differences in silhouette and movement style between the expected figure of Ko and the present bringer of tea, Goodman had closed the gap. As Redden, in instant response to the sudden danger signals, lunged for his Luger on the console table, Goodman flung the boiling water at his face, dropped the tray and, with a clean horizontal thrust of his left hand, stabbed the carving knife into Redden's kidneys at the point where shorts met shirt.

As Redden subsided across the console, he raised the Luger. Goodman's right hand, grasping the pencil-thick, steel shaft of the

448

shark hook, swung at the pistol and the barb tore into the tendons of Redden's hand.

The automatic clattered to the floor as Redden slumped backwards into the absent radio operator's swivel seat. His face registered neither pain nor surprise, merely a look of what Goodman took to be regret. A dark stain mushroomed down Redden's crisp white shorts.

This has taken me eight years, Goodman thought, his breathing gradually returning to normal. If only this act of Redden's dying could be prolonged and the viewing of it replayed, video-like, as a salve to the misery of his memories.

Goodman grasped Redden's head and pulled his face close. 'You murdered my wife and my little daughter in 1984 and again today. I will never forgive you. May your soul rot in hell for ever.'

He wanted to say more but a growing sense of revulsion made him fling Redden's head backwards and wipe his hands on his trousers to scour off the feel of the snake-like skin.

Redden's eyes bored into Goodman and he whispered, coughing a dribble of blood from the side of his mouth. His fingers curled in a beckoning sign and something in the set of his face made Goodman crane forward to listen.

'My men will kill you for this . . . You have wasted your time . . . *We* never touched your wife, your daughter . . . One of the drivers, an addict – he went back later to steal . . . for money . . . Whatever was done, he did alone.'

'You are lying,' Goodman hissed. 'You have crushed the life from everything that was ever precious to me.'

Again Redden gestured but his fingers barely moved. The coughing increased, followed by spasms and death. The cold blue eyes continued to stare across the cabin and a crisp voice came loud over the speaker. Goodman started back as though jolted.

'Jonas. Jonas here for Tuna. Over.' The call was urgently repeated and continued as Goodman left the boat and limped back to Observation Hill.

Devaux appeared around 3 a.m. with his arm in a sling. Four men – he assumed them to be a part of Redden's search groups – had been waiting at his flat. He had escaped with a single bullet wound but, unable to find his gangster acquaintances, decided to come back with two shotguns borrowed from a friend. This, he felt, would be better than nothing at all. When Goodman told him of his lone attack on the Hatteras, Devaux pounded his back, obviously surprised and impressed.

'You are a great man, Alex. But now we must move very quickly. When they find what you have done, they may put the island authorities on to you. Tell me, what do you want now?'

'England.' Goodman did not hesitate. 'I must go back there. But first I must phone my friends in London.'

They drove to Eight Mile Rock, where a friend of Devaux had agreed to hide Goodman for as long as necessary. Devaux went off to check all was well with Mary since she was unobtainable by phone. Goodman called The Home at Peckham and was surprised when there was no reply. For as long as he could remember there had always been someone on duty. There had to be, twenty-four hours a day, because of the cooler clients. He called London telephone enquiries, who confirmed the number was trouble-free and with no notified change of owner. So Goodman called Lee Troon, who agreed to check on The Family.

Devaux returned a worried man. Mary had disappeared. Her son, a fifteen-year-old layabout, said he had not seen her since the previous morning and she had left him no note. He had no idea where she could be. 'I think Redden's people have taken her,' Devaux said. 'You must not go back to Jensen Court. I will try to have your kit collected and brought here. Now I will arrange your travel from Freeport.'

That night they drove to Gold Rock Beach with a spade and pickaxe. They needed four hours to dig a grave six foot deep and five foot long in the rocky earth between the beach and the mangrove creek. Devaux had brought a sheet and a blanket. He retrieved Sara and Jyoti from the shallow scoop beneath the casuarinas. Already the furnace heat of the previous day had caused corruption but he wrapped both bodies in the covers so that Goodman would have no unpleasant last memories.

'She would have preferred cremation,' Goodman murmured.

Devaux shrugged and glanced skywards. 'I think she is happy up there. They are together. Only empty bodies down here now.'

'I agree, Johnny, but I have read a lot of Sara's Hindu booklets. We should have faced them to the north, on a stone *kunda* platform, and built a fire about them of wood primed with ghee . . . I will say the prayer she taught me for them both.'

The two men lowered the shrouded bodies gently into the grave and then stood back thinking their thoughts. The woods and the mangroves were silent but for the lapping scrape of waves on the nearby beach. The stars slid by as they had five hundred years before when the Conquistadors murdered the gentle Lucayan islanders on this same lovely beach: as indeed they had at the death of every human being since the beginning of Life. If stars had feelings, Goodman thought, they would scream for ever.

'O Sara and Jyoti,' Goodman said in a low, clear voice, 'may the power of your sight be absorbed in the sun, your soul into the atmosphere; may you go to the luminous region or to the earth or to the waters. Go in peace. I always will love you.'

They marked the site with a cross of white stones and, when Goodman dallied, loath to go, Devaux put gentle pressure on his shoulder. 'Time is short, Alex. You leave before dawn.'

On the way back to Freeport, Devaux explained his plans.

'They are watchin' the Seascape Ferry and the airport. They will know you are alone now and Mary will have described you to them, poor girl. You must fool them by going out as part of a group. I have fixed a disguise for you. Mary may have told them the name on your passport, so you must go out with a new one. They may know the details of this car, so time is vital. The island is too small to keep you hidden while we get Ah Troon to fix a new identity.'

'I agree, Johnny, but how the hell can you arrange what's necessary without his help?'

Devaux laid his finger against one nostril and winked. 'I done it before with a big cocaine guy they were watchin' the airport for. No problem! A British businessman called Freddie Laker lives on a boat in Xanadu marina. He has nightly return flights from New Orleans. Calls them junket flights. We'll get you out on one.'

Devaux explained that, back in the sixties, when the fledgling Freeport was desperate for dollars, the Port Authority had opted to build a casino, the Lucayan Beach Hotel, and to keep it 'clean' by staffing it only with British citizens. This proved impossible since no British citizens were expert at the three key games of roulette, blackjack and craps. As a result the Port Authority had hired American professionals, men with white socks, Gucci loafers and darting black eyes, men from Cosa Nostra specialising in crooked games.

By the 1970s the Port Authority had managed to replace these gangsters but, in order to make the casinos pay, they encouraged junkets or package groups of heavy gamblers willing to chance hundreds of thousands of dollars in a single night. These big-time players were enticed to Freeport's casinos by offers of free flights and accommodation.

By the nineties Freddie Laker had put together Laker Airways, which targeted well-off but less ambitious junketeers. He flew them out of New Orleans by the plane-load, normally hitting Freeport at 9 p.m. and flying back out around 5 a.m.

'There's two junkets leaving Freeport at 4.30 a.m.,' Devaux said. 'That gives us four hours. Now I need $4000, Alex. That's what it's cost me in bribes. All your luggage will be flown to Ah Troon, care of Taino Air. No baggage checks. No ownership proof required.'

'When?'

'It's already there. It went six hours ago.'

'That's wonderful. You're amazing, Johnny.'

'Thank the island's system,' said Devaux with a rueful smile.

'And me?'

'You will join Laker's second junket group back to New Orleans. You will have spent a happy night throwing your money away at The Princess. Don't forget that.'

'Under my name?'

'Of course not. Just before the flight boards, we'll give you a passport whose owner looks like you – vaguely. I have friends at The Princess too. They will introduce a very beautiful Bahamian girl to the chosen junketeer. He will be harmlessly drugged, lose his passport and miss his flight back to the US. At the airport you'll receive Customs Pre-clearance so you'll get no hassle in New Orleans. After that where will you go? Ah Troon in Miami?'

Goodman made a non-committal noise. He was learning the need-to-know principle. He wrote Devaux a cheque for the bribes and added a generous amount for himself and for Mary.

'Will she be OK?'

'When you're gone, I will do nothing but search for her. If necessary the Troons will come from Miami. Don't worry. We will find her.'

At 3.30 a.m., clad in lime-green fluorescent baggy shorts, matching shirt and red 'I Love Freeport' baseball cap, Goodman joined the chaos of junketeers debussing outside the Freeport Airport Departures Terminal. He clutched his newly acquired passport and passed quickly through Pre-clearance. Three police-men and two suited civilians, wearing dark glasses despite the fluorescent lights of the waiting lounge, stood watching each new arrival. Goodman had no way of knowing whether this was standard procedure. He studied the ancient *Newsweek* which Devaux had thoughtfully given him. The voice of one of the two civilian watchers came clearly to him as they walked slowly down the line of seats. He froze with apprehension for he had heard the man before; the same cold, curt tones, at the mooring bay of the Hatteras the previous night, speaking to Redden.

An age passed, or so it seemed to Goodman, before the flight was called and he joined the long shuffle to the gate. Redden's man and a police officer stood beside the lady checking the junketeers' names. Goodman sweated but, when his turn came, they checked only his name, not 'his' photograph. He would be OK now; at least until the drugged junketeer reported his passport missing. By then Goodman should be clear of New Orleans and using his Troon identity. He offered a silent prayer of thanks for Johnny Devaux.

From Miami, Goodman called Ah Troon and was given a message from Lee Troon in London. As yet nobody knew why but neither Sailor nor any other Family member was anywhere to be found. They had disappeared from the face of their known haunts. The agents they used for the cooler business had been told to send no further clients. James had called Lee Troon some weeks back sounding distracted but merely saying there was a problem which nobody could yet help them with. He would be in touch. Not a word from Sailor himself. Lee was mystified. If help was needed Goodman had only to call.

He took the next available flight to Heathrow and then a taxi direct to the Peckham Home. He let himself in. Somebody had ransacked every room, even torn up the floorboards, but, as Lee had advised, no clues had been left suggesting The Family's new whereabouts.

Goodman settled into his old room and reopened his London

bank account. Some hours after arrival his skin began to itch and red, suppurating blisters appeared all over his hands and forearms. Within a week they were gone, so he assumed he had brushed against poisonous leaves in the Grand Bahamian taiga. Before he made any move on Blackledge or Mafia, he resolved to locate The Family. He tried all Sailor's contacts with whom he'd done lab business and finally struck gold with Sonny Guha. He traced him through his mother, who still lived close to Woodberry Down.

Guha had fallen on hard times. His lab in Green Lanes had run on for a while after the fire-bombing but the local council, prompted by the staff of the trade union headquarters opposite, had targeted 'The House' and evicted Sonny along with his squatter clients before boarding up and then demolishing the entire building. Guha had lost favour with his Asian bosses and resorted now to small-time shoplifting and burglary. None the less he greeted Goodman with warmth and promises of 'whatever you need'.

'I'm OK for funds, Sonny. It's Sailor and the others I'm after. I went abroad for a few months and came back three weeks ago only to find they'd all disappeared. I was hoping you might have an idea where they'd gone and why.'

Guha stared at him. 'You've not heard?' He looked at his hands. His fingers entwined and wriggled together like worms. 'Look, I know where James is. He came here last week. But he's frightened. Doesn't want anyone knowing his current address.'

Goodman was excited. 'Wonderful, Sonny. You can tell me. You know I'm his friend. Thank God . . . I thought maybe he had died.'

'No. He looked fine. But . . . there has been . . . bad news. He'll tell you.' Guha tore a page from a tabloid and scribbled an address for Goodman, who left in a hurry.

The Highbury Hotel, in Highbury Grove, not far away, was not the most salubrious of residences but there was much happiness and relief on the faces and in the hearts of both James and Goodman when they met in room 30. James clasped Goodman's hands as he murmured his words of sympathy. Each man had lost those who meant most to him. They were both short of friends and bereft of love.

James sat on the bed. The room was simple but clean. Goodman joined him.

'It's Sailor, isn't it?' he asked quietly. 'Something's happened.'

James nodded. 'The Lord giveth and the Lord taketh away. Sailor was my brother and my friend. He was brave as a lion. You know that. They hurt him bad before they kill him. Then they kill Tosh. Now there is only me and Columbo. We knew you would come for us. I told Sonny but no one else, because things are very bad. The others are after us now. After you and all of us.'

'The others?'

'They are different. Government boys. Maybe American. Official people. Not like the devils of Mafia who killed Sailor and Tosh.'

Goodman broke down then. His grief flooded out and he sobbed uncontrollably. James laid a hand across his back. At least they had each other. Later, when the wave of sorrow and loss receded, they sat in silence.

'Why do you do that?' James asked when Goodman shrugged awkwardly at his jacket as though attempting to unseat a wasp from his shoulder.

'I have a sort of mole on my back. It bleeds and itches much of the time. Sara told me I should have it looked at.'

'Perhaps you should. Dr Khimji would be happy to give you a free opinion.'

'OK, I'll call him. But my trouble's in here.' Goodman tapped the side of his head. 'Two men are living free and enjoying themselves who should be locked away for life. I'm talking about Mafia and Blackledge. If I have a cancer that needs excision . . . it's them.'

'Mafia must die.' The kindly face of James was distorted. 'I will be glad to shoot him. But he's gone, you know. He's livin' full time in JA now.'

'Do you know where?'

'No, but I could find out. Sailor and I have close relatives there still.'

'James, my friend, I should be the executioner of Mafia. I have four murders to avenge. You have just two.'

'Alex.' James stood, moved to the linoleum of the passageway and performed a quick but skilful tap-dance routine. 'There are things you cannot do any more than I could understand your BCCI accountin' systems. If you go to Jamaica and try to move in on Mafia, you will surely die. I would fare little better and I am a black Jamaican. Believe me. You could not move without the eyes in the Yard walls identifyin' you and your motives. Brother will tell brother. The voodoo line. Allies to your face will be married to cousins of enemies and both sides will smile as a man in dark glasses guns you down.'

'I will take that risk. I have nothing to live for.'

'Please yourself but, number one, you are my friend and I don't want to lose you as well. Number two, it would achieve nothin', so I would have to go out there anyway.'

'And Blackledge?'

James looked at the ceiling for a while, deep in thought. 'No,' he said at length. 'We Rastas live by the Old Testament and heed two of the Lord's sayin's when it comes to killin's. Thou shalt not kill except that an eye for an eye provides an exception. Mafia was behind the killin' of my brother Sailor but Blackledge has caused me no bereavement. I will help you every other way, Alex, but I cannot be involved with the death of Blackledge.'

'I understand. Forgive me for asking.'

'All our funds are gone. As you know, when the labs closed, The Family started to run at a loss. The coolers kept us tickin' but only just. Art left us for the States; he was gettin' restless. I can't tell you who owns Sailor's London properties because they were loaned him in confidence and on condition the coolers were operated for drug-withdrawal work. Last month the lawyers gave me eight weeks to vacate the Peckham Home. You shouldn't go there anyway. Too dangerous. But what I'm sayin' is, Alex, there's no Family caboosh and we'll need five grand for Mafia.'

'No problem. My savings are still substantial even though I'm living off them. Also I have the CIA papers. The Hoover documents alone could fetch a big payment.'

'Don't count on that, man.' James waved a warning finger. 'You don't know where to "advertise" them for sale. And if you do, you'll get nothin' but trouble, surely as the Lord's risen. These boys as turned the Home upside down, maybe they were after these papers of yours.'

Goodman considered this. 'James, finding you is the one good thing in my life these past weeks. But we must find a quieter place than this hotel. I will set about that through Sonny Guha and I'll get cash from my bank immediately for your work to trace Mafia.'

'I will need to go to JA myself,' James thought aloud, 'and while

I'm out back-a-Yard I'll need phone contact. If you're goin' to get us a place, make sure it has communications.'

Heartened by their very togetherness, they embraced, then Goodman took his leave.

The following day Dr Khimji looked at the ulcerating mole on Goodman's back.

'Been sunbathing?' was his first question.

'A bit.' Goodman sounded defensive. 'I was in the Caribbean for a few months. Everybody sunbathes there.'

'Well, everybody shouldn't,' was the stern response. Khimji was never one for tact nor the softening of an ominous diagnosis. 'You have here a naevus, a pigmented mole, which may, if excised at once, give no further trouble. However, Mr Goodman, you must be warned that this tumour may already have spawned invasive cancers which available therapy may not be able to destroy.'

'What would excision involve?'

'I will arrange with a surgeon friend, who has reason to be grateful to The Family, to operate this week. Tomorrow if possible. A quick and simple process. Minimal time in bed. Then you must hope for the best. Tell me, was there always a mole there?'

'Yes, but smaller and no trouble.'

The doctor nodded. 'I thought as much. Your old naevus must have degenerated into a malignant form, probably catalysed by the big dose of UV radiation you gave it in the Caribbean.'

'If it has spread,' Goodman asked, 'can I expect to live for weeks or years . . . or what?'

'Impossible to answer that. You could survive for months only but some individuals live on for nine or ten years. Right now forget everything except getting the lesion excised.'

In the event, Goodman recovered quickly from the minor surgery and met up with Sonny Guha. He explained that he and James needed cheap and anonymous accommodation, preferably in Peckham, where James had friends.

'How are you fixed right now?' Guha queried.

'I'm still at the Home but too many people know about the place and it has already been raided. That's why James went to the Highbury Hotel.'

'How much does he pay there?'

'He doesn't. He just dropped in at their reception and gave them his UB40 and Housing Benefit forms. The DHSS pay the hotel £90 a week for him. He says several prostitutes use rooms that way and the government pays for their keep. Breakfast included.'

'How much are the two of you willing to pay?'

'How much are you thinking of?' Goodman had thought he trusted Guha, but now he realised he trusted nobody. Only James.

Guha tapped his knee thoughtfully. 'Well, Kilburn's good at present.'

'No good geographically, Sonny. We need a South London base. Like I say, Peckham would be best.'

'Shuggy may be able to sort somethin' out for you down that way. He specialises in unlet council flats. Thirty-five quid a week all in. OK?'

'Sounds good.'

They met Shuggy at The Finsbury Park Tavern, where the stocky Glaswegian lounged by a pool table, his hair spivved back, his eyeballs protruding like those of a startled rabbit and his jowls black with stubble. He listened to Guha.

'No problem. My pal Keith'll sort you out. But I'll need 120 smackers up front. That's for the first month, d'ye ken. Plus cash for the new lock and keys.'

They agreed to look at the giant estate blocks in North Peckham. Not the usual haunts of Shuggy and his mate Keith, but their system worked equally well on any housing estate where the authorities had lost control over the inmates. In fact flats in the Peckham area were being sublet so quickly and easily that they were being advertised daily in Lagos newspapers.

Keith, Guha had explained to Goodman, sussed out target sites by scouting along walkways by night and noting windows, usually on the upper, less popular floors, where there were never lights and, often, no curtains. Then he would knock at the relevant flat's door, ready to offer Hoover sales if someone answered. Once sure of no occupants, he would 'loid' back the catch of the old Yale lock with a strap of heavy celluloid cut from a two-litre lemonade bottle. Once inside, Keith would unscrew the lock's housing until the key-barrel popped out. This he would replace with one bought from a Yale locksmith. He and Shuggy were thenceforward the landlords. They always left matchsticks between the entry door and its frame on the hinge side to warn them if anyone else had entered in their absence.

Goodman paid Shuggy and, a week later, he and James moved into the Winchcombe Court block on the Gloucester Grove Estate. Not a wall inside or out but was sprayed with crude graffiti. 'Thirty quid a week!' James breathed. 'This place ain't fit for a tramp.' Their flat was on the fourth floor but the only nearby lift was out of order. Sailor had long since bequeathed the Home's furnishings to his brother and Goodman wondered how on earth they would move anything bigger than a chair into this place. Although interlocking walkways led from estate to estate for nearly two miles – a gift for criminals – safe parking facilities were non-existent.

The flat's previous occupants had owned a dog or dogs who had obviously never heard the word 'walkies'. The windows were jammed but the two men's joint body weight forced one open. They bought Ajax and swabs but agreed not to move in until the foul odour had gone.

James shook his head. 'You could start a guano factory. How could any folk live like this? And kids too by the look of it.' They found soiled nappies and human excrement in the bathroom and quickly traced the failed plumbing to a furred-up ballcock.

In the stairwell, off an ill-lit walkway close to their front door, they stepped over used hypodermic needles, condoms, more excreta and slivers of Kit-Kat foil paper blackened with the dribble lines of burnt heroin. James pointed to a sunlit corner where the floor was wet with the contents of somebody's bowels and fresh blood sprayed the concrete walls and ceiling. 'When they use heroin and crack,' James explained, 'they sometimes evacuate their bowels rapido. When they shove the needle into a main artery, it looks like a slaughterhouse. Used to happen in the coolers when they managed to smuggle the goods in past Tosh.'

'Watch those needles, James,' Goodman murmured. 'You don't want Aids.'

'Think of all the little kiddies as get brought up here,' James muttered. 'These bastards fling their needles about and innocent little kids play "doctors and nurses" with them. Alexo, man, you got us into a right jungle. Still it's cheap and anonymous. I can't argue with that.'

Guha helped James by getting him part-time employment as a cash-only minicab driver. At a Deptford Motor Auction sale they had bought a used banger for £400 and Guha called them whenever

459

he had a rushed client he couldn't or wouldn't supply but needed to get off his back. For £5 James would provide return transport between Peckham and Five Ways in Brixton, a street location turning over £500,000 in drugs daily. James, a proud man, would not consider living off Goodman or anyone else.

A cousin, with whose father James had grown up in St Andrews, Jamaica, was due at Gatwick on 13 September; a man with a history of political contract killings to his credit. James intended to hire him as Mafia's executioner and took half of Goodman's £5000 to Gatwick by way of up-front payment. He spent two hours waiting at Arrivals after the plane's announced landing but nobody appeared.

A week later Columbo's old friend, still working on the police HOLMES computer and responding to encouragement in the form of Goodman's cash, revealed that James's cousin had been arrested at Gatwick with £43,000 of cocaine hidden in small bags of nutmegs. The two halves of each nutshell had been skilfully glued together and the consignment was awaited by an international Yardie named Andy B. James was back at square one, with no other known contract killers in his address book. Using an unknown contract man could be as dangerous as firing a gun with a rusty barrel.

Standard Yardie practice was often to hire killers in Jamaica to knock off rivals in the UK and vice versa. The killer could return 'home' immediately after completing his contract and stand a lesser risk of pick-up by the police plus a better chance of avoiding snitches. Knowing nobody suitable in England, James made up his mind to return to Jamaica immediately, stay with relatives and, treading softly, set up a contract on Mafia after he had located him. Further tips from the HOLMES computer indicated that one of Mafia's eight children, a Clapham-based teenage daughter, was one of many mules running drugs between Kingston and London on a regular basis for her father. A fortnight later HOLMES divulged that Mafia was thought to have set up shop in Jamaica's second city, Mandeville, sixty miles west of Kingston, and his lieutenant, Kingston Williams, was expanding his boss's fiefdom in the local cocaine trade.

James, steeped in HOLMES-sourced information, left England and after visiting relatives and friends in St Andrews found a cheap bedsit in Mandeville where he based himself, telling his landlady he was on holiday from the UK and revisiting the place of his birth for the first time in fifty years.

James knew better than to ask direct questions about Mafia. He 'jawed the bone' in Mandeville pubs and discos. He dropped pebbles into conversations, watching where they would bounce, and in early November reaped gold dust. Mafia, using his real name, Stafford Douglas, had set up a jeep rental shop called Duggie's Car Hire as a business cover for his ongoing cocaine dealing. He had bought four Mandeville properties for rental and was building a palatial residence in exclusive Poinsettia Drive for himself and his wife Maureen. James took the bull by the horns and waited outside Duggie's Car Hire in Kingston Road until Mafia's Mercedes rolled on to the forecourt.

'He will almost certainly be hurting,' Goodman had advised James. 'He worked for Redden and Richter on a personal level. He reported direct and got his work direct. Their demise will have robbed him of a big part of his income and at a time when he's having to muscle in on the established JA drug scene. His expertise, his contacts, his scene, are all in the UK. Now he's got to start all over again in JA and it surely won't be easy. He'll need lots of money. Six hundred murders last year in Kingston alone. If he doesn't tread with care, somebody will do our work for us.'

James had based his own plans on the piranha-like behaviour of Jamaican dealers. A sign of weakness, of seeping blood, will turn the voracious pack in an instant on one of their own. He had more than enough money to carry out his first intention: to hire a local killer. But that method was fraught with danger. He knew of too many contractors being hit by boomerangs. What could happen was that the hired killer either ran off with his up-front cash, or, worse, squealed to the target and, in return for a larger sum, fingered the contractor, who in this case would be James.

So James had decided to avoid such risks by gathering his own intelligence on Mafia's current set-up, introducing himself and gaining Mafia's curiosity plus, ideally, his trust. HOLMES was the key. And the fact that, whereas he knew a good deal about Mafia, he was himself all but unknown in Jamaica.

Straightening his shirt, James walked into the foyer of Duggie's Car Hire. He told the receptionist he was interested in fleet rental.

Mafia saw him immediately and offered him a cool drink. James did not waste time.

'Mr Douglas . . .'

'Stafford.' Mafia lifted his hands. 'Call me Stafford.'

'Thank you. I am James. Stafford, I must tell you straight away I have no interest in jeeps. My expertise lies in the distribution of cocaine in the Peckham district of London. I know and respect your credentials in the UK and my colleagues have sent me to try to make a deal for trade.'

'James,' Mafia said, proffering a cigarette which James refused. 'I am flattered you come to me but how do I know your background? Maybe you are police. I have to say to you that I deal only in cars. I know nothin' of drugs in the UK or back-a-Yard.'

'Of course you don't, my friend.' James smiled. 'But there is no harm to either of us in your listenin' to my jaw. Then, if you wish to go to the local police about me, I will be arrested. You have good friends in Spanish Town. Very top policemen. They got you American contacts who gave you big work and big caboosh. But these Yanks are now dead . . .'

Mafia stood up, his face strained and tense.

'How do you know this, mister? Who are you with?'

'Stay calm, don't . . .' James's voice was soothing. 'I am on your side. I cannot say who informs me but you have no need to worry. If we wanted to put the police on you, we would do so.'

Mafia sat down. He was drawing heavily on his cigarette. James could sense his anxiety. For ten minutes he talked the scene back in Brixton, dazzling Mafia with hot gossip straight from HOLMES; exactly the sort of gold which, a year before, Mafia had himself been receiving from Goodman. Once Mafia was listening in silence, James sensed the timing was right.

'Stafford, I want one thing only: a reliable source of cocaine with reliable pricin' and a capable network of mules all the way to my people in Peckham. What do you say?'

Mafia sorted himself out. He would find out more about this old fellow later. Right now he could see the logic of seizing the golden opportunity apparently on offer. If this man and his backers had wanted to damage him, they could easily have done so. Since they had not, their motive was clearly to utilise his existing sources and network to fill their demand. If they had plans to take him over in due course, well that would be up to him to frustrate. Right now his best option was to go ahead and do business.

'OK, OK, my friend.' Mafia thrust out his hand. 'Sounds good. The Mandeville–Peckham Connection, eh?' They both chuckled and clasped hands.

'But Stafford,' James said with a frown, 'I also have a warnin' for you. They say your most senior friend in the Spanish Town police; him as got your business goin' back in the 80s. The word is that you have been pressin' too hard since you came back. This top policeman is not pleased with you. He's sayin', "Dis puppy think he is too big." The word is also that they may be wantin' to teach you a lesson. You know, keep you in line. I say this now only to warn you. We need to keep you healthy and fit, eh?' Again James chuckled and slapped the desk.

'Where are you stayin'?' Mafia asked.

James told him. 'I'll be there till I go back to the UK to report on our deal and to take a big first sample of your coke at a fair price.'

'How big?'

'Say a million dollars Yard price.'

Mafia nodded slowly, deep in thought. He looked pleased. 'Yeah, I see no problem. I will have to check out a few people, of course. Take maybe two, three weeks at most. OK?'

They shook hands again.

'I'll keep you informed, James.'

James went back to his lodgings a happy man. He would have liked to tell Goodman about his success but he trusted no telephone lines in Jamaica. The operators listened in. And he didn't know whether Mafia was merely acting. Any time now Mafia could simply send a hit man round. Perhaps he should change hotels. But no, he sensed that Mafia was hooked. James was an unknown factor but, for Mafia, a potential golden goose with big business opportunities and useful inside knowledge. Better kept alive surely.

James took his next step. He went to the police station in Spanish Town, Jamaica's third city, some ten miles west of Kingston and a den of corruption. He asked to see Inspector Mascel, the name recurring several times on the HOLMES Mafia file. He waited in the shabby waiting room crowded with the aimless and the shifty, the local sediment too poor to buy their way out of trouble. He steeled himself for the news that no Inspector Mascel existed, that he was dead or retired but, two hours after his arrival, a constable beckoned and led him to an office, dark with grime, with an officer behind a heavy desk; a senior rank judging by his insignia. This man is evil, James thought. He remembered Sailor a year back, returning from a visit to Kingston, saying: 'The worst villains work with the police. Jamaican cops are bent. They will kill for a dollar.'

Of course he was exaggerating. Most JA police are straight and brave, James reflected, remembering childhood propaganda, but *this* man is bad. I must be very careful.

'Yes?' The inspector's gaze was hard and impatient. 'You have some urgent message from Brixton, England? Why could you not have made an appointment, Mr. . . ?'

'James . . . sir. Mr James. I had to speak to you personally, not your staff.'

The inspector hesitated. A trace of curiosity, even apprehension, appeared in the set of his bloodshot eyes.

'Go on then,' he hissed. He could not place this feeble-looking, silver-haired Londoner in the normal scheme of things. There was an aura of the solid citizen about Mr James and a certain quiet authority which piqued his curiosity. Certainly no run-of-the-mill Yardie or local gangster on the make.

'Scotland Yard,' James had rehearsed with care, 'operate a computerised file on their Operation Dalehouse data bank aimed at Yardie crime. My colleagues have access to the data. I cannot say how or who they are but they have uncovered a UK police operation devoted to nailin' you.'

Mascel showed no emotion. He knew all about Dalehouse. He stared at James as though attempting to hypnotise him.

'To that end,' James continued, 'they sent a colleague of yours, a Kingston-born, British-educated Jamaican named Stafford Douglas to obtain hard evidence of your "corruption" which they will present to the Jamaican Police, copied to your Foreign Office, to ensure your arrest. They nailed Douglas three years ago and turned him. They've already used him to turn in other big names.' James named three well-known Yardie barons selected at random from HOLMES data.

'Why me?'

'Your use of corrupt HM Customs men at UK airports especially riles them.'

464

'What's all this to you?'

'My people want Douglas out of the game and they would like to do business with you.'

'Who *are* your friends?'

'They have decided to wait until Douglas is dealt with before they come over from Brixton to meet you. We have Douglas's networks in three UK cities in mind. Big business.'

Mascel nodded. 'I will need time. Where can I contact you? You were right to see me in person.'

James hesitated to give this man his hotel address in Mandeville but he had no option.

'When will you call me?' he asked. 'I cannot stay for long.'

'Maybe a week. Maybe more.' Mascel was curt, take it or leave it. 'It is not so simple.'

James had thrown his stones into the dark waters. Now he could only wait and hope the ripples would collide.

33

November 1992–November 1993

For a week Maureen Douglas received calls when Mafia was away. Different voices. One she recognised as a police officer – a lizard of a man who had dropped off a package for Mafia a couple of months back. Contradictory messages about meetings, rendezvous details, cancellations. Mafia was unusually tense; she would almost have said jumpy if she hadn't known better.

'No problem, just business,' he assured her.

'And all these calls?'

'It's a *big* deal. If it comes off there'll be new work in London. You and me'll be set up for good. But the other party's got their knickers all twisted. That's why all the phone fuss. Don't you worry none about it. I can handle these guys.'

The last of the calls came early on Thursday, 19 November. Maureen took it. 'They said, "Tell Stafford we're ready," ' Maureen told her husband. Mafia forgot his breakfast and walked a few houses down Poinsettia Avenue to where his builder lived. He returned in minutes with two duffle bags, pocketed his Smith & Wesson and drove off. Maureen had long since given up warning him to be careful. She was married to a cocaine wheeler-dealer in Jamaica; an occupation many times more hazardous than being a Grand Prix racing driver. She did not complain. They lived well off the proceeds.

Mafia stopped to collect Kingston Williams. Since the warning from the old guy James, Mafia had travelled nowhere without an armed bodyguard close by. And this morning the duffle bags in the boot had them both on edge, for they held $1 million in cash. And Mascel's boys would know he was carrying it.

Mandeville was high country, cooler than Kingston. Mascel had chosen a spot halfway between Spanish Town and Mafia's Mandeville home. The meet was by the side gates of the Little Ascot racecourse. Two of Mascel's men were there, out of uniform and dolled up like Tontons Macoutes.

Mafia and Kingston stayed in the car. Kingston's Uzi was ready. One of the men sauntered across.

'Hi, man. The boss said it'll be a while longer than he thought. The delivery was delayed. No fuss though. Maybe we all take a drink? OK?'

They cruised some local rum bars. Mafia was on edge. The money was in the boot and he told Kingston to stay 'on board' except when the car was immediately to hand. As the morning wore on and nothing happened, Mafia became abusive. This merely amused the policemen. Around noon they went off to 'make a call' and Mafia used their brief absence to prepare for the worst. He was clearly undermanned.

'I don't like this. Mascel's playin' stupid. Go get Marshall and the others,' he hissed at Kingston. 'The money's in two halves. Take one of the bags. Use a cab. Leave your Uzi under my seat in the Merc. Get back to the racecourse within two hours with whoever you can get. Mascel's muckin' us about and that's not his way. Everythin's been straight with him till now. That old Rasta, James, is maybe right.'

'My friend had to go,' Mafia explained to the two police when they returned. 'This has taken too long.'

'OK, don't fret. Everything's taken care of and the coke's ready right now. We got to go meet at the bar in Tamarind Tree.'

Mafia cursed himself for sending Kingston off but he was also relieved. Things were at last underway and the bottom line was nobody would be fool enough to shoot him when they learnt he carried only half the money.

He followed the policemen's car to the little village of Tamarind Tree and, in the backroom of a local bar, met up with two more of Mascel's men – nobody he knew – and took possession of the cocaine. He finger-sampled two packs and all seemed fine. Mascel's men counted out $500,000 from his bag. The atmosphere turned electric.

467

'Where's the rest?'

'What do you expect?' Mafia snarled. 'You boys have mucked me about all mornin'. I don't like it, so my man's taken the other bag off. You know where I live. I ain't goin' nowhere without your boss knows it.'

The four men stared at him; vultures in Raybans.

'So I'm goin' home with the coke to check it out. Then, before six tonight, I'll come back with the rest of the caboosh. We meet by the sea end in Port Esquirel. OK?'

The Mascel mob agreed with obvious reluctance. Mafia's neck hairs prickled as he left the bar.

Back home with a stiff drink he checked the individual packs one by one. It was a set-up. All but the topmost packets of each box contained cooking flour. Either Mascel was purposely provoking him or, more likely, one of his men had pulled the stunt, hoping perhaps that Mafia would send the boxes straight to the UK with only a rudimentary check. One of the four men at Tamarind Tree had probably sidelined the missing cocaine and was laughing his eyes out right now. Mafia smashed his glass on the concrete floor. He would kill the bastards. He would laugh last and longest.

Kingston did not respond on the mobile but that often happened; the hills or the heat interfered. Mafia drove straight to Little Ascot but Kingston was not at the racecourse. Impatient and burning on a dangerously short fuse, he scorched south towards Port Esquirel, calling Kingston's mobile as he went. He repeated to himself that Mascel's men would not try anything without the rest of the money. The Uzi was hard under his thighs as he drove. He felt invincible.

In Old Harbour Bay he swung into Goldbourn Lane and the sun dazzled his windscreen as a long black sedan drew out across the road and four men with sub-machine-guns closed about the Mercedes.

In that instant realisation came to Mafia that this was not just about the money. As his left hand closed about his Uzi, the nearest man shot him through the mouth.

Within moments the ambushers and the sedan had disappeared and the occupants of nearby homes shuffled, in morbid fascination, closer to the Mercedes to watch the blood dribble from the steering wheel and on to the fine white leather. Flour had spilled from packages on the passenger seat and some of it soaked up Mafia's blood as children with runny noses peered into the car's windows and sucked harder on their thumbs.

James, at his lodgings, picked up news of the killing on his radio. 'The Lord willed it,' he said aloud. Since Sailor's death he had increasingly spoken to himself. He hated to be alone. He called Goodman, who had agreed to stay near the phone at noon every day.

'Alexo, I'll make this short. I have done it. An eye for an eye. It is finished. I'm comin' back tomorrow.'

Two weeks later James went shopping and brought back to the apartment a copy of the *Weekly Gleaner* dated 8 December. Tucked away on page twenty-two, under a piece about ganja being smuggled out of Jamaica in cheese tins, a small article announced: 'Dead is Stafford Douglas, 42, of Mandeville . . . Robbed of his licensed firearm and an undisclosed sum of money . . . he died on the spot. The Old Harbour police are investigating.'

James watched Goodman. 'It will not bring back our dead,' he said quietly. 'Even God cannot change the past.'

'True,' Goodman agreed, 'but when Blackledge also meets his Maker, our loved ones may rest in peace and we may be able to think of the future, having buried the past.'

'One such death always leads to another,' James replied, handing Goodman a letter from his cousin in Jamaica which contained a news cutting.

Kingston Williams had been found dead at his home, robbed and shot through the head. 'The police are investigating,' said the newspaper.

Paul Blackledge's life had lost its zest. A local court had banned him for life from keeping dogs after the RSPCA had finally caught up with him at a Shropshire badger dig. The magistrate labelled him a social outcast, adding: 'He has a long record of violence to both humans and animals.'

Embittered by the injustice of the love of his life being confiscated, the dogs that he cared for so well and whose fighting prowess gave him such pride, Blackledge left the dog circuits and concentrated on crime. His wife, Jackie, a former school dinner lady, adored him. He could do no wrong. His parents and brothers, respected members of the Great Harwood community, knew nothing of his criminal activities. They were aware that he loved to fight but, as in Australia, fist-fighting was an accepted part of life in the North-West.

Now turned thirty, Blackledge was bald and paunchy. A few months back a friend of his, John Keaveney, had argued with him and shot him twice with a twelve-bore at the barn in Stanning Folly. Keaveney was now in prison for attempted murder and Blackledge limped slightly from his wounds. Now he trusted nobody and watched his back constantly.

He still enjoyed a solid reputation as a hard man and not only with his fists. He had a fine set of teeth and in a brawl with Barry Bridges, scion of a well-known Blackburn family, he had bitten off his opponent's nose to much public acclaim. 'A fair bite, that was,' he was fond of saying.

In the eighties Blackledge had worked mostly with a Dutchman, de Moeller, in the North and Mafia Douglas in London. But in 1990 he had met up with Tony Davis, an old friend from his slaughter-house days, with whom he had spent many a wild evening smashing up pubs and fighting doormen. Davis had introduced Blackledge to the Wilson brothers, John and David, the kings of the Darwen underworld.

Blackledge became one of the Wilsons' hard-man debt collectors. People who failed to pay the Wilsons their due were cornered by Blackledge, whose speciality was breaking limbs, as a warning. More serious offences were dealt with by the Wilsons themselves.

By the autumn of 1992, when Goodman turned his attention to Blackledge, the latter was making good money with the Wilsons but wanted more. Apart from street dealing in specific areas of Blackburn, mostly around the Duke's Brow turf, he continued gun sales to London Yardies and, for the Wilsons, strong-arm stuff at major acid raves in the North-West.

The Wilsons' dealings in Blackburn centred around the area of Johnson and Shadsworth Streets. That summer and autumn they derived excellent revenue from organising raves and selling soft drugs to all-night captive audiences. A nice change from the standard stuff of forgery, theft and protection violence.

On 7 December 1992 Blackledge drove his white Escort van to a hairdresser's in Johnson Street and picked up a Sicilian-born half-caste named Raymondo 'Luigi' Ballanca. Like Blackledge, Ballanca was trusted by the Wilsons with the large amounts of cash needed to

470

pay off their Colombian cocaine suppliers. At a meeting in the top flat of 107c Preston New Road in Blackburn the two men formed an unholy and perilous alliance. They would leach money from the Wilsons whenever the opportunity arose and suspicion seemed unlikely to fall their way. Ballanca's girlfriend Donna brought them mugs of coffee.

'Tell nobody,' Blackledge said, staring at Ballanca. 'Not even yer lass.'

'Not even her,' Luigi agreed. 'Nor your missus.'

Blackledge nodded. 'My Jackie thinks I'm a bleedin' saint.'

Both men laughed.

Columbo came to the Peckham flat without his habitual grin to the fore.

'Where's your smile, Col?' James stared over the bifocals he had recently started to use. 'The world must have fallen in.'

'Worse than that,' Columbo grunted. 'They're askin' for you and Alex on the street.'

'They?' James growled. 'Who's they?'

'I dunno exactly,' Columbo said, frowning. 'But sort of American government types like what you see on the box guardin' President Bush. That's how my mate described them. Not your typical pigs at all, he said. But they must've got on to us through the cops 'cos otherwise they wouldn't know where to ask, would they?'

James agreed and scribbled a note for Columbo. 'Remember Ears Norton, Sailor's CID friend? Yeah, well go see him. Ears promised me at Sailor's funeral that he'd always do what he could for us. Maybe there's a way he can discover who these Yank geezers are and what they're after.'

Goodman showed little interest that evening when James mentioned Columbo's disturbing news. The previous week they had finally completed their move to their new flat. Goodman had helped settle The Family's outstanding debts to local traders to the Peckham Home in the knowledge that James was determined to preserve Sailor's good name without posthumous blemish. But now Goodman's focus had switched entirely to the hunt for Blackledge.

In local public libraries he began to photocopy street maps of Blackburn and to read back copies of Lancashire papers. He located Blackledge's most recent address from a 1990 *Accrington Observer*.

Boosted by James's success in Jamaica, he decided to visit Blackburn, an equally alien environment, and to close cautiously on his quarry before deciding how best to move ahead.

Columbo returned after a fruitless search for Norton and volunteered to drive Goodman north.

'You need somebody streetwise to look after you, Alexo – somebody like me with connections. Plus I don't have no hot chicks on tap right now.'

'How about your business?'

'Business!' Columbo found his wide smile once more. 'Man, if you knew how business was, you'd know why even Lancashire will be a holiday.' His current job was as a sales assistant at a King's Road jeans shop. Purely, he explained, because he knew no better way of legitimately touching up the private parts of so many beautiful girls every day of the week. But he had been there over a month now, a record for him, and was getting itchy feet.

'Tito, my cousin, live in Salford,' Columbo announced. 'That's near Blackburn. I let him stay in the coolers once when he was down London, so he owe me. Alexo, we can use his place as our base. Good chicks in Salford, although they speak weird.'

Columbo was as good as his word. Tito turned out to be a full-time member of the Salford Lads, a drug-dealing gang, but he welcomed Columbo and Goodman with open arms and gave them free access to his basement flat. He was seldom there in person.

For three weeks Goodman, with or without Columbo, shadowed Blackledge, and although he lost him more often than not, on several occasions he managed to overhear him talking with friends, including a black called Danny, a giant of a man, in various Blackburn pubs.

Goodman was in a quandary. In the heat of the moment he had talked with Columbo about borrowing a pistol and a silencer from Tito. Yet the more he thought about it the more he realised one irrational but inescapable fact. Deep inside himself he was as repulsed as ever by the idea of killing anyone, even Blackledge, in cold blood. He had killed. He could still kill. But – and of this he was sure – he would prefer to use a professional.

So, after thanking Tito and his friends, Goodman and Columbo drove back to London. When Goodman sat down with James and talked about his dilemma, the older man was torn between amusement and genuine concern for his friend. 'I know you, Alexo, better than you know yourself. You ain't no born killer, that's your problem. Get yourself a contract man. That's the only way.'

Goodman agreed without arguing the point and James produced a heavy cardboard box from his bedroom. 'Tosh's things,' he explained.

Using her diaries and address book from the eighties and earlier, they identified three likely names in Ireland and one, 'Alpha' S. Arnold, from Stepney. There was a phone number from her 1984 diary which, when called, reached an answering machine. Goodman left their number and said he was calling 'on behalf of Tosh from Belfast 1984'.

Two days later a man with a neutral, classless voice called back. 'You phoned on behalf of Tosh?'

'Yes,' said Goodman. 'Are you "Alpha" Arnold?'

'I can reach him. What's it about?

'I am a friend of Tosh. She gave me your number,' he lied. 'We need your help.'

There was a silence. Then, 'We're working in Frankfurt. Can't leave. You'll have to come here.'

It was agreed. Goodman took a flight the next day from Heathrow to Frankfurt and a taxi to the Hauptbahnhof, where, as bidden, he sat in a sandwich bar reading a Dick Francis novel. After twenty minutes a thickset man in his fifties joined him at his table and beckoned to the waiter. In fluent German he ordered two coffees.

'You're with Tosh?' he enquired.

'Tosh died.' Goodman had decided he was no good at deception. 'I wanted to meet you but feared you might only wish to see her. I'm sorry but my need is great.'

'When did she die?'

'She was killed last year by one of a group of men I have been hunting for eight years. Her killer is now dead. I arranged it.'

'How did she die? No. First tell me about you. Start at the beginning. I have time.'

'I know nothing about you.' Goodman spoke with marked politeness. 'Are you "Alpha" Arnold?'

'I am the man known to Tosh, who was once my good friend, by that name.'

Goodman found Arnold's complete lack of expression unnerving. His features, his manner and his dialogue were middle-class British civil servant. There was nothing remotely sinister about him and yet, Goodman knew, he made a living through assassination. Goodman had no option and nothing to lose, so he launched into a heavily abridged version of his life after Kinver.

Arnold was attentive and when Goodman ended he said: 'So, because Tosh wrote in her diary that I once killed commercially, you assume that I still do. Your story may, of course, be cock and bull and you may be some form of law agent. But I have survived through the years on my instinct, my nose, and' – he paused – 'I believe you.'

'I am greatly relieved,' Goodman said, 'because I know nobody but you in your line of business.'

Arnold looked around. '*Kellner*,' he called to the waiter. '*Rechnung, bitte*.' He paid and walked Goodman some five minutes through the bitterly cold winds of downtown Frankfurt.

'I will see what can be done. I will need to ask many questions before I can decide whether to take on your work. So we might as well eat in civilised surroundings while we talk.' He indicated the sedate hotel ahead as they entered Westendstrasse. 'The Westend, old-fashioned and bursting with genuine antiques, including the staff. At this time of the year we can talk privately and in comfort.'

They were served an excellent lunch by three elderly waiters with penguin suits and nineteenth-century manners. Goodman told Arnold all he knew about Blackledge. After cheese and coffee Arnold said quietly: 'Successful anonymous termination will cost you £60,000 plus my expenses, which will be in the region of a further £5,000.' He looked up and Goodman nodded without hesitation: his Geneva account could easily cover the figure.

'Further,' Arnold added, 'I will not finish here in Germany until some time in October. Can you wait that long?'

Again Goodman agreed without query. He could trust this man. He felt sure Tosh would not have dealt with Arnold if he was in any way shifty.

'You pay me ten thousand now,' Arnold continued, and gave Goodman details of a Liechtenstein account. 'Twenty thousand by the first week of October and the balance, if I have been successful, immediately afterwards. Default of payment would be the ultimate stupidity.'

Goodman saw what he meant.

'When do you go home?' Arnold asked. 'May I call you Alex?'

'Of course, Mr Arnold, of course. I'm booked back early tomorrow morning.'

'Call me Alpha.' He said this in a take it or leave it sort of way. 'I don't meet many fellow-countrymen on this job and, to be frank, our German cousins can grate when taken in large helpings.'

'How did you meet Tosh?' Goodman asked.

'That's a long tale and one, I'm afraid, which must remain untold but she was a fine girl. One in a million. I was in Kinshasa with a group of British mercenaries early in 1976 and some Americans on the same job later drew me into the IRA–UVA weapons web. I wish to God they hadn't but the one bright spark, as far as I'm concerned, was meeting and working with Tosh.'

They talked about her for a while until there was no more to say. Tosh would clearly still be alive had she never met Goodman.

'Why are you out here, if you don't mind my asking?' he asked Arnold.

'Strangely enough, I don't.' Arnold almost smiled. 'You're about the most straightforward person I think I have ever done business with. I'm in mid-contract with a little-known – one might almost say unknown – Anglo-German group formed in 1949 to crush fledgeling Nazi groups in Europe when they get beyond the scope of the police and other government agencies. A group of yobbos in Germany, Holland and at home have formed Combat 18, the "1" and the "8" representing the alphabetical positions of Adolf Hitler's initials. Much of their activity is mindless violence at football matches, but six months ago three of their leaders mapped out plans for racist terror which could lead to spreading backlash and riots.'

'Don't the Germans have an SAS for that sort of thing?'

'Indeed they do. Grenzschutzgruppe 9, it's called – GSG9 – but their remit does not extend to knocking off troublesome citizens.'

'Much like the SAS shooting the IRA, surely?'

'Not quite. We are at war with the IRA, but GSG9 has no such mandate for a shoot-to-kill operation.'

As strangers thrown together often do, the two men talked for several hours. Later, as Arnold drove Goodman back to his airport hotel, he said, with evident sincerity: 'I enjoyed this evening. Come October I will do my best for you.'

*

475

Goodman became an avid reader at local libraries during the spring and summer of 1993, alternating between novels and books about ecology. He still hankered for involvement in conservation work but decided not to make a move until after the past was exorcised. Until October, and the coming of Arnold, he would merely live quietly with James, who was now fairly active with his taxi work and the local Rastafarian community.

In early October Goodman ordered Geneva to send his second cheque to Arnold's numbered account in Liechtenstein and, on the fifteenth, Arnold called him as though they had parted only the day before.

'I'll be in Blackburn for the next two or three weeks. If I need you, I'll let you know.'

In due course he called again and they met in a London pub on 3 November.

'You should have been with me yesterday,' Arnold said. 'Your friend Blackledge was drinking in The Packet House outside Blackburn with an erstwhile dog-fight pal, a big Irish lad named Gardiner. Real barefist battle of the Titans and our target lost convincingly.'

'What did you learn about him?'

For half an hour, and in great detail, Arnold described Blackledge's lifestyle, and his marital, extramarital and criminal activities with a wealth of intimate comment.

'How on earth did you discover all that?' Goodman was amazed.

'That's why you pay me more than a hundred times what you'd pay a local amateur. I do the job properly. No possible comeback on you. I use the best, the latest gear on the market. This watch of mine, for instance' – he indicated his heavy but ordinary-looking Seiko – 'is also a camera. And I can break in and "fix" any phone within two or three minutes given a typical household security system, leaving behind a bug which will relay all subsequent conversations to my recorder 400 yards away. I have tape recorders and bugs so small you wouldn't believe. All the information I've just given you, the target's current plans, was garnered through electronics, not magic.'

'Do you have a plan yet?' Goodman asked.

'Tomorrow the target and a young sidekick will be doing a cocaine delivery run. Then he meets Lynn Smith, his local lay I told you about, for a quickie at her place. That's when I go in. You'll get confirmation of his termination on the fifth – that's Friday. Just get the local press to fax you the details. Then wire the money' – he specified the exact amount – 'before close of play to my account. The timing is important to me.'

'Of course. I will be sure to be prompt. But, if things go wrong . . . ?'

'They won't.'

'You are confident.'

'This is my job. The target is sharp. Very sharp. Eyes in the back of his head but they're a bit puffy after his punch-up. Termination tomorrow night.'

'When will I next meet you?'

'You won't,' Arnold said, 'unless you have further work for me, in which case you know my number. I offer a healthy discount to regular customers.'

On 4 November Blackledge collected three heavily laden grocery bags from his Accrington Road flat in Blackburn. All the packs contained drugs, mostly cannabis, from his London source. These he took round to Ballanca's eyrie in Preston New Road. He drove with one eye on the mirror, aware that somebody close to him for some months had been snitching to the police and, with a car full of cannabis, he was feeling vulnerable. Especially since he was already on bail from Carlisle Crown Court for allegedly supplying cocaine.

Life was expensive. Blackledge loved his wife Jackie but keeping in with the Wilson brothers took time and effort and had driven a wedge between the married couple. He no longer lived at home with Jackie and their two kids. There were plenty of local girls aching to be gangsters' molls and he fancied a pretty brunette, Lynn Smith, whom he had met at a rave some months back. He had managed to tempt her away from her live-in lover, a Geordie car mechanic, with the lure of the rave scene. He had introduced her to Ecstasy, the tense atmosphere of pubs with the big boys spoiling for fights, the private discos. She had come with him for dirty weekends in London, staying at the Hilton and accepting his gifts of jewellery and smart clothes. He knew he had hurt Jackie. One day soon he would make it up to her. She always forgave him. Always had and always would, however many times he strayed. Dicking around was his style and he was not alone in that.

He unpacked the cannabis in Ballanca's living room and they worked out together how much of the Wilsons' cash they could safely sideline for their own business without inviting trouble. They spent an hour separating cannabis into sales packs and transferred the finished packages into a suitcase which Ballanca was about to carry down to a lock-up in Ashworth Close which he used for storage 'off the premises', when the phone rang.

'I'll take the case,' said Blackledge. He knew where the lock-up was although he had not been there before. Ballanca considered it a safe spot purely because nobody but he ever went there and no burglar would be seen dead raiding such a ramshackle place.

Blackledge noticed a clean and recent sort of smell in the lock-up that made him look around. Expensive aftershave, he guessed. He searched about, uncertain quite why or what he was looking for. Under a pile of wooden pallets he was surprised to see a cashbox-sized metal container. He snapped it open.

A tape recorder revolved within. He lifted the earphones already attached and heard Ballanca's voice on the telephone. He swore. They used the Preston New Road flat precisely because it was out of the way and secure. He assumed at first that the recorder belonged to the filth but that, on reflection, did not fit. *They* would use surveillance vans, not leave their hardware lying around on private property.

'The bastard,' he exploded. The realisation hit him like a lightning bolt. This must belong to the informer who was dogging his every move. Blackledge suspected the Blackburn police held a file on him which would identify the snitch. Blackledge's father's window cleaning company had long held a contract for cleaning the police station windows and Blackledge had been sorely tempted to exploit the situation. But he had refrained out of respect for his father. Now he would catch the grass red-handed and squeeze the truth out of him or her. He told Ballanca, who checked the lock-up for himself and was livid with rage. They altered their drug-run plans for the afternoon and, both armed, took turns to watch the outhouse.

'Alpha' Arnold slipped into the lock-up soon after dark, intent on replaying the day's voice-activated tapes before going in for the kill. A sharp blow to his temple dropped him cold and he regained consciousness to find commercial tape wrapped around his head and pinioning his limbs. Blackledge stood over him. Ballanca had left by himself to process the customer deliveries for the day's phone orders.

'You, mate, are going to sing,' Blackledge said through gritted teeth, 'and sing good. I'm short of time, so don't muck me around. You're a fuckin' grass. You been talking to the pigs for weeks. Because of you I've got a coke rap pending. So I'm right pissed off with you, see?'

No reply. Blackledge opened his clasp-knife and slit the adhesive tape over Arnold's mouth, cutting his upper lip in the process.

'I'm not who you think,' Arnold spoke quickly, urgently. 'I merely came in here looking for my dog.'

Blackledge hesitated. The man's accent was not local. This was an Oxbridge type and not by any stretch of the imagination a Blackburn police informant. In which case, who was he? A cold shiver ran through Blackledge. Could he be a contract man? If so, who was he working for? The Wilsons? Had they discovered what he and Ballanca were up to? Or Keaveney, directing things from jail . . . No, that was out of character. Who then? Only this man could tell him. Blackledge looked around the cluttered lock-up . On top of a lawnmower he spotted a battered one-litre fuel can. He unscrewed the lid and sniffed the contents. Petrol. At least a pint.

Blackledge again poked his knife though the tape and forced the blade into Arnold's mouth. He began to pour the petrol down his throat and Arnold had no choice but to swallow or choke. When the can was empty, Blackledge squatted down. With his knife in one hand and a lighter in the other, he grinned at Arnold.

'When I light the fumes in your mouth, the gas explosion will burn out your throat linin'. I know – I've done it before. You talk now or you never talk again.'

Arnold liked Goodman but he was not given to emotional loyalties. Self-preservation had always featured high on his priority list. Blackledge was obviously not playing around. Any story he told him would be quickly checked out. The issue was clear.

'I have a contract on you,' he managed to splutter through his burning lips. 'I'm being paid by a London man called Alex Goodman who says you killed his wife and daughter nine years ago.'

Blackledge remained expressionless.

'Where is this Goodman now?'

Arnold gave him the current contact details he had for Goodman.

'If I find you're bloody lyin',' Blackledge said through gritted teeth, 'I'll be back and you'll regret we ever met.'

James was away with Rasta friends and Goodman, unsure when he would return, left a note on the kitchen table giving Sonny Guha's address and phone number. The waiting to hear from Arnold was wearing him down. In need of good cheer he decided to visit Sonny, so he made the long tube journey to Manor House from New Cross and, walking through Woodberry Down, it was as though Sara was again at his side with her merry chatter. In Bethune Road he turned into the northern block of Lincoln Court and climbed the dark stairways to Sonny's top-floor flat. Fireworks exploded in the walkways and the two men watched from the window as rockets burst into fiery showers above the nearby East Reservoir.

At 6.30 p.m. Goodman sighed. 'I'd better get back home. I'm expecting a call. Thanks, Sonny. I always enjoy our get-togethers, you old reprobate. Keep out of harm's way, if you can.'

The front door burst in as Goodman, in the bathroom, collected his raincoat. Guha screamed but the sound was abruptly followed by a heavy thudding noise. Goodman slid into the adjoining room, out of the window and fled down the stairs. Back home he called Guha's number. The police replied. Mr Sumit Guha's body had been found in suspicious circumstances on the pavement outside Lincoln Court.

Something was wrong with the flat. In his sadness over Sonny's death and his feeling of guilt that he had done nothing to help, he had been distracted. Then he clicked. His note was missing from the kitchen table although James had not returned. Of course . . . Whoever had attacked Sonny had first been here for him and, finding the note, gone on to Lincoln Court. Sonny had died in his place. He remembered James's worries about 'the Americans'. How Columbo had heard rumours on the street.

Then the phone rang.

'Arnold here. Listen, Alex. You must get out of there at once. Things went wrong. Blackledge caught me, forced me to give him your address. Left me tied up but I got loose. I tried to call you earlier. Blackledge is probably on his way to you now.'

'Too late,' said Goodman. His voice full of bitterness and fury, he told Arnold about Sonny.

480

'I would suggest you leave immediately nonetheless,' said the hit man. 'He may well try your Peckham flat again.'

Goodman saw the point. 'What will you do?'

'Complete the contract. Try again. He will be doubly alert but I won't slip up twice. It may take time. Of course I will charge you the same. This weekend Blackledge is liable to run into domestic problems at his girlfriend's. I may try playing with that. Where will you be when I need to make contact?'

'Here,' said Goodman. 'I've nowhere else to go but I'll keep low and borrow a gun. Hopefully you will be successful before he comes here again.'

'I'm sorry about your friend,' said Arnold, then rang off.

Thirty minutes later the doorbell rang. Goodman felt the creeping approach of panic. He was unarmed. The bell kept ringing. If this was Blackledge he would surely let himself in as he must have done previously to have found Goodman's note. Maybe the caller was innocent. Arming himself with a kitchen knife, Goodman called out: 'Who is it?'

'Police. Peckham Crime Squad.'

Relieved, Goodman unlocked the door. A young, fresh-faced plainclothes officer entered. 'Sorry to disturb you, sir, but we have been watching a flat close to yours and about twenty minutes ago I saw two heavy-looking white guys listening at your door and walkway windows. I felt you ought to know about it. They ran off when I approached.'

'That's very good of you, officer. I'll make sure everything's well locked up.'

When the policeman had gone, Goodman called Columbo. 'Can you come soon, Col, and bring a gun? I hope all will be OK in a day or two but right now I need you urgently. James is away.'

Alan 'Geordie' Neale loved attractive brunette Lynn Smith and hated her dalliance with the notorious Blackledge. Alan's own marriage had ended four years earlier and his early bouts of car theft and minor burglary were a thing of the distant past. He had been straight for seventeen years now and made a living from repairing cars, working in the lock-up garage outside Lynn's council house in the quiet Blackburn cul-de-sac of Longton Close. Alan kept most of his personal odds and ends in the garage, including an unlicensed twelve-bore pump-action shotgun which, years earlier, he had bought with the intention of joining a local club.

For the past seven weeks, ever since Blackledge had enticed Lynn away from him, Alan had experienced a see-saw relationship with her. He knew she found Blackledge 'exciting' and was increasingly hooked by the joys of the rave circuit but she also felt guilty because her own three-year-old daughter Stevie depended on her and was very fond of Alan, who did much of the babysitting. Alan was quiet, gentle and boring; the antithesis of Blackledge. At 4 p.m. on Saturday, 6 November, Alan drove to Lynn's to take little Stevie to a Guy Fawkes bonfire in Witton Park. Nobody answered his knock, so he peered through the half-open blinds to the left of the front door.

Lynn and Blackledge were making violent love on the settee. Alan was stunned. Only three days earlier Lynn had assured him she was not serious about Blackledge and was considering letting Alan move in with her again. And now this. He drove his white Astra van aimlessly about town. His mind was in turmoil and he did not spot Arnold's rented Escort any more than he would have noticed an elephant close on his tail.

At 6 p.m. Alan returned to Longton Close and this time found Lynn by herself. Blackledge, it seemed, had just dropped by for the customary quickie. Alan, normally the most stable of men, exploded when he saw an expensive new gold necklace around Lynn's neck. He tore it off, slapped her face and screamed: 'You whore.'

His outburst must have hit home, for Lynn appeared contrite. She apologised and soon they were both sobbing in each other's arms. He asked if he could take little Stevie to the fireworks with his own children but Lynn's ex-husband had called earlier because the weekend was his time for their daughter.

Alan looked at his watch. 'I must go,' he said. 'I'm overdue at Jill's to collect the kids. I'll be back as soon as possible. We need to talk.'

Lynn nodded with a smile that seemed warm and positive. Alan was still shaken but happy to forgive her.

When he climbed back into his car he found an envelope on his seat addressed simply 'Geordie'. He tore it open, wondering how, since the car was both locked and undamaged, the sender had gained access. The message was scrawled in rough capitals. 'You're cold meat before Monday. Lynn's mine.' There was no signature. It could only be from Blackledge. So this was the crunch. He must either put up or shut up. A cold resolve gripped him. Why should he be bullied into submission? Blackledge, he had heard, was a killer. If he was to get Lynn back he would have to meet fire with fire, be able to protect himself and her. He realised she was probably with Blackledge and would soon be returning with him. He found his old shotgun, clamped it into his garage vice and used a hacksaw to shorten the barrel to fourteen inches. He loaded five cartridges and hid in the house all through the night and the following Sunday morning. He had no specific plan and no wish to tangle with Blackledge, of whom he was terrified. He only knew that he loved Lynn and would not give her up to any man.

Blackledge and Lynn spent that night in his flat. They watched a video, made love, drank and smoked cannabis. After a late breakfast of black coffee, Blackledge answered the doorbell only to find a folded typed note on the doormat.

'Touch her and you die, scum. I know what you and Ballanca are doing. The Wilsons will get you.'

Blackledge's lips pulled back in a terrier snarl and he crunched the note in his ham-like fist. It could only be from Geordie. He said nothing to Lynn. She might react by admiring the bastard for his rashness. You could never tell with women. But he was worried, very worried about the Wilsons.

'Look, love,' he said, ruffling Lynn's hair. 'Luigi dropped a lot of money with me. I got to get it delivered today. Neil Taylor's comin' round shortly with wheels. Why don't you get ready. On our way we can stop off at your place and collect your things. Then you can move in here while bloody Geordie's bein' a pain in the butt. I'll see he doesn't trouble you none.'

Blackledge stuffed a plastic shopping bag with £1000 bundles of notes totalling £53,000, and then Neil Taylor, a sycophantic dark-haired youth, drove the couple round to Longton Close just before 2 p.m. Neil parked the rented Vauxhall in the street outside and Blackledge accompanied Lynn into her house. On the mat she found a note in Geordie's handwriting: 'If I find the fat bastard tonight, we'll both die.'

'Is that supposed to mean me?' Blackledge laughed. 'Go up and grab what you need.'

483

Lynn, collecting her washing things from the bathroom upstairs, saw Alan with the gun. 'Don't scream, Lynn,' Alan hissed. 'I'll not hurt you.' She ignored him and grabbed at the gun barrel, so he slapped her. Then he heard Blackledge on the stairs and remembered the note on his car seat: 'You're cold meat before Monday.' Cocking the shotgun in a panic, he peered into the corridor. Blackledge, seeing him, yelled and powered towards him. Alan deliberately missed with his first shot but Blackledge kept coming. The next shot blasted the big man's shoulder. The bull-like Blackledge didn't even stagger. He did, however, see sense and turned to flee. Alan saw no blood. But he did see his future: a future of fear being stalked by Blackledge and his buddies.

The previous year, he remembered, Blackledge had walked away from two close-up shots from a twelve-bore. He had since acquired a legendary reputation. Alan knew he must cripple him now or he would himself be killed. He raced down the stairs and saw Blackledge running to catch up with the Vauxhall, which was moving away in a lurching manner like an unpractised relay runner taking a baton. Alan's third and fourth shots caught Blackledge in the kidneys and backside as he clung to the open door of the moving car. At last he collapsed and lay bleeding on the road. Children screamed, Alan retreated back into Lynn's house while Neil stopped the car and rushed off to use a neighbour's phone to call Ballanca and ask what to do with the money. The police arrived in minutes but, with an armed man overlooking the street, they kept back and moved householders out of harm's way.

Arnold, with binoculars, watched Blackledge's blood pools spread over the tarmac. The famous badger-baiter died slowly. Eventually a woman went to his aid but by then he was dead. Arnold called Goodman, who arrived from London with Columbo four hours later. By then the house was fully cordoned off by armed police since Alan was threatening to kill himself. Two hours later they watched Lynn Smith leave the house looking unconcerned. They took rooms at a local hotel and listened to the local news.

At noon the next day Alan Neale gave himself up. The police told him to dismantle the gun before coming out of the house. At this point he discovered that he was in fact unarmed, having unknowingly ejected his fifth and last cartridge in the street immediately after shooting Blackledge.

He was punished with life imprisonment, with a recommendation that he serve a minimum of fifteen years. In prison he received constant threats from friends of friends of Blackledge. He was moved between prisons to keep him safe.

Two weeks after the shooting, on a bitterly cold November day, they buried Paul Norman Blackledge in style. Hundreds of friends crammed the pews at the funeral in Great Harwood's church. One commented to the press: 'This is tragic. He was a lovely bloke.' Blackledge's estranged wife and their two young children led the mourners to the cemetery, where his grave was decorated with many wreaths. From the ranks of the silent crowd Alex Goodman noted floral tributes fashioned into the shapes of dogs and badgers.

Weeks later the Animal Liberation Front desecrated the grave. But for Goodman the bitterness and the anger had gone. He felt only an enormous emptiness where once there had been hatred and, before that, a heart filled with love, the heart of a simple accountant who would never knowingly have hurt a fly.

Epilogue

I met Alex Goodman eighteen times after March 1994, when I agreed to write his story. Since he was hostile to tape recorders, I resorted to laborious hand-written notes. He also refused to be photographed despite my argument that no publisher would accept his biography without at least a head-and-shoulders picture. Since he was adamant, I contacted a Flying Squad friend who took covert photographs at one of our London sessions.

For me, Goodman's most awkward hang-up was his refusal to furnish reasonable contact details. Once I was into the book I needed, at times, to check facts with him on an almost daily basis but had to make do with a weekly call from him. He gave me a series of addresses, mostly in South London, from which he collected my mail on an irregular basis, and this proved equally unsatisfactory.

By Christmas 1994 Goodman's health seemed to have deteriorated but my enquiries about doctors and hospitals met a blank wall. I became convinced he was covering some skin ailment with facial powder and dyeing his hair. Again my gentle questioning elicited no satisfactory answer. I assumed that fear of recognition and pursuit by various parties was responsible for his reticence.

I spent long hours checking out every detail of his story with hospitals, schools, MoD records and various agencies. For example, since I knew the exact date and even time of his admission to the Midland Centre for Neurosurgery, I checked with the hospital's records department but discovered that the 1984 card-index system had been computerised and much information not considered usable lost in the process. Luckily, Dr Bernard Williams, an eminent neurologist working at the Centre in 1984, was still there and he kindly showed me round. His own research drew a blank. He could find no proof that Goodman had been admitted; nor could he say that he had not.

I travelled to Bristol, Birmingham, Kinver, Peckham, Los Angeles, Miami and Grand Bahama to corroborate Goodman's data, knowing that no publisher would accept such a book and the consequent libel risks unless the information had been checked meticulously.

The psychological aspect was especially imponderable. I gave a brief outline of Goodman's story separately to three of Britain's most respected psychologists and two forensic consultants. One of the latter, Dr Shepherd of Guy's Hospital Forensic Department, London, told me that, in his opinion, Goodman's wife and daughter 'may never have existed' except in Goodman's imagination or that Goodman 'may himself be their murderer and his memory of the bodies is the one that he had when he buried them'.

This suggestion tallied with comments from one of the psychologists, who wrote to me: 'People have a sense that something happened but can't remember what. So they confabulate. They subconsciously invent things to fill the gap. Shrinks call it Pseudologia fantastica, meaning profound and psychopathic lying.'

Goodman's memory lapse, it seemed, might have been the result of a genuine physical problem of the brain, a real psychological malfunctioning, wilful deception or a mixture of all three. Therein lay my problem. I had written eleven books over twenty years, all based on my own experiences. But Goodman's world was utterly alien to mine and I was no psychologist.

The more I saw of Alex Goodman, the more I felt sympathy for him. None the less I found great difficulty in accepting that such an apparently harmless creature could possibly have withstood a mere fraction of the experiences he related.

At the end of February 1995 my literary agent, Ed Victor, grew worried lest Goodman should suddenly decide, after the book was published, that he didn't like the contents and wanted to sue the publishers. Ed drew up a legal document for Goodman to sign in the presence of one of Ed's fellow-directors, forswearing the right to libel action. Goodman duly met Ed's colleague and signed the affidavit.

On 2 March, at his request, I met Goodman in a West End coffee bar and saw at once that he was troubled. His worries came out in a rush. His friend Columbo had gone to Jamaica five months before and James had recently heard he had been crippled by a bullet during somebody else's shoot-out. James had spoken to Goodman in depth about Rastafarianism, about God and, importantly to Goodman, about life after death. Words which he had subsequently read in James's Bible had troubled him greatly: 'And ye shall know the truth, and the truth shall make you free.'

He clasped my wrist across the sticky Formica-topped table. 'You must write my story as I told it,' he said. His eyes were round and moist behind his spectacles.

'Of course,' I assured him. 'I have stuck to the facts as you presented them. As is the case with most biographies, I have invented dialogues and thoughts because these bring the bare skeleton of your story alive. But otherwise I have, as you will see when I send you the finished manuscript, kept rigidly to everything you said.'

Goodman nodded his approval, then pressed his hands against his temples. 'James is a great, great help to me. I accept now, thanks to him, that the Lord will forgive me. I will be shriven. But,' he insisted, 'I must know you will not alter this.'

I repeated my assurances, then asked him: 'Can you tell me what you have done with the BCCI and the Hoover papers?'

'Yes.' He looked briefly content. 'I want no more trouble. Yesterday I made phone calls. I am returning them all.'

'To whom?'

'To the owners.' He nodded as though to himself and would say no more. He looked empty, bewildered. I found myself wanting to part from him with some gesture of my sympathy for him. I had just completed shooting an advertisement for Clarks Shoes and offered Goodman the brand-new pair they had given me. He accepted the shoes and smiled. Nobody with a smile like that, I mused, could be capable of such aggression.

We then parted and, as at the time of writing, I have not seen him again.

The following day I took a call from an elderly-sounding man with a West Indian accent. 'James?' I responded instinctively.

'Yes. It is James.'

I felt that I knew him. 'How is Alex?' I asked.

'That is why I call. Last night, when we came back from the club, our place was upside down. Ransacked, you know. Brother Alex, he took it bad. Said it was all his fault. He had called people about his papers. Now he feared he would be the death of me, like the others. I know he calls you every week on this number. Has he called you today?'

I told him I had met Goodman the previous day.

'I know,' he said. 'But I fear he may do somethin' stupid.'

'Can I help you locate him?'

'Thank you. I would appreciate that. I cannot expect too much cooperation from the police without they ask me many questions.'

I could see what he meant.

'Do you have any idea where he may be?' I asked.

'Only that he has been in the past to All Saints.'

'A church? Have you tried the vicar?'

'Sadly,' James said, 'it would be better if you could do that. The vicar is also a police padre. A good man but, like I say, I must be careful.'

I promised I would do my best. James said he would call me back. He never did.

I called the Peckham police at once. During my research of Goodman's Peckham activities, Sergeant John Porter had introduced me to a number of his men at Peckham Centre and one of them, PC Pat Carey, had recognised my photograph of Goodman as the man he had met briefly the previous year when warning him of burglars.

PC Carey kindly agreed to help me locate Goodman. He traced a Nigerian in Peckham who for a while had acted as Goodman's mail drop but the man was unhelpful. Carey then checked out some two dozen All Saints churches in the London area since I had stupidly not asked James to be specific and Carey could find no 'police padre'. He finally located an All Saints in Lewisham with a Roman Catholic priest, Father Owen Beaumont, who remembered having met Goodman.

He told the police constable that Goodman had requested accommodation and he had advised him to report to the relevant 'housing officer' at another church nearby. Goodman had asked Father Beaumont to look after his belongings while he was gone but he never came back nor did he turn up at the second church.

Constable Carey checked the contents of Goodman's small bag, a

1930s gas-mask container, but there were no clues as to his whereabouts. Some items of theatrical make-up in the bag bore an address in Ealing Studios and Carey suggested I call them. I did so at once.

Profile Media Services were a small theatrical costumiers run by a Mary Hillman. She did not at first remember any Mr Goodman but checked back in her accounts and located his file.

'Ah ha,' she laughed. 'He hired some kit last year. We have his deposit but he's never returned our gear!' She had no contact details for him but agreed to call me at once if he ever came back. I could do no more. I checked the South London hospitals and mortuaries, but to no avail.

During my research visits to Blackburn I was threatened and, in the interests of my own family's safety, I have altered some names of Blackledge's acquaintances. I met Alan Neale in prison and he refused to give me any information. He was fearful of 'them'. Even at Blackburn Court one of Neale's friends was threatened with a kitchen knife. 'Your pal Neale killed Blackledge,' he was warned. 'We will kill you.'

I met a great many individuals during my ponderous attempts to retrace Goodman's footsteps. Some were helpful people whom I greatly respect and thank. Others were cruel bastards, the scum of the earth, mostly but not all white, who live by the law of intimidation and murder. I wish that I had never crossed their paths but, having done so, I admire all the more Alex Goodman and every other individual who has ever stood up to the menace of such people.

I grew to like Alex Goodman and I hope that he lives long enough to read his story. I find it difficult to judge him or his actions by any yardstick other than to ask myself how, if my wife were killed in a like manner, I would react in my own lasting grief. Would my response be in line with the teachings of the Old Testament or the New? I can only hope that such a question remains hypothetical.

London, August 1995

Index

'Home' 152, 244, 305–6, 310, 371, 423, 453, 456, 471; Jamaicans 180; North 135, 458–9; riots 180
Pedro 4–9
Pen Registers 157–8, 163
Pengelly, Sergeant David 184; Unit 502 184–8
Perrine 263; Assassin 265–7, 271–2; Mansion 263–5, 267–72, 274
Petty France, NCE members 307
Pirbhai 338
PLO 56–7, 59–60; boat 58
Pohl, Tony 213
Police Commissioners 183
Porsche club 203
Potter, John 35–6
Powers, Mike, Thailand 215
Price Waterhouse 163, 337, 342–3, 352
Professor 242–7, 294–302, 310
Puerto Triunfo 258–9
Punjab, eastern 18
Puri, Sushma 353

Qiryat Shemona 56

JR see Ridgway, John 'JR'
Rahman, Masi 219–20, 333–5
Ramón 258–9
Ramrez, Colonel Jaime 271
Rape Trauma Syndrome 50
Rappaport, Bruce 17
Rastafarians 137, 140
Raymondo 256
Reagan, Ronald 16–8, 158, 160; BCCI drugs 382; Executive Order 12333 38; Javed Abbas 21; Thatcher, Margaret *entente cordiale* 315; war on drugs 19, 214, 265–7
Redden, Albert 39; Abbas, Javed, tapes 24–7; Abeid, Agha Hassan 26–7; Anderson, John 267, 274; Bahamas 397–400, 404; Bahamas-based fleet 266; BCCI 26, 32, 316–17; bear fight 28–31; Casey, William, CIA contacts 18–19, 22, 25, 157, 264; cocaine empire 33, 162; competitors 217; contacts 158; European plans 32, 40; FBI 34, 264; HTA 276; Jamaican connection 33; Kinver Wood 192; LA office 390–4, 399; 'Mafia' activities 20; Mafia papers 20; Mason, Jed 284–5, 376, 382; Mexican cartel 211; Miami, HTA attack 264–5, 274–5; Operation Caesar 158–9; Pakistan

24–34; photograph 396, 410; Richter, Korbi 21, 37–8; Shaheen, John 280–1; Tricks 283; US, Customs officials 266; Vukov 431–5; Washington 158
Renkers Posse 394–5, 397, 400–4
Reynoso, Mr 412
Richter job 13
Richter, Korbi 4–5, 7–8, 399–400; BCCI 283, 308; death list 37; Duraz, Miguel 283; Goodman, Alex 382, 390–3, 396; heroin 40; Lasova, Kari 386–90, 392–3; Lebanon 59–60; 'Mafia' 365, 370–1, 377; Mason and Ridgway 394, 400; Mexico 211–23; Miami 265–71; Redden, Albert 20–1, 157, 161–2, 281, 387; telephones 12; Tricks call 53
Richter, Senior 21
RICO (Racketeer Influenced Corrupt Organization) 38; Redden-Richter 90, 276, 279
Ricord, Auguste 161–2, 261; Corsicans 270–1
Ridgway, John 'JR' 4–6, 8–9; BCCI insider 163–5, 314–18; bleeper-bug 41; Bradbury home 382; CENTAC 214, 279; Chemist 168–9; CIA friends 215; Fambridge 89, 316; Goodman, Alex 90–2, 115, 330–1; Lebanon 56–8; Los Angeles 156–65, 392–4; Mason, Jed 382–5; Mexico 12, 34, 38, 211–13, 264; Miami HTA meeting 261–5, 270, 272–3; Operation Caesar 12; Reagan, Ronald, war on drugs 214; Redden, Albert and Richter, Korbi 38–9, 41, 57, 89, 215, 278–9; Sara's flat 330; Seattle 275–82; Somogyi, Tibi 55; Tricks 37
riots 180, 182, 184; Birmingham, Liverpool 180; Bristol, Toxteth 182
Ripple Estuary 254
Rishton 241
River Crouch 82–4; Anchor pub 79–80, 85; Regional Force 84, 89
Robert Gordon 52, 54, 57–60, 82–3, 88, 90, 164
Roberto 265, 269–70, 273
Roberts, Constable Maxwell 187
Rodríguez, Gonzalo 260
Roehampton Hospital 293
Round Oak, British Steel Corporation furnaces 63
Rourke's Drift 187–8

499